*f*P

The
CYANIDE
CANARY

JOSEPH HILLDORFER
and ROBERT DUGONI

FREE PRESS ■ NEW YORK • LONDON • TORONTO • SYDNEY

FREE PRESS
A Division of Simon & Schuster, Inc.
1230 Avenue of the Americas
New York, NY 10020

FREE PRESS and colophon are trademarks
of Simon & Schuster, Inc.

For information regarding special discounts for bulk purchases,
please contact Simon & Schuster Special Sales at 1-800-456-6798
or business@simonandschuster.com

Designed by Dana Sloan

Manufactured in the United States of America

10 9 8 7 6 5 4 3 2 1

Library of Congress Cataloging-in-Publication Data
Hilldorfer, Joseph.
    The cyanide canary / Joseph Hilldorfer and Robert Dugoni.
        p.   cm.
    Includes bibliographical references and index.
    1. Elias, Allan.   2. Evergreen Resources (Firm)   3. Offenses against
the environment—Idaho—Soda Springs.   4. Fertilizer industry—
Accidents—Idaho—Soda Springs.   5. Trials (Offenses against the
environment)—Idaho.   I. Dugoni, Robert.   II. Title.
HV6404.I2H55   2004
364.1'42—dc22   2004050648

ISBN 0-7432-4652-7

ACKNOWLEDGMENTS

Not long before the Idaho jury returned its verdict in the trial of Allan Elias, Joe Hilldorfer turned and whispered into Dr. Joe Lowry's ear. Regardless of the ultimate outcome, he expressed how proud he felt that everyone had done the best they could, and that the presentation of the case had been as good as humanly possible. Considering this for a moment, Dr. Joe leaned forward on the courtroom pew and stroked his beard.

"You know, Joe," he said, "for a case to be successful, everybody has to do their job, and they have to do it well."

The same holds true for this book. Grateful as we are to have had thousands of pages of sworn testimony, court pleadings and transcripts, interviews, and newspaper articles from around the country, *The Cyanide Canary* came to life because of the cooperation and assistance of all who investigated and prosecuted Allan Elias. Everyone did his and her part, and did it well. We wish to specifically acknowledge EPA/CID Special Agent Bob Wojnicz, Assistant U.S. Attorney George Breitsameter, Assistant U.S. Attorney Celeste Miller, Caribou County Volunteer Fireman Daren Schwartz, and Assistant U.S. Attorney Michael Fica. Idaho State Police officers William Reese and Robert Clements, true professionals, got the ball rolling and also stood tall through the long and difficult legal battle.

In books, as in life, the spotlight finds certain people. On this project the spotlight found David Uhlmann. Though chief of the Environmental Crimes Section, David freely gave dozens of hours of his time to ensure the factual accuracy of *The Cyanide Canary*. Though quick to defer credit and praise each member of the investigative and trial teams, he shined the brightest, and we are grateful to him and acknowledge his considerable input. As with Joe, whose opinions expressed herein are his and do not reflect the official position of the Environmental Protection Agency, David's only caveat was an understanding that the opinions he expressed were his and did not necessarily reflect the official position of the U.S. Department of Justice. We are happy to note that here.

We owe much to Jennifer McCord, editor, consultant, and a true friend not only to us but all Northwest writers. Her unbridled enthusiasm for this project and her talents made it happen. Thanks to the Jane Rotrosen Agency, Jane Berkey, Donald Cleary, Kara Caesar, and Meg Ruley, who possess the three best qualities any writer could want in an agent—always available, always helpful, and always interested.

We are also deeply grateful to the vision of the talented people at Simon & Schuster/Free Press who saw *The Cyanide Canary* as an important story. Our thanks to publisher Martha Levin, editor-in-chief Dominic Anfuso, assistant publisher Suzanne Donahue, editor Bill Rosen, associate editor Andrea Au, art director Eric Fuentecilla, and all the production people, copy editors, proofreaders, and attorneys. Special thanks, though, are owed to editor Fred Hills, for his deft touch and mentoring. Fred, you made the manuscript better.

Joe also wishes to thank the "coffee club," Mike Burnett, Gerd Hatwig, Lorinda Wallace, Sandy Smith, and Glenn Bruck. Not only did they help with the investigation, they provided advice, support, and a friendly ear throughout. Thanks also to everyone at the NEIC Lab, and its preeminent scientist, Dr. Joe Lowry, the trial team's chief expert, personal chemistry tutor, and Joe and Bob's lunch companion throughout the trial.

Thanks to our respective spouses and families, who did without husbands and a father far too often so we could pursue this project, and as a result allowed two strangers who grew up on opposite sides of the country to become the best of friends. This book is proof positive we weren't working out all the time.

During the course of this project many told how Scott Dominguez's courage and Ron and Jackie Hamp's dignity and grace inspired them to fight so hard and to sacrifice so much in search of justice. We, too, found inspiration in his courage and their dignity during the long and arduous process of researching and writing this story. We are deeply grateful for their full support of this project and happy to donate a portion of the proceeds from the sale of this book to help Scott continue his courageous fight.

For Cristina, and our two children. Your encouragement, inspiration, and self-sacrifice are the foundation upon which this book was written.

ROBERT DUGONI

To Dixon McClary and the late Robert A. Boodey, two founding fathers of the Environmental Protection Agency's Criminal Investigation Division; to my fellow special agents, who wage the daunting and often thankless battle to bring to justice those who pollute our waterways, the air we breathe, and the land upon which we live; and foremost, to Mr. Scott Dominguez, who touched the hearts of all who had the privilege of trying to find a measure of justice for him, and who taught me the meaning of courage.

JOSEPH HILLDORFER

ABOUT THE TITLE

In the early 1900s, coal miners burdened with heavy picks, shovels, and candles for their headlamps, carted canaries into the bowels of the earth with them. The small bird's internal organs were highly sensitive to the lethal gases the mining operations could disturb: methane, carbon dioxide, and carbon monoxide. If a canary fell from its perch, the miners knew they had scant minutes to get out of the mine before being overcome as well, or having a flame ignite a thunderous explosion. So valued and respected were these tiny creatures that the miners brought glass cages with air tanks to revive them and carried them to safety. The term *cyanide canary* became a common expression. While the beloved birds have since given way to technology, the coal miners' compassion was strictly a human quality, neither improved upon nor necessarily shared by all men.

NOTE TO READER

In retelling this story in full, the authors recognized that it would be necessary to reconstruct from other sources many scenes and events at which Special Agent Joe Hilldorfer was not present. To ensure the accuracy of these events, we relied upon thousands of pages of sworn trial testimony and interviews, which are discussed more fully in the notes at the end of the book.

DRAMATIS PERSONAE   *[In alphabetical order]*

Cecil D. Andrus—Former two-time Democratic governor of the state of Idaho and secretary of the interior under President Jimmy Carter.

Kim Barnett—Former employee at AEI, Inc., in Pocatello, Idaho.

George Breitsameter—Assistant U.S. attorney and senior litigator in the Boise, Idaho, U.S. Attorney's Office. A Chicago native and the son of an OSHA investigator, Breitsameter was one of the prosecutors for the government in *United States v. Elias.*

Mike Burnett—A special agent with the Region 10 Environmental Protection Agency/Criminal Investigation Division (EPA/CID).

Matt Christiansen—Caribou County volunteer fireman and member of emergency rescue team who responded to Evergreen.

Officer Bryce "Bob" Clements—Idaho State Trooper who interviewed Evergreen employee Darren Weaver and performed HAZMAT inspection of tank materials at Evergreen.

Theresa Cole—Scott Dominguez's fiancée.

Scott Dominguez—In August 1996, Dominguez was twenty years old, the youngest employee at the Evergreen Resources phosphate fertilizer plant in Soda Springs, Idaho, when his employer Allan Elias sent him into an acid storage tank without any safety equipment.

Joe Eizaguirre—Compliance officer, Department of Labor, Occupational Safety and Health Administration (OSHA).

Allan Elias—The owner of Evergreen Resources, a phosphate fertilizer plant in Soda Springs, Idaho. The son of a New York garment industry owner, Elias moved to Soda Springs via Pocatello, Idaho, and

Tucson, Arizona. In Pocatello he established AEI, Inc., a business to extract silver from mining waste. When that venture failed he moved to Soda Springs and founded Evergreen Resources.

Michael Fica—Law clerk to U.S. Federal District Court Judge B. Lynn Winmill.

Barb Franek—Compliance officer, Department of Labor, Occupational Safety and Health Administration (OSHA).

Bob Griffin—Former Kerr-McGee manager charged with the task of solving Kerr-McGee's hazardous waste problem at its facility in Soda Springs, Idaho.

Jackie Hamp—Scott Dominguez's mother.

Ron Hamp—Scott Dominguez's stepfather.

Joe Hilldorfer—A special agent with the EPA/CID in Seattle, Washington, Mr. Hilldorfer was the lead investigator for the government in *United States v. Elias*. He is an accomplished former FBI agent in Seattle and New York City.

Craig Jorgensen—Allan Elias's longtime attorney in Pocatello, Idaho.

Dr. Joe Lowry—Chief deputy scientist for the EPA's National Enforcement Intelligence Center in Lakewood, Colorado. Lowry was the government's primary scientific expert at the trial of *United States v. Allan Elias*.

Fred Mancini—Former employee at Evergreen who was nicknamed "Feel My Head Fred" by the EPA special agents.

David Marshall—A former assistant U.S. attorney, Marshall is a defense attorney in Seattle and was one of Allan Elias's defense attorneys in *United States v. Elias*.

Kenny McAllister—Kerr-McGee employee and Elias's defense witness.

Dixon McClary—The special agent in charge of EPA's Region 10 in Seattle. A former DEA agent, McClary left the DEA in 1982 to become one of the founding agents of the EPA/CID.

Celeste Miller—An assistant U.S. attorney in Boise, Idaho, and one of the prosecutors for the government in *United States v. Elias*.

Ron Myers—Caribou County volunteer fireman.

David Nevin—Considered the premier federal criminal defense attorney in Idaho, Nevin was Allan Elias's lead defense attorney.

Dr. John Wayne Obray—The Caribou County Memorial Hospital emergency room doctor who fought to save Scott Dominguez's life.

James Oesterle—EPA District 10 regional counsel.

Kelly O'Neil—The EPA/CID special agent working in Portland, Oregon, who received the call of an impending disaster at the Evergreen Resources plant in Soda Springs.

Roger Parker—A former Evergreen employee.

Officer Bill Reese—The Idaho State Trooper who delayed his family vacation to report the incident at Evergreen Resources to the EPA.

Danny Rice—A former Evergreen employee injured working in a confined space.

Officer Joe Rice—A sergeant with the Soda Springs Police Department, Rice testified at the suppression hearing in *United States v. Elias*.

Dr. John Warren Roberts—One of Scott Dominguez's treating doctors at the Bannock Regional Medical Center in Pocatello, Idaho.

Kyle Schick—The owner and operator of Western Analysis, a testing laboratory in Salt Lake City, Utah. Schick tested the samples sent to his lab by Allan Elias.

Boyd Schvaneveldt—A staff safety and health specialist at Kerr-McGee, Soda Springs, Idaho.

Daren Schwartz—Caribou County volunteer fireman. As the first rescuer to arrive at Evergreen, he became the incident commander.

Roger Sears—Pocatello, Idaho, fireman and member of the state's hazardous material response team (HAZMAT).

Brian Smith—An employee at Evergreen Resources, Smith entered the tank to save Scott Dominguez.

Sean Stevens—A former employee at Evergreen Resources.

John Stoor—Caribou County volunteer fireman.

William Stout—A Van Waters & Rogers salesman, Stout sold cyanide to AEI, Inc., Elias's company in Pocatello, Idaho.

Gene Thornock—An employee at Evergreen Resources, Thornock entered the tank to save Scott Dominguez and was nicknamed "Caveman Gene" by the EPA special agents for his cavemanlike scream of frustration when he could not save him.

David Uhlmann—A graduate of Yale Law School, in 1996, Uhlmann was a thirty-four-year-old federal prosecutor with the Environmental Crimes Section of the Department of Justice in Washington, D.C. He became the government's lead prosecutor in *United States v. Elias*.

Lorinda Wallace—An EPA/CID special agent in Region 10.

Darren Weaver—An employee at Evergreen Resources.

Ivan Williams—Williams transported the acid storage tank from AEI, Inc., in Pocatello to Evergreen Resources in Soda Springs, Idaho, and later cut it up and hauled it away at Elias's request.

Judge B. Lynn Winmill—The federal district court judge who presided over *United States v. Elias* in Pocatello, Idaho.

Bogdan "Bob" Wojnicz [*Voy-Nitch*]—A special agent with the EPA/CID. Joe Hilldorfer's co–case agent in the investigation of *United States v. Elias*.

CHAPTER ONE

SCOTT DOMINGUEZ pulled up the extension ladder, balancing it like a circus performer high off the ground as he stepped along the rounded surface of the acid storage tank. He fit the legs of the ladder into the twenty-two-inch-diameter entry hole and let the rungs slide through his palms until he felt it hit bottom. It was like dropping something down a manhole. Darkness swallowed it.[1]

He sat down atop the eleven-foot-tall, thirty-six-foot-long rust orange tank dangling his steel-toed Redwings in the hole, thinking about the morning, and regretting his comment.

Theresa Cole, his fiancée, had driven him to work at Evergreen Resources, a phosphate fertilizer plant in Soda Springs, Idaho, at 6:45 that morning. She stopped the car near the construction trailer at the front of the plant, their normal routine. Dominguez kissed her good-bye, opened the car door, and turned to get out, but something made him stop.

"I'm afraid to go to work," he said.

He knew his comment had worried her, and he hadn't meant to do that. It was just that his boots were still wet from standing in the knee-deep sludge and water in the tank the day before, and he didn't feel well. His throat had started bothering him after he and Darren Weaver had climbed out of the tank, unsuccessful in their efforts to break up the sludge using a fire hose and brooms. The sludge kept clogging the $1\frac{1}{4}$-inch spigot, making the water level in the tank rise, so they decided to quit and wait until the morning when they could talk to their employer, Allan Elias, about cutting a bigger hole. By the time Dominguez got home, his throat burned and he felt like he was coming down with something. He begged off hiking with Theresa and his nephews and spent the night on the couch.

In the morning he'd felt better, but still not himself. He knew Allan was going to make him go back inside the tank, something he didn't want to do. He thought about phoning in sick, but didn't want to lose his job. Besides, he felt better now, though his throat was still bothering him.

He'd tell Theresa everything was fine when she picked him up to go to lunch at the Quick Stop in town.

Dominguez sat back beneath a cornflower blue, summer sky and wiped a trickle of perspiration from the side of his face. The temperature would likely hit the mid-nineties by early afternoon, but at just after ten in the morning it remained comfortable. Atop the tank he looked out over the Evergreen plant. To anyone driving along North Hooper Road, the rugged beauty of southeast Idaho's Bear River valley gave Evergreen the feel of a high-plain cattle ranch, but upon closer inspection, nature could not camouflage Evergreen's dilapidated and tattered condition. It looked damn near abandoned—a junkyard of rusted tanks, cut-up railroad cars, and twisted bits of metal and plastic containers littering a pocked and scarred moonscape of craters and dirt piles. Pipes and smokestacks extended from the tanks and battered barnlike buildings at odd angles, a maze of metal that turned and digressed seemingly without purpose. Two mountains of mining waste rose above the building rooflines, one a coal black, the other a starch white. The piles had been trucked in from the waste ponds of the Kerr-McGee processing plant, which was just a mile down North Hooper Road.

Twenty years old, Dominguez had two years invested at Evergreen, his first real job after graduating from Soda Springs High, and he didn't want to get fired. He needed the money if he and Theresa were to get married. He wanted to replace the promise ring he gave her with a diamond, and maybe start saving for college—something they continued to talk about. He couldn't do that working as a stock boy at the Quick Stop, or helping his mom out at the B&H Cleaners she owned in town. The real money was at the industrial plants along North Hooper Road, like Kerr-McGee, Monsanto, and Soda Springs Phosphate. Problem was, most wouldn't hire a twenty-year-old without experience.

Allan Elias did.

Elias had a big contract to process Kerr-McGee's mining waste and turn it into fertilizer, and Dominguez understood that if Elias could get the plant up and running Kerr-McGee would buy it. If that happened, he would have an inside track working for a premier company in town, giving him and Theresa a real start in life. So he wasn't about to lose his job, even if that meant going back inside the tank, which was inevitable since he and Weaver were the only two Evergreen employees who could physically fit through the small opening. Lean-muscled like a flyweight boxer, Dominguez was just 130 pounds, with the wiry strength of a high school wrestler and nimble enough to keep a Hacky Sack in the air for two hundred kicks. Taller, but thin as a pipe cleaner, Weaver also had no problem fitting in the entry hole. Evergreen's other two employees, Brian Smith and Gene Thornock, were each twenty years older and carried the extra years in their chests and bellies. When they met Monday in Elias's construction trailer to discuss cleaning out the tank, Gene told Allan he couldn't fit in the hole, and Brian, well, he just flat out said he wasn't going in without safety equipment. Allan told Gene to stay on the outside and Scott and Darren to clean the tank from the inside. Brian was to turn the water to the fire hose on and off.

They met again Tuesday morning to tell Elias about the sludge clogging the spigot and that Gene wanted to cut a bigger hole, and that touched off another conversation about the lack of safety equipment.

"They should be wearing full rubber gear, and they should be wearing SCBA's," Smith said, referring to a self-contained breathing apparatus, which worked like scuba gear. "And the tank needs to be ventilated with air blowers. It's supposed to be tested for oxygen and gasses." Even then, Smith said, "they should not be going in the tank. It should be washed from the outside."

"You're not going to be directly involved in the tank cleaning," Elias replied, telling Smith he'd be working on the granulator, which was across the plant near the fire hydrant. "You can turn the water to the fire hose on and off."[2]

"My throat is kind of hurting," Dominguez said.

"Yeah, it kind of irritated my throat . . . and my eyes, too," Weaver agreed.

"What about getting respirators?" Dominguez asked, hoping Allan would get respirators from Kerr-McGee, which is where they had borrowed the fire hoses.

Elias just got angry. He was renting two railcars to store sulfuric acid, and he couldn't transfer the acid into the storage tank until it was cleaned out.[3] At over six feet tall with round shoulders and a thick chest, Elias was physically imposing. When he got mad his eyes bugged, his face flushed red, and his mouth became a great gaping hole.

"You guys lose everything I buy for you," he said, though none of them knew what he was talking about since they had never seen any SCBA's at the plant.[4]

"Well, what about the permit? You also need a confined-space permit and everyone has to sign off on it," Smith said.

"I don't need a permit. There's nothing in that tank but mud and water. It's as safe as ordinary shampoo."[5]

"I'll hand-write it."

"No," Elias replied. "I'll take care of it."[6]

It was what he always said. He never did.[7]

"I saw a mask in one of the railcars," Dominguez said.

Elias turned to him. "Well, go get that."[8]

They left the trailer and walked down the dirt road between the two storage barns. Scott left them standing by the tank and climbed into one of the railroad boxcars in the boneyard. He found the trunk with the mask piled amid junk, carried it to where Elias and the rest of the employees waited, and popped it open. The respirator looked like something from World War I, a mask with a hose attached to a canister.

"That's not a respirator," Smith said.

Scott turned the oxygen valve and heard a hiss.

"Good. Just use that," Elias said. "That way I don't have to go get more oxygen."[9]

"What about the rest of the safety equipment?" Smith asked, referring to the protective clothing, the air blowers to ventilate the tank, and the equipment needed to test the air inside.

"I'll take care of it. You guys just get in there and do the job. I'll see you in two hours. Have it done before I get back," Allan said. He walked back toward the trailer, got in his truck, and left.[10]

But getting the job done turned out to be easier said than done. The claylike sludge continued to clog the opening, even after Gene cut a six-inch square in the side. The water also flowed underneath the tank, forming puddles around the freshly poured, three-foot-tall concrete saddles holding it off the ground. Brian said the blue-green tint to the water indicated phosphoric acid, which could weaken the concrete. If the saddles collapsed, the tank would crash through the plant like a knocked-down bowling pin. So they had to shut it down again while Gene built a sluice to direct the water and sludge away from the back of the tank. The sluice protruded out the back of the tank like an eighteenth-century gold miner's trough.

Atop the tank, Dominguez looked down into the hole. Maybe there was nothing to worry about. Maybe all the talk about safety equipment and confined-space permits was just Brian's way of getting out of going in the tank. Allan assured them there was nothing in it that could hurt them, that the sludge had the pH of ordinary shampoo. He'd even put some in his mouth and spit it out.[11] Dominguez trusted him.

With the opening cut and the sluice built, he stood, climbed onto the ladder and stepped down a rung. Then he stopped. To the east the smoke-stacks of Monsanto billowed artificial clouds. Scott Dominguez closed his eyes for a moment, feeling the sun warm on his face; the air soothing his throat and lungs like a cool glass of water. When he opened his eyes he took one last look down North Hooper Road, a desolate two-lane high-way that stretched like gray taffy to the horizon.

There was no sign of Allan.

Friday, March 15, 1996[1]
Federal Courthouse
Tacoma, Washington

CHAPTER TWO

SEVERAL MONTHS EARLIER, Joe Hilldorfer stood alone admir-ing the opulent Dale Chihuly glass sculpture that floated from the ceiling in the foyer of the magnificently renovated railway station that now served as Tacoma's Federal Courthouse. A special agent with the Environmental Protection Agency's Criminal Investigation Division (EPA/CID), Hilldorfer had come to the courthouse to witness the sen-tencing of Boomsnub Chrome & Grind, a Vancouver, Washington, chrome-plating company. His two-year investigation had led to an in-dictment of the company and two of its officers on charges of illegally dumping thousands of gallons of the cancer-causing agent hexavalent chromium into the soil, then lying to cover up the crime.

Hilldorfer adjusted the knot of his tie, which felt as if it was strangling him. For an FBI agent, suits and ties had been mandatory; as an EPA agent, he rarely put one on, even for court. Today he felt he needed the karma from his years with the Bureau, when the directive from his superiors had been simple—AIJ, "Put the assholes in jail." Despite Boom-snub's history, and the evidence Hilldorfer's investigation uncovered, his instincts told him he was going to find something far less pleasing inside Judge Robert Bryan's courtroom than the sculpture that sparkled over-head like thousands of distant stars.

In the 1980s the Washington State Department of Ecology (WDOE) had learned that chromium was being released into the soils at the Boom-snub facility. Boomsnub's officers led the WDOE to believe the problem was the result of a prior two-thousand-gallon spill, but wells dug on and off the site and soil samples revealed extreme contamination levels and a plume of chromium that was spreading along a thick layer of clay that protected the Troutdale aquifer. Concern grew that the plume would compromise the drinking water to the second largest county in Washing-ton State.

The WDOE instituted a $3.4 million, four-year effort to solve the problem, including the installation of a pump and treatment system at Boomsnub to catch spills of rinse water and chromic acid, but the plume continued to spread.

Hilldorfer and his co-agent, Mike Burnett, became involved on Octo-ber 10, 1993, when the WDOE called to say that the pump and treatment system had a meltdown. Hilldorfer and Burnett tracked down a former Boomsnub employee who said the company had been deliberately dump-ing chromium waste into the state's treatment system and that he had been reporting other problems to the WDOE. Based on his statement and the problems documented in the WDOE file, Hilldorfer and Burnett ob-tained a search warrant to raid the facility. Boomsnub officials blamed the employee, calling him a "terrorist" and "vandal." While they admitted to putting waste in the state's system, they said it was only to clean up the spill. Additional inspections of the treatment system, however, revealed levels of chromium waste so high that it had dissolved brass fittings, which resulted in a discharge of up to twenty thousand gallons into the city of Vancouver's sewer system. Boomsnub's waste containment vault was also leaking, but the company said it had not fixed it because they were preparing to move into a new facility. Hilldorfer suspected more to their story, and documentation seized during the search proved that the plant manager had been systematically dumping the chromium waste di-rectly into the state's system.

The EPA obtained an emergency shut-down order. The subsequent emergency removal action to knock down the plant and clean up the mess would leave taxpayers with an estimated $31 million clean-up bill—at the time the largest Superfund project in Washington State.

In February 1995 a federal grand jury indicted Boomsnub and three of its top officials on eight counts of environmental crimes including conspiring to violate hazardous waste laws. When trial appeared imminent, expectations grew that Boomsnub would be fined millions of dollars and the officers sentenced to significant jail time. Dixon McClary, the special agent in charge of EPA's Region 10, didn't think so. He began to utter a mantra when he passed Hilldorfer's cubicle.

"I smell a plea."

Hilldorfer had ignored him. There was no reason for the government to plea the charges. The evidence of criminal activity by the company and its officers was strong. Then, late on a Friday night, a fax came in to the Region 10 office in Seattle. The Department of Justice and Boomsnub's lawyers had reached an agreement. In exchange for guilty pleas on two counts, the DOJ would drop the remaining counts. Still, Hilldorfer remained optimistic. Under federal sentencing guidelines Boomsnub faced a $500,000 fine for each remaining charge, and the officers were facing maximum sentences of five years in prison and individual fines of $250,000.

Lowering his gaze from the sculpture, Hilldorfer checked his watch. It was time. He walked to Judge Bryan's courtroom, swung open the heavy wooden doors, and took a seat in the gallery next to Burnett. At twenty-seven, Burnett was ten years younger than Hilldorfer and had become like a brother during their prolonged investigation. Except for a brief greeting, neither man said much. Others in the gallery included the regulators from WDOE; Thor Cutler, the EPA on-scene coordinator who had excavated nine thousand tons of contaminated dirt from the Boomsnub site; and the citizens from the Clark County Citizens Action Committee. Beyond the wooden railing sat the prosecutors from the U.S. Attorney's Office and the officers of Boomsnub and their counsel.

Today was judgment day. They had all come to see Boomsnub pay the piper.

Judge Bryan entered the courtroom from a door at the side and took the bench, arranging the papers on his desk before sitting forward to discuss the charges and the plea agreement. After hearing argument Bryan sat back and said the remaining charges were no worse than someone driving through a stop sign.[2] A pall fell over the gallery as heavy as a gray wool blanket, suffocating the optimism that had glimmered like the Chihuly glass sculpture, and leaving Hilldorfer bereft and hollow. He thought he had prepared himself for the worst.

He was wrong.

Burnett turned to him for an explanation. The citizens of the Clark County Action Committee shifted in their seats looking as if they'd been dropped in a foreign country, straining to understand the language. Thor Cutler's face pinched in a bewildered, sickened-pale expression. He had spent a year and a half of his life documenting the removal of the carcinogenic waste from a seventy-foot hole in the ground as meticulously as an archaeologist because Hilldorfer told him this one was going to trial. This time people were going to jail.

It wasn't.

No one was.

As Judge Bryan continued to discuss the charges, Hilldorfer could no longer hear him over the din of his burned-out EPA colleagues.

What did you expect? People don't go to jail for environmental crimes; you know that. They get a slap on the wrist—six months at most at one of the federal clubs.

You're wasting your time.

He had shut them out. He wanted to believe his investigations were different, that they were as important as his investigations with the FBI.

They weren't. A federal judge had just told him so.

He stood. "I'm out of here."

Burnett gave him a puzzled, uncertain look. Protocol required agents to remain in the courtroom to show support for the prosecutor. Hilldorfer couldn't do it. He didn't need to hear Judge Bryan say what he already knew. No one was going to jail. They'd get probation and pay a small fine, and everyone would say justice had been served.[3]

CHAPTER THREE

GENE THORNOCK POKED the broom handle at a clump of sludge. The blockage gave way like a dam bursting and was swept down the wooden sluice by a powerful stream of water. He bent down and looked inside the six-inch-square opening, but with his eyes adjusted to the bright sunshine he couldn't see much inside the tank, though he could hear the force of the fire hose and Scott's and Darren's voices.

"Hey, you guys okay in there?"

A burst of water shot out the opening, causing him to stumble backward off-balance, the water deflecting off the edges and spraying him about his face and neck.

"Hey!"

Weaver's cackle echoed at him from inside the drum.

At thirty-eight, Thornock was nearly twice Weaver's and Dominguez's age, but at the moment circumstances dictated he was junior man on Evergreen's payroll. He started at the company in 1994 when his sister told him the owner was rebuilding the plant and needed an experienced welder. Thornock took one look at the broken-down equipment and saw job security, but it didn't work out that way. Elias never seemed particularly interested in fixing the equipment. For two years it was just one odd job after the next until Allan fired him, saying the work "ran out." Thornock hooked on as a welder at Mark III, another company in town, but they laid him off during a shutdown and he was again in need of a job. Much as he didn't want to, he went back to Evergreen and Allan rehired him.

Thornock turned from the tank at the sound of the backhoe approaching and stepped back from the sluice as Brian Smith lowered the bucket and scraped another pile of sludge toward the boneyard. As the clatter of the engine softened, the backhoe getting farther away, Thornock heard a different sound, a hissing, like a small rattler shaking its tail at his feet. When he looked down he saw sludge and water foaming around the soles of his leather work boots, as if eating its way through the soil.

◆   ◆   ◆

DARREN WEAVER shot a blast of water at the square opening, heard Gene Thornock yell in protest, and laughed loud and long. Weaver would have blasted whoever was outside the tank, but the fact that it was Thornock made it better. He didn't particularly like him—or Brian Smith for that matter.[1]

With no further sign of Thornock, Weaver returned to spraying the sludge clinging to the bottom of the tank while Scott Dominguez used a bar to try to break it up. Weaver stood near the ladder. Scott stood toward the front of the tank, grinning the way he did—like he was up to something but wasn't about to tell you what. They had been at it, off and on, for about forty minutes. They initially took turns in the tank, about fifteen- to twenty-minute shifts, and had tried using the old chemical masks with cartridge filters, but the masks only seemed to trap the fumes, making breathing more difficult. So when Weaver came out of the tank after a shift he tossed the mask to the side along with his safety glasses, which kept fogging over from the humidity in the tank.

"It don't work," he told Dominguez. They went into the tank together, taking turns holding the hose.

Weaver changed his grip to relieve the tingling in his forearms. Though it wasn't that hot in the tank, perhaps eighty degrees, his red-russet hair dripped with sweat and his T-shirt and jeans were clinging to his skin. He was also having trouble catching his breath. His chest hurt.

He yelled to Dominguez. "Is it getting harder to breathe in here?"

Scott looked at him as though he hadn't understood or heard the question.

Weaver shouted over the force of the water. "Is it getting harder to breathe?"

Dominguez nodded. "Yeah."

There was no way they were going to get the job done by noon, as Allan wanted.[2] Weaver pointed to the ladder. "Let's take a break." He shouted toward the opening. "Gene, tell Brian to shut off the water."

Thornock didn't respond.

"Gene!"

Weaver started up the ladder. The hole at the top looked as small as a dinner plate and he felt dizzy. He looked back down expecting to see

Dominguez following him, but Scott was not at the bottom of the ladder. He still stood at the front of the tank, looking confused.

"Scott?"

Dominguez looked up at him. "I can't breathe," he said and toppled face forward into the sludge and water.

"Scott!"

Weaver climbed back down the ladder yelling at Thornock to shut off the water. He stumbled to Dominguez and turned him over onto his back. Dominguez's eyes had rolled back in his head, two hollow sockets of frightening white.

"Scott! Scott!"

A wave buckled his knees. He lunged for the ladder, clinging to it like a man cast overboard in a storm. Something was wrong. He had to get out. He pulled himself up the rungs and popped out of the hatch gasping and out of breath, struggling to get to his feet. Atop the tank he shouted and waved his arms, trying to get Brian Smith's attention.

"Scott's down! Scott's down in the tank!"

BRIAN SMITH FLIPPED his salt-and-peppered ponytail off his shoulder. Rings of sweat saturated his armpits and the collar of his T-shirt. He forced the lever forward, heard the gears grind and gnash and slammed the clutch pedal to the floor, causing the bucket to jerk and the backhoe to bounce. Smith was adept at driving heavy equipment, but at the moment he was seeing red. He threw the gear into reverse and the long scorpion arm on the back rocked up and down as he corrected his angle, lowered the teeth of the bucket, shifted forward, and scraped another pile of sludge toward the boneyard.

They had no business being in there. That's what he'd told Allan that morning. Working in a tank was not something to screw around with; they needed respirators and rubber gear, and the tank needed to be ventilated.

It was like talking to a wall. The stubborn son of a bitch did what he always did. Nothing. He didn't want to spend the money.

"I'll take care of it." That's what Elias always said.[3]

When he swung the backhoe toward the tank Smith saw Gene Thornock running across the plant like his ass was on fire. He looked back to the tank, saw Weaver standing on top waving his arms like he was flagging down a passing car and knew there was a problem. When he dropped the bucket and killed the engine, Weaver's voice rang out to him.

"Scotty's down! Brian, Scotty's down!"

Smith bailed from the cab and ran to the edge of the tank, hollering for Weaver to drop the ladder. Weaver kept yelling the same thing. "Scott's down in the tank."

He climbed a ladder welded to the side of the molasses tank, got a running start, and jumped across to the storage tank, grabbing Weaver's hand as he landed. He dropped to his belly and stuck his head in the hole but couldn't see Dominguez.

Weaver rushed on. "He's not breathing. I asked if it was getting hot and he just blacked out."

The tank shuddered as Thornock jumped from the molasses tank, joining them at the hole.

"He's at the front." Weaver pointed. "Right there."

Smith caught a shape, a gray outline in the dark. Scott. "I'm going down and see if I can get him out. You stay here."

At five foot seven and a well-built 180 pounds, it would be a tight fit. Smith stepped onto the ladder, raised his hands over his head, took a breath like a diver about to submerge, and squeezed through the opening. The heat and humidity hit him like a furnace blast as he made his way down the ladder and dropped into the sludge. Dominguez leaned against the side of the tank like a punch-drunk boxer struggling against the ropes to get to his feet.

Smith shook him by the shoulders. "Scott! Can you hear me?"

Sludge covered Dominguez's body, his breathing raspy, irregular gasps for air that emitted foam from his mouth and nostrils. The pupils of his eyes were black spheres, a vacant, empty look. Smith lifted him to his feet, but Dominguez's legs buckled as if they had fallen asleep and couldn't carry him. Still, he was trying, which meant he was coherent.

"Scotty, you gotta help me. Stand up." Smith leaned Dominguez against him and dragged him across the tank to where Thornock had climbed halfway down the ladder to help pull Dominguez up, but the angle was awkward.

"I'm going to have to carry him up," Smith said.

He gripped Dominguez's Levi's with his left arm, grabbed the rung with his right hand, and stepped up, breathing heavily, pulling air into his lungs. He adjusted Dominguez's weight on his hip and reached for the next rung, repeating the process.

Thornock reached down through the hole, encouraging him. "Come on, Brian, get him up here."

He gasped, but it was like breathing thin air at a high altitude. The hole above him doubled, two moons shifting, and his head felt like a helium balloon floating at the end of a string. He stepped up another rung. If he could get Dominguez high enough, Thornock could pull him up while Smith pushed.

The smell.

Keep going.

He grabbed another rung, his thick legs straining, his chest heaving.

Burnt almonds?

Keep going.

Burnt almonds. Cyanide.

Oh shit.

He reached for another rung and felt Dominguez give out, his body collapsing like a puppet cut from its strings, the weight pulling him down. He squeezed the rung, struggling to hang on, his strength waning, his arms and legs giving out. Sweat poured from him. He couldn't breathe. He couldn't step up.

"Come on, Brian, get him up here. Just a couple more. Come on."

He couldn't do it. He had to go down. He stepped down, dropping the last two rungs, his boots slipping in the sludge. He set Dominguez down against the side of the tank, physically spent.

"I got to get out, Scotty." He knelt at Dominguez's side. "I got to get out or there's going to be two of us here. You hang on. Do you hear me?" He gripped Dominguez's shoulders. "I'll get help. I won't leave you here. You hang on."

Smith started back up the ladder. It was like climbing a mountain with a sixty-pound pack on his back. His arms and legs strained, his mind fighting the desire to just quit, to rest.

No. Stopping meant dying.

He stepped up another rung and felt Gene grab him by the shirt and pull him out.

"I couldn't get him. I couldn't breathe. You stay here. I'm going for help."

Smith scooted to the edge of the tank and slid over the side, his legs buckling as he hit the ground and fell forward onto his hands and knees. He picked himself up and started across the yard, weaving like a man crossing the deck of a boat in a storm. Three times his legs betrayed him and he fell. Each time he picked himself up and continued. When he reached the trailer he climbed the wooden steps, flung open the door, and lurched inside for the phone on the desk and dialed 911.

"This is Evergreen Resources. We have a man down in a tank."

GENE THORNOCK watched Smith stumbling across the yard and turned to Darren Weaver. "I'm going in."

He stepped onto the ladder, raised his hands over his head, took a deep breath like Smith, and dropped through the hole and down the ladder. Dominguez was slumped against the side of the tank, not moving. Thornock put Dominguez's arm around his neck and lifted him to his feet. "Come on, Scotty, we're getting you out of here."

Dominguez's limbs were like cooked spaghetti. "Scott, come on. You got to stand up. Stand up."

Dominguez did not respond.

Thornock put him down, climbed the ladder, and popped out the hole. He pointed to the Air-Pac Weaver had discarded. "Darren, give me that Air-Pac. We need it."

Weaver climbed off the tank and retrieved the Pac. A moment later he handed it to Thornock, tied to a rope, and Thornock went back into the tank.[4] The fresh air had revived him, but as he descended back into the tank he felt the oxygen being sucked from his lungs. He stuck the mask over his mouth and nose and took a deep breath, then slipped the mask on Dominguez, placing the small oxygen tank at his side. His plan was to tie the rope around Dominguez, but he couldn't hold his breath. It felt as if someone had stuck a vacuum down his throat and sucked the air out of his lungs.

Tie the rope.

He couldn't do it. He felt his strength leaking from his body. His legs felt leaden, as if the sludge had hardened around his boots, anchoring them in place. His muscles quivered.

"I have to get out. I'm sorry, Scott. I'm so sorry."

◆   ◆   ◆

WEAVER LOOKED UP from the hole toward the trailer, hoping to see Brian Smith. Allan Elias sat parked in his truck looking up at him through the windshield. "Allan, go call nine-one-one. Call nine-one-one."

Elias looked at him with a puzzled expression.

"Scott's in the tank," Weaver yelled. "He ain't breathing."

Elias backed the truck down the road between the two warehouses, got out, and climbed the steps to the trailer door.[5]

BRIAN SMITH MADE his emergency call at 10:45 A.M. Caribou County emergency dispatch was adamant that he stay on the line and Smith was pacing the cluttered office, phone in hand, like an animal in a cage.

"I got to get back."

"The engines are on their way."

From outside the trailer Smith heard a primal wail of pain and frustration that echoed across the valley and exploded inside the trailer as the door flew open, and the floor shook with the weight of a man entering. Allan Elias.

"What the hell is going on?" Elias yelled.[6]

Smith heard the sirens of the emergency trucks coming down North Hooper Road and dropped the telephone. "The emergency crews are here. I'm leaving."

"What the hell happened?"[7]

Smith knocked Elias out of the doorway and rushed past him. "Scotty's down in the tank. We can't get him out."

Tuesday, August 27, 1996
Seattle, Washington
9:04 P.M.

CHAPTER FOUR

THE FERRY to Bainbridge Island crossed the slate-gray waters of Seattle's Elliott Bay. Behind it the fluorescent orange loading cranes that lined the Port of Seattle like huge praying mantises were at rest, no longer lifting and stacking the colorful cargo containers onto transport ships. Seagulls continued to circle and dive at the robotic giants.

"You want more wine? Joe?"

Hilldorfer took in the view from the deck of his West Seattle home, the Northwest summer sun warming his neck as it slid behind the Olympic Mountain Range and painted the skyscrapers of downtown Seattle a golden hue.

"Yabba dabba dabba. The house is on fire. Joe?"

"Huh?" Hilldorfer looked across the wrought-iron patio table. His wife, Joanne, awaited an answer to a question he had not heard. She looked at his plate of tomato-garlic pasta and he stabbed at the noodles with a fork. "Probably too many sun-dried tomatoes. I should have stuck to the recipe."

Joanne laughed and held up the bottle of Australian chardonnay. "Wine. Do you want more wine?"

He smiled and held out his glass. She poured it half-full. "Sorry."

"Is everything all right?"

It wasn't, but he wasn't about to ruin a beautiful summer evening, a good bottle of wine, and a not too bad attempt at a gourmet pasta dish. He took a sip of wine and looked back out at the view. "I'm fine."

"Uh-huh." She sounded unconvinced. "You didn't finish your dinner."

She knew him well. Though he carried a lean and muscled 185 pounds on his six-foot-one frame, that was largely due to a regimented workout schedule and fast metabolism. He could clean two plates on any night and she'd still find him eating a bowl of chili in the kitchen at 3:00 A.M.

"You're thinking about Boomsnub again, aren't you? You have to let it go, Joe. You did your job. You did everything you could. What happened wasn't because of anything you did."

Given the outcome, he wasn't so sure. At the moment he wasn't sure of a lot of things, except that he didn't feel like talking about it.

She picked up their plates and left him alone on the balcony. Minutes later he heard her calling to him from the kitchen. "Joe, you want me to get that?"

The phone was ringing. They screened their calls at night. He had a feeling he knew who it was—an ears-burning, speak-of-the-devil-type intuition. The answering machine picked up and he heard his own voice telling the caller to leave a message before Dixon McClary's controlled cadence spilled out onto the deck.

"Joe? Joe, pick up your phone."

Joanne answered the extension in the kitchen and untangled the cord as she walked out onto the deck. Hilldorfer finished his glass of chardonnay, stood, and took the phone.

"Hey, Dixon, what's up?"

"What do you remember about Evergreen Resources?"

The name rang a bell but Hilldorfer couldn't place it. "Evergreen Resources?"

"The fertilizer plant in Idaho. Soda Springs. Didn't you take a ride out there once?"

Soda Springs. That had been a year ago. He took a trip to Idaho to talk to the Department of Environmental Quality (DEQ) about some matters. It came back to him. They had complained about an owner of a fertilizer plant with multiple environmental infractions, mostly acid spills, but said the guy was also a lawyer and as slippery as new leather shoes on a waxed floor. They hadn't been able to get any serious charges or fines to stick. Hilldorfer vaguely remembered taking a long drive to look at the plant, a dump of a place, but nothing had come of it.

"Yeah, I did. What's going on?"

"Kelly got a call from an Idaho State Trooper named Bill Reese. Apparently there's shit bubbling all over the ground from a storage tank. I'm sending him over from La Grande." McClary referred to Kelly O'Neil, a special agent stationed in Oregon.

Another acid spill. Great. Soda Springs was at the far reaches of Region 10 and not easy to get to. Hilldorfer held out hope McClary was calling just to determine if he had any information that would be helpful to O'Neil, but already his mind had started the to-do lists—airline and hotel reservations and the "agent's checklist," a phrase his first partner at the FBI, Randy "Bird-Dog" Scott, condemned him to never forget. "Spectacles, testicles, wallet, credentials, and watch."

"Call Wojnicz," McClary said. Bob Wojnicz (pronounced *Voy-nitch*) was the Region 10 EPA duty agent that night. "He took the call at home and may have more information. HAZMAT's driving down from Pocatello," he said, referring to the hazardous materials team. "DEQ and OSHA [Occupational Safety and Health Administration] are already out there with the local and state police. I want you both to meet Kelly as soon as you can get a flight."[1]

It was a large response for an acid spill. "What's going on, Dixon?"

"I just got off the phone with Idaho State Police, Joe. They're saying the owner sent his workers into the tank without any safety equipment. They're in the hospital. One isn't expected to make it through the night."[2]

Tuesday, August 27, 1996
Solutia Chemical Plant
Soda Springs, Idaho

CHAPTER FIVE

THE SECOND-OLDEST city in Idaho, Soda Springs began unceremoniously as a way station for settlers heading west along the Oregon and California trails. Three hundred miles from Boise, nestled in the southeast corner of the state between the Utah and Wyoming borders, it sits at an altitude of 6,000 feet at the big bend in the 165-mile Bear River. The town's existence is attributable to its beauty. Western-bound travelers weary from the mountainous terrain and parched from crossing dry and dusty plains found comfort and respite in the lush valley. They let their animals graze on the tall grass, washed their clothes in the river, and drank from warm springs of water that percolated up from one of nature's great laboratories. A furnace of gasses burst through fissures of earth in geothermal effervescence—hot springs of water spouting three feet in the air. Strongly impregnated with gas, it tasted like soda water, giving the town its name.

General Patrick Edward Conner founded Soda Springs in 1863 with fifty-three Mormon families. Twenty-six years later prospectors searching for gold made a different discovery. The town was in the center of an enormous phosphate bed that had likely formed 250 million years earlier, when a prehistoric inland sea covered much of what became the western United States. The combination of wave action, temperature, topography, and chemical deposition left phosphate-rich sediments across southeastern Idaho, the southwest corner of Wyoming, and northern Utah.

Eventually the phosphate field would be estimated to contain 40 percent of the known phosphate rock reserves in the United States.

The first commercial phosphate mining began in 1906 near Montpelier, Idaho. Miners dug narrow pits to remove rock and dirt, called overburden, to reach the phosphate and produced about eight hundred tons a year. By 1946 modern mining and processing of phosphate fertilizer and elemental phosphorus began. Coke, quartz, and rock were heated in large furnaces to produce white phosphorus. A ubiquitous chemical, it was soon used in everything from toothpaste and soft drinks to detergents, fire retardant fabrics, and weed killers. As demand increased, the value of phosphate rock doubled that of silver.

By 1976 the total production of phosphate ore in Idaho exceeded 75 million tons, and southeastern Idaho had become the top producer of elemental phosphorus and phosphate fertilizers. By 1996 the industry was at its peak, employing three thousand people generating $400 million in annual sales. It was the largest mineral industry in the state and second largest in the nation.[1] Approximately half the Soda Springs workforce was employed within the phosphate industry at half a dozen plants located just to the north of the town on State Highway 34.

With a total population of 3,600, Soda Springs was the seat of Caribou County, but it remained rural, small-town America with modest houses, pickup trucks and RVs in the driveways, a drive-in theater, and a local cafe that served pork chops and pie.[2] A one-stop town, it didn't even require an exit. Highway 30 just became Second Street as it entered the town and continued for a span of perhaps ten blocks east to west past the Caribou Lodge, with its large caribou mounted atop the sign, and retail businesses like John Deere Tractor. Then Second Street, and the town, ended.

DAREN SCHWARTZ moved to Soda Springs in the mid-1970s, driving sixty-five miles up Highway 34 from Preston, Idaho, a small town on the edge of the Utah border. He went to work for Monsanto, where he paid his dues in the furnaces breaking out "slag," the concrete-hard residue from the mining process. In August 1996 the plant was officially called Solutia Chemical Company, though most still referred to it as Monsanto. After several promotions, Schwartz now spent half his time teaching other employees how to safely use heavy equipment and the other half as the plant's fire chief. The latter job had evolved from his work and training with the Caribou County Fire Department, a volunteer organization he joined when it formed in 1988.

At 10:46 A.M. on Tuesday, August 27, Schwartz was inspecting fire extinguishers at the plant with summer relief student Scott Twiss. Schwartz had just snapped an extinguisher back into its place on the wall, checked it off his list, and was about to pick up another relief student he'd left at a remote area of the plant when his voice pager beeped. Voice activated, the message was short, and chilling.

"There is a man down in a tank at Evergreen Resources."

Ordinarily Schwartz would have never left Monsanto or taken its equipment without talking to the plant manager, but he knew Evergreen's reputation as a risky place to work. He interpreted the page as a "Code 3"—life and death. With rescue operations all about speed, he had no time to lose. Evergreen was a quarter of a mile, at most, down North Hooper Road. Schwartz would save time if he responded directly instead of driving into town to the Caribou County firehouse to get the truck.

He turned to Twiss. "This is a serious call. Get in the truck."

He rushed to the back of the truck and pulled on heavy rubber pants and boots then jumped into the cab and exited the plant with lights flashing and sirens wailing. "County Control this is One Frank Four, I'm en route to the scene."

Others would follow. The Soda Springs dispatch service notified all of the town's emergency services—fire, police, and medical emergency personnel; however, none were likely to beat Schwartz. It would be his scene.

Dispatch had not said whether the man had been knocked unconscious or had been overcome from some type of chemical. If it was a chemical, Schwartz knew the longer the exposure, the more likely the man would suffer severe injuries. Either way this would be the real deal. Except for a house fire in Grace where they had retrieved a body, the Caribou County volunteers had never encountered a rescue situation, let alone one in a confined space with a potentially very hazardous chemical.

Two minutes after he left Monsanto's driveway, Schwartz turned left off North Hooper Road onto a dirt road and drove past Soda Springs Phosphate. When he crested the rise and crossed the railroad tracks he saw Allan Elias standing near a construction trailer at the front of the plant. Elias pointed left and Schwartz drove between two dilapidated storage barns toward a series of tanks where two men staggered like drunks failing a field sobriety test. A third man stood atop a weathered tank shouting and waving his arms. As Schwartz parked, one of the men on the ground dropped to his knee, fell to a sitting position, and teetered over onto his back.

Schwartz jumped from the cab and hurried to the back of the truck, his mind working linearly. Given the condition of the two men on the ground, the material in the tank was likely toxic. He'd need a respirator. He slipped on a turnout coat and grabbed an SCBA.

"You're not going to be able to get in the tank with the Air-Pac on. You can't fit. Forget it." The man standing behind Schwartz had a ponytail extending down his back. His breathing was labored and distressed, his face pale and damp. "You're going to need to cut a hole. Forget that stuff. Just get up there and help him."[3] He, too, dropped to his knee, like a mountain climber who had run out of gas at the top of his ascent and was reluctantly giving in to extreme fatigue.

"It's going to be okay," Schwartz assured him. "We have help coming."

He needed to move quickly but not rush. Rushing led to accidents, and accidents at industrial plants, which stored volatile chemicals, could kill those who worked there and those trying to help them. He needed to know what kind of chemical he might be dealing with. He looked for Elias but did not see him.

The man atop the tank, who was on his knees and leaning precariously over the edge, continued yelling at him, telling Schwartz to get a ladder. Schwartz grabbed a ladder from the truck, propped it against the side of the tank, and climbed on top.

"He passed out and went down, we couldn't get him out, he's not conscious, he's barely breathing," Darren Weaver said.

Brian Smith had followed Schwartz up the ladder. "Listen, goddamn it, you can't fit. You're going to need a torch to cut him out."

Schwartz looked down at the narrow entry and understood what Smith had been telling him. The opening was frighteningly small. At six foot two Schwartz was built like old-growth timber, thick and straight. He wouldn't fit, not wearing the bulky turnout gear, maybe not even without it, but there was no way he or anyone else was going in without safety gear. Sixty percent of fatalities in confined spaces were to would-be rescuers.

He looked for the entry permit, which would have the oxygen level in the tank and the LEL—the legal explosive limit. Without knowing those two things, using a torch to cut the tank could be like throwing a firebomb into a gasoline tanker. Required by law for disasters just like this, the permit was supposed to be posted in a place readily available to responders, but Schwartz did not see one.

With Smith continuing to berate him and Weaver rushing on about what had happened, Schwartz dropped to one knee and looked into a pool of black ink. It seemed somehow alive, something from a horror film that had swallowed a man whole and was now baiting him to tempt the same fate, to lean forward just far enough for the darkness to spill out and drag him down. He angled his head, trying to use the ambient light, but he couldn't see anything beyond several rungs of the ladder.

"He's right there," Weaver pointed. "He's against the side of the tank."

As Schwartz's eyes adjusted to the darkness the shadows became distinct from the sheer black curtain and he made out the edges of a light-colored T-shirt, a faint outline like a charcoal sketch of a body stone-still against the side of the tank.

He shouted Dominguez's name into the hole but did not get any reaction. He turned to Weaver and Smith. "Is there any other way in?"

"No!" Smith said, his face flushed and his eyes watering. "You need a torch. You have to cut him out."

The situation was surreal. There was no permit. There was no tripod or harness to pull Dominguez out. There was no safety equipment at all. The men were dressed in jeans and T-shirts. What the hell was going on? Schwartz stood and shouted instructions down to Twiss, telling him to get the tripod and harness equipment off the Monsanto truck.

Smith was adamant. "You need a torch, goddamn it!"

"We can't use a torch if we don't know what's in there. You'll blow everyone up."

"It isn't going to explode. Just get me a torch. I'll cut him out."

Schwartz looked again for Elias but did not see him. Across the railroad tracks, at Soda Springs Phosphate, a man stood on an elevated platform taking pictures. Other employees had started to cross the tracks, just what Schwartz did not need. An already dangerous situation was getting worse. Schwartz heard the sound of approaching sirens and saw emergency vehicles, ambulances, and police cars streaming dust down the dirt road. They'd need room to work.

"You need to get off the tank. You need to get down."

The two men protested.

"We're going to do everything we can for him, but we can't work with you up here in the way. You need to get off the tank and get medical attention. You need to let us do our job."

Ron Myers and John Stoor parked Caribou County Fire Engine 102, a one-ton Ford Chassis, next to the Monsanto truck and got out dressed in their turnout gear. Schwartz yelled down at them to help Twiss with the retrieval equipment.

Seconds later, Myers was atop the tank, setting up a tripod over the hole. "What have we got?"

"One man down in the tank. I haven't seen him move," Schwartz said. "I think he might be dead."

Myers shined a flashlight in the hole. Somewhat claustrophobic, the prospect that a man was trapped inside the tank and that it might be his job to go in and get him out made him break out in a cold sweat.[4] He angled the light toward the east end of the tank and found Dominguez. Schwartz was right. Dominguez was not moving. He did not appear to be breathing.

Schwartz mapped out the rescue scenarios. Stoor, an EMT and the smallest of the three men, would go into the hole with the harness attached to a rope. He'd slip the harness on Dominguez and Schwartz and Myers would pull him up using the winch. Working quickly, Stoor strapped on his SCBA, adjusted the flow of oxygen, and started down the ladder but it became readily apparent he was not going to fit.

"Take off your tank." Schwartz helped Stoor slip off the tank. "Leave your mask on. We'll hand you the tank once you get in."

Schwartz felt the tank shake and turned to see Matt Christiansen coming toward them. At six foot five with broad shoulders, Christiansen looked like an NBA power forward. No way he'd fit. "We're going to need a backup plan if we can't get him in," Schwartz said. "We may need to cut a hole in the end of the tank. Round up some oxygen acetylene hoses and a cutting torch."

Schwartz turned his attention back to Stoor, who held his facemask over his nose and mouth and was starting back down the hole, Myers holding his oxygen tank. Stoor got halfway in the hole when the edges of the tank began to constrict around his turnout gear, making it bunch around his waist. He wouldn't fit.

"No good," he said. He tried to step back up but found he couldn't move. "I'm stuck."

Schwartz and Myers grabbed him under each arm and tugged on his turnout gear, eventually cutting it to get precious inches of room to get him free. Schwartz's only option was to cut a hole, but could he? There were now as many as thirty people at the scene. Fire trucks, ambulances, and police vehicles littered the lot. He tied an Industrial Scientific monitor onto the end of a rope, dropped it into the tank, and began swinging it back and forth. The monitor checked oxygen, carbon monoxide, and hydrogen sulfide levels in the tank. An enriched oxygen environment increased the potential for a fire, and a combustible gas in an oxygen-enriched environment was a recipe for disaster.

Christiansen and Mike Allen, another volunteer firefighter, waited near the sluice, torch in hand. Stoor and Myers knelt, peering into the hole. Schwartz fought the urge to pull the meter out. As much as he wanted to get Dominguez out of the tank, he could not risk the lives of his men. If the meter detected unsafe levels it would sound an alarm and flash red lights. After a few minutes, when it had not gone off, Schwartz pulled the monitor from the tank. The oxygen level was 18.5—depressed not elevated. OSHA allowed an LEL limit of 10 percent. The monitor read 2 percent. It was well within the limit, but only for the area of the tank Schwartz could reach. It was impossible to get an accurate reading for the entire tank. Myers and Stoor looked to him. It was his call.

He took a breath then yelled down to Christiansen. "Cut a hole."

Christiansen sparked the torch, adjusting the nozzle to a hissing, triangular blue flame that would cut as sharp as a blade. Schwartz, Myers, and Stoor climbed down the ladder. Schwartz grabbed David Hirsbrunner, an EMT on site, and told him to get on top of the tank and monitor Dominguez's condition through the opening even though he remained convinced Dominguez was dead. He directed Stoor and Myers to bring the fire hose to where Christiansen was cutting the opening. Spraying the edges, which would be red hot from the torch, would cool them faster and save time on the entry. Stoor and Myers would go in the tank, place Dominguez on a backboard, and pass him back through the hole.

The plan in place, he looked at his men. "Take a breath. I'm not seeing any movement in there. I think he's dead." He walked over to Joe Rice, a Soda Springs police officer, and told him the same thing. "Keep everybody back," he said. "We're doing a body retrieval."

As Rice began moving the crowd back from the tank Schwartz started back toward Christiansen. Hirsbrunner suddenly yelled down at them.

"Hey, I think I saw him move."

◆   ◆   ◆

THERESA COLE wiped down the meat counter in the deli section of the Common Cents Convenience Store, a drab commercial building of cinder block at the corner of Main Street and North Hooper Road. The morning had dragged. Lunch was an hour away.

"I'm afraid to go to work today."

Scott's words haunted her. Evergreen had a bad reputation. People got hurt there, at least two since Scott started. The stories made her nervous. The acid scared her. Scott's clothes came out of the washing machine riddled with holes, beyond repair. It got so that each time she did a load she looked to determine what had gone from being a shirt to a rag. He'd gone through multiple pairs of jeans and ruined at least one pair of his good leather Redwing boots. But she didn't care about the clothes. She cared about him. His hands bore the red marks of acid burns and a scar from an injury working the conveyor belt. One morning he'd burst back into their apartment wearing nothing but his long johns. Sprayed with acid, he had to tear off his clothes because they were burning his skin. Evergreen had no showers. On another occasion he'd been sprayed in the face. She begged him to see an eye doctor, but he refused to go. He said Allan Elias would fire him.

Cole looked up from the counter and saw a familiar car turning into the parking lot. Stacey Thornock pushed open the driver-side door, jumped out, and ran into the store with a wide-eyed look of panic. Before she spoke the first syllable, before the first sound left her lips, Theresa knew. She felt it in that place where hope suppressed unwanted feelings and the irrational belief that bad things only happened to others, never to you. Something had happened. Something bad. Something to Scott.

"I just heard on the scanner," Thornock said. "One of the guys at Evergreen fell into an acid tank."

Theresa dropped the towel and ran.

Inside the car, Stacey told her she had been at home listening to the police scanner when she heard a report of a man down in a tank at Evergreen. They gave no name. They gave no indication the man was dead or alive. They gave no details. Both women knew there was a one-in-four chance it was Scott or Gene, but Theresa knew the odds were actually much worse. She knew Scott and Darren Weaver had been inside a tank the day before, cleaning it out, and it was unlikely things had changed.

"I'm afraid to go to work today."

She wished no harm to anyone, but prayed it was not Scott.

The car pitched down Evergreen's dirt road, kicking up dust, and bounded across the railroad tracks, stopping near the office trailer. The two women shot out of the car running. Cole saw Allan Elias sitting in his yellow truck near the trailer. For a brief moment it was a welcome sight. There had to be a mistake. Allan wouldn't be sitting in his truck if something had happened. But even as her mind held on to that thin line of hope, it could not ignore the emergency vehicles and rescue people surrounding the tank down the road.

She knocked on the driver-side window. "Allan, who fell in the tank?" Elias shook his head.

"Who fell in the tank?" she repeated.

"I'm sorry."[5]

Cole turned and ran down the road, her heart pounding in panic. Behind her Elias yelled. "Don't run."[6]

The emergency vehicles were everywhere—rescue units, fire engines, navy blue police cruisers, and two ambulances—the words *Caribou County* stenciled in blue beneath the universal symbol for medicine, two snakes wrapped around a staff with wings at the top. They had backed down the road and now waited with their doors open. A cluster of men huddled on top of a tank. She didn't see Scott. Another group stood near the rear of the tank dressed in thick pants, jackets, and hard hats. No Scott. She felt lost and alone, frightened and helpless, left to stand spinning in a circle, her eyes darting left and right, searching, hoping to see Scott's golden brown hair and that shining bright smile. But she didn't see him, and with each passing second the ache in the pit of her stomach consumed more and more of her hope, leaving behind a spreading agony of dread.

She saw a familiar face. He sat on the ground, knees pulled to his chest, head hung, chest heaving. Darren Weaver.

"Darren, where's Scotty?"

Weaver shook his head from side to side.

"Darren, where's Scotty?"

Weaver did not answer.

"I'm afraid to go to work today."

Cole looked up and saw Stacey running across the yard toward medical personnel working on a man on a stretcher. It was Gene. Cole scanned the faces standing around the stretcher and saw him mixed with the medical personnel, his hands at his mouth like a schoolboy in prayer.

Brian Smith.

Statistics became reality and it rushed over her like an unseen wave.

Scotty was in the tank.

SCHWARTZ LOOKED UP at Hirsbrunner as if struggling to comprehend a sudden apparition in the sky. "He's alive," he said, almost disbelieving, then to the others. "He's alive."

The blue flame hissed, melting the metal, leaving behind a keloid scar in the tank. Christiansen cut a thirty-inch rip across the top then started down the side. Schwartz repeated his instructions to Stoor and Myers to get the fire hose and an extension ladder ready, then shouted up to Hirsbrunner. "Anything?"

"No," Hirsbrunner yelled back.

Christiansen started down the final side. Six minutes had passed. The final cut would be another two. All eyes now focused on the blue flame inching toward the intersection of the original cut. When they met the piece of metal fell in. Stoor and Myers hit the edge of the hole with a blast of water, the tank emitting a hiss. Then they plugged in their air. Stoor climbed the ladder first, Myers followed. Schwartz watched them enter the tank on hands and knees and disappear into the darkness.

The depth of the sludge at the entrance was only three to four inches, but as Stoor and Myers continued back to Dominguez it deepened, perhaps two feet. Stoor reached Dominguez first. A mask covered his nose and mouth, what Stoor thought to be a five-minute Air-Pac. It was ancient. He grabbed Dominguez's wrist and pressed down with his thumb. "I have a pulse," he said to Myers. It was faint. He yelled at the opening. "He's alive."

Myers was nervous. This was not a training exercise. He couldn't just pull off his mask and laugh if something went wrong.[7] He kept his head down, not wanting to look at Dominguez.

"Are you okay?" Stoor asked.

"I'm fine," he said. "How about you?"

"I'm okay. Grab his legs."

They carried him to the hole. Christiansen and Schwartz handed

Myers a backboard and they rolled Dominguez onto it and passed him out feet first.

As Dominguez came through the hole his limbs hung over the backboard limp as a rag doll. Eyes open, face a pale blue, he looked dead. Though he did not appear to be breathing he was foaming at the mouth. Gurgling sounds rumbled inside his chest. Schwartz had two firefighters prepared to decontaminate Dominguez, but given his condition and the pool bubbling on the ground, an indication the sludge might be water reactive, he changed his mind.

"Forget the water. Get him loaded in the ambulance. Go."

The EMTs quickly bagged him and started CPR, hurrying toward the ambulance.

THERESA COLE collapsed. The air caught in her throat, choking her, then burst from her in hysterical sobs. Missy Weaver, an EMT, helped her to the back of one of the emergency trucks, but now the sight of Scott being carried out of the tank, lifeless, was too much. Cole rushed to him crying and calling his name.

The EMTs shouted to get her out of the way. Schwartz interceded, grabbing her by the shoulders. He turned to Joe Rice. "Joe, get her out of here."

Rice put his arm around Cole's shoulder and escorted her to the police car. As he helped her into the backseat she turned and looked out the back window. The EMTs loaded Scott into the ambulance. Then the doors abruptly shut.

Tuesday, August 27, 1996
Evergreen Resources
Soda Springs, Idaho

CHAPTER SIX

AT 11:10 A.M. DOMINGUEZ was en route to Caribou County Memorial Hospital. Schwartz switched gears. His men stood covered in a foreign substance and their eyes betrayed their calm demeanor.

They were afraid. He needed to know what was in the tank to safely decontaminate them and because he knew that Scott Dominguez's survival, as remote as that appeared, depended on doctors being able to effectively treat him. He had privacy showers set up for Stoor and Myers to change out of their clothes and wash off.

Then he went to find Allan Elias.

Elias's absence from the scene had been the subject of discussion among the rescuers. Normally the problem was trying to keep the owner away from the accident as he overwhelmed rescue personnel with information about the plant and the chemicals stored there.[1]

Schwartz found Elias standing near the office trailer.[2]

"Do you have any information on what's in the tank?" Schwartz asked.

Elias shook his head. "There's nothing in that tank but mud and water."

"Obviously there has to be something more in the tank. I mean, we have somebody hurt. Water didn't hurt him. What could possibly be in there?"

"I don't know. I'm telling you there's nothing in that tank but mud and water."[3]

At a loss, Schwartz hurried back to the fire truck and used the cellular phone to call Chemtrek, the Chemical Manufacturers Association. Chemtrek kept Material Safety Data Sheets (MSDS) that identified the chemicals in products and how to treat persons exposed. Schwartz explained the situation and told Chemtrek someone at the site suggested there might have been cyanide in the tank. Chemtrek told him that without more details they couldn't help him.

Schwartz went back to Elias. "Is there cyanide in the tank? Is that a possibility?"

Elias shook his head. "I told you, there's only water and mud in the tank."

"Please, think of any possibilities that might be in the tank. Is there anything remotely that you can think of that might be in the tank that would have caused this injury?"

Elias said no. He said he had checked the pH before the men started working in the tank and it was five, and that he had sniffed the tank and smelled something. "That's why I told them to wear this respiratory protection." He pointed to the Air-Pac on the ground. "I told them to wear it but they told me it wasn't needed, that the stuff was junk. Look at this stuff. It's brand new. You see that don't you?"

To Schwartz the equipment looked far from brand new. In fact it looked antiquated. Elias also wasn't making sense. Why was Elias telling him there was nothing but mud and water in the tank but that he had insisted on breathing equipment?

"Later on they came back and told me that it wasn't necessary, that those respirators weren't doing them any good, and that they were going to go ahead and do the work without the protection on," Elias continued.[4]

Schwartz left and reported back to his men. They were stunned, Christiansen the most vocal. "How can he say there's nothing in there? There has to be something in there." He pointed to the ooze bubbling into the ground. "What about that?"

Schwartz shook his head. "He's acting cooperative, saying he wants to cooperate, but he's not providing any information. Maybe you could try. Ask him if he has any MSDS sheets that might help."

Christiansen found Elias still standing near the trailer. "Do you have any MSDS sheets that would tell us what's in the tank?"

He got the same response. "No. There is nothing in that tank that required an MSDS sheet."

"Well, there's something in the tank. Don't you have an MSDS sheet?"

"I'm telling you there is nothing in that tank that requires an MSDS sheet."

Frustrated, Christiansen asked Elias a third time. "Look, there's definitely something in the tank that caused this situation. Do you have any MSDS sheets at all on the entire facility?"

Elias shook his head. "There's nothing in the tank that required an MSDS sheet."[5]

DR. JOHN WAYNE OBRAY'S path to chief of surgery at Soda Springs's Caribou County Memorial Hospital was not the typical college to medical school to residency journey. Growing up in Logan, Utah, he attended medical school at the University of Utah then entered the U.S. Army. He did a five-year residency in general surgery and a residency at the West Point military academy in New York before following his heart back out West. He settled in Soda Springs, becoming a fixture in the community during his eighteen years there. Though he was the chief of surgery, the needs of a rural community had made him a jack-of-all-trades, doing just about everything except delivering babies.[6]

On August 27 he received a telephone call from the EMTs advising that they were en route to the emergency room with men injured in a tank at Evergreen Resources.[7] Obray kept an office and clinic near the hospital. As a member of the hospital staff he was required to take a rotation covering the emergency room, and he had treated a number of employees injured in industrial accidents. Given the relatively small size of its work crew, the number of injuries at Evergreen was disproportionately higher than the larger mining and processing facilities.[8]

Obray arrived at the emergency room shortly before 11:00 A.M. Quickly thereafter the first ambulance delivered an Evergreen employee named Gene Thornock. The EMTs advised that another man was en route, but that a third, Scott Dominguez, was unconscious inside the tank. Obray knew Dominguez and his family well, having been the family physician to Scott and his two brothers and sister. He'd treated Scott for wrestling injuries and a laceration, and he'd watched Scott and his older brother, Anthony, wrestle in high school and followed their careers in the local papers. They were both outstanding.

Thornock said he and another worker, Brian Smith, had made multiple attempts to rescue Dominguez from the tank, but when he entered the tank he had trouble breathing and felt as if he was going to pass out. Once he got out of the tank he'd start to feel better. He was complaining of headaches but his vital signs—his blood pressure, heart rate, and oxygenation (amount of oxygen in his blood)—were normal and he appeared fully alert and in no respiratory distress. He was, however, covered in a pond-gray material.

"Is your skin burning?" Obray asked.

"No."

Having a poor sense of smell, Obray turned to nurse Debbie Little. "Can you smell anything?"

She shook her head. "No."

"Scott's in bad shape," Thornock said. "He was breathing real slow."

It puzzled Obray. Thornock appeared strong and healthy, as was

Dominguez. What chemical could take down healthy men so quickly? Knowing he was about to receive a critically injured patient, and being the type of doctor who looked for conditions he could treat, Obray continued to question Thornock about the sludge.

"Do you know what this stuff is?"

Thornock shook his head.

Having a limited knowledge of the work performed at the local plants, Obray knew the men worked with hydrochloric acid and phosphoric acid but dismissed them because he had very sensitive skin and he had no irritation despite getting the sludge on his hands. He also knew the employees at the plants worked with ammonia, and hydrogen sulfide. Both were pungent. The sludge had no discernible odor.

"Did you smell any noxious odors or gas?" he asked Thornock.

"No."

He speculated the substance could be chlorine, but chlorine would have irritated the mucous membranes, eyes, and throat. It was also visible as a brown vapor.

"Did you see any gas?"

"No."

At approximately 11:15 A.M., with still no clear answers, Obray triaged Thornock to the hospital floor where he was put in a shower then taken to Room 108A.

Eleven minutes later Obray received a call from dispatch. Four Adams, the call sign for the Caribou County ambulance, was 1076 with a twenty-year-old male in severe respiratory distress. It arrived minutes later. Thornock had not exaggerated Dominguez's condition. The emergency medical technicians rushed him into the emergency room beating on his chest and bagging him. They told Obray that Dominguez had a pulse when he was pulled from the tank, but they could not find one in the ambulance for several minutes, then Dominguez began thrashing about, fighting to breathe before he again went still. They thought Dominguez had gone into "cardiac arrest," which was why they were continuing to perform CPR.

Unconscious and deathly still, Dominguez was coated with the slimy, semi-liquid substance. Obray immediately intubated him—forcing a tube down his throat into his lungs to establish an adequate airway. Dominguez did not respond with a cough reflex, confirming his serious condition. Obray put a small device over one of Dominguez's fingernails to measure his oxygen level and was surprised, given Thornock's recount of the tank, to find Dominguez's level to be 100 percent. He was getting more than enough oxygen. Why was he comatose? As Obray worked, so did the nurses. They started an IV in Dominguez's right hand and hooked him up to a cardiac monitor, which displayed a heart rate of 120 and a normal sinus rhythm. His blood pressure was 123 over 79. A catheter was put into his bladder.

By 11:30, Dominguez was breathing at a normal rate of twelve breaths a minute, but remained unconscious. Obray pulled back Dominguez's eyelids and shined a penlight into each eye. The nurse recorded Dominguez's treatment and Obray's assessments. "Pupils are undilated and asymmetric. Responsive to light."

The condition of a patient's pupils can tell a lot. If they are dilated and fixed, unresponsive to light, it indicates an irreversible brain condition, usually caused by severe trauma or a prolonged lack of oxygen. If dilated, it indicates severe anoxia or lack of oxygen to the brain. If one pupil is asymmetric it can indicate swelling or bleeding within the brain. Dominguez's pupils were round and light responsive. What was wrong with him?

Obray put a nasogastric tube through Dominguez's nostril and fed it into his stomach to decompress it. Without a gag reflex, if Dominguez vomited it could go into his lungs. Again Dominguez showed no reaction to the invasion. It was becoming apparent he was beyond what the Caribou facility could do to treat him.

Obray had mentally eliminated the likely chemicals that could have caused the injury with the exception of one. Thornock said he couldn't breathe inside the tank, couldn't get enough oxygen, but when he left the tank he would recuperate. Dominguez also appeared to be getting more than enough oxygen, but his body was not utilizing it. The only chemical Obray knew capable of dropping healthy men so fast, that caused irregular breathing and prevented the body from effectively utilizing oxygen, was cyanide. A person exposed eventually lapsed into a coma, seizures, respiratory arrest, and, ultimately, cardiac arrest. But with the improvement in worker conditions in the United States, cyanide injuries were increasingly rare. It had become, essentially, a third-world problem. Cyanide poisoning required a specific antidote, a kit with two chemicals—sodium thiosulfate and sodium nitrate, which bound with the cyanide in the blood and allowed the cells to once again utilize oxygen.

The hospital did not carry one.

At 11:40 A.M., Obray took an intermediate step that could also act to bind the cyanide in the blood. He broke five ampules of amyl nitrate— smelling salts—beneath Dominguez's nostrils and held them over the endotracheal tube. It had no observable effect. At 11:48 A.M., Obray called Life Flight, the helicopter transport service, and told them he needed a patient transferred to the Bannock Regional Medical Center in Pocatello. He then called Bannock and requested that they accept Dominguez for transfer and have Life Flight fly down a cyanide antidote. If Obray was right he did not have much time. The flight from Pocatello was only fifteen minutes, but with the time to assemble the crew it would take between thirty and fifty minutes for the helicopter to arrive. Administering the antidote on his end would save time, which was continuing to slip away.

When he got off the phone with Bannock, Obray called Poison Control in Boise, told them the clinical situation, and said his educated guess was that the likely agent was cyanide. He asked if they had any other idea what might cause this type of loss of consciousness. The poison control center could think of nothing else.

"What if I give him the cyanide antidote? What if I give it to him and he hasn't been exposed to cyanide? Can I hurt him?"

Given the severity of Dominguez's condition, Poison Control said, "No."

Obray continued to break the ampules and hold them over the endotracheal tube. At 11:53 he did it three times without response. Then he picked up the phone in the emergency room and called Kerr-McGee looking for his friend Joe Hulse. Obray had a hunch. Kerr-McGee was a mile from an abandoned plant called Dregerstrom. Dregerstrom had used cyanide to extract gold and silver from mining ore, and he remembered that ten to twelve years earlier someone from the plant had brought a cyanide kit to the hospital. The mine eventually took the kit back to the plant, worried the hospital was too far away in the event of an emergency. Hulse was not at work. Obray hung up and called Hulse's cell phone, catching him at home having lunch. He quickly brought him up to speed and asked him to see if he could find a cyanide antidote kit at the old Dregerstrom site.

Hulse said he would try.

Obray then called the local police and asked Captain Joe Rice to also search for the kit.

At 11:56 A.M., Dominguez was suctioned and suddenly opened his eyes, but it was a nonpurposeful stare and he did not otherwise move.

Hulse called back. "John, no luck. I couldn't find it."

Obray heard voices in the background. "Where are you now?"

"I'm at Evergreen."

"Is Elias there?"

"Yeah, he's right here."

"Put him on," Obray said. "I want to talk to him."

Obray asked Elias about the sludge. Elias said it was being used in a fertilizer operation and had no further information. Obray hung up and went back to focusing on Dominguez. He checked the results of a blood draw and an arterial blood gas, drawing blood directly from the artery to measure the pH in Dominguez's blood, the carbon dioxide level, and the partial pressure of oxygen. The carbon dioxide was normal. The oxygen was 365, nearly six times normal. Dominguez was getting more than enough oxygen, but his body was not utilizing it.

As Obray reviewed the results Joe Rice rushed into the emergency room. They'd caught a break. The Soda Springs policeman had found the Dregerstrom kit. Obray put it on the table and opened it, his relief becoming further frustration. The kit had expired. It was useless.

A nurse advised him that Allan Elias had arrived at the emergency room. Obray found him standing in the hallway, looking in.[9]

"How is he?" Elias asked as Obray approached.

Obray shook his head. "It's very bad," he said. "I think he's going to die." He looked over his shoulder at Dominguez, tubes protruding from his nose, mouth, groin, and arms. Then he turned back to Elias. "Do you have any more information about what could be in the tank? Because I think it's cyanide."[10]

CHAPTER SEVEN

WITH NO DIRECT flights to Pocatello, Hilldorfer and Wojnicz flew to Boise, Idaho's capital, and took a twin-engine prop plane the remaining three hundred miles. Though the flight was at a civilized hour, Hilldorfer had been up since five o'clock packing, getting to the airport, and thinking about what lay ahead.

What he continued to like best about law enforcement, and did well, was interviewing what he universally referred to as "the bad guys." It had been easier at the FBI; the moniker carried significant weight when it came to getting people to talk. Most people didn't even know what EPA meant, let alone that the agents had law enforcement powers. Telling someone you were a special agent with the EPA wasn't going to make them talk, and getting the bad guy to talk during the initial interview was critical. If they refused, by the time an agent could realistically obtain a search warrant, at a minimum twenty-four hours, the guy had usually "lawyered-up," which meant their attorney was talking for them.

Hilldorfer likened the first interview to walking across a high school gymnasium and asking a girl to dance. How the agent projected himself in those first few moments could be the difference between walking onto the dance floor or walking off it alone. If the agent made it onto the dance floor he then had to choose the right interview technique to keep the person talking. One wrong question could end the dance.

Forty-five minutes after takeoff, Hilldorfer and Wojnicz stepped down a metal staircase into a dry desert heat and retrieved their luggage at the side of the plane. Wojnicz switched his glasses for a pair of reflector aviator sunglasses as he considered the Pocatello airport, which was one gate.

"Looks like a Costco."

With a dark complexion, military-short salt-and-pepper hair, and a pencil-thin mustache, Wojnicz looked like a homicide detective from a television show. Hilldorfer was several inches taller. His German descent showed in aquiline features, blue eyes, and a fair complexion.

Inside the terminal Wojnicz rented the fastest car he could get, an Intrepid, slipped on a pair of driving gloves, and before Hilldorfer could fasten his seat belt and say a prayer to Saint Christopher, the patron saint of travelers, they were speeding at a hundred miles an hour on U.S. 34 through Pocatello. Midge, at the Avis counter, told Wojnicz the drive to Soda Springs was sixty-three miles and took an hour.

"Forty minutes," Wojnicz predicted. Hilldorfer didn't doubt him.

Wojnicz put his fanny pack with his nine-millimeter Glock on the seat. He'd expressed surprise when Hilldorfer walked through airport security without declaring a weapon. Agent protocol required that an agent be capable of responding to an emergency with deadly force.

"You didn't bring your gun?"

Hilldorfer shook his head. "Didn't want to hassle with the forms. Besides, I knew you'd come armed for both of us." In truth he no longer considered the Environmental Protection Agency's Criminal Investigation Division blood-and-guts law enforcement. Not what he had known at the FBI. Not what his father had done.

The son of a cop, born just a stone's throw from Three Rivers Stadium in the blue-collar suburb of Pittsburgh's North Side, Hilldorfer grew up knowing the good guys and the bad guys intimately. The Hilldorfers were fixtures in North Side, once a German immigrant and Union stronghold. In the 1860s his great-grandfather "Diamond" Joe Hilldorfer owned a market house in downtown Pittsburgh and a large plantation-style home in the lower North Side where he raised champion bulldogs and prized roosters.

His son, Ben, took a job as a butcher in his father's market, earning $20 a week until apparent tax problems and generosity to strangers put Diamond Joe out of business. Ben went to work for Donahue Markets as a butcher in downtown Pittsburgh, met his future wife at church, and moved into her father's house on Perrysville Avenue. They had three children—a daughter and two sons. He named the first son Ben, and the second after his father, Joseph P. Hilldorfer II. After stints in the U.S. Army, both his sons returned to the North Side. Joe bought a house on Veteran Street, two blocks from his parents, where he also raised three children—two daughters and his son, whom he also named Joe.

In the late 1960s and early 1970s, North Side grew progressively more run-down and crime-ridden. Determined to get his children out of the deteriorating public school system, Joe Hilldorfer rose at 4:30 A.M. to drive a school bus before his shift at the police department. The extra money paid to send Joe and his two sisters to the Annunciation Grade School. The only problem was, to get to Annunciation, Joe still had to walk past the public schools and down Charles Street, which had become the great dividing line between the haves and have nots. Tall and thin, he was a clear target.

He spent a lot of his time with his grandfather on Perrysville, going there for homemade milkshakes and ham salad sandwiches and discussions on topics such as handling the bullies in the neighborhood.

"Best not to fight if you can help it because there can be consequences," his grandfather told him. "But if you can't get out of it, make sure you hit them as hard and as fast as you can under the bridge of the nose. If you get the first one in, you have a chance to finish what they started."

It normally worked.

He also learned how to hunt and shoot. Each fall the Hilldorfer men—his father, grandfather, and uncle—went to the family cabins at Sandy Lake and at Indiana, Pennsylvania, to shoot rabbit, squirrel, and grouse. Joe learned he could shoot, but he didn't enjoy killing animals. What he really liked was going to Baker's Town just outside Pittsburgh to "run the dogs," a summer ritual to prepare the animals for the fall hunting season. He and his grandfather would kick up brush piles, spook a rabbit, and watch the beagles chase it for miles through thickets, brush, and streams, never giving up until they'd circled the rabbit back to the hunters for what was usually a single shot.

Hilldorfer attended North Catholic High School, an all-boys school where sports were like a religion, and grew from a lanky five foot nine, 130 pounds, to a lean-muscled six foot one, 185 pounds. He lettered in basketball and soccer. After graduating he became the first Hilldorfer to attend college, taking criminal law classes at a local community college where he found a mentor in a blind African-American professor named James Spruill. Spruill spoke frequently about the cost that white-collar criminals exacted on society, and the disparate way the justice system treated them and violent criminals. Hilldorfer started to seriously consider a career in law enforcement. He set his sights on the FBI.

In 1977 he graduated cum laude with a degree in criminology from Indiana University of Pennsylvania and took a job teaching local police officers firearms shooting skills to pay for his master's degree in criminal justice the next year. Diplomas in hand and eager to get his career started, he drove to the local FBI offices where he was promptly told a federal hiring freeze was in place. The FBI wasn't accepting applications. Plan B was law school.

At the University of Pittsburgh School of Law, Hilldorfer continued his focus on criminal law, working at the public defender's office and the district attorney's office. When he passed the Pennsylvania bar he thought his career was set as a public defender.

But law enforcement was in his blood.

A law school acquaintance called out of the blue and told him the FBI was taking applications. Hilldorfer never hesitated. He spent an afternoon in interviews at the Federal Building and endured an extensive background check. On June 30, 1984, he was riding a bus with forty other candidates to the FBI training facility in Quantico, Virginia, where he would spend eighteen weeks surviving a physically and mentally rigorous boot camp that weeded out many who had been on that bus.

At his graduation in November 1984 they handed him an envelope containing a card that said Seattle, Washington. He knew nothing about Seattle except that it was wet, had a reputation for good fugitive work, and the people who lived there drank a lot of coffee and didn't cross the street against a red light.

In Seattle the FBI became his family. They picked him up at SeaTac airport, found him a hotel, got him situated in the city, and assigned him a training agent, a salty old dog and decorated Marine with a metal plate in his head named Keith Wilson. On Hilldorfer's first day on the job Wilson pulled him aside and told him the three essential rules: "One, you got to know how to get the car out of the garage. Two, you got to know where to have coffee every morning where the supervisor can't find you. Three, your hair grows on Bureau time. Get it cut on Bureau time if you want to have a life."

With that advice Hilldorfer met his first supervisor, Ron Beinner. Beinner handed him a daunting stack of forms detailing what seemed like an endless number of ways the Bureau would evaluate his performance, but like Wilson, Beinner cut to the chase. "The only thing that matters, Joe, is the AIJs. Put the assholes in jail and you'll be all right."

Hilldorfer asked to be assigned to the White-Collar Crime Squad but was sent to Squad 5, the Reactive Squad, also known as the Animal Squad because it responded to armed robberies, hijackings, kidnappings, and other violent crimes. It was a rare assignment for a rookie. Hilldorfer worked out religiously to fit in. He lowered his body fat to 4 percent and improved his shooting skills, becoming a SWAT team sniper, which was where the legends in the Seattle Bureau worked, men like "Granola" Jake Jay, "Shogun" Mike Byrne, and Larry "The Weasel" Montague. Agents in the office started calling Hilldorfer "The Animal."

In 1988 the Bureau transferred him to the New York Field Office. As luck would have it the transfer came at the same time he met the woman he loved, an assistant U.S. attorney in Seattle. Joanne gave New York a try but it wasn't for her. She moved back home to Seattle and waited. In New York, Hilldorfer's career took off. He joined the Foreign and Counter Intelligence Squad, I-22, working undercover with access to a suite of rooms at The Plaza and a chauffeur-driven stretch limousine. It was heady stuff and Hilldorfer loved it, but being away from Joanne was like dying. For two years they commuted every holiday and long weekend. When the Bureau ultimately refused his request for a transfer back to Seattle he stood at a crossroads. Again, fate intervened. Dixon McClary called. McClary was the special agent in charge of the EPA/CID's Region 10 office in Seattle. He said he'd heard Hilldorfer might be looking to make a change to get back to Seattle and asked if Hilldorfer might be interested in the EPA/CID. Hilldorfer hadn't even heard of it, but he agreed to meet with McClary the next time he was in Seattle. In between, he sniffed around. What he heard from other FBI agents wasn't encouraging. They said going from the FBI to the EPA would be like going from the United States to Pakistan.

He met McClary in a Starbucks parking lot in West Seattle. Puffing on a cigarette, McClary had tough, weathered skin and a deep smoker's voice. He looked and sounded like the advertisement for the Marlboro Man. McClary had been one of the Criminal Investigation Division's original sixteen agents after a career with the Drug Enforcement Agency and was a true believer in the environmental justice program. When the program opened its doors on December 2, 1970, Bill Ruckelshaus, the EPA's first director, had proclaimed it the eight-hundred-pound gorilla in the closet, a strong deterrent to those who would violate America's environmental laws.[1] The original agents were considered the best of the best, men and women from every law enforcement agency in the country. McClary had worked hard to try to make the program succeed despite limited manpower and funds, and it was obvious he also knew Hilldorfer's reputation for working big cases with the Bureau's clout and limitless resources. Not wanting Hilldorfer to have any false illusions that he'd have the same resources at the EPA, he was blunt.

"You sure you want to come work for this chicken-shit outfit?"

WOJNICZ TOOK an exit for Highway 30, a two-lane road that funneled between barren rolling hills of lava rock formations, abandoned mining shacks, and dilapidated farmhouses long since abandoned and teetering on the edge of collapse. Fifteen minutes later they came over a crest in the road to a vista that afforded them a breathtaking view. A valley of rich farmland sparkled green and gold in the glint of a summer sun. It spread out like a huge patchwork quilt, farm roads crisscrossing it at right angles. In the distance a range of snowcapped, sawtoothed mountains loomed. But amid the beauty, Hilldorfer saw distant stacks emitting trails of smoke like burning cigarettes, and watched a procession of eighteen-wheel commercial trucks streaming past them in the opposite direction. Things were rarely what they seemed.

Wednesday, August 28, 1996
Soda Springs, Idaho
1:00 P.M.

CHAPTER EIGHT

THE TWO AGENTS decided to drive straight to Evergreen to try to talk with some of the employees. Experience had taught them that employers, who bore the potential for liability, tended to color what had happened to protect themselves, or they outright lied. Employees were the best witnesses if you could get them talking.

Just past a golf course on Highway 30, Hilldorfer spotted police lights atop a black suburban parked in a dirt-and-gravel parking lot of a roadside diner, Betty's Café. He knew from working environmental crimes in small towns in eastern Washington that word of a local tragedy spread like a wildfire in a field of dry grass, and local law enforcement was usually in the center of the blaze. It was also important to have as much information as possible before conducting an interview, and talking to the local police could be a good place to start. At the moment they were flying blind.

"Pull over. Let's see what the locals have to say."

Wojnicz pulled in behind the suburban, which had a shovel mounted on the back and the words *Idaho State Police* on the door panel. An Idaho State Trooper dressed in full uniform got out and met them at the back of the SUV, introducing himself as Bob Clements. Hilldorfer recognized it as the name McClary mentioned on the telephone.

"You drove down with Kelly O'Neil," Hilldorfer said.

At six foot one and maybe ten pounds shy of two hundred, Clements was in good shape. He had a trimmed mustache and equally well kept sandy brown hair. "I got one of the employees in there," he said, nodding to the car and keeping his voice low. "Kelly's at Evergreen. He's going to need your help."

Clements was obviously concerned about spooking the witness in the car, which told Hilldorfer he knew what he was doing. While employees could be the best witnesses to a workplace injury, they were also the most reluctant. If they testified against their employer, at the very least they lost their job. In a small town word of an employee cooperating with government agencies like OSHA, DEQ, and the EPA got around. It put their livelihood and the well-being of their families at risk.

"Just point me in the right direction," Hilldorfer said, not wanting to interfere with Clements's interview.

Clements pointed down Highway 30. "Head straight on out. Drive through town and take a left on Third East and a right on Hooper. You won't miss it."

The two agents got back into their car; at just after 1:00 p.m. they drove through Soda Springs. It reminded Hilldorfer of the one-stop towns that had sprung up along the highway in remote stretches of eastern Washington. It looked like a town that had stopped growing in the 1950s, the shops in need of a coat of paint, but it was quaint, small-town America. Hilldorfer half-expected to see a kid with a crew cut and black PF Flyer tennis shoes turn the corner on his Schwinn bike.

They followed Clements's directions, eventually turning left out of town onto Highway 34, North Hooper Road. As they crested an incline the scenery became familiar from his previous visit. Hilldorfer knew they were close. "Slow down. It's up here on the right."

A white wooden sign, weathered and faded, was staked in the ground. The words *Evergreen Resources* in an equally faded robin's-egg blue marked a dirt road.

"That's it."

Wojnicz hung a right and kicked up dust down a dirt road parallel to a plant Hilldorfer recalled as Soda Springs Phosphate. A Paul Bunyanesque character stood at the end of the road screaming at a reed-thin police officer on the opposite side of the tracks with his arms folded as if he were watching a rabid dog behind an invisible electric fence.

"You come across these tracks, John, and I will arrest you," the officer said.[1]

Hilldorfer surprised himself by not only recognizing the agitated man but remembering his name. "That's John Hatfield. He owns Soda Springs Phosphate." Hatfield had approached Hilldorfer on his prior trip to tell him about numerous acid spills at Evergreen. It had been clear to Hilldorfer that there was no love lost between Hatfield and Elias.

Hatfield rushed the car like a protester, screaming into the window. Red in the face and foaming at the mouth he was projecting spittle like an actor trying to hit the back wall with every word. "No one is doing nothing. I've been telling people for years about this goddamn place and nobody does nothin'. How does this happen? I keep telling people someone is going to get killed and nobody does a goddamn thing."[2]

"Drive through," Hilldorfer said, realizing there was no point engaging Hatfield in his current state.

They flashed their badges at the officer and he waved them through. Wojnicz parked alongside cars near a double-wide trailer and they stepped out to a foul smell, like burning rubber. Wojnicz looked at Evergreen's dilapidated equipment and shook his head.

"What a dump. It looks like Barter Town in *Beyond Thunderdome,*" he said, referring to the Mel Gibson Mad Max movie. "Christ, the guy could have got hurt almost anywhere around here."

The police officer had followed them and identified himself as the Soda Springs chief of police, Blyn Wilcox. "I told him I will arrest him if he crosses the tracks," he said, nodding to Hatfield. "What can I do for you?" he asked, his tone not exactly friendly.

"We're here to investigate the accident that happened yesterday," Hilldorfer said. "We're looking to interview Allan Elias."

Wilcox looked them up and down while rubbing the top of his head. More bald than balding with a face wrinkled like a dried apple, he looked to be at least in his seventies. "Well, you can go interview Allan and do what you got to do," he said. "But you boys better not spend the night in Soda Springs or go to any of the bars in town. You might get yourself in some trouble."[3] Then he turned and walked back to the tracks.

Hilldorfer looked at Wojnicz. "Did you just hear what I heard?"

Wojnicz smiled. "Yes, I did," he said. "Always nice to be welcomed."

They started for the trailer and stopped at the same time, looking down at the ground, which was cracked like concrete but had the color and consistency of warm tar, an elasticity that compressed beneath their weight. As they stood pressing down on the ground the trailer door flew open suddenly and a tanned, heavyset man burst out like a bull from a chute. He passed them without a word and stormed down a path between barnlike structures to where a group stood near a series of tanks.

Kelly O'Neil stepped out of the trailer behind him and walked down the three wooden stairs. O'Neil was perhaps five foot six and maintained the lean build of a former high school gymnast. With thinning hair showing gray, round glasses, and heavy eyebrows he looked more like an aggrieved accountant than an investigator. He also had a temper, and when he got angry his Irish heritage showed in his face, which lit up as red as a Christmas light. At the moment it was glowing.

"What's going on?" Hilldorfer asked, shaking hands.

"This guy's upset. I don't know if he is going to talk anymore."

O'Neil employed an admittedly aggressive interview style that could be officious, and it rubbed some people the wrong way. But O'Neil was an experienced agent, and Hilldorfer knew he and O'Neil would have the same agenda.

"Did he give consent?"

Getting consent to take samples of the material in the tank was the number one priority. If Elias gave consent they wouldn't have to run out and get a search warrant.

O'Neil rubbed a hand across a chin darkened by a five o'clock shadow. "He gave consent, but he gets upset and just goes off. I'm afraid he's going to pull the plug and tell us to get the fuck out of here."

Hilldorfer looked down the path at Elias pinballing between the group gathered by the tank, his arms waving. "Then let's get the sample and get out of here. Who's coming?" Hilldorfer asked, meaning to take the sample. It wasn't going to be him. The toxic stuff frightened him. It was well known in the office that "Joe don't do moon suits."

O'Neil checked his watch. "Bill Frutel should be here in about an hour. He's on his way from Boise." Frutel was an EPA on-scene coordinator. Hilldorfer and Wojnicz both knew him. O'Neil then explained that Bob Clements made the initial call to Dixon McClary, who tracked down O'Neil in a hotel in La Grande, Oregon. O'Neil checked out of his hotel at 10:00 P.M. and drove to Boise, arriving at 1:30 A.M. He was on the road with Clements to Soda Springs at 5:00 A.M., stopping to pick up Dave Hull, an inspector from the Department of Environmental Quality in Pocatello. DEQ had information on Elias at Evergreen and at a former site he owned in Pocatello, Idaho, called AEI, Inc. Elias had also given O'Neil a history of Evergreen and his version of the events.

"But Elias is squirrelly," O'Neil said. "Whenever I ask him for documents or try to ask him something specific he says he's preparing a report for the police."

Having just met the local police, Hilldorfer suspected that was a likely problem. "We ran into Clements on the way in," he said. "He's got a witness in the car."

O'Neil told them the witness was Darren Weaver, an Evergreen employee, and that Weaver had walked into the trailer unannounced while O'Neil and Clements talked with Elias.

"Elias didn't want Weaver talking to anyone. He took him behind that building for about twenty minutes."

"What did he talk about?"

"Don't know," O'Neil said. "I had Clements follow him when he left Evergreen to try to find out what he and Elias had talked about."

As O'Neil talked Elias stormed back up the road. Hilldorfer estimated him to be just over six feet with arms and legs that seemed short for a stout torso. He looked like a pop-eyed toad. With an olive complexion, dark hair, and a meaty face, Elias was dressed in unblemished navy blue western jeans, cowboy boots, and a long-sleeved dress shirt open at the neck.

"I just tested the liquid coming out of the tank and my pH paper continues to be five," he growled at O'Neil. "That DEQ guy told me the emergency responders indicated a pH of two. They're wrong." He looked at Hilldorfer and Wojnicz as if just seeing them. "Who are you?"[4]

Hilldorfer introduced himself and Wojnicz. Elias dismissed them and turned back to O'Neil. "I want to talk with you in private."

Elias didn't seem the least bit intimidated to have federal investigators and regulators at his plant. He sounded defiant. O'Neil followed him back inside the trailer and emerged five minutes later with a message. "He says he's not content having so many investigators at his plant."

"What does that mean, 'not content'?" Hilldorfer asked. "Does he want us to leave?"

"No, I asked him that. He said he doesn't want people all over his plant. He'll give us a few minutes to 'gather our thoughts,' but he's thinking about ending it."

Hilldorfer's training and experience told him Elias was drawing lines in the sand, a security zone, and that he needed to feel in control. It was best to let him think that was the case. They all agreed that Hilldorfer would go back inside with O'Neil. Wojnicz would wait outside.

Hilldorfer followed O'Neil up the steps. When they reached the door O'Neil stopped. "I got a bad feeling he's going to pull the plug."

Hilldorfer shook his head. "Don't worry about it. We'll do a little rope-a-dope in there."

The inside of the trailer was typical of trailers on construction sites. Dimly lit by bare fluorescent tubes, it had a low, tiled ceiling that made Hilldorfer want to duck his head. Shelving made from wood scraps lined cheap paneled walls and overflowed with junk, making the space even more narrow and cluttered. Dust had settled on metal desks indicating infrequent use, and while Elias had a telephone Hilldorfer saw no file cabinets, fax machines, computers, or other office equipment he normally associated with a functioning office. He found this curious.

Elias stormed from the back of the trailer as they entered. "I have a little bit more to say and that's going to be the end of the interview." Elias pointed to O'Neil. "I want you to write down just what I say." He turned to Hilldorfer. "You have a business card?"

Hilldorfer handed a card to Elias. He considered it as though he was committing it to memory. "I told Kelly you're going to hear what I have to say and that's going to be the end of it. I got too many things going on today."

Hilldorfer stuck out his hand. "Allan, I'm sorry you've been through so much today. You must be having a hard day."

Elias paused, seeming uncertain what to make of the comment. He took the hand. "There's been a lot of people here. I don't want a bunch of people running all over my plant."

Hilldorfer got the impression that if he could, Elias would run around the plant lifting his leg and marking his territory, and it was a concession Hilldorfer was, at the moment, willing to give. "We're not going to be running all over your plant. I understand you're trying to run a business and I'll be as sensitive to that as I can. We don't want to do anything more than necessary to disrupt your business."

Elias appeared to calm. "You're not disrupting my business. I sent my employees home. They're not here." Hilldorfer detected a New York City accent; Elias sounded like Larry King, the talk-show host, but with a temper.

"That's fine, and you don't have to talk to us. If you want us to leave, that's your right," Hilldorfer said. "But we need to get a sample of what came out of that tank because I understand a number of your employees almost died yesterday. You don't have to give us a sample, but I came all the way from Seattle to find out what happened, and I *will* call an assistant U.S. attorney in Boise to get a search warrant to get a sample because that's my job."

Hilldorfer waited. He had asked Elias for a dance. Now he stood in the middle of the gymnasium waiting for the answer.

"There's no need to get a search warrant or the U.S. attorney," Elias said. "I want to be the most cooperative guy you ever dealt with. Certainly you can get a sample. Certainly I'll talk with you."

The fact that Elias had been able to change emotions as if flipping a switch indicated he was testing the waters to see how far he could push the agents. Con men Hilldorfer had interviewed in Seattle and New York while with the FBI did the same thing. But the same qualities that made them successful were also their biggest weaknesses. Bright, articulate, and charismatic, they needed to feel they were in control, and because they believed they were smarter than everyone else they believed they could talk their way out of any situation. Hilldorfer had learned that whether they told the truth or lied didn't matter. It was the story they had to live with and more times than not it became the grave they dug for themselves. Hilldorfer was content to just let Elias talk.

Elias took a seat in a swivel chair behind a desk and proceeded to re-

peat much of the information O'Neil had already told him. He said he
bought the underground storage tank in 1988 from a commercial facility
in Pocatello for a few thousand dollars.

Mindful of O'Neil's statement that Elias wouldn't respond to specific
questions, Hilldorfer interrupted him. "What was the name of the company?"

Elias waved him off. "I'm not going to answer detailed questions until
I finish what I have to say."

Elias said he had used the tank in a former business called AEI, Inc., in
Pocatello, Idaho, which he described as "DEQ permitted"—a term that
indicated he was familiar with environmental regulations. He said AEI
reclaimed precious metals from something called "treater dust" that Elias
got from FMC, a company just across the street. Elias said the tank was
used in a cyanide circuit system to recover silver from the dust and that
fertilizer was made from the waste. The bottom of the tank, Elias said,
had accumulated a sludge material of heavy metals from that process.[5]

Hilldorfer had no idea what Elias was talking about, having barely
made it through high school chemistry, but with O'Neil taking notes like
a stenographer, he was content to let Elias continue uninterrupted.

"The process was a success, too." Elias held his hands about a foot
apart and said he had produced a bar of silver the size of a twelve-inch
gold bar. "And it would have continued to be successful except for some
bothersome regulations that forced me to shut it down."

Elias said he put the tank out of commission for about a year, then had
the liquid material drained and moved the tank to Evergreen where he
had used it to store "wash water." A month before the accident he sent
an employee into the tank to get samples "without any problems" and
said the samples had a pH of 5.0. He sent the samples to a lab to be analyzed for silver concentrates.

To Hilldorfer it sounded like Elias was marshaling a defense and he
recalled DEQ telling him Elias was a lawyer.

Elias explained that he directed his employees to remove the sludge at
the bottom of the tank using shovels and a fire hose. He said the sludge
contained gypsum, a product that came from phosphate ore, which Evergreen obtained from Kerr-McGee, and he intended to let it dry in the sun
then mix it with other material he got from Kerr-McGee to make fertilizer. To Hilldorfer it sounded like a scam, but it was readily apparent that
Elias knew that if the material could be classified as a "product" it was not

a hazardous waste regulated by the Resource Conservation and Recovery Act, known by its acronym RCRA (Rick-ra). In 1976, Congress had taken a bold step in the hazardous waste battle by enacting RCRA, a wide-scale series of laws the EPA was fond of saying created a "cradle to grave" regulatory system because it governed hazardous waste from the point of generation until its final disposal.[6]

"I had a two-hour safety meeting with them yesterday morning," Elias said, referring to his employees. "I told them I wanted the sludge removed from the tank but that I was concerned with how they did it. I told them there were regulations concerning confined spaces that absolutely had to be followed, and that we had to fill out an entry permit before anyone entered the tank."[7]

Elias said one of his employees, Brian Smith, had confined-space entry training at a former job and volunteered to take care of the permit. He said Scott Dominguez, the injured employee, told him that he got new chemical canisters for the respirators from a company called Bisco, so there should have been no problem with respiratory protection in the tank.

"I specifically instructed them to use the SCBAs," Elias said, adding that he told another employee, Gene Thornock, to remain on top of the tank in visual and verbal contact with "the two younger guys," and "to be sure to use the safety harnesses and ropes in case Dominguez or Weaver had a problem while they were inside the tank."

Hilldorfer made mental notes for a search warrant. If Elias directed his employees to dump the tank contents on the hard pan and the material was hazardous, which the evidence certainly indicated, that alone was a barebones RCRA violation giving him probable cause for a search warrant. But Elias had also admitted he instructed the employees on the clean-out method, an unusual admission for an employer. Employers normally distanced themselves or outright blamed their employees for any illegal acts because OSHA regulations were aimed at punishing employers, not the employees.

Elias said he took all four employees down to the tank to talk about the "cleaning operation," where he took a pH test.[8] "Scott brought the SCBA tanks and told me he had checked the level of oxygen in each one and the gauges indicated they were full, but I wanted to see for myself, so I instructed him to crack the valves on each tank to make sure." He said Dominguez and Weaver told him they knew how to use the tanks and that they would have the job completed by 10:30 when he returned from a meeting. Then he left the plant.

"I was totally confident everything would go smoothly. They said they knew what they were doing and I had no reason not to believe them."

Elias said when he returned at 10:30, Dominguez was unconscious in the tank but the rescuers were reluctant to cut a hole because they couldn't determine if the atmosphere in the tank was explosive even though he kept telling them that it wasn't.

"I couldn't stand it. It was taking so much time for them to make a decision I finally grabbed a cutting torch myself to cut the hole but they stopped me. We had a big fight about it."

Elias stood and walked into the back room and returned with a red, three-ringed binder that he said contained an OSHA pamphlet detailing safety requirements for a confined-space entry and that he had talked about confined spaces with OSHA regulators at both AEI and Evergreen. "I know everything there is to know. I've got booklets on confined spaces, electrical tag-outs and all kinds of things, and I'm always referring to them. I read the one on confined-space entry requirements to prepare for the tank cleaning operation. That's why I'm so familiar with it."

"Can we get copies of all those?" Hilldorfer asked.

"They're not here. They're at my other office. I'm preparing a report for the police department. I'll attach them with my report."

O'Neil looked up at Hilldorfer. He'd heard the same story. But that wasn't what Hilldorfer was concerned about at the moment. His instincts about Elias having another office were accurate. "Where is your other office?" Hilldorfer asked, needing the information for a search warrant.

"I don't want to discuss that right now."

"Will you take us there so we can look at the documentation?"

"I told you I'll provide them to you as soon as I have a chance to finish my report and copy them."

"We could go to your office and copy them and get them back to you by the end of the day."

"It's not here in Soda Springs."

"Can we make copies of the binder?" Hilldorfer asked.

Elias shook his head. "I'm using it to prepare my report. I'll attach everything pertinent to that."

Elias gave a history of Evergreen and explained that he needed the storage tank to store sulfuric acid to manufacture fertilizer. He described himself as "a self-taught chemist" but wouldn't say what degrees he'd actually obtained. Then his story took another turn.

"This is really almost a hobby for me," he said, estimating that he spent only five to forty-five minutes a day at the plant because it was not profitable for him to spend any more of his time there. "I come in real early in the morning and I'm out the door by eight," he said, offering that the business lost $25,000 a month.

Elias said that after the accident his employees admitted to him that Smith had not filled out the confined-space permit as he said he would and that Weaver told Dominguez it was okay to go into the tank without wearing the respirator.

Again, Hilldorfer wasn't buying his story. "Could we see the four respirators they were using?"

"I only have one. I think they must have taken the other ones with them when they went home yesterday."

"Can we see the one that's here?"

"I'm not sure where it is."

"What about the safety harnesses?"

"I'm not sure where they are at the moment either. I'd have to find them."

"But you're sure you told the employees to use them."

Elias was adamant. "I discussed it with Brian that morning and with Darren and Scott. They agreed it was a good idea."

"And you told them to wear the respirators?"

"I ordered them to wear them." Elias sat back and shrugged. "What am I going to do? I can't prevent stupid employees from doing stupid things when I'm not there looking over their shoulders. There's no managing stupidity. When I left them I told them to do this one by the book, but they were lazy and stupid and now I'm the focus of an investigation by you guys."

But Hilldorfer knew Elias was not about to let them investigate what happened. He clearly believed that if he solved the entire puzzle for them they would simply go away.

"It's curious to me that Darren was able to work in the tank with no problems yesterday, you know? That they were both in the tank with no problem."

Hilldorfer bit because he knew Elias wanted him to. "Why do you think that is?"

"It's clear to me they hit a pocket of cyanide, and that immediately de-pleted the oxygen inside the tank."[9]

Elias said he told a Dr. Obray at the emergency room that he thought Dominguez had been overcome by hydrogen cyanide gas, but that the hospital was not equipped to treat him. He also said he provided Obray or one of the emergency responders with an MSDS sheet.

Hilldorfer looked at his watch. It was almost 2:30 P.M. Frutel had likely arrived.

"Are you still willing to allow us to get a sample and take some photographs of the tank."

"I haven't withdrawn my consent."

Hilldorfer no longer trusted Elias. "I appreciate that, but I would feel more comfortable if you would provide written consent."

Elias waved it off as unnecessary and reiterated he'd given his consent.[10]

Hilldorfer and O'Neil ended the conversation and walked outside. Bill Frutel arrived in his on-scene sampling van ten minutes later. Frutel had been around the EPA forever and at six foot four, 230 pounds, with a buzz cut and reflector glasses, he looked more like a state trooper than a state trooper. Clements had also returned and he and Frutel put on the "moon suits." Hilldorfer told them he wanted samples from inside the tank, from the material dripping out the back of it, and from the puddle on the ground. Then he walked away to watch at a safe distance.

Elias, however, seemed unfazed by the potential danger. He followed Frutel and Clements with pH paper, yelling and screaming that he was getting different results, that his pH readings were higher. Hilldorfer and Wojnicz suspected he was doing it for show, that he was going to argue that he had reasonably relied on his pH paper. Frutel and Clements fi-nally told him to back away. Elias sought out Hilldorfer. He began a con-voluted explanation using arithmetic equations and dimensions about the length and diameter of the tank and the volume and the amount of mate-rial inside it, and said that because of the size of the tank he would have had to have divided the entire sludge bed into a grid and take representa-tive samples from each quadrant in order to thoroughly test it. Hilldorfer made sure Wojnicz was listening as Elias explained there were two "strata" inside the tank, the lower one, which contained cyanide sludge from the leaching system at AEI, and a second, top, layer that formed when the particulate in the Evergreen wash water settled on top. He said

Weaver and Dominguez must have broken through the top layer and hit a pocket of contaminants that depleted the oxygen in the tank, calling it "horrific." In case Hilldorfer and Wojnicz missed his point, he stated it explicitly. "There was no criminal intent. I gave them everything they needed to do the job safely." He held up one of his pH strips. "Based on my sampling I thought it was safe enough for me to sit in there in my rocking chair and read a book."[11]

At 4:38 p.m., Frutel and Clements finished taking samples and Elias said he was leaving. He approached Hilldorfer. "Are you staying here overnight?"

"No," Hilldorfer said. "I'm staying in Pocatello."

"I'd like to meet with you," Elias said. "I'm going to be in Pocatello tomorrow; how about a cup of coffee? There's a place there called the Allegro. It's a good place, you'll like it."

"Okay," Hilldorfer said. They shook hands and confirmed a meeting at 10:15 a.m. Then Elias walked to his pickup truck and left.

Thursday, August 29, 1996
The Ameritel Hotel
Pocatello, Idaho

CHAPTER NINE

THE FOLLOWING MORNING, Hilldorfer paced the lobby of the Ameritel Hotel eyeballing his watch. He had told Wojnicz to meet him in the lobby at 10:00 but Wojnicz was five minutes late. According to the woman behind the desk, the Allegro Coffee Shop was ten minutes from the hotel, a few exits south on Interstate 15 near the state police building. Hilldorfer did not want to be late. When Wojnicz stepped off the elevator Hilldorfer was already walking toward the door.

"Let's go."

Wojnicz remained skeptical. "I don't think he's going to show."

"I don't want to take that chance."

Elias was smart and clearly thinking like a chess player, two moves down the board. He had already spoken to Weaver and he had refused to provide Hilldorfer and O'Neil with the addresses for Smith or Thornock.

The agents had to assume he was trying to reach his employees. After leaving Evergreen the afternoon before, Hilldorfer and Wojnicz found Smith's and Thornock's addresses in a phone book in town, but neither man was home. After striking out they ran the license plate on Elias's truck and obtained a home address, Hilldorfer playing a hunch it was Elias's "other office."

The address turned out to be a stone's throw from Evergreen, but if it hadn't been for the Lincoln parked out front with the California plate that came back registered to Evergreen, they would have thought the address a mistake. Elias's "home" sat on an otherwise vacant lot with no vegetation, driveway or walkway of any kind. Perhaps thirty feet by twenty feet, it was a single-story brick-and-wood-faced structure with a flat roof and three doors and windows that faced Highway 34. It looked like a commercial building more appropriate for a Laundromat or dental office. It didn't look much like home, and it certainly didn't fit the profile of someone said to be a Beverly Hills millionaire, but Hilldorfer was starting to realize that Allan Elias did not fit the profile of a midnight-dumper of toxic materials either.

THE SON OF a New York garment district business owner, Elias grew up in the affluent Long Island town of Great Neck. By all accounts, he was a whiz kid, graduating with a finance degree from the prestigious Wharton School of Business at the University of Pennsylvania at just nineteen years of age.[1] He went to work for his father in the garment industry for eleven years. In 1968 he and his wife, Midge—his high school sweetheart—left New York and moved to Arizona, where Elias enrolled at the University of Arizona Law School. He graduated and was admitted to the Arizona bar but never appeared to actually practice law. He attended the University's School of Architecture long enough to become a licensed building contractor and began a career in real estate. In between, he and Midge raised three children.

In Tucson he made a quick splash in the real estate market, doing well enough that a Tucson magazine profiled him on its cover as a "one-man superstar" who had arrived in Tucson at thirty years of age after cutting his teeth in "that camp of killers and climbers, the Big Apple." The magazine depicted a young man in a superman costume bursting through a wall fist first and cape flying, and said Elias had become "the City's financial Bruce Jenner" with a "four-in-one leap"—a single purchase of three shopping centers and a medical building. His subsequent purchases included hotels and a country club; then he built what was at the time Tucson's tallest building, the twenty-two-story Arizona Bank Plaza. He also bought a controlling interest in Union Bank, becoming its chairman and president and hiring what was described as an impressive team. According to the article, that team referred to him as "the coach" and said the bank operated "like any other well-managed business. The only difference is that our product is money; we're retailers in money."

Elias was also said to have syndicated and speculated in land, and liked to show off at a restaurant he owned on the east side. But there was at least some indication that more than a few Tucsonians in finance, development, and other businesses didn't think as highly of him as the article suggested. In any event, Elias left Arizona around 1979 and built a house in La Jolla, California. According to Midge he spent his time losing great amounts of money buying and selling commodities, and somewhere along the way became interested in metallurgy. In the early 1980s they moved to Las Vegas and he made his way to Moapa, Nevada, where he set up a "pilot project" that used a cyanide circuit system to recover precious metals from industrial waste generated by the Moapa Power Plant. Elias obtained a patent for the process and leased property from the power company while trying to recover silver from flue dust. Though the process worked, it had a poor silver recovery rate and was not commercially viable. After a year and a half, he shut the project down.

At that point Midge informed him that she couldn't stand being in Las Vegas "another day" and said she was moving to Los Angeles, where she eventually bought a Beverly Hills condominium. Elias moved to Idaho to pursue the flue dust he needed to continue his precious metals recovery business. Among the dust samples Elias had tested during the pilot project in Moapa was waste from FMC, a mining company in Pocatello, Idaho. He leased a facility directly across from the FMC plant on East County Road and set up shop, intending to extract precious metals from the treater dust and make fertilizer out of the leftover by-product, believing it would revolutionize the waste-handling business. But the bottom dropped out of the silver market, and then treater dust lost its Bevill exemption, meaning it had been exempted from RCRA regulations under certain circumstances, and it became subject to regulation as a hazardous waste. AEI, Inc., filed for bankruptcy and Elias left Pocatello. He didn't go far, sixty miles down the road to Soda Springs.

FROM THE OUTSIDE, the Allegro Coffee Shop looked like a renovated Taco Bell. Inside it was more quaint. Wooden benches lined the perimeter walls with small round tables and chairs arranged to provide intimate seating. At 10:20 A.M., Hilldorfer surveyed the tables. Elias was not there.

Wojnicz pulled an automobile magazine from a rack near the door. "Told you he wouldn't show."

"He's got an hour's drive. Let's give him a few minutes."

"With everything going on do you really think he'll come?"

"If he thinks a meeting could benefit him, he'll come."

"You think he's looking to make a deal?"

Hilldorfer shrugged. "Just a feeling, but it wouldn't surprise me."

They walked to a wooden counter and glass case containing basic pastries, ordered coffee, and took seats with a view of the parking lot. When at 10:30 Elias had still not shown, Hilldorfer stood. "Let's go find him."

On the drive to Soda Springs they watched the cars passing in the opposite direction for Elias's yellow truck or the white Lincoln. Usually a good judge of character, Hilldorfer was sure Elias would show. They drove back through town onto North Hooper Road and as they approached the crest in the road they spotted Elias's yellow truck parked in front of his home like a battered beacon. Elias stood out front talking with two people.

"There he is," Wojnicz said.

Wojnicz turned off the highway and parked at the curb. Barb Franek and Joe Eizaguirre, the two OSHA inspectors who had been at Evergreen the day before, were having a loud discussion with Elias, who was red in the face and berating them.[2] As the two agents approached Elias swiveled to Hilldorfer.

"And you stood me up for coffee this morning," he said, not missing a beat. "After I drove all the way to Pocatello and back."

It wasn't bullshit. Elias was pissed. He'd been at the Allegro. "Hey, Allan, I was there. I thought you stood me up."

"I drove there and back," Elias barked.

"Well, I was there. I was about five minutes late. I apologize." He stuck out his hand. "It's no big deal. It's good to see you again. Maybe we can have coffee in the future."

Elias shook his hand, then left to answer a phone ringing inside one of the doors to his home. Wojnicz wandered over to get a better look inside, and, as they suspected, it appeared to be an office with a desk, and cabinets and boxes lining a hallway.

"What's going on?" Hilldorfer asked Franek.

"He won't talk to us. He won't give us any information at all. Every time we ask him for something he tells us he's putting it in a report to the Soda Springs Police Department."

"We got the same song and dance yesterday."

Elias came out of the building and made a point of shaking Hilldorfer's hand in front of the OSHA inspectors. "I've been the most cooperative and friendly person the EPA has ever met, haven't I?"

Hilldorfer chuckled. "Well, I wouldn't call you the most cooperative person I've ever interviewed, Allan, but I would like those lab results you mentioned yesterday for the tests you had run on the material in the tank."

"I don't know where they are at the moment and I haven't had time to look for them."

Though he had calmed, Elias had a short fuse and Hilldorfer knew the more he pushed him the less cooperative he would be. He nodded to Wojnicz and they turned to leave. He wasn't surprised when Elias walked them to their car.

"Maybe we could have coffee tomorrow," Elias said.

"I'm not going to be around tomorrow. I'll have to do it another time," Hilldorfer said.

"I'll fax you those lab results, and if you have any other concerns or want anything else, give me a call," Elias said.

Hilldorfer shook his hand. "I'll do that."

"Don't hold your breath," Wojnicz said when they got back inside the car. "You're likely to suffocate."

BAILEY CREEK, IDAHO, was rolling green hills with modest homes of various styles, from Cape Cods to country rustic. The address for Gene Thornock was a one-story rambler. Flat, without much architectural consideration, the house looked like a modular and was in need of a fresh coat of paint. The landscaping was like the house—basic, neat, and tidy but otherwise uninteresting. Hilldorfer suspected it was a rental.

Hilldorfer intended to "door-knock" both Thornock and Smith— show up at their homes without any advance notice. He rarely called a witness to set up an interview. It was too easy for people to say "No" on the phone, and it gave them time to prepare what they had to say. But door-knocking witnesses also had its drawbacks, like spending long hours sitting in a car waiting. In remote areas that could be all day because people commuted long distances to find employment. He'd also had a few doors slammed in his face.

They had made several drive-bys during the day with no indication anyone was home, then returned at dusk and saw a car parked in the driveway and lights on inside. "Someone's home," Hilldorfer said.

They parked in the street and walked down the driveway, but Hilldorfer didn't get a chance to knock before the door was pulled open. In a small town it was not unusual for the residents to begin calling when strangers, especially federal investigators, started asking about the locals. Gene Thornock stood barefoot in the doorway wearing a tank top T-shirt and jeans. He was perhaps five foot nine and stocky. He looked like the hardworking, blue-collar workers Hilldorfer grew up with on Pittsburgh's North Side. Beside him stood a woman with strawberry blond hair. She kept a hand on his back, as if holding him upright.

"Mr. Thornock, I'm Special Agent Joe Hilldorfer. This is Special Agent Bob Wojnicz. We're with the EPA."

Thornock's hand was thick and rough and his arms scarred and banged up from hard labor. At the moment he looked as if he'd been to hell and back, his eyes bloodshot and weighted by bags, his hair an unkempt thicket, his face unshaven.

"I can't talk now," he said softly, his body sagging against the door frame. Hilldorfer's first thought was that Scott Dominguez had died.

"We just came back to get something to eat. I got to get back to Scott."

Dominguez was still alive. "I'm really sorry to bother you," Hilldorfer said. "Could I ask you just a few questions before you go?"

"I really can't think too good right now."

Hilldorfer appraised Thornock as sincere, not uncooperative, but he also knew Thornock was already mentally closing the door and could physically shut it in an instant. He didn't want to risk alienating Thornock by forcing him to answer a lot of questions, but they were leaving town early in the morning and he knew it was likely Thornock would return to work for Elias. This was his only opportunity to find out what happened before Elias spoke to him. He would have to walk a fine line and read Thornock's reaction as he went. He began a series of rapid-fire questions.

"Did you work for Allan Elias at Evergreen?"

"Yep."

"On the morning of the accident, did Allan have a safety meeting?"

"Nope."

"Did he have a meeting at all?"

"Yep."

"What was the meeting for? What was discussed?"

Thornock shrugged. "Just told us what to do. I can't really talk. I got to get back."

"What did he tell you to do, Mr. Thornock?"

"Just empty the sludge in the tank onto the ground."

"Did he provide you with any safety equipment to do that work?"

Thornock looked up. "No," he said, his voice emphatic.

"Did he have safety equipment at the plant?"

"No. Nothing." Thornock shook his head. "I got to get back to Scott now."

Hilldorfer pushed on. "Did Scott or Darren Weaver have respirators?"

Thornock sighed. "An old one. Didn't work very well, though. I wouldn't call it a respirator." Thornock's voice cracked. "We couldn't get him out. The fumes were just too strong. I tried holding my breath but . . . they took me to the hospital, too." His chest heaved. The woman rubbed his back. The door was nearly shut. "I haven't slept since it happened. I can't talk any more now."

Hilldorfer knew he had pushed as far as he could. He turned to Stacey Thornock. "Your husband is a hero, Mrs. Thornock. I understand he went into the tank to try to save Scott Dominguez. I don't know many men who would risk their lives like that. It took a hell of a lot of courage." He shook Thornock's hand. "I really appreciate you talking to me. I hope I can talk to you again."

Thornock nodded. Then he stepped back and closed the door.

Allan Elias was lying, but they were a long way from determining how much and why.[3]

◆   ◆   ◆

THEY LEFT BAILEY CREEK and found their way to Grace, Idaho, which was a turnoff from Highway 30 marked by a small roadside sign staked in the ground. They drove along a narrow road wedged between miles of flat pasture until scattered buildings appeared without warning. If Soda Springs was a bedroom community, Grace was an annex to the bedroom, a one-block main street of stucco buildings looked to have been built in the 1920s. Intersecting it were half a dozen side streets. The two agents could see the town's edges in each direction. As they circled, looking for Smith's address, they could see that the homes were modest but well cared for, a fair share being prefabricated or mobile homes, some with impressive flower gardens. The streets, however, were unmarked and it took nearly an hour before Wojnicz, who had a sense of direction like a bloodhound, pulled up to a trailer home with a manicured lawn.

"This has to be it."

Hilldorfer got out of the car with the mind-set that Smith would be predisposed, like Thornock, not to talk. He had a series of short questions at the ready. As they approached the front door Hilldorfer heard a television or radio filtering through a screen door. His knock triggered loud barking and the appearance of a shaggy-haired dog followed by an attractive woman dressed in cut-off jean shorts and a tank top. Hilldorfer and Wojnicz held up their credentials to the screen and introduced themselves.

"We're investigating a tragedy that happened in Soda Springs the other day to a young man named Scott Dominguez. We'd like to talk to Brian Smith."

Hilldorfer immediately sensed the woman put up a barrier, shaking her head before he had finished his sentence. "He hasn't slept and he's not in good shape. Now's not a good time to be talking to him."

He was about to have the door shut in his face when a man appeared behind the screen. Brian Smith looked to be the same age as Thornock, late thirties or early forties, and thick-bodied. A ponytail hung past his shoulders.

"I'm Joe Hilldorfer," he said, deciding against a long-winded explanation. "I need your help."

"You need my help?"

Hilldorfer nodded. "Yes I do, Mr. Smith."

Smith stepped forward and pushed open the screen door. "Come on in."

The agents took seats on a couch. Smith sat in an oversized chair and his wife, who introduced herself as Kathy, sat on the arm. The furnishings inside were modest but, like the yard, spotless.

"I need to know what happened out there that day," Hilldorfer said.

Smith's eyes watered and it seemed only pride prevented tears from rolling down his cheeks. His wife rubbed his back and gave Hilldorfer an angry "I told you so" glare.

Hilldorfer tried a different tack. "Can you tell me what you did at Evergreen?"

Smith cleared his throat and seemed to ease his way into the conversation. A millwright by profession, he explained that he had worked in many of the local plants over the years. Shortly after Elias bought Evergreen he asked Smith to take a look at the plant and tell him how much work it needed to make it suitable for fertilizer production.

"I told him it was a mess and it was going to require major work and repair before it could do anything at all."

Elias hired him. Smith said the portion of the plant set up to make phosphoric acid was in operation when he started, but shortly thereafter Elias shut that down, too.

"Do you know why?"

"My understanding is Kerr-McGee bought it. And I heard they paid Allan a bunch of money for it, too."

Smith explained that Kerr-McGee was looking to have fertilizer made out of its mining waste and that the dark mound of dirt at the plant was "black ore," called "calcinite" or "gyp." "That's the stuff Allan's supposed to use to make fertilizer." The white mound was "MAP"—magnesium ammonium phosphate—and also came from Kerr-McGee.

"Does he actually make any fertilizer?" Wojnicz asked.

Smith shook his head. He said Kerr-McGee was putting a lot of pressure on Elias to do a five-hundred-ton trial run because it was under pressure from the EPA to show that the process would work, but there was no way Evergreen could do it. Smith said it would be "damn near impossible." Instead, Kerr-McGee had recently begun building its own fertilizer plant, but, in the interim, he understood they were paying Elias to take the gyp.

Smith clearly knew a lot about the industry. Bright and articulate, he would not only be a key witness for the government, but a key source of information for Hilldorfer and Wojnicz on the industry and how it worked. At the moment, however, Hilldorfer was focused on getting enough information for a search warrant.

"Can you tell me about the incident, how it happened?"

Smith took a breath as if to gather himself for an arduous task. He said he was working on something called a granulator and not directly involved in the clean-out project. "I didn't want nothing to do with that tank. I'd been involved in accidents with acid and confined spaces."

"At Evergreen?"

"And other places I've worked, but yeah, people have been hurt at Evergreen before. Lots of them."

He said Elias was anxious to empty the tank because he was paying a daily fee to rent two railcars of sulfuric acid. The tank had a "greenish colored" sludge at the bottom, which to Smith indicated phosphoric acid residue, and he had repeatedly told Elias that morning and the day before that he needed to take certain safety precautions, like getting proper safety equipment and filling out a confined-space entry permit, before he could clean out the tank.

"What did he say?"

Smith shook his head. "He said he'd take care of it. He never does."

"He didn't ask you to fill out the permit?"

"No."

"Did he say he wanted the job done by the book?"

Smith thought for a moment. "He might have said it, but he didn't have any of the equipment for doing it by the book."

Smith said he was driving the backhoe when he looked up and saw Thornock running across the yard and Weaver standing on top of the tank yelling. "We couldn't get him out. The fumes were just too much." He closed his eyes and took a breath, fighting back tears. When he spoke his voice had softened. "That's the hardest thing I ever had to do in my life . . . to sit him down and leave him there. I just couldn't get him out." He opened his eyes and looked at Hilldorfer. "It haunts me every time I close my eyes."[4]

Tuesday, August 27, 1996
Bannock Regional Medical Center
Intensive Care Unit
Soda Springs, Idaho

CHAPTER TEN

THE DAY OF the accident, Life Flight arrived at Caribou County Memorial Hospital at 12:25 P.M.[1] Obray administered the cyanide antidote at 12:28 P.M. Within minutes Dominguez began to move his arms and legs and to resist ventilation. There was also a dramatic change in the level of his consciousness. His eyes shifted back and forth, though without purpose or direct eye contact. At 12:39 P.M., as the medical team prepped Dominguez for flight, Obray did a stimulus test. Dominguez could move his limbs, but his responses were delayed as much as half a minute.

Concerned Dominguez could pull the tube out of his throat, the medical team bound his wrists and started out the door when a nurse stepped in and advised Obray that they had received another call from Evergreen. Someone wanted a blood sample taken for cyanide. Obray quickly had Dominguez's blood drawn from his left arm and marked the sample to be sent to a SmithKline lab.

The helicopter departed Soda Springs at 1:22 P.M. and arrived at the Bannock Regional Medical Center in Pocatello at 1:43 P.M. During the flight Dominguez was spitting up gray and red tissue into his breathing tube.

Dr. John Ratcliffe admitted Dominguez to the intensive care unit and placed him on a respirator, noting that his pupils remained unresponsive to light and he had limited response to painful stimuli. He was in such critical condition that not even his family was allowed into the room. They had to stand in the doorway observing him like some horrible experiment gone wrong.

At 9:30 P.M., though his condition had not markedly improved, Dominguez's family was allowed into his room. They spent a long and tortured night in a bedside vigil. The following day Dominguez's level of consciousness seemed to increase slightly. He opened his eyes upon hearing his mother's voice, but he still did not respond to questions or commands or withdraw from painful stimulation. Late that night a nurse asked the family to limit the number of visitors in the room to two at a time. When she did, Scott slowly lifted his arm from the table and held up two fingers. The nurse hurried to inform Dr. Ratcliffe. When Ratcliffe arrived Dominguez was able to repeat the gesture, but the rest of his condition that day, and the next, did not improve. He remained immobile, in critical condition, his eyes dark fixed spheres, like a doll.

By Sunday, September 1, Dominguez began to display signs he was suffering grand mal seizures. His body would become suddenly rigid, his face a deep purple, and his eyes would roll back in his head, his eyelids fluttering rapidly while he clutched and grabbed at the sheets, breathing rapidly and biting down on the endotracheal tube for as long as two minutes. Doctors ordered a CT scan and EEG. The results were a further blow to the family, revealing multiple pockets of dead brain tissue.

The SmithKline test results came back Monday, September 2. On the day of his injury Dominguez's blood contained nearly three times the amount of cyanide considered toxic. In contrast, the second blood test, drawn at 11:30 P.M., after the cyanide antidote kit had been administered, revealed that his cyanide level dropped from .13 to .07 milligrams per deciliter. There was little doubt Dominguez had been poisoned by cyanide, but that was now of little consolation. Doctors upgraded his condition from critical to serious, but he remained in the intensive care unit, his survival anything but certain.

Monday, September 2, 1996
EPA Headquarters
Sixth and University
Seattle, Washington

CHAPTER ELEVEN

MONDAY MORNING at the Region 10 offices in Seattle, Hilldorfer briefed McClary on the investigation and McClary "rewarded" him with the task of putting together the affidavit needed to support the application for a search warrant. McClary also gave him a pitch—as much as McClary ever gave a pitch. He said he'd met Terry

Deerden, the assistant U.S. attorney (AUSA) in Boise in charge of the criminal division. Deerden was from Arkansas with ties to the Clinton administration. He kept a collection of caps in his office from police agencies around the country.

"I think he respects cops," McClary said. "He says the AUSA handling this is a workhorse named George Breitsameter. He's supposed to have a lot of trial experience and Deerden says he's very well respected. Give him a call and let him know what's going on." McClary paused. He knew Hilldorfer was frustrated, that Boomsnub had taken a lot out of him. In his own career McClary had investigated charges against Weyerhaeuser, the Pacific Northwest lumber giant, and watched politics in Washington, D.C., end the investigation in its tracks. "Maybe things will be different this time," he said.

Hilldorfer would reserve judgment. Too many prosecutors had sounded good on paper then folded in the trenches.

The first order of business was determining whether Evergreen had filed reports for the lawful storage or disposal of hazardous waste. While he waited to hear back on that inquiry he received a call from Boyd Roberts of the Idaho DEQ in Boise. Roberts said there'd been another acid spill at Evergreen the Friday after the accident. It was almost incomprehensible under the circumstances.

"How did you guys find out about it?"

"One of the employees made a report to the police department. Said he was sick of Allan's bullshit."

"No kidding," Hilldorfer said, making notes of a potential cooperative employee witness. "Who was the employee?"

He heard Roberts shuffling papers. "Gene Thornock."

Roberts said Elias gave them a "reportable quantity"—an amount below the limit for a spill to be a fineable offense, which was his pattern. The Department of Environmental Quality had responded to multiple reports of acid spills at Evergreen, most of them filed by John Hatfield, but on each occasion Elias managed to evade prosecution or fines by calculating the spill to be below the reportable quantity.

"Not a lot we can do. The employees back him up or won't talk to us. A lot of times we can't even find them. They're not on-site and he just says he's not in operation." Roberts added that worker turnover was so high at Evergreen that the employees weren't around long enough to be good witnesses anyway.

"You guys ever see any safety equipment on-site, respirators, clothing?" Hilldorfer asked.

"Never."

Roberts described the conditions at Evergreen as deplorable, the employees dressing in nothing more than jeans and T-shirts. "He doesn't even have a change-out area. I tell you, Joe, given the working conditions there and the lack of safety equipment, our office kept saying, 'This man will kill someone someday. It's just a matter of time.' "

Now he almost had.

For the better part of the next two weeks Hilldorfer sat in his cubicle with a telephone to his ear, ignoring the million-dollar view down University Avenue to the Puget Sound. A criminal check on Elias for outstanding warrants was negative, as was the EPA records department search for RCRA violations at Evergreen and AEI, Inc. Given Roberts's statement that Elias was well familiar with the regulations, this wasn't surprising. The only records that existed for Evergreen were EPCRA documents filed before Elias bought the plant. The Emergency Planning and Community Right to Know Act required businesses storing chemicals on-site to file paperwork so the community, especially fire responders and emergency personnel, knew the potential dangers. Since Elias had bought the plant, the EPCRA reports had ceased. There was, however, documentation that EPA had initially pursued RCRA allegations against AEI for dumping cyanide waste into sumps, but Elias contested the charges and the EPA dropped the investigation.

RCRA governed "solid waste" like garbage, refuse, sludge from a waste treatment plant, or other discarded material from industrial, commercial, mining, and agricultural activities. If the waste was sufficiently corrosive, reactive, or toxic to be capable of injuring a person or posing a substantial hazard to the environment, it was designated "hazardous" and had to be disposed of at "permitted" facilities. Elias had no permit to store or dispose of hazardous waste at Evergreen, which meant if the waste in the tank met the RCRA standard as hazardous, Elias's dumping it on the ground was, at minimum, a nuts-and-bolts violation.

HILLDORFER RETURNED to Boise on Monday, September 16, 1996, armed with a twenty-two-page affidavit laying out the evidence he hoped would convince a magistrate to issue warrants to search Evergreen and Elias's home office. The first search warrant was critical to an investigation. As much as Hilldorfer and everyone else wanted to get back to Evergreen quickly to search the plant, he had to be sure the affidavit left no doubt there was probable cause for a warrant. At the moment Hilldorfer was convinced Elias was not concerned they were coming back to raid his facility, arrogant enough to believe he had satisfied them with his story. Why wouldn't he be? From what Hilldorfer had learned he had more lives than a cat, leaving DEQ and OSHA frustrated. But in a small town word could spread quickly, and if Elias learned Hilldorfer was coming back with a warrant, Hilldorfer didn't put it past him to purge his files or create whatever evidence he needed. If he did, finding out what had happened would be infinitely more difficult.

Hilldorfer met George Breitsameter, the assistant U.S. attorney handling the case, in his office on the third floor of the six-story, salmon-brown Wells Fargo Building, one of the tallest in downtown Boise. Breitsameter's office was modest in size and decor, a government-issued desk, credenza, and two chairs for visitors. The usable space beneath the window was cluttered with boxes, files, and scattered papers. Breitsameter sat beneath a framed poster depicting photographs of Abraham Lincoln at various points in his life from the clean-shaven young man to the bearded president of the United States with mournful eyes. He also kept a bust of the nation's sixteenth president atop a glass bookcase of memorabilia collected during his five years as a state prosecutor and ten years as an assistant U.S. attorney, all of them in Boise.

Like Lincoln, Breitsameter was born and raised in Illinois. He and a law school friend had moved to Idaho after each decided they didn't want to fight the commute or be treated like beasts of burden as associates at the big Chicago law firms. Skiing in Idaho had much more appeal. Now forty-one, Breitsameter had since married and become the senior trial attorney in the office.[1]

As he reviewed the affidavit, which was about twenty pages longer than he was used to, Breitsameter wiped a trickle of sweat from his brow after a bike ride to work. He'd worn out his knees running the steep dirt trails of Camel Back Hill near his home, which also precluded skiing; biking was his current exercise choice. With brown hair pushed off the tips of his ears Hilldorfer thought Breitsameter looked like a young Walter Matthau, and he had a disarming, down-home manner that bespoke confidence and gave Hilldorfer an instant comfort level.

They went that afternoon to a federal magistrate in Boise. Breitsameter had no trouble securing the search warrant. Now it was up to Hilldorfer.

It was time to kick a few brush piles, score up a rabbit, and let the dogs run.

HILLDORFER AWOKE early the following morning anxious and apprehensive, which was how he always felt when about to execute a search warrant. Things usually went off without a hitch, but the potential remained for the shit to hit the fan, and this was his fan.

He met his search warrant team in the breakfast room of the Ameritel Hotel in Pocatello. It was a young group. Brad Campbell, an EPA special agent and former customs agent, had come up from Portland. Hilldorfer brought Mike Burnett, his co-agent on Boomsnub, and Lorinda Wallace, the newest hire in the Seattle office. In her early twenties, Wallace was, like Hilldorfer, the offspring of a cop. She had graduated Phi Beta Kappa from the University of Washington but passed up a scholarship to Yale Law School to be an EPA special agent. They drove to the Idaho State Police barracks, a one-story building in Pocatello, where Hilldorfer met Bill Reese for the first time. Reese had responded to Evergreen the day of the accident. Though Reese had little experience with environmental crimes, something in his gut told him what happened that day was wrong and he had delayed his family's vacation, staying up most of that night trying to track down the EPA. He had become Hilldorfer's eyes and ears into the Soda Springs community. With a buzz cut, bullet-proof vest bulging beneath an indigo blue uniform, and cumbersome black utility belt fully loaded with the usual police paraphernalia, he looked like the all-American cop.

Reese told the group Elias owned at least one handgun, a .357 Magnum, and possessed a volatile temper. Elias and John Hatfield had been at each other on a couple of occasions. Hatfield had been arrested for punching Elias in the face and said it was the best money he'd ever spent. He'd also shown up at Elias's home one night and challenged him to a fight. Elias pulled the gun but only managed to shoot his own television set.[2]

"Some of you have seen this already," Hilldorfer said as he handed out copies of the warrant giving them authority to search Elias's home office and Evergreen. "The first thing we need to do is find Allan and secure his weapon. Once we do that, we'll search both the facility and his residence at the same time."

Reese and Campbell would search the facility for safety equipment, including the four new SCBA's Elias claimed to have on-site, or note the lack thereof. Reese, who was trained as a HAZMAT specialist, and Wallace, who had received one of her degrees in science, had the duty of going through Elias's "lab" at the back of his trailer.

"Search it top to bottom. I want to know exactly what is and is not in there. I don't want any surprises later," Hilldorfer said.

Wallace would also be the seizing agent, a tedious job that usually fell to the youngest agent. She had the task of filling out the forms noting everything seized and where it had been specifically located.[3] It had to be accurate. Burnett was given the task of taking pictures.

"We'll low-key this thing. Guns out of sight," Hilldorfer said, reminding them their weapons were to remain hidden under sports coats or in bags. He wanted nothing that defense attorneys could argue had intimidated Elias. He thought of giving them a speech, telling them this was a serious case, but it sounded preachy. "We'll rendezvous at the Soda Springs Police Department," he said.

The caravan set out along Highway 30 to Soda Springs. Hilldorfer had delayed giving notice to local law enforcement, having not forgotten the reception he and Wojnicz received from the Soda Springs chief of police. Once inside the town limits, he pulled into the parking lot of the Soda Springs Police Department, a stone-block building with black metal railing that looked like something out of Smallsville, USA, and went inside and asked for Chief Wilcox. The officer at the desk said Wilcox was out on a personal matter so Hilldorfer advised the officer on duty that they would be executing a search warrant at Evergreen that morning then walked back outside.

Campbell approached him looking a bit sheepish. "Sorry, Joe."

"What's the matter?" Hilldorfer asked.

"Kelly O'Neil called over yesterday and told them you'd be executing the search warrant today."

"He did what?"

"Breitsameter said he wanted to be sure you touched base with the locals."

Hilldorfer clenched his teeth to keep from exploding. "And I was going to do it, goddamn it. Today. This morning." He got back into his car seething at O'Neil for stepping on his warrant and sensing the worst. As he drove down Evergreen's dirt road he saw Elias's yellow truck parked near the trailer, and pulled into the parking lot with a sick, unsettled feeling in his stomach. He grabbed a copy of the search warrant, and stepped out of the car, but hadn't taken five steps when the door to the trailer flew open and Allan Elias walked out to greet him.

Wednesday, October 30, 1996
EPA Headquarters
Sixth and University
Seattle, Washington

CHAPTER TWELVE

FIVE WEEKS AFTER executing the search warrants Hilldorfer sat at his desk reviewing a box of materials seized from Evergreen. He was waiting to hear back from the Manchester Lab for the test results from the samples taken from the tank the day after the accident. Otherwise, the investigation was on hold. Breitsameter had made the decision to take the matter before the Boise grand jury, which was the only grand jury in the state, and he wanted to wait until a new grand jury sat in January so the government didn't get halfway through the presentation of evidence against Elias and have to start over with a new grand jury.

Breitsameter was a big proponent of the grand jury process. A panel of citizens, the grand jury in Boise was called to sit once a month for eighteen months to hear evidence on cases being pursued by the U.S. Attorney's Office and decide if there was enough evidence to indict a defendant. It gave the prosecutor a bellwether of the community in which the charges would be tried. It also provided the prosecutor with subpoena power to get documents and to force reluctant witnesses to testify under oath. Just as important to Breitsameter, it allowed the government time to get its case together. Until a defendant is indicted, the prosecutor controls the flow of information and works at his pace. After the indictment, the defense lawyers, the court, and other outside factors muddy the waters and the schedule. Breitsameter liked to say he'd never been accused of prematurely indicting a case.[1]

Hilldorfer had his doubts this one would make it that far.

When he stepped out of the car to hand Allan Elias the search warrant he saw no panic, shock, disbelief, or anger. He would have settled for mild surprise. Elias just smiled, like greeting an acquaintance. "I'm glad you're back," he said shaking Hilldorfer's hand. "I want to show you my locker room of safety equipment." He sounded like the proud father of a newborn child.

They were burned.

Hilldorfer followed protocol, identifying himself and providing Elias with a copy of the search warrant, and inside the trailer he went through the litany of things he was legally obligated to tell Elias about the search warrant and the authority it gave Hilldorfer to seize items. "We'll leave you a copy of the inventory of everything we take."

Elias sat calm as a Sunday afternoon. He even pointed out typing errors in the warrant, like an attorney reviewing a legal document.

This was a salvage operation.

"I want all your documentation of the lab tests you said you ran of the material in the tank."

Elias opened a desk drawer and pulled out a case containing the pH testing kit with unused thin strips of paper. "This is all the sampling information that I have."[2]

"I also want the red binder."

Elias provided it to him and also handed him an MSDS binder.[3] Then he stood and walked them out to one of the barnlike buildings with several lockers. Inside were hard hats, a harness and rope, some beat-up rubber gear, and a couple of full-body protective suits. It wasn't perfect, but it was more than DEQ and the Evergreen employees said Elias had the day of the accident, which was nothing.

Sitting at his cubicle in Seattle, Hilldorfer pulled the red binder from the box and flipped through OSHA documentation that on its face appeared to confirm that all of the Evergreen employees had been provided hazard and safety training. *Appeared* was the operative word. Lorinda Wallace had been the first to notice something about the documents that didn't look right.

"Hold it to the window," she told Hilldorfer.

When he did he noticed that Wite-Out had been used to make changes to the face of the documents. The information beneath it could be read when held to the light. Any reference to cyanide had been covered.[4]

"He was in a hurry," Hilldorfer said.

"Looks that way," Wallace agreed. She also pointed out that the signatures of the employees acknowledging they had received safety training were all the same handwriting and made in the same-colored ink even though they were purportedly signed between 1993 and 1996.[5]

Elias had also produced a confined-space entry permit dated and signed the day of the accident, which was at odds with Elias's statement to Hilldorfer during their first meeting that he had delegated that task to Smith and that Smith had failed to complete the permit. Hilldorfer was certain it, and the locker room, were fabricated after the accident and the permit backdated, a crime if he could prove it.

Hilldorfer had also found a phone number and address for a laboratory in Salt Lake City, presumably where Elias claimed to have had the samples tested. If he had, they'd be the only tests, other than the Manchester Lab tests. Idaho DEQ had called Hilldorfer on October 23 to tell him the tank had disappeared along with the material in it. Elias maintained he had properly disposed of the waste but he was refusing to provide them with any details of where or how.

Hilldorfer's telephone rang. He put down the binder to answer it.

Dr. Bruce Woods told him he had the Manchester Lab results, as promised.

"Give me the good news, Bruce," he said, but as he listened he began to get the same sickening feeling he had when Elias walked out of the trailer smiling.

MINUTES LATER, Hilldorfer met Woods in the conference room outside Dixon McClary's office. Blown-up photographs of locations where Region 10 had executed search warrants lined the walls. The agents called it a rogues' gallery of Northwest environmental dumping. Prominently displayed were several shots of the Boomsnub facility, the brilliant, sun-colored, hexavalent chromium dripping down the containment pond walls.

Hilldorfer was beside himself. "How can that be, Bruce?"

"There are hits, Joe, they're just not at a level to meet the regulatory requirement."

The lab results showed the presence of cyanide but at levels below the regulation that made it hazardous. Hilldorfer pulled out the Code of Federal Regulations that governs what does and does not constitute an RCRA hazardous waste. He read it out loud: " '. . . a cyanide-bearing waste when exposed to pH conditions of between 2 and 12.5 that can generate toxic gases, vapors or fumes in a quantity sufficient to present a danger to human health or the environment is a hazardous waste,' goddamn it. We know from Dominguez's medical records that the cyanide level in his blood was three times the lethal level, and the emergency responders and Bill Frutel both tested the tank and said the atmosphere had a shitload of cyanide. So what happened?"

"I don't know what to tell you, Joe. It doesn't meet the guidelines. Maybe the reaction already occurred and it dissipated."

"Shit, Bruce, where does that leave me? I got this stuff dripping on the ground, bubbling in a pond, it nearly killed one kid and two other employees who tried to rescue him, and you're telling me it doesn't test positive?"

Woods shrugged. "Those are the results."

If that were the case, Hilldorfer would have a hell of a time convincing anyone to prosecute Elias. "I'm going to talk about this with Jim."

Jim Oesterle was the Region 10 Criminal Investigation Division's attorney. Officially he worked for the regional counsel's office, but the agents thought of him as their lawyer. He'd taken over the role of psychotherapist and guidance counselor and often refereed fights between the agents and the Department of Justice. Calm by nature and level-headed, Oesterle was often the voice of reason. He had also gained the agents' respect because he left a high-paying private practice to come to the EPA because he cared about the environment.

Oesterle met Hilldorfer and Woods in the conference room. He had thick black hair, wore glasses that partially hid equally full eyebrows, and had the thin build of a long-distance runner. It was not uncommon to see him limping down the hall because a knee or ankle was bothering him after running some ungodly distance meant to be traveled by car. Dixon McClary also joined them. No one knew the criminal law and sampling regulations better than McClary. As one of the first CID agents, McClary had worked with EPA's scientists to create the tests that set out the Code of Federal Regulations thresholds for materials to be considered hazardous. He agreed with Hilldorfer's analysis that all of the circumstantial evidence indicated the substance in the tank was a hazardous waste, and he and Oesterle had the same solution.

"Let's call Dr. Joe."

Hilldorfer had never met or spoken with Dr. Joe Lowry, the EPA's chief deputy scientist at their main lab at the National Enforcement Investigation Center in Lakewood, Colorado, but he knew his reputation. Investigators and U.S. attorneys spoke of Lowry with respect that bordered on reverence. About the only bad thing anyone ever said was Lowry was in such demand he was virtually impossible to get hold of. It was therefore not surprising when the group could not reach him. They left a message for Lowry to call Hilldorfer.

"If there's an explanation, Dr. Joe will know it," McClary said.

It was little solace, and Hilldorfer figured he'd be stewing on the matter for days waiting to hear back from Lowry, but a few minutes after getting to his cubicle his phone rang. Lowry was on the line. He had already heard of the Dominguez case.

"What've you got, Joe?" Lowry's voice was bass-drum deep but had a soft quality that at times made him difficult to hear.

Hilldorfer explained the situation. "The Manchester Lab is telling me we don't have squat. How can that be?"

If Lowry had an explanation, he didn't share it. He laughed. "Tell Kathy Parker to run the tests again. Tell her I want to know exactly what she did to test the sample. Then send me the sample and everything else you have, all the paperwork on the tank, the blood tests, everything."

With that, Lowry hung up.

Hilldorfer set the phone down and contemplated whether or not to call George Breitsameter. As he did he looked out the window at a low gray sky. Wisps of clouds hung down like leafless branches of an old tree, reminding him of the ominous winter skies in Pittsburgh, foretelling they were about to be hit with heavy snows. He decided not to call Breitsameter. The last thing he wanted was for the Department of Justice to start getting cold feet.

CHAPTER THIRTEEN

IN LATE OCTOBER, George Breitsameter flew to Washington, D.C., for an ethics seminar at the Department of Justice. The timing was fortuitous. Breitsameter had two significant environmental prosecutions pending in Idaho, the Elias case and one involving the INNEL, the large nuclear site in the Idaho desert. The Boise U.S. Attorney's Office recognized Elias to be a significant case. The EPA was calling it a poster case to illustrate that environmental crimes were real crimes, with real injuries to real victims. Breitsameter didn't doubt it. His commitment, however, didn't change the fact that the number of cases he was prosecuting remained daunting, and the RCRA statutes were complex and fluid. An attorney could spend a career prosecuting environmental crimes and still not understand all the nuances. What Breitsameter needed was help, and he had a specific person at the Department of Justice's Environmental Crimes Section in mind.[1]

IN NOVEMBER 1982, as the EPA was still developing its criminal enforcement program, the Department of Justice created an Environmental Crimes Unit within the Environment and Natural Resources Division.[2] A three-attorney unit, its exclusive domain was criminal enforcement of environmental laws. The unit went right to work, gaining significant publicity for prosecuting A.C. Lawrence Leather Company, the third-largest leather tannery in the world, and five of its corporate officers for dumping untreated wastewater into a nearby stream then falsifying records to hide the crimes. The company paid a fine of $475,000, but despite vehement urging by the prosecutors that the corporate executives were educated, privileged people who had cheated and betrayed the public, the judge demurred. Nobody went to jail.

Over the course of the next six years the unit handed out nearly five hundred indictments against individuals and corporations resulting in sentences of 270 years and $26 million in criminal fines. The DOJ boasted an environmental crimes conviction rate of 95 percent. Things seemed to be going so well that on April 24, 1987, Attorney General Edwin Meese III elevated the unit to full section status, increased its budget, and doubled its manpower. By 1992 the Environmental Crimes Section, or ECS, was twenty-eight attorneys.

In 1996, David Uhlmann was a thirty-four-year-old lawyer at the ECS whom Breitsameter had met at environmental conferences around the country where Uhlmann had been a featured speaker. Uhlmann had also stepped in for the Boise U.S. Attorney's Office to prosecute an environmental charge against the Wilber Ellis Company, a large fertilizer company in Boise.

Uhlmann was developing a serious résumé prosecuting environmental crimes, particularly in the West. He and Dennis Holmes, a respected senior litigator in the U.S. Attorney's Office in South Dakota, had recently convicted the John Morrell Meat Packing Company and two of its senior officers for dumping improperly treated wastewater into the Sioux River, then falsifying records to conceal the violations. At the time, Morrell was the largest employer in the state and had hired the best lawyers and law firms money could buy. The company pled guilty to multiple violations of the Clean Water Act and paid a $3 million fine. But the senior vice president, Timothy Sinskey, and the plant engineer, Wayne Kumm, went to trial. The three-week trial had been an all-out battle with Uhlmann and Holmes fighting a wave of defense lawyers defending Sinskey and Kumm—at one point there were thirteen. Uhlmann and Holmes convicted both men.[3]

Breitsameter met Uhlmann in his office at the ECS at Sixth and Pennsylvania, with a spectacular view up Pennsylvania Avenue that culminated in a postcardlike snapshot of the gleaming white Capitol building. They walked to The Markett, a take-out restaurant associated with the well-known D.C. restaurant The Mark at Seventh and D Streets, then walked down Seventh Street across Pennsylvania and Constitution Avenues to a park bench in the Mall between the National Gallery and the Air and Space Museum with the Capitol rotunda looming to their immediate left and the spire of the Washington Monument to their right.

Breitsameter explained the INNEL matters first and Uhlmann told him he'd see about getting an ECS attorney to help.

"The other matter is the Allan Elias case."

Uhlmann didn't miss a beat. "I'll help you with that." He knew about Elias from two independent sources. Neil Mcaliley, an attorney with the ECS, had been working a case in Oregon at the time Dominguez was hurt and sent Uhlmann a September 3 e-mail at 1:18 P.M. "FYI good-sounding knowing-endangerment case growing in Idaho." Mcaliley was under the impression that several employees had died. Kelly O'Neil, who worked the Wilber Ellis case in Idaho with Uhlmann, had also told him about it.

Uhlmann's response confirmed Breitsameter's suspicion that the ECS also considered Elias a significant case. Neither he nor Terry Deerden wanted to lose it. "We want to keep it in the office, and I know you can't handle them all yourself either. I'm looking for help."

Uhlmann was in the middle of a battle to get the Morrell defendants sentenced and preparing to try the owner of a Memphis company that had abandoned dozens of toxic drums in a poor black community. His wife, Virginia, was also about to give birth, and he intended to take a paternity leave. "You're right, I can't handle them all, and I understand you want to keep the Elias case," he said. "We can work the case together."

It was the answer Breitsameter was looking for.

That afternoon, Uhlmann went back to his office and immediately found Deborah Smith, the assistant section chief to whom he reported. "I just had lunch with George Breitsameter," he said. "He has some environmental crimes he's working in Idaho and would like our help. I don't have a lot of time, but I want the Elias case."

Winter 1996–97
EPA Region 10 Headquarters
Seattle, Washington

CHAPTER FOURTEEN

DURING THE WINTER, as they waited for the new grand jury to sit, the Occupational Safety and Health Administration, the Environmental Protection Agency, and the Department of Justice argued about who would investigate and charge Allan Elias. Both OSHA and

EPA technically had jurisdiction; there being evidence of both an environmental crime and an employee injury.

Hilldorfer and Breitsameter met with Ryan Kuehmichael, the area head of OSHA, and Barb Franek, one of his inspectors, on December 11 and January 10. Kuehmichael and Franek recounted a long and frustrating history with Elias. Dominguez was not Elias's first employee injury—far from it. OSHA had charged him multiple times for violations at both AEI and Evergreen. In 1988, OSHA cited AEI, Inc., for failing to have a cyanide antidote kit on the premises and for failing to keep MSDS sheets on hazardous chemicals. Elias had also been cited at Evergreen for confined-space entry violations.[1] Each time he had managed to avoid any significant fines or convictions and OSHA was understandably reluctant to let go of their best opportunity to bring an immediate administrative action and perhaps a civil action. They wanted to impose a $700,000 fine, arguing it was important for their program to issue as strong a penalty as possible to mark their presence in the community.

Breitsameter didn't like either option. He feared that an administrative or civil action would give Elias access to civil discovery tools like depositions and subpoenas and undermine his strategy to use the grand jury to control the criminal investigation. It could also potentially raise double-jeopardy issues if OSHA succeeded in getting a civil judgment. He was also certain any OSHA fine or civil judgment would be hollow. Elias would never pay it. He'd file bankruptcy.

Breitsameter had to convince OSHA that while he empathized with their history with Elias, it shouldn't issue its penalties. He was the right man for the job. His father, whom Kuehmichael knew, had worked as an OSHA instructor at the OSHA institute in Chicago when it was formed during the Nixon administration. Breitsameter made a commitment to OSHA that if it relinquished jurisdiction to the EPA and the DOJ, he would ensure that an OSHA charge was included in the indictment against Elias, and that it would be prosecuted very seriously.

The more time Hilldorfer spent with Breitsameter the more impressed he was with his legal knowledge and his people skills. He likened him to a Jimmy Stewart–type lawyer—an everyday guy who didn't make it a habit of trying to stand out. His demeanor was even-keeled and rational, and he didn't take himself too seriously like some U.S. attorneys. He was also a diehard Chicago Cubs fan, which meant he had staying power, and a rabid Bulls fan, which meant he could pick a winner. His

Midwestern accent came through in certain words like chocolate, which sounded more like "chocklit."

Some time after the winter meetings Breitsameter called Hilldorfer. OSHA conceded. That was all well and good, except McClary had yet to assign the case to an agent, and he didn't appear to be in a hurry to do so. Hilldorfer sensed O'Neil wanted it, but Wojnicz had a right to it since he'd been the duty agent and took the call. Much as Boomsnub had been a disappointment, Hilldorfer also wanted the case. He saw the investigation of Allan Elias as a challenge and he liked the thought of going toe to toe with him. Still, he knew better than to ask McClary for the case. McClary knew Hilldorfer's frustrations with devoting long hours to an investigation only to see it go south. If Hilldorfer asked for the case, he couldn't bitch if it didn't go as planned. McClary would simply tell him he had wanted the case and had to live with it.

McClary began hovering around Hilldorfer's cubicle talking about the case, but neither man seemed willing to make the first move. After a week, McClary finally ended the suspense.

"I'm assigning you to be the case agent," he said. "But I'm going to give it a Portland referral number."

It was politics. The Seattle office would work the case, but the Portland office would get credit for the referral to the Department of Justice. It might have been to appease Portland, or it might have been because Portland needed the "bean"—as agents called cases. Unlike the FBI, which was about "putting the assholes in jail," the EPA was about numbers.[2]

When the Criminal Investigation Division was established within the EPA there was significant discussion concerning how cases would be referred to the Department of Justice for prosecution. The intent of the system was to insulate regional EPA administrators from being manipulated by big business and the political clout it swung.[3]

As a result, the EPA instituted a system in which the Department of Justice made the ultimate decision as to whether or not to prosecute a case and the regional EPA office was given a "referral" when it directed a case to the DOJ or to the local U.S. attorney for prosecution and/or for further investigation by the grand jury. CID agents began referring to the process as counting "beans" because the number of cases referred to the Justice Department was the only quantifiable means to measure the individual efforts of each of the ten regional EPA offices and their agents. Funding was decided, to a large part, based on those numbers, which pressured investigators to refer as many cases as possible. Unlike the FBI, where cases are weighted by their degree of complexity and importance, with a premium placed on the quality of the conviction—putting the asshole in jail—referring cases to the DOJ became an EPA "body count." When prosecutors declined nearly two thirds of the cases referred, either because they did not consider the case serious enough to warrant the expenditure of limited judicial resources or because the case had not been investigated thoroughly, it led to considerable friction between the EPA special agents and the DOJ prosecutors.[4]

That would not be a problem for Hilldorfer. There was no doubt the DOJ considered the Elias case serious. The only question then was whether the EPA could pull together enough evidence to convict him. That task now fell squarely on Hilldorfer's shoulders.

He popped open the lid on a box of materials OSHA had forwarded to the Region 10 office. OSHA had obtained taped statements from Gene Thornock, Brian Smith, and Darren Weaver just two days after the accident. Having talked with Thornock and Smith, Hilldorfer knew they were distraught and upset, which was not a good time to record an interview. Anger and emotion made witnesses say things they later regretted on the witness stand. A good defense attorney would use it to imply bias. Hilldorfer made a note that the tapes needed to be transcribed, then he put them aside and flipped through the reports filed by Barb Franek and Joe Eizaguirre. As he did, he noted a reference to the emergency room physician who had treated Dominguez, Dr. John Wayne Obray.

No cyanide in the tank.

He read it twice. It made no sense. Elias had told both Hilldorfer and O'Neil, and later Wojnicz, that the tank contained cyanide from the operation at AEI, and Dominguez's blood left no doubt that was the case. How could the emergency room doctor have reached a different conclusion?

Hilldorfer called Obray's office but was told the doctor was unavailable. When he pushed the issue the woman replied that Obray had already talked to OSHA. Hilldorfer explained he was conducting a criminal investigation but it seemed to have little effect. The woman took his name and number, but he could tell from her tone that he shouldn't miss lunch waiting for a return call.

It was another red flag—one that would fly prominently next to the red flag raised by the Manchester Lab, and it reminded Hilldorfer of another of his grandfather's expressions: "Be careful what you wish for."

Tuesday, February 4, 1997
SeaTac Airport
Seattle, Washington

CHAPTER FIFTEEN

AT 7:25 A.M., FEBRUARY 4, 1997, Hilldorfer and Wojnicz boarded Alaska Flight 2700 to Boise. Wojnicz had arranged a meeting the following morning with Dr. John Ratcliffe, the doctor who had treated Dominguez at the Bannock Regional Medical Center in Pocatello. Later that afternoon they would meet at the U.S. Attorney's Office in Boise, at which time OSHA would formally bow out of the case, and they would begin discussing the investigation and potential charges with Breitsameter.

Hilldorfer knew McClary would be reluctant to have two senior investigators working the same bean, which would hurt Region 10's overall production numbers and eat up its limited budget resources. But having worked cases in rural parts of eastern Washington, he also knew finding witnesses in sparsely populated towns could be difficult, and he preferred to have another agent present when he conducted interviews to corroborate the witness's statement. Agents did not tape interviews. Pulling out a tape recorder was a surefire way to get someone to stop talking and it only gave defense attorneys another means to attack the agent's interview. Agents took notes, then wrote their interviews into witness statements. Those statements were often all that a prosecutor had at trial to conduct cross-examinations.

So, subscribing to the theory that it was better to seek forgiveness than permission, Hilldorfer took it upon himself to ask Wojnicz to be the co-agent on the case.

As he suspected, Wojnicz didn't blink. Like Hilldorfer, he had taken an interest in the Dominguez investigation after meeting Elias. It had been Wojnicz who put into perspective the lethal combination of cyanide and acid that had nearly killed Dominguez. "Hydrogen cyanide," he said. "That's what the Nazis used to gas the Jews at Auschwitz."

Wojnicz was the son of Polish immigrants. In 1939, when the Germans and Russians were carving up Poland like a slab of meat, his father, Joseph, joined the Polish underground and eventually joined a Polish faction of the English army under General Wladyslaw Anders. Shot in the leg and captured by the Germans, he caught a break when they kept him in the field because he was a machinist and adept at fixing equipment. He stayed alive long enough to escape, made his way toward the advancing American forces, hailed a jeep and was nearly shot as a German soldier. Fortuitously, the jeep driver turned out to be a Polish immigrant from Chicago.

After the war Joseph Wojnicz moved to London where he met his wife. Bogdan "Bob" Wojnicz and his sister were born in London and lived there until the summer of 1960, when the family boarded the *Queen Elizabeth* to America, and watched the Statue of Liberty from its deck. They moved to an apartment in the Bronx and later to Brooklyn, tough neighborhoods that quickly taught Bob to fight and talk like a native New Yorker. His father joined the Machinists Union, working for a factory that made machine parts. When the machinists went on strike, Joseph Wojnicz took Bob to walk the picket line, often in bitter cold, and to explain the importance of what they were doing. The lessons hit home the day a machine spit hot oil in Joseph's face and he lost an eye.

With a voracious appetite for reading and an interest in electronics, Bob Wojnicz graduated from the Brooklyn Vocational Technical School at sixteen. He turned down MIT to apply to the electricians' union, but when he saw the line of applicants snaking for several city blocks he rethought college. Eventually he obtained an accounting degree from Queens College in New York, then hopped in his van and drove west. He fell in love with the open green space of the Northwest and settled in Portland, Oregon, taking a position as an accountant for a paper mill. A year into the job the IRS called to tell him it had accepted his application. He moved to eastern Washington to help open an IRS office, began working with special agents from the IRS's Criminal Investigation Division, and realized he preferred their job over his own. With no available positions in the IRS/CID he decided to attend law school and moved to Seattle, obtaining a law degree from the University of Puget Sound. Like

Hilldorfer, he would never practice law. The IRS/CID called with an un-expected opening.

For twelve years he investigated tax protestors, early identity theft and fraud cases, and drug money-laundering cases. In May 1994, looking for a change, he switched to the EPA/CID Region 10 Office. Months into the job he hit an agent's jackpot. An employee informant led him to CH_2O Inc., a company in Olympia with a suspected history of dumping chemical wash water from its drum-cleaning operation. The informant said CH_2O had dumped thousands of gallons into a sewer drain at a nearby apartment complex and down a sewer near the company president's home, and was now dumping it down drains at a warehouse the company had recently purchased. Wojnicz's investigation led to indictments of the company and certain of its management employees, including the president. All pled guilty but the president, who was convicted after an eight-day trial and received a one-year sentence and $75,000 fine.[1]

Wojnicz quickly realized that what motivated people to cheat the IRS was exactly what motivated people to commit environmental crimes. It was all about saving money. It was all about greed.

Wojnicz maintained the fastidious appearance of someone who worked with numbers. He kept his Carhart work jeans and buttoned-down shirts pressed and tucked, and each morning at the office he used an X-Acto blade to cut out the television guide from the USA Today, then checked off the programs he intended to watch that night. He was also a bargain hunter the likes of which Hilldorfer had never seen. If there was a "screaming deal" to be found, Wojnicz found it. His voracious appetite for reading had given him an encyclopedialike knowledge of facts; some of which were so obscure, Hilldorfer likened him to Cliff Claven, the dedicated postal service employee from the hit television show Cheers.

As different as the two men were, they got along. That was important when they would be spending a lot of time together on the road, and they would.

At the moment the biggest hole in the case was the fact that the samples did not meet the EPA's regulatory threshold to be a hazardous substance. Dr. Joe Lowry was working on the issue, but Hilldorfer believed the best answer was to invoke the language in the statute. The substance in the tank was hazardous if it had "the potential to cause bodily injury." In his mind, what they needed was a doctor to say Dominguez was injured by cyanide. Unfortunately his efforts to contact Obray remained unsuccessful. Unable to reach Obray, he and Wojnicz decided to start with Ratcliffe.

THE TWO AGENTS walked into a reception area of oversized soft chairs and well-read magazines. The Family Medical Center in Pocatello was overrun with kids, frazzled mothers, and people wearing casts and gloomy expressions. Looking at the number of patients waiting to be seen, Hilldorfer worried that Ratcliffe would not afford them much time. He equated being a doctor in a clinic to his father's observation about being a bus driver on a route. If you fell behind at one stop it meant you'd be behind the rest of the day.

The nurse at the counter didn't offer any comfort. "He's very busy," she said. "Take a seat."

"Charming," Wojnicz said as they sat for what they anticipated would be a prolonged wait, but as each reached for a magazine a silver-haired man in a white doctor's coat walked into the waiting room and introduced himself as Dr. John Ratcliffe. Of slender build with a ruddy, outdoor complexion and easy smile, Ratcliffe asked that they follow him to the Bannock Regional Medical Center so he could get Dominguez's file.

The center was a maze of corridors, stairwells, and elevators that seemed never-ending. Hilldorfer considered each passing minute one less they would have with Ratcliffe. The path led to the records department where a woman behind the counter sat with a pursed expression and a no-nonsense attitude when it came to her files. Despite having Ratcliffe present, she would not give up the file until she checked their subpoena and the release of records form signed by Jackie Hamp, Dominguez's mother.

The file finally in hand, Ratcliffe escorted them to an empty office no bigger than a cubicle, then left again to find three chairs. They had barely sat when Hilldorfer rushed forward, but if Ratcliffe was concerned about time he didn't show it. He joked that he worked part-time, forty to sixty hours a week, because he loved the outdoors, particularly skiing, which explained his ruddy cheeks. He told them he was impressed that they had come to see him so soon after the injury, that normally he wasn't called until the day before a trial.

"As you're reviewing the file, one of the things we're interested in,

Doctor, is whether you have an opinion if Scott's injury was due to cyanide," Hilldorfer said.

Ratcliffe looked at them over bifocal glasses. "Yes, definitely."

"Could you explain how you came to that conclusion?" Hilldorfer asked, feeling immediately more relaxed.

"Several factors. His condition when he arrived, his reaction when treated for cyanide exposure, and the manner in which he sustained his injury would all lead to that conclusion."

Ratcliffe explained that cyanide was usually inhaled into the body as hydrogen cyanide gas. "It is an extremely rapid-acting poison that prevents the body from using oxygen and can kill in minutes. In layman's terms, it shuts down the chemical machinery inside the cells that converts oxygen into energy, effectively suffocating a person from the inside."

The records indicated that when administered a cyanide antidote Dominguez immediately became more conscious, but that the exposure had damaged a place deep inside Dominguez's brain called the basal ganglia, a sort of switching station that coordinates body movement, and caused a condition called necrosis, in which the brain tissue is killed. Scott Dominguez's basal ganglia were now riddled with pockets, holes, where brain matter used to be. Those holes caused a delay between his thoughts and the corresponding body movement.

Hilldorfer had just begun to feel like his first red flag was solved when Ratcliffe continued.

"His condition could also have been exacerbated by a lack of oxygen. I understand that a respirator was placed over his face by one of the employees attempting to save his life and that it ran out of air. It may have also caused oxygen deprivation that in conjunction with the cyanide caused his brain injuries."

Ratcliffe's answer would give Elias's defense "wiggle room"—a basis to argue that cyanide was not the cause of Dominguez's injuries, that it had been a lack of oxygen. He was back to square one.

"But all of the objective evidence, and based on his employer's explanation regarding the manner in which Mr. Dominguez was injured, indicates it was cyanide."

Hilldorfer and Wojnicz exchanged a glance.

"When did you speak to his employer?" Hilldorfer asked.

"He came to the medical center about an hour after Mr. Dominguez was admitted."

Hilldorfer and Wojnicz did not know this. "Do you remember the conversation?"

Ratcliffe told them that Elias told him the tank was once used to store gasoline and was purchased from an excavation company. From 1988 to 1989 the tank was used by a silver extraction company, which Ratcliffe's notes reflected as GEI Corporation but was likely AEI, to store sodium cyanide solution. What was interesting to Hilldorfer was that Elias's version of the history of the tank was clearly intended to distance himself from it. It was almost as if he were speaking of someone else.

"It was sold to Evergreen Fertilizer Company in 1990," Ratcliffe continued. "At that time they used it for phosphate processing and used it in the processing of phosphate ore. It was drained approximately three months ago, at which time it was inspected and a solid precipitate was found at the bottom. He had a sample sent to Western Analysis in Salt Lake City to determine the presence of silver and also presumably to analyze whether cyanide was also present. He said that the cyanide test was negative."[2]

Elias's story was like a linen shirt thrown in the laundry. Every minute there appeared a new wrinkle. Hilldorfer's initial opinion that Elias was calculating was proving accurate. He didn't believe for a minute that Elias made the trip out of concern for Dominguez. Elias had never expressed any concern about Dominguez. To the contrary, he called his employees "stupid" and blamed them for his legal troubles. Elias's reason for making the trip was more likely about continuing to set up his potential defenses.

"Doctor, are you referring to notes?"

Ratcliffe handed them a single sheet of paper from the file. "I asked an intern to take notes while I talked to Mr. Elias."

Ratcliffe paused. Hilldorfer had interviewed enough witnesses to know it was to invite the obvious question. "Why did you do that?"

Ratcliffe removed his glasses and shook his head. "As soon as he started talking to me about the tank and that he had it tested, I had a gut reaction that he just wasn't telling the truth. He came across as somewhat of a used-car salesman. He was evasive. When I asked him questions he was nonresponsive. I got the feeling he wanted to give me his version of what had happened but not answer my questions."[3]

CHAPTER SIXTEEN

SCOTT DOMINGUEZ spent two weeks in intensive care at the Bannock Regional Medical Center before being transferred to Room 407. He continued to sweat profusely and his face remained frozen in a wrinkled, wide-eyed look of fear. He still did not respond to verbal stimuli but he could moan, a ghostly painful wail. His arms and legs shook uncontrollably.[1] After a consultation on Friday, September 6, his doctors concluded he was not a candidate for rehabilitation and recommended he be placed in a nursing home, provided physical and occupational therapy, and monitored to determine if he would remain "vegetative." It was devastating news for the family. That evening, two young boys, family friends, came to Dominguez's room to visit. As they spoke to him, Scott's eyes slowly pooled until a tear trickled down the side of his face.

Whether or not that had anything to do with it, Dominguez's mental status improved dramatically over the weekend. By Monday, September 9, his nurses were able to get him out of bed and walking the hallways in a gingerly gait. His seizures had also subsided and he spoke his first word, a whisper in response to his mother's question.

"No."

Since Dr. John Roberts had never cared for a patient with a cyanide-related injury,[2] he had nothing to compare Dominguez's recovery to. For whatever reason, Dominguez was now considered a candidate for rehabilitation. At 9:00 A.M., September 10, he was transferred by airplane to the University of Utah Hospital in Salt Lake City for an intense multidisciplinary hospital rehabilitation program.

Dr. Roberts examined him ten days later and described his condition as "Parkinsonian"—that is, similar to a person with advanced Parkinson's disease. Dominguez moved as if his muscles and legs were rigid; nurses said that moving his limbs was like bending wax or a piece of wire. He spoke barely above a whisper and was difficult to understand. Though he was walking, his balance remained poor. In addition to his physical injuries, Dominguez was no longer the self-initiating young man he had been. He was content to sit, his demeanor flat and monotone, but he was also now emotionally volatile. He could be smiling one moment and wailing the next, seemingly without reason.

Roberts prescribed Sinemet, the same medication given Parkinson's patients, and over the following two weeks Dominguez's neurological status and his ability to move and communicate continued to improve. He could answer "yes" and "no" to questions, eat independently, and dress if given straightforward commands, though he tended to "freeze" in the middle of tasks, which made the process laborious, sometimes taking hours. Still, he had come a long way given where he had started.

The hospital discharged him September 25, 1996, and he returned to his parents' home with Theresa to continue what would be an arduous and intense rehabilitation schedule for them all, while enduring a frustratingly slow legal process.

Thursday, March 6, 1997
The Ameritel Hotel
Pocatello, Idaho

CHAPTER SEVENTEEN

THE WOMAN behind the counter at the Ameritel Hotel in Pocatello greeted Hilldorfer by name before he reached the counter.

Home sweet home.

Wojnicz was in Georgia again at the Federal Law Enforcement Training Center. Hilldorfer would make this trip alone. This would be his first meeting with Scott Dominguez and his family. He knew from telephone conversations with Jackie Hamp, and from his interview with Dr. Ratcliffe, that Scott remained in very poor condition. He had not slept well, anxious about what to expect. The family would have questions, and rightfully so. On the telephone Hamp had expressed frustration with the pace of the legal process, though her criticism was soft-spoken and almost apologetic in tone. She felt no one was listening to her or helping Scott, and she told Hilldorfer that she was starting to dislike lawyers. The latter comment was the reason Hilldorfer made a quick detour to the Ameritel instead of driving straight to Soda Springs. He had been wearing a suit and tie to project a professional appearance to the family. A stewardess on the plane asked if he was a lawyer.

At the hotel he changed into a pair of jeans, a sweater, and a Gore-Tex jacket, but he had not brought his waterproof boots. He'd likely ruin his dress shoes in the melting snow. Though it remained cold, spring was beginning to break winter's hold. The brown landscape with errant patches of snow did not have the picturesque beauty of the summer and fall or of the fresh snowfalls that blanketed the landscape during his trips in February.

Hilldorfer drove into Soda Springs, made a right on Main Street, and located the row of single-story, white-brick-facade buildings across the street from the Soda Springs Chamber of Commerce. The B&H Dry Cleaners was the last door on the right, next to a vacant lot. Hilldorfer parked at the curb. Mid-morning on a weekday, the sidewalk was empty. Main Street rarely produced a moving car. He stepped out and immediately felt the cold seep through the bottom of his shoes and the open collar of his shirt. It was not the cold he knew growing up in Pittsburgh or living in Seattle, a dampness that made his socks feel perpetually wet. The cold of southeast Idaho sucked the moisture from his skin, leaving his flesh a chapped red, his nostrils dry, and his lips cracked and bleeding within hours of exposure.

Condensation covered the inside of the glass door and three wood-framed windows that faced Main Street. When he pulled open the door it brought a chemical smell like the inside of a new car. Hilldorfer introduced himself to a young woman at the counter and asked to speak to Jackie Hamp.

She turned and yelled to the back of the cleaners, "Mom."

Hamp appeared from between racks of clothes hanging encased in sheets of plastic. She looked surprisingly close to what he expected from their telephone conversations. Five feet four inches tall, she had blond-brown hair like her daughter, wore no makeup on a pleasant face, and looked comfortable in jeans, a T-shirt, and tennis shoes. She also looked tired. Small bags lingered beneath hollow blue eyes that probably sparkled when given sufficient sleep, but now seemed dull and flat. She moved toward the counter as if physically drained.

Hamp had a right to be tired. On August 27 she had been at home in Soda Springs when her mother unexpectedly arrived at the house saying she didn't know why, but she felt something was wrong. Then the telephone rang—it was Hamp's sister calling to tell her of reports that some-body had fallen into a tank of acid at Evergreen. Jackie knew her mother had come because something terrible had happened to Scott. She rushed to Evergreen but was not allowed near the tank and was not allowed to see Scott at the Caribou County Memorial Hospital emergency room. When she finally did see him, at the Bannock Regional Medical Center, the hospital wouldn't let her near him for several maddening hours. The next two weeks had been a life-and-death ordeal.[1] The long drives and nights had understandably worn her thin, and even now she continued to get up multiple times each night, sometimes every fifteen minutes, when Scott cried out in pain, unable to turn over on his own.

Hilldorfer introduced himself and they made small talk for a few minutes in front of the counter. Then Hamp asked him about the investigation.

"We think the best chance for justice for Scott is to try and convict Allan Elias on an environmental charge," Hilldorfer said. "You're going to be seeing a lot of me in Soda Springs along with my partner, Bob Wojnicz. We're trying to get as much information as we can. Although we're pursuing environmental charges, make no mistake about it: This case is about what Allan did to Scott. We'll present that information to a grand jury in Boise and if everything goes as we think, we'll secure an indict-ment against Mr. Elias."

"What does that mean?"

"That means that if they agree there is enough evidence, he'll be charged and put on trial for injuring Scott."

"How long is all this going to take?" She asked the question politely, her tone almost deferential.

Hilldorfer empathized with Jackie Hamp's frustration, but he had no encouraging words or guarantees that Elias would go to jail for what he had done to her son. He could make no promises about justice, which he no longer saw as something cast in concrete, a pedestal on which one could stand and feel comfortable. It was more like a piece of Styrofoam floating on water, unstable and ever fluid. What he could do was ex-plain the process and let her know Scott had not been and would not be forgotten.

"I'm not going to lie to you, Jackie. It's going to be a slow process. I'm going to ask you to be patient, as hard as that might be at times. The investigation has to be thorough because we only get one bite at the apple and Allan is probably going to get some good legal help. But I've also met the federal prosecutor and I'm told he's outstanding."

"Most of the people injured at Evergreen were young, like Scott," she offered. "They didn't know better, and Allan could intimidate them easier. He threatened to fire them all the time, for anything. Scott said he fired an entire night crew once because they didn't get the job done by the morning. That's why Scott did things. He felt he had to or Allan would fire him."

"I'd like to get the names of those employees, as many as I can."

"My husband can probably help with that." She gave him a half-hearted smile. "I'm just glad something is being done. It seemed like everyone was worried about everything except what happened to Scott."

"We haven't forgotten about Scott," Hilldorfer said. "How's he doing?"

She gave him a resigned shrug. "He's shown some improvement from the therapy and the medicine." Hamp led Hilldorfer back to the entrance. "You can follow me to the house. He should be done with his physical therapy by now."

He followed her by car to a modest, two-story home with champagne-colored siding and maroon trim, but what he noticed were the cars that filled a gravel drive. The family had gathered to find out what was being done for Scott and when Allan was going to jail. It caused a trickle of sweat to roll down Hilldorfer's side. He followed Hamp through the front door to a room at the back of the house and a group of waiting faces. It reminded Hilldorfer of a Catholic wake, the family gathered in mourning, all orbiting around a presence in the room.

Hamp introduced him to her parents and sisters, "Scott's aunts," as well as Scott's sister and two brothers, and his girlfriend, Theresa Cole. Ron Hamp, the man who had raised him from an infant, was at work at Monsanto. Cole looked like a porcelain doll, maybe five feet tall with alabaster skin, a shock of thick blond hair, and opulent blue eyes. But if the family had questions, or was angry about the legal pace, they didn't express it or show it. They seemed content just to meet him.

Hamp stepped to a couch where a woman knelt on the floor bending and lowering the limbs of a young man lying supine. Hilldorfer stepped closer and looked down upon an angelic face of unblemished skin and eyes the color of dark chocolate. Scott Dominguez reminded him of a young Tom Cruise, the actor. His beauty, however, was in striking contrast to what was also so readily apparent. Scott remained seriously disabled. The arm the woman manipulated was reed thin, Dominguez's body a gaunt skeleton of cheekbones and sharp protruding points.

Hamp knelt. "Scott, this is Joe Hilldorfer. He's a federal agent with the EPA. He's going to be investigating Allan."

Hilldorfer stepped forward. Dominguez stared at the ceiling, as if blind, his face a blank canvas. "Hi, Scott, it's very nice to meet you. I don't want to interrupt your therapy. I just wanted to introduce myself and see how you're doing."

Dominguez's eyes shifted and locked on Hilldorfer, holding his gaze for a full minute before the young man's face broke into a radiant, ear-to-ear smile. He began to stutter, like a car engine struggling to turn over on a cold morning, its owner refusing to let go of the key.

"Um um um um um um um um um um um um." The smile faded, replaced by a pinched expression, as if he was stricken by pain. The stuttering continued. "Um um um um um um um um um um um."

Hilldorfer looked to Hamp, uncertain what to do. She waited patiently. The others in the room also remained focused on Dominguez. A few wiped tears from their eyes. Hilldorfer was certain Dominguez would never make it to the witness stand.

Then the stuttering stopped and a ghostly voice emerged as soft as a whisper and as hoarse as an eighty-year-old man with a three-pack-a-day habit.

"I'm fine. Um, um, how are you?"

Hilldorfer stepped closer and knelt. "I'm fine, Scott. Thank you for asking." He made small talk for a few minutes, patiently waiting for each response, sometimes as long as a minute. Before each response Dominguez struggled to swallow, as if something in his throat blocked the words. When he spoke the stuttering was a raspy, ghostlike chant.

"Scott, do you remember anything that happened that day? Do you remember what happened to you?"

Dominguez closed his eyes. "Um um um um . . . Allan. Allan made me go in the tank."

"Did he give you any safety equipment, Scott? Did he give you anything to wear or to help you breathe?"

"Um um um um. No."

"Did he have a safety meeting?"

"No. No . . . meeting . . . just go in . . . clean the . . . shit . . . on the bottom."

As Hilldorfer spoke to the young man he realized that what had happened was far worse than he had inferred from Dr. Ratcliffe's explanation. He equated the term *brain damage* to mental retardation and had assumed Dominguez could not comprehend his injuries or how they had impacted him. That was not the case. Scott Dominguez's brain was functioning, but it was like a corroded engine, the gears reluctant to move. Ratcliffe's use of the term *Parkinsonian* suddenly made perfect sense. The holes in his basal ganglia caused a delay while his brain found different paths to communicate with his body, but Scott Dominguez knew what had happened to him, and that it had left him a prisoner in his own body. The grimace etched on his face was wrought from the frustration of not being able to get out.

The thought made Hilldorfer shiver.

Though he had many more questions, he had the answer to the question most important. Dominguez could testify. It would not be easy, but he could do it and if he did, he would be a powerful witness. He gently held the young man's hand. "Thank you for allowing me to interrupt your therapy, Scott. I'd like to come back and introduce you to the attorneys I'm going to be working with. I'd like them to meet you, too."

The smile returned. "Yes," he whispered.

Hilldorfer said his good-byes. Hamp walked him to the front door. As they spoke he spotted a photograph of Dominguez hanging on the wall. Dressed in a blue graduation gown, his smile held the promise of a bright future.

"Could I borrow that? The grand jury might want to know what Scott looks like."

Hamp removed the photograph from the frame and handed it to him. "I'm so glad you came all the way from Seattle, Joe. Thank you. It means so much to us. If there is anything we can do, just let us know."

He handed her a business card, thanked her again, and walked back to the car. Before leaving he looked back at the house, his mind leaping forward to a nondescript courtroom with a nondescript judge sitting at an elevated bench, and the thought that someday he would be trying to explain to Jackie Hamp and her family why Allan Elias would never spend a day in jail.[2]

HILLDORFER'S PESSIMISM was based on statistics. From its inception, the percentage of EPA cases declined by the Department of Justice remained substantially higher than its overall declination rate.[3] The reasons were many, with fingers pointed in every direction. The EPA blamed the DOJ's declination for creating a disincentive to investigate cases. The DOJ fired back that the EPA was too concerned with bean counting and the investigations were, at best, incomplete. Both pointed fingers at the Environmental Crimes Section, complaining it did not foster a cooperative working relationship and had too much discretion to decline prosecutions.

In truth, there was enough blame to go around, and Congress and the White House were not immune. The promulgation of more and more environmental statutes cast a wider and wider net over industrial facilities—amendments to RCRA in 1984 extended the EPA's regulatory reach to include generators of relatively small volumes of hazardous waste, expanding the universe of RCRA-regulated facilities from about 15,000 to 200,000. By contrast, the EPA and ECS budgets—and concomitantly, their manpower—remained relatively stagnant. In 1996 the EPA still had less than 150 agents working nationwide. Other resources needed to fully investigate criminal matters also remained limited, especially given the technical needs of criminal cases.

A lack of resources was not the only problem. By the early 1990s critics also began to question whether the threat of jail was as big a deterrent as the Department of Justice was boasting. Though the ECS reported that more than nine hundred environmental criminal indictments had resulted in nearly seven hundred guilty pleas and convictions during its first ten years, critics argued that guilty pleas and convictions did not equate to actual jail time. Statistics kept by watchdog agencies indicated that less than 10 percent of the prosecutions were resulting in convictions and actual time spent in jail. Defendants were receiving jail sentences on average of between only four and six months, and even those numbers could be considered misleading because the time of incarceration did not take into consideration that some of the sentences were suspended and other defendants got out early on probation.

Despite the emphasis on criminal convictions and tough talk, fines remained the primary enforcement weapon.[4]

Monday, March 10, 1997
EPA Headquarters, Region 10
Sixth and University Streets
Seattle, Washington

CHAPTER EIGHTEEN

HILLDORFER RETURNED to his office the following Monday after spending much of the weekend thinking of Scott Dominguez and talking about the experience with his wife. He wondered what it did to a young man to hold the world by the tail one day and have it stripped from his hands the next? What did that do to his family?

He stepped into his cubicle and emptied his briefcase, settling in to prepare written witness statements of his meetings with both Jackie and Scott. He held up Scott's graduation photo, struck again by the young man's eyes. They radiated so much promise, so much life. He stood and walked across the hallway to Sandy Smith's office, knocked on the door, and handed her the picture. Like McClary, Smith had been one of the first EPA/CID agents after a storied career with the DEA in San Francisco. Tall, athletic, and attractive, Smith had a grown son about Dominguez's age and had taken an interest in the investigation, encouraging Hilldorfer by referring to it as the most important case in the office.

"Oh my God, he's such a good-looking kid. Did you talk with him?"

"Yeah."

"Do you think he can testify?"

Hilldorfer nodded. "I think so. Maybe."

Smith stared at the photograph for another moment then handed it back to him. "He'd be a powerful witness."

"You want to get a cup of coffee?" Hilldorfer asked.

They walked to the hallway elevators.

"Hang on," Hilldorfer said. He went back to his cubicle and left Dominguez's photograph on his desk, face up for others to see.

◆   ◆   ◆

THROUGHOUT THE SPRING Hilldorfer and Wojnicz began the arduous process of tracking down witnesses who had worked at Evergreen before and after Dominguez's injury. Ron Hamp, Scott's stepfather, provided the first name, Casey Johnson. After that it was like a line of dominoes falling. Everyone seemed to have another tale of an employee getting hurt at Evergreen.

On March 18 the two agents traveled down a dark and deserted country road in Eagle, Idaho—a small town forty minutes outside of Boise. Just after twilight and without the benefit of any ambient light, it was darker than dark except for a strange glow atop the mountains that stumped even Wojnicz. They found the parking lot adjacent to the small grass park. Telephone poles on the ground served as curbs. As they parked, a pencil-thin young man got out of the cab of a truck and identified himself as Casey Johnson. Hilldorfer suggested they go to a nearby picnic table to talk. Johnson wore stiff blue jeans, a gray sweatshirt, and baseball cap and leaned against the edge of the table, his face in profile. He had suggested the location for their meeting—it and his first question spoke volumes.

"Will Allan find out I've been talking to you?"

"For now this is just between us, but if this goes to trial, yes, you may be called to testify," Hilldorfer said. "If that happens, we have to provide a statement to the defense about what we talk about tonight." Sensing Johnson becoming reticent, Hilldorfer sought common ground. "I talked to Scotty's father. He indicated you might have some information for me about Evergreen after Scotty's injury, about what Allan said happened?"

"Yeah, Allan told us about it first day I was there." Johnson's words were drawn out, a near drawl. "He said 'Those guys were fucking idiots and have caused me a lot of problems,' is what he said."

"Did he say why they were idiots?"

"He just said he had safety equipment available but they didn't use it."

"Was there safety equipment when you worked there?"

Johnson smirked. "No. There was shit, a bunch of junk around the site. That was it."

"Was the tank still there?"

"It *was,* but Allan had someone come in, cut it up, and haul it off."

"Do you know who?"

"No."

"What happened to the stuff in the tank?"

"Just said to dump it on the ground and had Sean bury it."

"Sean?"

"Sean Stevens. But then he had to dig it up again."

"Yeah, why was that?"

"Allan said someone from DEQ was coming to do an inspection, so he had Sean scrape it up and put it on a black tarp and cover it with dirt so the inspectors couldn't see or smell it. He told us not to say anything. He said the inspectors were 'idiots.'"

It confirmed Hilldorfer's suspicion that someone was warning Elias about inspections at the plant. Johnson gave them the names of other employees who worked at Evergreen while he was there, Kenny McAllister, Jamie Dunford, Sean Stevens, and Vance Turner, who he said Elias was calling a "foreman." As DEQ had warned, Evergreen's entire workforce had turned over.

"How'd you get hurt, Casey?"

Johnson unfolded his arms and slipped his hands into the pockets of his jeans, looking down as he explained how Elias told them to hook up an acid pump to a tank, but didn't tell them how to do it. When they asked, Elias said, "You'll figure it out." The acid melted the hose thread.

"When we turned the pump on the shit sprayed twenty to thirty feet in the air. It burnt my face and Kenny's leg."

Johnson described the pain of the acid burning his face and said there was no safety tub or shower to flush the injury and that the acid had temporarily disfigured him. "I got a videotape to prove it."

He was taken to the hospital but Elias called him and told him he wanted him back in two days and not to report the injury to OSHA. Johnson said that whenever an employee expressed concern about getting hurt Elias would tell them the acid was too weak to hurt them.

"Then one time he puts the acid into a plastic bucket to show us . . . and the acid melted the bucket. We all started calling the place 'Everdeath.'"[1]

JOHNSON GAVE THEM the name Roger Parker, and on a subsequent trip Hilldorfer and Lorinda Wallace, who was in Idaho working another EPA case, tracked Parker down at a technical college in Pocatello. They slipped into an empty classroom of tired-looking desks and walls in need of a fresh coat of paint. Parker, who had short wiry hair and a wispy mustache, told them he worked for Elias for about eighteen months in 1995, then quit to start a landscaping business. When the business didn't do well he called Elias for his job back. Elias told him "no." The day after Dominguez's injury Elias called him out of the blue and asked him to come back to work. Elias said the injury happened because he left the "stupid son of a bitches to do the job alone."[2]

But Parker said he knew exactly what happened in the tank. "Because he wanted me to do the same thing."

He said that in 1995, Elias had him drain liquid from the tank onto the ground behind the railroad tracks and told him and Scott Dominguez to clean out the sludge with shovels. Parker's recollection of what might have been clearly unnerved him, like a man who changed flights at the last moment, then heard his original plane had crashed. "I was afraid to go inside it; so I told Allan I couldn't fit in the opening."

"Did Allan ever tell you there was cyanide in the tank?"

"Not cyanide. He said the sludge might have silver in it."

Parker confirmed Johnson's statement of frequent acid spills at Evergreen, and described the quantity as "thousands and thousands" of gallons. He said that if given dates he could probably tell Hilldorfer the true amount spilled.

"The true amount?"

"Allan was a genius at calculating numbers real quick, and he always seemed to know when DEQ was coming. By the time they got there he had a whole system figured out, a plan of attack."

Parker said Elias would call the employees together and gin up an excuse for the spill while he sent someone to measure the amount of acid left in the tank. Once he knew the amount left in the tank he calculated how much could have spilled so as to be below the reportable quantity, added that to the amount left, and reported the total to the DEQ inspectors. The employees were told not to talk to DEQ. If they got cornered they were to say that the spilled material was going to be reused in the fertilizer process so it wouldn't have to be shipped off as waste. After DEQ left Elias had them bury the waste in the boneyard. He bragged that he was so good at avoiding DEQ and beating OSHA fines that local businesses and even a law firm had called him to find out how to beat OSHA.

Parker said acid wasn't the only thing Elias had them bury in the boneyard, that he had them bury drums of lab-packing waste. He also said Elias found out regulatory officials were coming to test a stream that caught Evergreen's groundwater runoff and directed them to put rock and lime near it to skew the results. "He used to joke about it. He called it his 'garden.' "

Parker said Elias claimed to have an "out" if anyone accused him of dumping hazardous waste, a clause in his contract with the city of Soda Springs that said the ground was contaminated before he bought it by waste blowing over from Soda Springs Phosphate.

It was no wonder Hatfield disliked Elias, and it was further confirmation that Elias calculated his defenses.

"I heard he was trying to rehire the guys working there when Scott was injured," Parker said. "I heard he was going to give them raises and try to persuade them to go along with his story that Scott was to blame."

Parker gave them the name Danny Rice, who he said suffered a head injury at Evergreen, and when Elias found out that the employees had called an ambulance, he "went crazy."

HILLDORFER AND WOJNICZ found Rice on June 11 living in a beautifully maintained log cabin home in Soda Springs. He had a cherubic face with a mullet haircut, short on top and long in the back, and sang country-western songs in the local bars. Rice told the agents that he had been in desperate financial straits when he asked Elias for work in January 1995. He didn't last a month. Elias ordered him to clean out the inside of a granulator but provided no safety equipment. Fortunately, Rice had brought his hard hat with him from California and had the common sense to wear it and to tie a rope around his waist before he went into the machine. While he was inside, an unlocked rotating hammer fell suddenly and hit him in the head.

"If I hadn't been wearing my hard hat, it likely would have killed me."

He said Elias called him in the hospital and Rice told him he was getting dizzy spells and didn't think he'd be back to work for a while.

"You know what he said? He screamed at me. 'Fuck the headaches; fuck the dizziness; if you're not back to work on Wednesday, you're fired.' " Rice shook his head. "I heard he yelled at Gene and Ed for calling the ambulance; said they should have just thrown a blanket over me. Ask them. I vowed right then I'd never go back to work for him."

When Rice left the hospital he reported the injury to OSHA and said that after he did, Elias "changed his tune."

"He offered to hire me back, but I said 'No way.' I wasn't working for him ever again. I'd rather be broke and unemployed than go out there and get killed."

Rice was working at another facility when he heard the emergency call of a man down in a tank at Evergreen. "I felt sick to my stomach when I heard that. I knew someone was going to die there. I told that to OSHA; that if they didn't stop him someone was going to die."[3]

HILLDORFER ALSO WANTED to talk with Vance Turner, though there was no indication Turner had been injured at Evergreen. He suspected Elias was calling Turner a "foreman" because he intended to argue, despite what he told Hilldorfer and O'Neil when they interviewed him, that he was not involved in the day-to-day operation of the plant, and at the time of Dominguez's injury he'd left that responsibility to Brian Smith.[4]

Turner lived in Montpelier, Idaho, a small town a half-hour southwest of Soda Springs, near the Wyoming border. As was becoming standard procedure, Hilldorfer and Wojnicz drove in circles, unable to find the area where Turner lived. Wojnicz finally broke one of the unwritten codes of men and stopped to ask directions. They pulled into a parking lot of beat-up Ford trucks parked in front of an old brick building, a gun shop; not exactly the kind of place Hilldorfer expected to throw out the welcome mat to two federal agents.

"Uh, Bob, I don't think this is a good idea."

Wojnicz stepped from the car unconcerned. "Best place to get directions. This is where the locals hang out."

It felt as if they had walked into a bastion of pure Northwest Militia. The men inside dressed in camouflage and thick-soled, high-laced black boots, or cowboy boots and blue jeans with belt buckles the size of small cars. Dressed in his Carhart jeans and a flannel shirt, Wojnicz blended. In slacks and a blue sport coat Hilldorfer was the proverbial sore thumb. The chitchat stopped when they entered, the men giving them the hairy eye, but if Wojnicz noticed, he didn't let on. He walked to an antique glass case and began pricing guns, talking up the owner with his considerable knowledge about weapons. Hilldorfer headed for the restroom. When he returned Wojnicz stood in the middle of the group in animated discussion. It looked like they were ready to elect him mayor. Hilldorfer walked outside and waited. Two minutes later Wojnicz emerged wearing a shit-eating grin.

"Did you find the place?"

"What do you think?"

Hilldorfer laughed. "Yeah, but I'll bet you didn't tell them you used to work for the IRS, did you?"

THOUGH HE SAT in an easy chair in his own living room, Vance Turner was clearly not comfortable. A big man with a full head of hair, he fidgeted and didn't make a lot of eye contact with the two agents.

"Does Allan know I'm going to be talking to you?"

Hilldorfer gave him the same response he gave Johnson. Then he asked, "We understand Allan hired you as a foreman."

Turner seemed to become even more uncomfortable. "Well, I was the most senior guy there, and I kind of ran the place . . . but I wasn't no foreman."

Hilldorfer decided to bait him a bit. "People said Allan called you a foreman."

"How can I be a foreman if every time I tried to do anything Allan jumped all over me? It was pretty clear he was the only one with any authority. You did it his way, or you were fired."

"Is that the reason you left?"

"It was the most unsafe place I ever worked at."

"Unsafe how?"

"Just terrible."

Turner said he tried to make the equipment safer by adding guards and trip cords, but Elias told him it was too time consuming and too expensive. "He said people are numbers, that there are always more out there. If someone gets hurt, you could always replace them, that someone always needs a job bad enough."

◆   ◆   ◆

THE TWO AGENTS had made it a habit with each trip to stop and talk with Gene Thornock and Brian Smith. They had yet to make contact with Darren Weaver, who they understood had moved to Salt Lake City, but Hilldorfer wasn't concerned. They could track Weaver down as they got close to trial and his OSHA interview had been transcribed. Of Evergreen's three employees, Weaver was clearly going to be a star witness for the government. He told OSHA that after leaving the hospital emergency room he returned to Evergreen to pick up his truck and found Elias inside his construction trailer talking to himself. Elias asked him, "How should I act? Should I show remorse about what happened? Should I be defensive?"

Elias said he was concerned OSHA and the EPA would shut him down, which would leave Weaver and the others without jobs. Weaver said he told Elias he "wanted nothing to do with it. I just came out here to get my truck. I'm going to Pocatello to see Scott."

The following morning Weaver confirmed he returned to Evergreen and walked into the trailer while O'Neil and Clements were interviewing Elias and that Elias had pulled him outside behind one of the warehouses. Elias told him it would be better if he blamed the employees for the accident because OSHA and EPA wouldn't charge them. He wanted Weaver to confirm Elias had safety and rescue equipment on-site and told them to use it, but they had ignored him. He also wanted Weaver to say they had been trained to work in confined spaces. Instead, Weaver left and told Clements that Elias had "tried to kill them."[5]

It was explosive stuff. Trying to get Weaver to adopt a bullshit story would be evidence that Elias was guilty and had blatantly tried to obstruct justice by getting a witness to lie.

While in town the agents tracked down Thornock. Things had not been easy for Thornock since quitting Evergreen. Work was scarce and he was driving long distances to try to make money. He seemed to move between each visit, and often did not have a phone. Keeping track of him was a challenge.

The agents had taken a liking to him, despite his gruff exterior, and called him "Caveman Gene" after Smith told them Thornock had screamed "like a caveman" when he couldn't get Scott out of the tank.

Thornock confirmed Roger Parker and the Idaho DEQ's statements that there was an acid spill the first day he went back to work after Dominguez's injury.

"The first thing he did was gather us together to get us to lie. That was it. I wasn't going to lie for that man."

Thornock quit, walked to the Soda Springs Police Department, and made a report. "I didn't want to see anyone else get hurt there, and I knew right there that Allan was never going to change."

He told them Elias wanted them to scrape up the dirt and bury it in the boneyard "with all the other dirt he had us bury."

"What other dirt?" Hilldorfer asked.

Thornock said that when he first started working at Evergreen trucks loaded with what looked like cooked dirt began arriving and Elias told them to bury it. Hilldorfer and Wojnicz had not heard this before.

"Do you know where the dirt came from?"

"Allan said it was from a place in Pocatello. He said he'd tried to get silver from it."

If it was the spent treater dust from AEI, as the agents suspected, it was a hazardous waste. Elias was not permitted to transport or handle it. It was another clear RCRA violation. The magnitude of the violation, and it sounded significant, would dictate the magnitude of the criminal charge.

"How many trucks were there?" Wojnicz asked.

Thornock shrugged. "A hundred or more. They were belly loads."

Thornock gave them the name and address of Jerry Farrel[6] another employee working at Evergreen when the trucks arrived. Farrel lived in a single-wide, green-and-white mobile home, part of a cluster of mobile homes just a stone's throw from the back of Evergreen. When the two agents drove up the front door swung open and a young man with a military-style crew cut stuck his head out. He sat in a folding chair playing solitaire on a TV dinner tray and smoking a cigarette, like a bouncer at a club.

"C'mon in," he said without getting up. "It's going to be a few more minutes."

They stood in the front room watching the young man flip cards, having assumed Farrel had gone out for a moment, until they heard a thumping against the wall that separated the living room from the rest of the trailer. It became rhythmic, the vibration shaking the trailer like a nearby train passing, accelerating to a crescendo before slowing to a stop. If the young man noticed, he didn't let on. He just sat smoking and flipping cards. A moment later the door to the room opened and a man with an amazing beer belly and hair that stood a foot off the top of his head walked out with a hand in his white brief underwear, adjusting himself.

Hilldorfer refused to look at Wojnicz for fear they would break out laughing. "Jerry Farrel?"

"Yep."

Hilldorfer made the introductions. Farrel removed his hand from his shorts. Neither Hilldorfer nor Wojnicz hesitated to shake it.

Farrel collapsed into a worn couch next to the kid in the folding chair and told them he worked for Elias for about a year, hiring on to do welding. He confirmed the employee injuries and the acid spills and just shook his head, bemused, when they asked about safety equipment and meetings.

"Allan's idea of a safety meeting was to walk in and say, 'This is your safety meeting—be safe—good-bye.'" Farrel demonstrated with a dismissive wave. "He acted like we was ripping him off if we asked for safety equipment."

He also said Elias ordered him to remove an air-monitoring instrument from a stack at Evergreen so they could "bring it into the trailer and figure out how to make it read wrong." Then he asked, "Are you the same guys went out there after Scott was injured?"

"Yes," Hilldorfer answered.

"Well, you guys missed a big drum of cyanide out there."

It was like being slapped in the face. If the agents had found cyanide on-site, it would have been damning proof of Elias's lies to OSHA and to the firefighters that he had no hazardous chemicals on-site that warranted his keeping MSDS sheets, and it would have made it all the more unreasonable for him not to have any safety equipment or a training program.

"Allan had it hidden in the corner of one of them storage trailers, the one at the back. It was covered under junk and pillows, but don't bother looking for it now. I been told it ain't there no more."

"Do you know where it went?"

Farrel shook his head.

They asked him about the belly loads of waste and Thornock's estimate of the number of truckloads.

"Hell, there was a hundred trucks, easy."

To obtain a second search warrant Hilldorfer needed independent corroboration that the material came from AEI and therefore was likely hazardous waste illegally transported and dumped, but Farrel couldn't confirm that with any certainty. Like Thornock he said it just started showing up at Evergreen one truck at a time. They thanked him for his time, shook his hand again, and walked back down the steps toward their car.

"The truck driver's name was Joe."

Hilldorfer and Wojnicz turned. Farrel stood on the front step of his trailer in his underwear.

"I don't know his last name. He was bossing us around and Gene wanted to punch him in the nose. Joe something."

It was a start, but trying to find a truck driver named Joe in the state of Idaho was going to have to wait. Hilldorfer had finally gotten past the gatekeeper. Tomorrow afternoon they had an audience with Dr. John Wayne Obray.

Thursday, June 12, 1997
Soda Springs, Idaho

CHAPTER NINETEEN

THE NEXT MORNING the two agents drove back to Soda Springs and stopped by B&H Cleaners to say hello to Jackie Hamp. Hamp stood behind the counter, and when the two agents walked in they knew immediately something was wrong.

"Theresa and Scott broke up," Hamp said, knowing Hilldorfer had not yet had the chance to talk to Cole. "She's leaving to live with her mom and stepdad in Louisiana and go back to school."

"Where is she?"

♦   ♦   ♦

THE DENTAL CLINIC where Cole worked was in an older section of Soda Springs. The agents identified themselves to a woman at the front desk and apologized for coming during the middle of a business day, but said they needed to speak to Theresa Cole. The woman dismissed it as "not a problem" and went to get her.

Cole walked into the lobby dressed in a white dental outfit. The moment she saw Hilldorfer her eyes widened and she smiled wanly. "I've been hoping for the chance to talk to someone about this."

The woman gave them permission to use a partitioned cubicle in the back of the office.

As Cole spoke it became clear she'd been carrying her feelings inside like an overpacked suitcase. Once she opened up, everything spilled out. She cried as she told them how she and Scott met in high school and became sweethearts. They moved in together and he gave her a "promise ring." They planned to marry within the year.

"I was going to be a dentist and he was going to work for one of the big companies in Soda Springs or go back to college," she said. "Now all that's changed."

Tension had developed between her and the family and she and Scott had moved back to their own apartment, but it was clear caring for Scott and the bleak outlook was more than a young woman with her entire life ahead of her could handle. "I cared for Scotty. I visited him constantly while he was in the hospital, and I did as much as I could with his rehabilitation, but I had to work, too, you know?" Cole wiped away tears. "We broke up," she said softly and told them she was going to Louisiana with "the hope of getting my life together again."[1]

As Cole talked, Hilldorfer caught sight of two men moving purposefully toward them and could tell from their pursed expressions they weren't coming to greet the agents. The man in front, short and bald, stormed into the cubicle wide-eyed and red in the face. "Who the hell do you think you are? I want your business cards. How dare you come in here and interrupt a business."

Quick to anger, Hilldorfer stood up asking himself the same question. *Who the hell did this guy think he was?* He looked like a constipated accountant dressed up in a miner's outfit, flannel shirt, jeans, and work boots.

Without prompting, the man identified himself as Robert Geddes, and said he was an Idaho state senator who worked at Monsanto.[2] Hilldorfer assumed the dentist, who stood behind Geddes, had called, upset that federal agents were in his office talking to one of his employees, and wanted to know who was going to pay her salary.

Hilldorfer bit his tongue. He wanted to tell them both to kiss his ass, but he also knew that anything he said could come back to damage Dominguez's case. So rather than escalate the confrontation, he did what he and Wojnicz referred to as "making nice."

"I apologize, Mr. Geddes." He looked at the dentist. "We certainly didn't intend to interrupt anyone's business, sir." He and Wojnicz showed Geddes their credentials. "We're in town investigating a tragedy that happened at Evergreen; perhaps you heard about it?"

Neither Geddes nor the dentist responded.

"Ms. Cole was a witness to that incident and we were recently advised she would be leaving town soon. We wanted to catch her before she left. Your office manager indicated it would be all right if we did that here." Hilldorfer turned back to Cole. He had her contact information in Louisiana and didn't want to get her in any trouble. She was clearly intimidated. "Theresa, thank you so much for your cooperation. I'm glad to have met you. Best of luck to you."

Outside the building the two agents both let loose their anger in a stream of profanities.

"Fuck him. Give him his little moment of power," Hilldorfer said, dismissing Geddes but not the message he had delivered. The city of Soda Springs was starting to pay attention to the two agents' continued presence, and not everyone was rolling out the welcome mat.

AS THEY DROVE from the dental clinic, Hilldorfer shifted his focus to their meeting with Dr. John Obray. He had been given conflicting impressions of Obray. His own attempts to reach him had left him frustrated.

Joe Rice, the Soda Springs Police Department sergeant, however, said Obray was anything but pretentious, known to have a whiskey with friends at a local bar in town, and that the police considered him nothing less than a local hero, a man unafraid to make on-the-spot life-and-death decisions. They still spoke of a shooting at a local bank and how Obray, desperate to keep the victim alive, cut open the chest, thrust his hands into the chest cavity, and began massaging the heart.

As Wojnicz pulled into the parking lot of the medical clinic on South Third Street, Hilldorfer saw a grizzly bear of a man standing outside the building puffing on a cigarette. When they approached the man looked up, as if expecting them, but perhaps not right then.

"Dr. Obray?" Hilldorfer asked.

Obray took a final puff on the cigarette, dropped it, and ground out the butt on the pavement with the sole of his shoe. Then he shrugged and gave them a sheepish look. "I ain't nobody's role model," he said. "Come on in."

Inside Obray's office Hilldorfer considered a picture of the doctor sitting on a horse with a rifle slung across his lap. He wore boots, chaps, and a cowboy hat that shaded a cherubic face that appeared untouched by the dry desert air and harsh sun. Hilldorfer knew nothing about horses, but was seeking common ground. "Great picture; that's a good-looking horse."

Obray looked up at the picture as if just noticing it. "Let me tell you about that horse."

He described an elk-hunting trip with friends and told the agents how he had taken the horse up a mountain trail to a spot that overlooked the valley so he could get a clean shot at a caribou. "I get off that horse and make my way to the overlook, and when I turn around that horse takes off and runs. Left me miles in the middle of nowhere. I'm still limping from hurting my leg walking back down the mountain. If I could have, I would have shot that horse."

Obray smiled and sat down at a modestly cluttered desk in an office of light-colored furniture. On the desk rested a file. He picked up a pair of reading glasses.

"I know you spoke with OSHA," Hilldorfer said, mindful of his prior conversations with Obray's wife. "I'm sorry to make you repeat things, but would you walk us through it?"

Like Dr. Ratcliffe, Obray dismissed the intrusion and seemed in no hurry to rush them out the door. "Let me tell you about Scott Dominguez. He's a good kid, a fantastic athlete. Everybody in town used to go and watch him and his brother wrestle. It's terrible what happened to him."

He told them how he had arrived at the emergency room already advised of the incident at Evergreen and took them through the details of his treatment of Gene Thornock and Brian Smith. He told them he was trying to eliminate possible chemicals, when Dominguez arrived in a critical state and he turned his attention to keeping him alive. After stabilizing him, Obray went back to trying to figure out what could have caused his condition. He had eliminated every chemical he could think of except cyanide, which required a specific antidote. He called his good friend Joe Hulse and asked him to see if he could find a cyanide antidote kit at an old mining facility in town. Not long afterward Hulse called back to tell him he couldn't find the kit but he was at Evergreen. Obray asked to talk to Elias.

"I asked him what was in the tank."

"What did he tell you?"

"He said it was some kind of accumulated material that they were going to wash out and make fertilizer out of. He said he had tested the pH and it was eight. But other than this vague reference to some kind of product, he didn't give me any help."

Obray explained that lab work continued to show Dominguez was getting more than enough oxygen, but that his body was not utilizing it, both consistent with his hypothesis of cyanide exposure. Hilldorfer asked Obray why, if that was the case, he had concluded there was no cyanide in the tank.

Obray looked genuinely confused and said that he had never made that conclusion.

Hilldorfer showed him the note in the OSHA file. *No cyanide in the tank*.

"I received that information from Mr. Elias."

"He told you there was no cyanide in the tank?"

"When I spoke to him on the phone I specifically asked him, since I thought the exposure had been to cyanide, 'Was there a possibility there was cyanide in the tank' and he said, 'No.' "[3]

Hilldorfer tried to slow his mind, which was rushing forward like a swollen river. Obray said Elias then came to the emergency room.

"We were standing just outside the door and he asked what Scott's condition was and I told him it was very bad, in fact, I thought he was going to die. And I asked him again if he had any more information about what was in the tank because I thought it was cyanide?"

"What did he say?"

Obray started looking confused. "He said he didn't have any information on what was in the tank."

"I take it then, Dr. Obray, that Mr. Elias didn't give you any MSDS sheets on cyanide?"

Obray shook his head. "No, why would he have?"

Hilldorfer looked at Wojnicz. Neither said anything, but Obray apparently deduced the basis for their questions. "There's no way he was lying," he said, though the possibility was, perhaps, beginning to dawn on him. "He stood at the entrance to the emergency room with Scott on the table. He had tears in his eyes. He would have had to have been the greatest actor in the world."[4]

THE TWO AGENTS drove from the clinic in silence, and back to Pocatello through the Caribou National Forest and Portneuf River valley. Obray told them that while his "naive deductive reasoning" may have saved Dominguez's life, it was no cause for joy. The prolonged cyanide poisoning had caused severe brain damage that would get worse with time, not better. "For all practical purposes it ruined his life."

Hilldorfer stared out the window with a sickening thought. Could Elias, calculating from the start, have thought it better for him if Scott died? Scott would be the most compelling witness, the one able to tell everyone what happened that day in the tank.

He turned to Wojnicz. "You want to know my opinion?"

Wojnicz looked over at him.

"I think Allan gets back to Evergreen and finds out Scott is down in the tank, but his immediate concern isn't about Scott; he's worried about himself. So, he lies to the fire responders and says there's nothing in the tank but mud and water. When Obray asks him directly if there could be cyanide in the tank he can't say yes because he's already said he doesn't know. So he says 'no.' But while he's at the emergency room he sees that they're drawing Scott's blood. He's a lawyer. He knows it's evidence that will show Scott has cyanide in his system. So he follows the helicopter to Pocatello and has an hour to change his story. He tells Ratcliffe, 'You know, maybe there could have been cyanide in the tank,' but says that he had it tested and it showed there was no cyanide. The problem is, Ratcliffe doesn't seem to be buying it and someone is taking notes. Now he's admitted the possibility of cyanide being in the tank and that it came from

AEI. When he goes home that night he knows there's going to be an investigation and there's no way he can get rid of the tank that quickly. So he changes his story again. The next day he admits to us that he used the tank in a cyanide-leaching system at AEI, and says he told that to all the doctors and rescuers and he even gave the fire responders an MSDS sheet. If anyone asks him why he told Obray there was no cyanide he'll just say Obray got it wrong, otherwise why would he have so freely admitted the potential of cyanide being in the tank to federal investigators? His only mistake was that maybe he didn't test the sludge well enough. That was the reason for all the bullshit about the strata he told us, you remember? That's why he said, 'There's no criminal intent.' That's his defense: He tested the sludge and reasonably believed the tank was safe enough for him to sit in it in his rocking chair reading a book."

Tuesday, June 17, 1997
Salt Lake City, Utah

CHAPTER TWENTY

THE WEEK AFTER his meeting with Dr. Obray, Hilldorfer flew to Salt Lake City and then drove to Boise to work with Breitsameter. Everyone who heard the story of Dr. Obray expressed shock, but for Hilldorfer the case had crystallized. Every chance he could he gave his closing statement. Elias lied to an emergency room doctor while watching Scott die. What more evidence of guilt was needed?

Flying to Salt Lake City and driving to Boise was a concession to McClary's diminishing travel budget. Flights to Salt Lake City were cheaper than the $368 direct flights to Boise, and the case remained a long way from indictment; no evidence had yet been presented to the grand jury. Hilldorfer knew McClary was trying to be diplomatic. McClary knew what it was like to be an agent humping an investigation, but he also had a region to manage and knew firsthand that EPA investigations were a lot like fishing. It was never the small ones that got away; it was always the big ones. McClary was undoubtedly envisioning Elias getting away and having nothing to show for a costly investigation but an unbaited hook. Hilldorfer knew McClary didn't believe it was a fair way to assess an agent's or the region's performance because he'd been in meetings with McClary when EPA officials from Washington, D.C., visited. McClary told them it was a mistake to play the referral game, that they had to look at the quality of the investigations because someday Congress would take a close look at the number of referrals, compare it to the number of convictions, and red flags would be raised all over.

At the moment, however, referrals remained the game they all had to play, and McClary wanted an indictment before the end of the fiscal year in October. Hilldorfer couldn't promise that was going to happen.

Hilldorfer's final appointment on his way out of town was to pay a surprise visit to Western Analysis, the lab to which Elias claimed he sent the samples from the tank. Wojnicz had flown to New York to help his father move to Washington where he could care for him, but he had been adamant that Hilldorfer not go to Western Analysis without him. He wanted to hear for himself what the tests revealed about cyanide. Hilldorfer picked him up at the Salt Lake City Airport on June 18.

Western Analysis was located in a single-story commercial building in an industrial park. Hilldorfer pulled open the door and asked the lab technician, Kyle Schick, if the lab had any records on materials submitted by Allan Elias of Evergreen Resources in Soda Springs, Idaho.

Schick said he did.

Schick could have been a poster boy for the Mormon Church. With nearly white hair and boyish features he looked like a kid, and he came across as an everyday-honest guy. He told Hilldorfer and Wojnicz that he first did an analysis for Elias in February 1996 on a sample Elias said was fertilizer. Elias wanted to know if it was "safe for putting on fields." The second analysis was done in late July 1996. This was likely the sample retrieved from the tank by Weaver.

"He usually calls to discuss the type of lab work he wants done before he sends the sample. He said he was sending a sample that he wanted tested for silver concentration."

That much the agents already knew.

"Did he ask you to test it for cyanide?" Hilldorfer asked.

Schick looked at the records. "He specifically asked for a fire assay, a silver test. There was no TCLP or pH test."

"And what does that mean?"

"It means he didn't ask that it be tested for cyanide."

Son of a bitch, Hilldorfer thought. Elias had never even checked.

"What did the tests show?"

"The sample had a low concentration of silver but too low to be of value."

"And you're sure you did not do any tests for cyanide?"

Schick reconsidered the records. "It's not in here and I don't recall taking any special precautions. At a minimum, if we had suspected that the sample contained cyanide we would have done the test under a hood. There's nothing in the records indicating the fire assay test was performed with any special precautions."

"You said you did another analysis?"

"Mr. Elias called me again on October 12."

With a timeline formulated in his head, Hilldorfer knew the call was two weeks before Idaho DEQ called him and told him the tank and its contents had disappeared.

"What did he call for that time?"

"He said he had tailings and he suspected he had a cyanide problem. He was going to mail me a sample to test. He picked my brain for information for about fifteen to twenty minutes."

"What about?"

"He was interested in the behavior of cyanide at different pH levels."

"Did he tell you where the sample came from?"

"He said they were tank solids from a process that used cyanide leaching on mining tailings, but said that it had been stored out in the open and exposed to the weather for seven years."

"Did he tell you the material was kept in a twenty-five-thousand-gallon tank with only minimal ventilation?"

Schick shook his head. "No."

"What did you tell him?"

"I told him that pH was important when dealing with cyanide because a low pH will drive out cyanide gas, but in the case of a sludge the absence of cyanide on the surface didn't mean that the sludge was safe to work with because at higher concentrations the sludge on top would keep the cyanide from any liberating action and you could have cyanide in the lower levels."

"Did you test that sample?"

"We didn't. We farmed it to another lab, American West. It's better equipped to do that kind of testing."

"Did they send you their results?"

Schick shuffled through papers. "The sample was high in silver. A TCLP test showed silver at about seven parts per million. The regulatory level is five, so the sample was in fact a hazardous waste."

"What about cyanide? Did they test it for cyanide?"

Schick nodded. "That was quite high also, about one thousand parts per million, which is ten times the maximum level considered safe."

"And did you call Mr. Elias and give him those results?"

"Yes."

"And did you have any further conversation with him?"

"He wanted to know what he could do to get the cyanide out of the sludge."

I'll bet he did, Hilldorfer thought.

"What did you tell him?"

"I told him that pH adjustments to the material could help in reducing the cyanide level, but that it would be very risky because of the possibility of a cyanide gas release. At a pH over 9.5 or below about 7.7, cyanide becomes very unstable and very dangerous."[1]

Tuesday, July 8, 1997
Boise, Idaho

CHAPTER TWENTY-ONE

JULY 8 WAS Joanne's birthday, and it had traditionally been accorded a big celebration by her family. Her parents were flying out from Hawaii for the party, but Hilldorfer wouldn't be there, and he'd then made the typical guy mistake—he'd made matters worse. Without time to get Joanne a proper birthday card before rushing to the airport, he'd modified a Christmas card. Now in Boise he realized it was the wrong thing to do, and rationalizing the importance of this trip was not easing his conscience.

David Uhlmann, the young prosecutor from the Environmental Crimes Section in Washington, D.C., had come to Boise for the first time in the Elias case. At long last the government would present evidence to the grand jury. After much debate Uhlmann and Breitsameter decided against a shotgun presentation of witnesses and opted instead to have an agent lay out a road map of the evidence against Allan Elias. That agent would be Wojnicz. Hilldorfer would be saved for the trial.

Hilldorfer had been anxious to meet the man in whose hands he knew he would eventually have to place Scott Dominguez. Breitsameter spoke highly of Uhlmann, and Hilldorfer's telephone conversations left him with the impression that Uhlmann was a prosecutor who took cases the distance. That, however, conflicted with a conversation he had with Kelly O'Neil. O'Neil had told Hilldorfer, in essence, to watch his back. He said his investigation of the Wilber Ellis Company, a fertilizer manufacturer in northern Idaho, for discharging rinse water laden with fertilizer residue into the Cow Creek, had been progressing until David Marshall appeared as defense counsel. At that point he said Uhlmann backtracked, pleading the company to a bullshit misdemeanor.[1] Marshall was well known to Region 10 special agents, having at one time been an assistant U.S. attorney in Seattle. He worked many cases with Dixon McClary and was well-versed on environmental regulations. The special agents joked that Marshall had "gone to the dark side," but his reputation was no joke. Hilldorfer couldn't recall anyone trying a case against him. Every case pled out before trial.

As a result of O'Neil's admonition Hilldorfer wasn't sure who David Uhlmann was.

DAVID UHLMANN was a product of a turbulent era in a turbulent city. He grew up in Washington, D.C., and lived through the assassinations of Robert Kennedy and Martin Luther King, and the race marches through the streets of the city. The assassinations convinced him never to become a politician, but the marches and the ideals they embraced, fostered by staunchly Democratic parents, ingrained in him a keen awareness of the need for social justice.

At thirteen his parents divorced and his father moved out. Beyond being emotionally difficult, it resulted in financial strain for Uhlmann and his mother and two sisters. He attended public high school until his junior year, when he received a partial scholarship to St. Albans, an up-scale prep school in Washington, D.C. He resolved to take full advantage of the opportunity. Despite his childhood misgivings about becoming a politician, and the fact that he was new to the school, he defeated Bill Mondale, the son of then–vice president Walter Mondale, for Liberal

Party president of the school's government club. Uhlmann had labored over his campaign speech, borrowing a line from John F. Kennedy that would begin to define him as a person and shape his future career choice.

"To whom much is given, much is expected."

When Uhlmann became active in drama others began suggesting he had the skills to be a good trial lawyer, something Uhlmann had never considered. His perception of a trial lawyer was Atticus Finch, the Gregory Peck character in *To Kill a Mockingbird*. Finch embodied everything Uhlmann's parents taught him about the fight for social justice—the defense lawyer defending the wrongfully accused black man against blatant prejudices.

He attended Swarthmore College outside Philadelphia, working to pay for his education but still managing to graduate Phi Beta Kappa with High Honors from a history honors program. He also found a niche as a journalist, becoming the editor in chief of the college newspaper, *The Phoenix,* but ultimately decided against it as a career. Being an objective observer did not fulfill his yearning to be an active advocate. He applied to law school and was accepted everywhere he applied except Harvard, Yale, and Stanford—his three top choices. He chose Columbia then deferred his admission for a year to save money. He took a job working for ICF, an environmental consulting firm, and became part of a program started after the Love Canal disaster in New York State that sent him to Superfund sites around the nation to speak with local residents and the media about their environmental problems. The exposure made him see the environment as a worthy social cause.

The following year Yale put him on its wait-list and he deferred Columbia again to take a position at ICF's offices in California. On his second day in San Francisco, Yale called. Two students failed to show for the first day of classes. "You're the next person on the waiting list. Are you still interested in coming to Yale?"

Uhlmann explained his situation and asked for time. Yale gave him twenty-four hours. Torn, he called his college mentor, Alex Hybel, and rattled off the positives and negatives he had quickly considered. The professor listened patiently then cut to the chase.

"David, my boy," he said in his thick Argentinean accent, "it's not how you enter in life. It's how you exit."

Uhlmann boarded a plane for Yale the next day. In his three years there he did well enough to seek a highly coveted clerkship with a federal district court judge and picked Judge Marvin H. Shoob of the Northern District of Georgia. An activist judge, Shoob had presided over several prominent cases including the Cuban refugee riots in an Atlanta jail and the anti-trust litigation against the airlines for fixing airfares. His two years with Shoob would become an apprenticeship in courtroom dynamics and provide him a lifelong mentor. A trial lawyer for thirty years before taking the bench, Shoob gathered his clerks after each trial to discuss what had been effective tactics by both the prosecutor and the defense attorney, and he urged them to ask the same questions of jurors after their own trials.

The only negative part of the experience for Uhlmann was having his idealistic vision that all defense lawyers were defenders of social justice, like Atticus Finch, shattered. Most of the defense attorneys who appeared before Shoob did not seem interested in seeking truth, just in obstructing it. They used smoke-and-mirror tactics to obscure the fact that their clients were plainly guilty. At the same time, Uhlmann realized he did not have the hardcore prosecutor mentality—what he referred to as "the anger"—needed to go after hardened street criminals each day. While he did not condone crime born of poverty, he sympathized with many of the defendants who stood before the bench. Given few opportunities in life and even fewer choices, drugs and crime became their only visible means to escape poverty. In stark contrast were the white-collar criminals who appeared before Shoob. Most were the people about whom Kennedy spoke—people who had been given opportunities. Their crimes were those of the well educated and well heeled, crimes of greed, arrogance, and a blatant disregard for the rules that governed the rest of society—crimes that Uhlmann realized did arouse the anger in him. It pissed him off.

When his two years with Shoob came to an end he looked for a place to apply that passion and chose the attorney general's honor program—and sought an entry-level position at the Justice Department's Civil Rights Division or Environmental Crimes Section. Hundreds applied; less than twenty were accepted. The ECS offered him a job. In 1990 he became the twenty-second lawyer in a section just three years old and still trying to get a handle on how to enforce the environmental legislation that exploded in the late 1970s.

His first day he had neither an assignment nor an office but eventually became part of the *Exxon Valdez* team; he then caught another career break when he asked to work a case near Rock Springs, Wyoming, and met an aggressive, senior litigator in the Wyoming U.S. Attorney's Office named David Kubichek. Like his time with Judge Shoob, trying cases with Kubichek would be career-shaping. They prosecuted a series of environmental crimes on public lands. In between Uhlmann tried cases in the U.S. Attorney's Office in D.C., amassing twenty to twenty-five trials in six months. Before each one he called Judge Shoob to discuss the case.

Emboldened by his trial experience, Uhlmann returned to Wyoming in August 1993 to try his first environmental criminal case with Kubichek, and quickly learned that not everyone within the judiciary shared his passion for bringing hazardous waste polluters to justice.[2]

INTENDED OR NOT, Hilldorfer found himself alone with Uhlmann making small talk over the clatter of tables being cleared and set in the Dong Khanh Vietnamese restaurant on Broadway Street in downtown Boise. Ironically, July 8 was Uhlmann's mother's birthday, and he, too, was regretting not being home for the celebration.

"What's good?" Uhlmann asked, taking a menu from a heavyset Caucasian woman.

Hilldorfer explained that Wojnicz usually ordered the spicy eggplant. He stayed with the garlic chicken.

"How is it?"

"Not bad."

"Sounds good." Uhlmann closed his menu and sipped water. Physically unimposing, he was perhaps five foot eight with a slender build, 150 pounds. He wore a white shirt from the day's grand jury proceedings, but had removed his tie and jacket and put on blue jeans, which made him look even younger than his thirty-five years. He had the ruddy complexion, youthful looks, and coltish energy of someone in their late twenties. Hilldorfer knew Uhlmann would be the lead trial attorney on the Elias case. He had the ability to command the room without dominating it and the intelligence to support his opinions.

After ordering Uhlmann told Hilldorfer that he and his wife, Virginia, had recently had a baby girl to add to their family of two children from her prior marriage. He took a four-week paternity leave but had found the time to try four environmental cases. Hilldorfer sat back. This was when most attorneys told their "war stories"—tales of how they overcame seemingly insurmountable odds to win their cases.

"The first environmental case I ever tried, I lost." Uhlmann laughed at the recollection though it was a begrudging laugh that clearly had come with time, and not from humor.

The admission caught Hilldorfer off-guard. "What happened?"

"I was working with an AUSA in Wyoming named David Kubichek prosecuting environmental crimes on public lands." Uhlmann spoke with the ease of someone who had told the story before and had a habit of adjusting his wire-rimmed glasses and leaning forward on his elbows. "Someone dumped three dozen fifty-five-gallon drums of lacquer thinner waste in the middle of nowhere outside Rock Springs with their caps off so the material inside would evaporate. An expert told me that if someone had lit a match you would have seen the flames for miles."

"How did you find out about it?" Hilldorfer knew from his own experience that determining the perpetrator in a dumping case on public land was particularly difficult because the area was expansive and remote.

Uhlmann picked up his chopsticks and pulled them apart, holding them like a drummer. "The train goes through Rock Springs. The conductor reported seeing the drums to the Cheyenne sheriff's office. They got the Bureau of Land Management involved, and they called the EPA. It took the agents about five minutes to figure out the drums most likely came from an automobile junkyard three miles away, but when they went out there the owner denied he had anything to do with it."

"How'd they get him?"

"The train conductor also gave them a description of a truck he'd seen out there and it matched a description of a truck registered to the junkyard. One of the agents asked if he could take a look inside and found a cap in the back that fit perfectly into the top of the fifty-five-gallon drums. The owner confessed and told the agents in great detail about what he did and how he did it."

"But he didn't plead?"

Uhlmann shook his head. "No."

"What went wrong?" Hilldorfer asked, though he was thinking, *How the hell could you have lost at trial?*

Uhlmann told him that the judge, Clarence "Bud" Brimmer, hated the case and apparently wasn't too fond of lawyers from Washington, D.C., at one point questioning whether a witness from the Bureau of Land Management was getting "chits" from Washington for bringing the case. "He wouldn't let me speak in his courtroom during the arraignment. He would only let Kubichek talk."

"What did you do?"

Uhlmann shrugged. "We picked a jury. I actually felt pretty good after giving my opening statement, but from there it went downhill fast. The trial became just an absolute circus, Joe. Brimmer excluded the defendant's confession and wouldn't allow me to use it to cross-examine the defendant."

"Why?"

"He said he didn't consider it complete. He referred to it in front of the jury as 'artfully contrived.' Then he let the defense attorney just badger my witnesses on cross-examination. When I finally stood up and objected that the questions were argumentative, he stood and leaned over the bench." Uhlmann put his hands palms down on the table and pushed himself out of his seat, leaning across the table to imitate Brimmer. " 'The question was not addressed to you, Mr. Uhlmann. Sit down.' " He laughed. "I sat down, turned to Kubichek, and said, 'Does that mean my objection is overruled?' "

Hilldorfer was laughing, but only because it was too close to home.

"Then he allowed the defendant's wife and son to testify about what a great husband and father he was, and how he never would throw anything away. And he let them sit with him."

"At counsel's table?"

Uhlmann nodded. "It was like trying a case against the Beaver Cleaver family. I was actually proud we managed to keep the jury out overnight, but we ultimately lost."

"That was your first trial?"

Uhlmann sat back. "First environmental trial." He shrugged. "It wasn't a complete loss. When I got back to Washington I went to dinner at a friend's house. There was a woman there I liked and the trial was great material, like a comedy routine. Two years later I married her."

Hilldorfer smiled. It was a good story, and intended or not it told him everything he needed to know about David Uhlmann. A graduate of Yale Law School, Uhlmann could have thrown up his hands after that trial and said "What's the point?", which was how Hilldorfer felt after Boomsnub. Uhlmann could have jumped ship to one of the big Washington, D.C., law firms and likely earned triple his government salary. Instead the two of them were sitting in a restaurant miles from home, missing their families, trying to secure an indictment that would lead to the trial of another local businessman in another small town with no guarantees Elias would ever spend a day in jail.[3]

September 1997
EPA Region 10 Headquarters
Seattle, Washington

CHAPTER TWENTY-TWO

LATE THAT SUMMER, as the end of the October fiscal year approached and Elias remained far from a bean in Region 10's referral jar, the political pressures began to heat up for Hilldorfer and Wojnicz. Kelly O'Neil had been promoted to assistant special agent in charge (pronounced *A-SAC*) for Region 10, the number two man beneath Dixon McClary. O'Neil began leaving Wojnicz "love notes" asking him about the status of his other pending investigations and confronting them both about Wojnicz's continued involvement in the Elias investigation and their declining referral numbers.

"Joe's a big boy, Bob. Why do you have to go up there? He can handle it."

They discussed it with McClary, but the hard place in which McClary was stuck was getting tighter as his travel budget continued to get squeezed. He, too, began to question the need for two agents. Hilldorfer found it both upsetting and amusing.

"It's not like we're putting in requests to go to Tahiti," he'd say. "Do you really think we want to spend another weekend in southeast Idaho? This isn't a party."

As the pressure intensified, Hilldorfer called on Breitsameter and Uhlmann to "lean on the purse strings," something he never had to do at the FBI, and when the budget crunch reached a critical stage Breitsameter had Terry Deerden write a letter touting the outstanding job being performed by Hilldorfer and Wojnicz. It was a double-edged sword. Each year McClary had given Hilldorfer a strong job evaluation and a yearly bonus for "sustained superior performance," which included the number of referrals he made to the DOJ. Hilldorfer had admittedly neglected those other files, which his evaluation that year reflected.

Complicating things further, Uhlmann and Breitsameter were seriously considering charging Elias with knowingly endangering Scott Dominguez, the environmental crime equivalent of proving a charge of attempted first-degree murder. Knowing endangerment required proving Elias *knew* his conduct would place Dominguez in danger of death or serious bodily injury, and if proven the potential penalties were stiff: a $250,000 fine against the individual, a $1 million fine against the corporation, and imprisonment for as long as fifteen years. The problem was that a knowing endangerment charge had never been successfully prosecuted against an individual. The only agent Hilldorfer knew who had investigated such a charge was Sandy Smith. When Uhlmann and Breitsameter appeared intent on going after Elias, Hilldorfer sought out Smith to find out what had happened.

HILLDORFER SAT AT a table in the carpeted corridor between the One Union Square and Two Union Square buildings lined with fast-food restaurants and, since it was Seattle, a Starbucks *and* a Tully's coffee shop. The tables should have had government bar codes given how often the EPA agents were there. Sandy Smith was still at the counter waiting for her specialty coffee, which usually took twice as long to make. When she joined him at the table they talked about Scott Dominguez.

"Well, it doesn't look like I'm going to get it indicted this year," he said, "but they might actually pursue a knowing endangerment charge."

Smith nodded but didn't otherwise respond.

"I understand you had one."

"Yeah, I had one," she said without enthusiasm. "PureGro."

"How'd it go?"

She shook her head, watching the flow of people through the hall and sipping the rim of her cup. Then she looked back at him. "You sure you want to know?"

A LACK OF jail time to environmental criminals was not the only criticism being leveled at the Department of Justice in the early 1990s. Local U.S. Attorney's Offices, of which there were ninety-three, were accusing the Environmental Crimes Section of being unwilling to prosecute difficult but meritorious cases, especially against major corporations and their executives. Critics reported numbers that appeared to back up the allegation, citing statistics that the vast majority of the prosecutions for federal criminal environmental violations were to mom-and-pop businesses with less than 6 percent against Fortune 500 companies.[1]

The allegations indicated a growing mutiny by the local U.S. Attorney's Offices against a protocol established when the environmental statutes were promulgated. That protocol required every U.S. Attorney's Office to obtain approval from the assistant attorney general for the environment and natural resources before indicting an environmental crime. While the rationale for the policy—nationwide uniformity in the interpretation and application of the statutes—might have been worthwhile, local U.S. attorneys, who had autonomy for nearly every other crime they prosecuted, viewed the approval requirement as a stranglehold and further indictment of the Department of Justice in Washington's (referred to as Main Justice) arrogance.

The external criticism fueled the fires of dissidents within the ECS. The section had been founded by a handful of prosecutors who considered themselves true environmentalists, but when environmental crimes became the politically hot white-collar crime, there was no shortage of people who wanted to offer opinions on charting the ECS's direction. Experienced prosecutors without environmental backgrounds, like Section Chief Neil Cartusciello from the Southern District of New York U.S. Attorney's Office, were brought in to run the program. It led to an inevitable clash with the founding attorneys, and their disagreements spilled into shouting matches in the hallways. Uhlmann and his other line attorneys, those prosecuting the cases, found themselves in the middle of a civil war. They referred to the hardcore group of attorneys who backed management as "Loyalists," and to the hardcore group who supported the environmentalists as "Dissidents." Neutral, they called themselves the "Swiss."[2]

The issue became public when Professor John Turley of the Environmental Crimes Project at the George Washington University National Law Center issued a preliminary report on the ECS to Congressman Charles E. Schumer (D-N.Y.), chairman of the Subcommittee on Crime and Criminal Justice. Turley's report alleged that the ECS scrutinized environmental violations to eliminate all but the most egregious violations, and that the declinations were politically motivated, reflecting pressure from the White House and industry.[3] The report accused the ECS of being too willing to accept trivial financial settlements in cases involving serious and long-standing environmental violations.

Shortly thereafter, Congressman John Dingell's (D-Mich.) Subcommittee on Investigations and Oversight of the House Energy and Commerce Committee sought to investigate six cases in particular for the stated purpose of determining whether the ECS was declining cases because of political pressure from the White House and lobbyists. One of the featured cases was an eastern Washington case known as "PureGro."

AS HE SAT listening to Smith, Hilldorfer quickly understood why she had been hesitant to tell him her experience. It was like listening to someone relive a car accident.

PureGro was a wholly-owned subsidiary of the large California-based corporation Unocal, one of the largest agricultural chemical application and distribution companies in the United States with a facility in Pasco, Washington. On May 18, 1987, the local health department notified the Washington State Department of Agriculture that people living in the outskirts of Pasco were experiencing breathing difficulties, nausea, and rashes. One couple, Jack and Velma Downs, complained of a foul smell and became ill after witnessing PureGro employees apply a pesticide to a field directly across the road from their home. An investigation revealed that the pesticide had been taken from a tank at PureGro used to collect a variety of pesticide and fertilizer wastes and contained the residue of incompatibly dangerous chemicals. Two weeks later, Jack Downs died of a heart attack.

The local district attorney considered the matter for many months but ultimately declined to press charges. The Washington State Attorney General's Office, however, took notice and assigned Assistant Attorney General Ken Ackerman to the case. Ackerman, an experienced trial attorney, made the decision to prosecute under federal law so that he could bring felony charges against the company and its individual officers. Smith said she began working with Ackerman and an aggressive, twenty-eight-year-old assistant U.S. attorney named Becky Dewees. They interviewed dozens of witnesses and presented the evidence to a grand jury in the Eastern District of Washington. In September the

grand jury returned a six-count indictment against PureGro for violations of the Resource, Conservation and Recovery Act, including a
knowing endangerment charge. A Department of Justice press release touted the case as "the first indictment against a Washington corporation alleging violations of the 'knowing endangerment' clause of
RCRA" and praised the EPA investigation and the Washington attorney
general.

The Environmental Crimes Section conducted a prosecution review
in Washington, D.C., to discuss the strengths and weaknesses of the evidence and the legal theories being pursued. According to the congressional investigation no one expressed doubt about the merits of the case.
In fact, before being indicted, PureGro offered to plead the corporation
guilty to a felony and to pay a substantial fine if the charges against the individual defendants were dropped. ECS management and Washington
State officials had rejected the plea as too lenient for a case considered one
of the section's most important.

Prior to the scheduled trial, Dewees went to Mexico on vacation, got
hit by a car while riding a bike, suffered a head injury, and nearly died.
The Dingell committee's probe concluded that the accident resulted in
chaos inside the ECS. Unit Chief Criselda Ortiz called Dewees in the
hospital and reportedly told her to get back and get the case prepared for
trial. When that became impossible and the case was ultimately assigned
to Ortiz, the committee heard evidence that she was unwilling or inca-
pable of prosecuting it. The committee reported that despite having minimal working knowledge of the case, Ortiz excluded Ackerman and
Smith from discussions with defense counsel. It also reported that she
reinterviewed witnesses, some of whom had already testified before the
grand jury. Her motive, in Ackerman and Smith's view, was not to prepare the case for trial but to discredit the witnesses to justify dismissing
the case.

"I was horrified," Smith told Hilldorfer. "These were my witnesses,
Joe. These people came forward to testify and they were cross-examining
them like defense attorneys."

Smith complained about the attack on the witnesses, but was told she
had "lost her objectivity and that there were fatal weaknesses in the government's case."

Ultimately the ECS engaged the defense attorneys in plea discussions
without the knowledge or involvement of Smith or Ackerman and dis-

missed all charges against the individual corporate officers. PureGro pled guilty to a misdemeanor and paid a $15,000 fine.[4]

Smith looked up from her coffee, which had grown cold. Hilldorfer didn't know what to say. It was like opening up a deep wound and watching it bleed all over again. At the same time he felt sick to his stomach. For an agent it was a helpless feeling. There was nothing they could do.

Smith picked up her coffee and stood. "I cried, Joe. I just cried," she said and walked away from the table.

Summer/fall 1997
Soda Sprigs, Idaho

CHAPTER TWENTY-THREE

HILLDORFER AND WOJNICZ returned to Soda Springs to continue a series of interviews with people who had done business with Allan Elias. Like the interviews with his employees, they were consistent in their impression of the man and the end result of their dealings with him.

Kim Barnett had been an employee at AEI, Inc., and told them he had known Elias since 1983 when he became involved with the project in Moapa, Nevada, to extract silver from waste produced by the power plant. Barnett said Elias was motivated by one thing: "He wanted to be rich."

Barnett gave them the name of Hans Rasmussen and said he was also involved in the project. The two agents tracked Rasmussen to a lab in St. George, Utah. According to Rasmussen, the "pilot project" involved the use of a cyanide circuit system to recover precious metals from industrial waste generated by the plant, and Elias had a patent for the process that attempted to recover silver from flue dust. The process worked but had a poor silver recovery rate and was not commercially viable. After a year and a half, it was shut down.

Among the waste Elias tested during the pilot project was treater dust from FMC, a mining company in Pocatello, Idaho. Sometime in 1985, Barnett said Elias called him "out of the blue" and told him he was running the same process on a larger scale in Pocatello, had leased a facility directly across from the FMC plant on East County Road, and wanted Barnett to come and work for him. Intrigued, Barnett moved to Pocatello and began to work at Industrial Refining, which later became AEI, Inc.

According to William Moore,[1] FMC's director of environmental affairs at its Pocatello facility, Elias approached FMC's Philadelphia office in the late 1980s with a proposal to recover gallium and silver from FMC's "precipitator dust," also known as "treater dust." Moore said FMC was cautious because it frequently received proposals from individuals with strange ideas about what they could do with FMC's mining by-products and FMC had been burned in the past, having on one occasion been stuck with a $600,000 clean-up tab on an operation in Utah. Arnold Bernas, a technical person at FMC, was assigned the task of reviewing Elias's proposal and reported that the proposal came across as technically deficient but credible.

Barnett said the "ore" came to the plant wet and black in color and was dried on the ground. Salt was added to the dry ore and the mixture was heated to about seven hundred degrees, broken up and mixed in an impact mill, then sent through a calciner to burn off the carbon at about fifteen hundred degrees. Now white in color, when the material cooled it was placed in an intermediate tank and combined with a water-and-cyanide mixture for about sixty seconds. The resulting slurry was then piped to a sand filter constructed from an old railroad gondola car, which caught the solid material. The liquid by-product, nearly clear, was piped to vertical storage tanks, then to a precipitator tank where it was collected and heated to extract the silver. After the silver was extracted the solution was piped back to a twenty-five-thousand-gallon storage tank.

The solids caught in the sand were scraped off and treated with acid, ostensibly to make fertilizer, though Barnett said they contained untreated cyanide, which he described as "one of those loose ends."

Moore said FMC agreed to give Elias a trial period and entered into a written "research agreement" that specified the type and amount of waste FMC would provide. FMC had some oversight role in Elias's operation, and Moore said that while the chemistry and metallurgy worked in theory, the business had "serious operational and cash-flow problems." Elias had quit paying the owner of the Industrial Refining property, Tesco American.

On August 25, 1997, Hilldorfer and Wojnicz interviewed William Brugger, the president of Tesco American, in his office. Brugger didn't mince words about his perception of Elias. Brugger said Elias approached Tesco in 1985 to lease the property. Elias showed Brugger newspaper clippings of his business accomplishments in Tucson and a video that showed Industrial Refining would run an environmentally clean operation that would not generate any solid waste. Soon after entering into the lease agreement with Tesco, Industrial Refining defaulted on its payments and Tesco initiated eviction proceedings. Those proceedings were stayed when Elias took Industrial Refining into bankruptcy. Undeterred, Elias started AEI, Inc., and managed to obtain a $150,000 loan from the Southeast Idaho Council of Governments, known as SEICOG, which had a program to fund and promote local businesses. Elias and his wife, Midge, personally guaranteed that obligation. Brugger said Elias then approached him about purchasing the site. A real estate contract dated February 2, 1989, was drawn up and Elias paid Tesco $100,000 up front.

Though AEI had some success with the silver recovery process, as in Moapa, it was not cost-effective. The price of silver was about equal to the cost to recover it from the FMC waste.

Then in January 1990 treater dust lost its Bevill exemption and became subject to RCRA regulations as a hazardous waste—the "bothersome regulations" Elias had complained about during Hilldorfer's initial interview. FMC cut off any further sales to Elias and notified him and their other vendors of the changes in the law making the treater dust a hazardous waste. Dave Buttleman, an FMC employee with degrees in environmental engineering, specifically recalled several meetings with Elias telling him that since the FMC waste was now regulated as a hazardous waste, Elias would have to obtain permits to handle and store it. When Buttleman subsequently observed that Elias was not properly storing the waste on containment pads, FMC made the decision not to provide him with any more material.

Elias, however, had mounds of treater dust, now regulated as a hazardous substance, and a review of Idaho DEQ, OSHA, EPA, and bankruptcy records by Wojnicz and Hilldorfer revealed he was receiving increased pressure for environmental violations at the facility. His solution was simple. Mark Cates, an employee at AEI, told Hilldorfer and Wojnicz that Elias told him he could no longer use the dirt, which he described as dark, like coffee grounds, to make fertilizer, and directed Cates to bury it behind the AEI facility. Cates did.

About the same time that Elias was losing his source for treater dust and taking AEI into bankruptcy, Gary Dahms, a chemist, and Gary Greer, a mechanical engineer, both with experience in the fertilizer business, were talking with Kerr-McGee about buying its calcine tailings. Dahms and Greer told the two agents they reached a ten-year agreement with Robert Griffin of Kerr-McGee to buy calcine waste for $3 a ton if they could establish an alternative method to treat the waste and turn it into a fertilizer. They sought to take over the Evergreen plant, but were concerned about a dusting of material spread about an inch deep that had blown over from Soda Springs Phosphate. Soda Springs Phosphate had also been using FMC waste to make fertilizer before the change in the RCRA regulations. Tests revealed the dust to be high in cadmium. Dahms and Greer negotiated a provision in a lease with the city of Soda Springs that held them harmless for any preexisting contamination from Soda Springs Phosphate. The agents called it "Elias's license to kill."

According to Dahms and Greer, they invested about $2 million in Evergreen with between $600,000 and $700,000 of that amount spent to build the facility and put in a rail spur so railcars could access it. By 1991 they had a system in place to successfully make a low-grade fertilizer out of the calcine tails but needed MAP (magnesium ammonia phosphate), another of Kerr-McGee's waste products, to mix with the calcine tailings to raise the phosphorus level so it could be sold as fertilizer. For a reason Dahms and Greer never learned, Griffin suddenly refused to sell Evergreen any more MAP. They told Hilldorfer and Wojnicz they later came to believe he was selling it to Allan Elias, who at the time was still operating AEI in Pocatello. When Griffin cut off the MAP, Dahms and Greer were backed into a corner. They had no option but to sell Evergreen. Lo and behold, they said, Allan Elias appeared out of the woodwork as a willing buyer.

According to Brugger, Elias had again defaulted on the payments to Tesco, despite a personal guarantee. According to SEICOG he also defaulted on that loan. Brugger said Tesco initiated foreclosure proceedings on the property, and Elias again sought bankruptcy protection, this time for AEI, Inc. The bankruptcy court approved a reorganization plan, but Elias and AEI failed to pay Tesco and Tesco eventually obtained a personal judgment against Elias. According to Brugger, Elias then sought to lessen his liability to Tesco by arguing that the property value of the AEI site was diminished *because it was contaminated with massive amounts of hazardous waste.* Brugger told the agents he considered this nothing more than a scare tactic to forestall collection efforts, so he commissioned an environmental assessment of the AEI facility. To his dismay, the assessment confirmed that the site was now contaminated with tons of hazardous waste. Contrary to Elias's representations to Brugger, his company had not been an environmentally clean operation. Caught in a nightmare, Tesco tried to get Elias to clean up the site. Elias would only agree if, in return, Tesco agreed to reduce the amount of his personal monetary obligation. When Tesco agreed, Elias's new problem was how to clean up the site.

According to Gordon Brown and Boyd Roberts, the Idaho DEQ had also given Elias a mandate to clean up the treater dust, which they described as looking like dark coffee. As that deadline approached, "around the spring of 1996," they inspected the facility and found that the piles of waste had simply vanished. Elias refused to provide them with any information about what happened to it.

"Well, I think we know where it went," Hilldorfer said. That was about the same time Thornock and Farrel recalled belly loads of "cooked dirt" arriving at the Evergreen facility.

As for the storage tank, the agents learned Elias contacted a Pocatello resident named Clayton Kroger who was in the storage tank business and had recently dug up two tanks used to store diesel fuel. Elias asked Kroger if he could use one of the tanks temporarily at AEI. Kroger sold Elias a case loader and steel and moved the tank to the facility. Kroger's records reflected Elias made some initial payments then quit, owing him roughly $4,500. Some years later Kroger went to AEI looking for his tank but it was gone and the facility gutted.

After Elias took AEI, Inc., into bankruptcy he moved sixty miles southwest to Soda Springs and on March 8, 1991, signed a note to purchase Evergreen from Dahms and Greer for just $68,000. Dahms and Greer said Elias made periodic payments but only if Greer physically went to the facility to collect it. Then Elias simply stopped paying altogether. Determining that the amount owed wasn't worth the cost of litigation, Greer and Dahms simply walked away.

What was now clear to Wojnicz and Hilldorfer was that Elias had been engaged in a massive shell game of hide the hazardous waste. A DEQ official was quoted in a newspaper article as saying Elias was Soda Springs's version of a "walking, talking Three-Mile Island."[2] And, in what Hilldorfer and Wojnicz referred to as the ultimate display of balls, sometime in the summer of 1997, with the grand jury proceeding progressing against him, Elias wrote to the city of Soda Springs and notified it that he wished to renew his lease at Evergreen for ten more years.[3]

By the time the agents had completed the interviews one lingering question stood above the others. Why would Kerr-McGee get in bed with someone with a history like Allan Elias? Hilldorfer had a list of Kerr-McGee employees he wanted to interview, with Robert Griffin at the top, but there was something else nagging him, something he hadn't quite been able to put his finger on. Then it hit him.

It had been quiet. Too quiet. They had been so busy tracking down information and trying to untangle what was a knotted ball of string they had forgotten to play chess, forgotten to think several moves down the board. He only hoped Elias had been just as busy.

He was wrong.

August 1997
Region 10 Headquarters
Seattle, Washington

CHAPTER TWENTY-FOUR

W E'VE lost Weaver."

George Breitsameter's words hit Hilldorfer in the chest like a fifty-pound sack of cement thrown off the back of a truck. He and Wojnicz were on a late-afternoon conference call, what they referred to as their monthly "debriefings" with Breitsameter and Uhlmann.

"What happened?" Hilldorfer asked.

"Terry Deerden just walked into my office and gave me some paperwork. There's a note attached to it."

> Terry—You said you lawyers like to accumulate paper, well this might be of interest and then again, it may not.

The note had been personally delivered to the U.S. Attorney's Office in Boise by Cecil D. Andrus, the former two-term Democratic governor of the State of Idaho and the U.S. secretary of the interior.[1]

◆   ◆   ◆

HILLDORFER AND WOJNICZ boarded Southwest flight 361 to Salt Lake City the following morning. It was time to talk to Darren Weaver, and it wasn't going to be pleasant. One of the papers Andrus had delivered with his note was an affidavit by Weaver, and it was a bomb. Weaver had done a complete one-eighty from what he had told Clements and the OSHA investigators the day after the incident. He now claimed there was safety equipment on-site, but that he and Dominguez failed to wear it. He also had blame for Smith and Thornock.[2] It was just what the government did not want. Elias could plead the Fifth Amendment and never have to take the stand to testify, instead using Weaver like a ventriloquist's dummy to mouth-fart his defense for him. He told his employees to use safety equipment but they had ignored him.

"You can't manage stupidity."

It would be Elias's theme.

At a minimum their potential star witness had been greatly compromised. That was a problem. But they all knew that one witness going south could be indicative of something more problematic—like other witnesses going south. If Elias had compromised Weaver could he have also reached Smith and Thornock? And why would Andrus, the former secretary of the interior, stand up for a toxic polluter? Having attended high school in Washington, D.C., during the Carter administration, Uhlmann knew Andrus's background as an environmentalist. His involvement raised a red flag that Elias had the means and the contacts to mount a no-holds-barred defense. Whatever he could do to win, he would.

Hilldorfer and Wojnicz found the trailer court where Weaver lived, but no one appeared home and they didn't want to park out front for concern the neighbors would begin making phone calls. They drove north on North Hooper Road past Evergreen and turned west onto an unpaved road, parking next to a fenced area at the back of the Monsanto plant in the shadow of a man-made mountain of cement-colored material that looked like hardened lava rock.

As dusk approached, Wojnicz got out of the car. "I got to take a leak."

Hilldorfer sat in the passenger seat, waiting, when a brilliant orange glow suddenly burst in the sky. As bright as an artificial sun cresting the horizon, it grew more brilliant until the entire sky erupted in a blinding flash of light and heat that pulsed through the car. He thought a meteor had struck until he saw a fire-orange-red river flowing down the side of the mountain, carving a path like molten lava spewed from a volcano.

Wojnicz danced away from the fence, struggling to get his fly zipped, and jumped back into the car. "Holy shit. What the fuck was that?"

As the light faded, they stepped out of the car and looked up at a huge metal bucket receding from view. The lava flow was molten slag from Monsanto's mining process. Hilldorfer had grown up in Steel Town USA, but he had never seen anything like it before. If there was any doubt about what fueled the economy of Soda Springs, it vanished with the orange glow in the sky.

They laughed about the incident before turning their attention back to Darren Weaver. Hilldorfer had been debating the best way to approach Weaver. He had to assume Elias coached Weaver to either not say anything to the investigators or exactly what he should say if confronted about the affidavit. Neither was the option Hilldorfer wanted; he'd get nothing or a crafted story. He knew the affidavit was bullshit but had to find a way to get Weaver to admit it. Thornock and Smith both said Weaver was a hothead, and Hilldorfer knew from experience that one surefire way to get a hothead talking without thinking was to make him lose his temper. He needed to get Weaver mad enough that he'd explode like the orange glow. If he did, Weaver might forget what he'd been told and just talk.

The trailer court was bleak, with no trees and little if any landscaping. Two dozen metal-sided, single-wide trailers had been crammed together at the end of an industrial area off North Hooper Road near Evergreen, and looked to have been randomly placed, like a child would drop blocks, haphazardly and without thought. A car was parked in front of Weaver's trailer and the agents ran the plate, which came back a match.

"He's home," Wojnicz said.

Hilldorfer held the affidavit in his hand as he walked up the porch steps and knocked hard on the door. Weaver answered.

"I'm Joe Hilldorfer and this is Bob Wojnicz. We're federal investigators with the EPA. We need to talk with you. We know you worked with Scotty."

Weaver shook his head. "We're getting ready to eat. Now is not a good time."

"I'm over here from Seattle. I need to talk to you right now."

Weaver paused, as if considering what to do. Hilldorfer waited for the door to slam but something told him Weaver's defiance wouldn't let him do it. Weaver stepped aside. "I don't have much time."

Inside the trailer, a woman Hilldorfer presumed to be Weaver's wife corralled a young girl crawling on the floor. He waited until they left the room then held up a copy of Weaver's affidavit. "I need to talk to you about the affidavit you signed for Allan Elias. It's bullshit, Darren."

That hit the switch. Weaver went ballistic. "How dare you say the word *bullshit* in my fucking house."

"Darren, this affidavit is bullshit. It is not true."

"How dare you say the word *bullshit* in my home." Weaver was spitting his words and stabbed at the air with his index finger.

Having obtained the reaction he intended Hilldorfer sought to keep Weaver talking by letting him save face in his own home. "Hey, I'm sorry I said the word *bullshit* in your fucking home, Darren, but let me explain why this is bullshit." He tapped the affidavit with his finger. "You talked to both the state police and to OSHA the day after Scotty almost died and what you told them is not even close to this affidavit you signed for Allan. I need to understand how two stories about the same event can be so different."

Weaver closed his eyes. If he was going to tell them to get out, now would be the time. He took a breath.

"Yeah, I did talk to the police and OSHA, okay? And I like Scotty. I'd never do nothing bad to hurt Scot. And I was never going to go back to work for Allan and I feel guilty about going back there, all right? I haven't even seen Scott since that day in the hospital. I don't go places he might be." Weaver was dressed in jeans and a soiled T-shirt. He looked like he'd just gotten off work. "I was fucked up for months after that day and I still have nightmares about it. I had to go to Salt Lake City just to get another job, okay? I wasn't going to work for him, but I didn't like it there, I didn't get along with my boss, so I had to move back and I called Allan to get my job back."

"And Allan said he'd give you your job back?" Hilldorfer said, the picture becoming clearer.

"Not right away. He said he was concerned I might be a spy or something for EPA or OSHA, and he said it would make him feel better if I signed something for him." Weaver said he didn't want to sign the affidavit, but that Elias insisted and told him the pay was higher, and he was giving a bonus if he could make fertilizer from the Kerr-McGee waste. "He said no one would ever see it." Weaver pointed to the affidavit. "He said it wouldn't see the light of day. It was just for his files."

Hilldorfer was having trouble feeling any sympathy for Weaver, but he realized the young man probably didn't have a lot of options with a wife and a baby to feed. Elias had manipulated him. "I still don't understand how this can be so different from what you told OSHA and the State Police, Darren. Tell me how this can be so different?"

Weaver thought about it a moment, then said, "It's like the red bike, you know?"

"No. Explain it to me."

"You know, it's like that bicycle you had when you were a kid, and you don't remember it but someone keeps telling you it was red and it had baseball cards through the spokes, and they can describe it so well that pretty soon you remember it was red."

"Okay."

He said he told Elias he couldn't remember what happened that day, "but Allan said he'd help me to remember what happened that day."

"How did he do that?"

"He'd give me choices like, you know, a, b, or c, and he'd say which one made sense, and you know he had a real good memory for details."

When they agreed on the choice, Elias would make Weaver repeat it then he'd turn on a tape recorder and tape it. He had his longtime counsel Craig Jorgensen type up the affidavit.

Hilldorfer knew Weaver was gone. The government could never use him now. The only thing he could do was make sure Weaver could not testify for the defense either. "So which version is true, Darren? Is it this, or is it what you told OSHA?"

"What I told OSHA. That's when it was most fresh in my mind. I just signed that to make Allan happy. I would've signed anything because I needed my job back and Allan said it was only for his peace of mind. He said it wasn't going to go anywhere. As far as I was concerned that was the end of it. It's all behind me. I got a good job now."

"Where are you working?"

"Mullen Construction. I'm getting seven twelves a week. I couldn't get enough hours at Evergreen."

"Where's your job site?"

"Kerr-McGee. Mullen's building a fertilizer production plant."

Christ, Hilldorfer thought, Kerr-McGee again. Was it coincidence that the government's best witness, a kid that had to go all the way to Salt Lake City to find work, was now working as many hours as he wanted for a company doing a project at Kerr-McGee's plant? He handed Weaver a grand jury subpoena. Weaver objected, but Hilldorfer told him that if he didn't appear there'd be a warrant out for his arrest. He wanted to shake Weaver's hand far less than he wanted to shake Jerry Farrel's hand, but he did it because it was important for Weaver to tell the truth to the grand jury. That would be the end of his involvement in the case. Scotty's best witness had just become his worst.[3]

September 1997
Boise, Idaho

CHAPTER TWENTY-FIVE

THE MORNING OF September 10, Hilldorfer ran into Weaver in the U.S. Federal Courthouse in Boise after Weaver had testified before the grand jury.[1] Weaver approached him with a big smile on his face. "Got it all straight," he said.

Weaver told the grand jury, "There was no way I was going to get this job back without signing this affidavit." He also testified that portions of the affidavit were false and that Elias had told him he was going to blame the employees for what had happened. "The state police report and my statement to OSHA was the truth."

"Good for you," Hilldorfer said without enthusiasm and walked away. He had his mind on things that still mattered. That afternoon they had an appointment with Cecil Andrus.

Hilldorfer and Wojnicz wanted to cold-call Andrus, but Breitsameter and Celeste Miller, the assistant U.S. attorney in the Boise office who was also working on the case, wouldn't allow it. Miller told the agents they couldn't door-knock a former governor and secretary of the interior. She walked into the cherrywood conference room with a book on the history of Idaho and read a passage describing Andrus's background and career that referred to him as an environmentalist and visionary. Bill Reese had also told Hilldorfer that, as governor, Andrus used the State Police for his protective detail when he traveled in-state and was well liked by the officers because he had a remarkable ability to remember everyone's name.

Andrus worked as a consultant for an organization called the Gallatin Center, which was just down the street from the U.S. Attorney's Office. He met the two prosecutors and two agents in the company's lobby and escorted them to a conference room. Well-dressed and well-groomed in a suit and tie, Andrus was balding, with silver hair and a tanned complexion. He walked with a politician's confidence and shook their hands like they were all well acquainted. If he had any concern, it didn't show.

Despite Miller's tutorial, Hilldorfer was having a difficult time seeing Andrus as anything but the epitome of the problem with environmental crimes—politics. No powerful figure would come out of the woodwork to help a common everyday thief or murderer. None of the beautiful and powerful people in Los Angeles had rushed to O.J. Simpson's defense. But environmental crimes were different. This was business, big business, with a lot of money at stake and a lot of money to spend. Politicians depended on big business and big business depended on politicians. It was the American way. When Hilldorfer started at the EPA one of the investigators shook his hand.

"Welcome to the world of environmental crimes, the best justice money can buy."

Breitsameter conducted the interview.[2] Andrus said he'd known Betty Richardson, the Boise district attorney, since she was knee high and handing out his campaign literature. He held his hand so it was three feet off the floor, a gesture Hilldorfer interpreted as a not-so-subtle way of letting them know who they were dealing with. Andrus said he had a relationship with Kerr-McGee as a "consultant" and golfed with Bob Griffin, Kerr-McGee's manager in Soda Springs, whom he had known for a number of years. There was that name again. Kerr-McGee seemed to be the center of a vast root system with Griffin clearly the key, but getting him to talk openly now was probably highly unlikely. He had undoubtedly "lawyered-up."

Andrus explained that Griffin called and said he had a problem. Kerr-McGee wanted to buy the Evergreen plant to make fertilizer and the permitting process was nearly done but they had a problem: a workman's comp injury at the facility. "He wanted to know if there was an ongoing criminal investigation into Evergreen or its owner. Basically that was it."

"And did you know the owner of Evergreen?" Breitsameter asked.

"I can't recall his name."

"Could it have been Allan Elias?"

"That's it. That's correct. Elias was the owner."

Given Reese's comment about Andrus's ability to remember names, Hilldorfer wasn't buying Andrus's inability to remember Elias's name. He had it on a $5,000 check, the amount he was paid to deliver the papers on behalf of Elias, and because the agents had not door-knocked him, Andrus knew they were coming. He had ample opportunity to consider the matter. Hilldorfer hoped the lack of memory was Andrus's way of distancing himself from Elias. The last thing the government wanted was the defense calling Andrus to imply that Elias was a pillar in the business community.

Andrus said he told Griffin it would be no problem finding out because he had a long-standing association with Betty Richardson. He said Griffin mailed him documents in January. They included a memorandum of law concerning Dominguez's accident, an analysis of a purported sample from the tank, a legal analysis, and a version of the facts. Andrus then appeared unannounced in Richardson's office and asked her if there was anything going on with a plant called Evergreen Resources in Soda Springs, whether the owner had anything to worry about. He said Richardson looked at the credenza in her office, turned white as a sheet, and said she couldn't divulge whether her office had an ongoing criminal investigation and asked Deerden to join the meeting. Andrus deduced from her response and demeanor that was, in fact, the case.

"I asked him if I could give him some documents that pertained to the incident and he said, 'You know us attorneys, we always like to look at papers.'"

Andrus said he later got a call from Elias about additional documents proving he didn't do anything criminal, including the signed statement from Weaver. Andrus said he read it and it seemed to exonerate Elias from any wrongdoing. So he called Terry Deerden and told him he'd be bringing over more documents. Deerden wasn't there. Andrus dropped them off.

Breitsameter asked if Andrus gave Griffin any advice regarding Kerr-McGee's potential purchase of the Evergreen plant.

"I told him it would be better to wait until the matter was settled. Sometime later I learned they had decided not to buy it."

Summer and fall, 1997
Soda Springs, Idaho

CHAPTER TWENTY-SIX

AT HOME, DOMINGUEZ continued a rigorous five-day-a-week rehabilitation that included physical exercise, occupational rehabilitation, and speech therapy. Initially he could not walk on a treadmill, even at half a mile an hour; his balance was so poor he would fall over. His walking and balance had improved, but he could not walk backward and would still spontaneously fall forward. While his enunciation was getting better, his speech remained very weak, monotone and robotic and interrupted by extended pauses, and his face continued to get stuck, his eyes unblinking, giving the appearance of a "mask." His family worked hard to keep a normal life, taking him on hikes and fishing, but the intensity of the rehabilitation had been hard on them all. The breakup with Theresa had depressed Scott further and he was started on an antidepressant. He had begun smoking again and drinking, something the doctors sternly recommended he not do.[1]

HILLDORFER AND WOJNICZ turned their attention to getting a second warrant to search Evergreen for the belly loads of waste they suspected Elias had trucked in from AEI. That meant finding a truck driver named "Joe." They might as well have been looking for a needle in a haystack.

They spent hours going through Idaho phone books making cold calls to local trucking companies asking if they had a driver named "Joe" or knew anyone who had hauled materials for Allan Elias; AEI, Inc.; or Evergreen Resources. When that failed they took to door-knocking trucking companies in the area and waiting at rest stops to ask the truckers directly. The best they got were a couple of false leads.

"We have to think like Allan," Hilldorfer said as they sat parked at another truck stop. "Allan wouldn't go with a reputable company because they wouldn't haul a bunch of hazardous waste up the highway."

"Yeah," Wojnicz answered, "but if we're thinking like Allan we have to assume he would have lied and said it was just dirt."

"You're right, but he still probably wouldn't use a reputable outfit."

"Too cheap."

"Exactly. Allan would want a deal, something for nothing. He'd find someone he knew. Who have we talked to who actually liked Allan?"

"Weaver?"

"Weaver just wanted his job. You weren't with me that trip. Lorinda was. Ivan Williams."

Williams was a contractor who took over AEI after Elias went bankrupt, and he continued to do odd jobs for him. Hilldorfer and Lorinda Wallace had talked to Williams in April looking for information on how the tank got from AEI, Inc., to Evergreen. Shortly after the interview Williams submitted an affidavit saying Hilldorfer got their interview completely wrong. Williams was on their list of people they needed to serve with a subpoena to appear before the grand jury.[2]

Wojnicz started the car. "At least it won't be a wasted trip."

Williams was not at home but his wife gave them directions to his job site, a hole in the ground about fifteen miles outside Pocatello where he sat in the cab of a Bobcat. Hilldorfer stood outside the car and waved until Williams shut off the engine and climbed out of the cab, a burly man with a head of curly silver hair.

"Do you remember me, Ivan? I'm Joe Hilldorfer with the EPA."

Williams smiled like they were old friends and shook hands.

"Why'd you file that affidavit, Ivan?"

Williams dismissed it. "Oh, no big thing. I talked to Allan about it. Sounds like you were confused about a few things."

"Right. I guess I was. I have to serve you with this subpoena, Ivan."

Williams took the papers still smiling, like enjoying a private joke. "Okay."

Hilldorfer shook his hand again and turned for the car as Williams climbed back up onto the Bobcat.

"Oh, Ivan, by the way . . ."

Williams looked down at him.

"Your buddy Joe, the truck driver, said to say 'Hello.' "

"Joe Colton?"

Bingo.

"Yeah. Joe Colton. Does he still work out by the airport?"

Williams looked confused. "The airport? Far as I know he's always worked out of his home in Inkom."

Hilldorfer nodded. "Well, he said to say hello. Take care."

He got into the car amazed that the ruse had actually worked, but he was now worried Williams would call Colton, find out he'd been had, and warn him that federal investigators were looking for him.

"Bob, I never thought I'd say this to you, but step on it, hard."

THEY HAD NO trouble finding Inkom. On their first trip to Soda Springs, Wojnicz had pointed out a beautifully manicured baseball field plunked down in the middle of dried yellow grass and scrub brush along Highway 15. The field sat in the shadow of an enormous cement plant imbedded in the side of a mountain, its stack belching white smoke. The cement plant was pretty much Inkom.

They found a phone book in a gas station and a telephone number but no address for Joe Colton, which became irrelevant since most of the roads did not appear designated.

As they drove, Hilldorfer spotted a woman putting a real estate sign in the trunk of her gold Continental and had Wojnicz stop. The woman didn't know a Joe Colton but pointed behind them to some homes dotting the hillside. "You might try up there."

Most of the homes were not numbered. It was exasperating. "How do people get their mail around here?" Hilldorfer asked. Out of options, he called the number from the phone book. No one answered, but it gave him an idea. There were perhaps a dozen houses in the area where the woman directed them. "Let's go house to house. I'll knock on the door. If no one answers, you call the number on your cell phone and I'll put an ear to the door and see if I hear it ringing."

Wojnicz wasn't crazy about running up his cell phone bill and trying to get McClary to approve reimbursement. Hilldorfer had a more immediate concern. Thornock and Farrel said the truck driver had been difficult and Hilldorfer didn't like the idea of sticking his ear to the door for someone to shoot at. But they didn't have any other options.

Wojnicz pulled off the road and Hilldorfer went to the first home, knocked on the door and waited. When there was no answer he gave Wojnicz a thumbs-up and pressed his ear to the wood. He didn't hear a phone ringing. He moved to the second house and repeated the exercise. Again he heard no phone. When no one came to the door at the sixth house he gave Wojnicz another thumbs-up and heard a phone ring. Not convinced, he put a hand across his throat to signal Wojnicz to hang up. The phone stopped ringing. He gave him the thumbs-up to call again. The phone rang.

Unbelievably, they'd found the needle in the haystack.

Hilldorfer got back in the car smiling. "Let's come back so we don't have a bunch of looky-lou's watching us."

Wojnicz agreed, but nature was calling again and he got out of the car and walked around the side of Joe Colton's house.

They returned at dusk and found the lights on and a car parked out front. They took up positions on different sides of the door frame and Hilldorfer did a law enforcement knock—loud enough to shake the house and get somebody's attention. It worked. A curtain pulled back revealing the bearded face of a very big man in a flannel shirt and bib overalls. Hilldorfer and Wojnicz held their gold badges to the window.

"Joe Colton?"

"Yeah."

"We're federal agents. Can you open the door, please?"

Colton opened the door.

"Mr. Colton, I'm Joe Hilldorfer, I'm a federal agent from Seattle. Can I please have a few minutes of your time tonight?"

Colton considered him. "So you're the guy knocking on my door earlier today?"

As Hilldorfer suspected, the neighbors had eyes and ears. "That would be me."

Colton turned to Wojnicz. "Then you must have been the guy pissing on the side of my house."

This was not going good, but like with the patrons in the gun shop Wojnicz seemed to know exactly the right thing to say. He managed a sheepish smile. "That would be me."

Colton laughed. "Well, come on in."

Tuesday, September 16, 1997
Evergreen Resources
Soda Springs, Idaho

CHAPTER TWENTY-SEVEN

ON SEPTEMBER 16, Hilldorfer and the team from the first search warrant, Mike Burnett, Lorinda Wallace, and Bill Reese, converged on Evergreen together with Wojnicz and Glenn Bruck, an EPA regional technical coordinator, and contractors hired by the Superfund. They had no trouble getting the second search warrant. Joe Colton had not only confirmed hauling truckloads of ore from AEI to Evergreen, he kept logbooks of each trip. He was also visibly upset when told the waste might have been hazardous, afraid he could lose his license.

Elias showed up half an hour after the search team arrived and Hilldorfer gave him the same speech, then accompanied Elias back to his home to secure his weapon. With no warrant to search the house Hilldorfer waited outside. Elias emerged with his gun, the phone, and a smug smile.

"There's someone on the phone I want you to talk to."

"Who is it?"

"My attorneys."

Hilldorfer expected Craig Jorgensen.

"Joe? It's David Marshall."

Hilldorfer winced.

"I'm going to put David Nevin on the phone with you."

Hilldorfer was unfamiliar with Nevin. Marshall said he wanted it clear that Elias did not consent to the search in the event there was a problem with the warrant.

"I understand that, David."

"And I want you to wait before you start digging until we can get there."

"No. That's not going to happen, David. We're starting today and we're starting right now."

MARSHALL AND NEVIN showed up the following morning. Overnight, Breitsameter filled Hilldorfer in on Nevin's reputation. The U.S. Attorney's Office in Boise considered him one of the best criminal defense attorneys in Idaho, perhaps the Northwest. He had achieved some notoriety representing Kevin Harris, the man accused of pulling the trigger and killing the U.S. marshal that led to the tense standoff in Ruby Ridge, Idaho. Though Jerry Spence received most of the accolades, Nevin got Harris off; he walked out of the courtroom free.

Hilldorfer and Wojnicz immediately dubbed Nevin and Marshall Elias's "Dream Team." Marshall, with round, wire-rimmed glasses, resembled a red-headed Teddy Roosevelt in appearance and build, and there was something about Nevin's cocksure attitude, brown hair, and fit, boyish look that reminded them of the Kennedy clan.

Marshall asked that they be provided splits of every sample taken by the government. Hilldorfer politely told him to pound sand. "We don't give splits in criminal cases and you know that, David, but you're free to watch where we take our samples. Since it's Allan's property your consultants can take as many samples as you want."

After four days of digging, however, they had not found the material and Hilldorfer was beginning to look like he had egg on his face. Wojnicz had left for a prearranged vacation with his fiancée—the lifelong bachelor was finally getting married. Hilldorfer was also anxious to get home. His mother and sister were coming into town that Monday from Pittsburgh and he had not seen either for quite some time. He called McClary from his hotel and asked that someone be sent to relieve him, but McClary told him he couldn't get any additional travel money. Frustrated, Hilldorfer hung up and called Brian Smith.

"I need your help," he said for the second time.

The following morning he picked up Smith and they drove to Evergreen, careful to remain on the other side of the railroad tracks in case anyone had a problem with Smith being on the site. Smith got out of the car, smiled, and pointed to one of the search team's backhoes.

"You don't need my help. You'll find it today," he said. "It's right there."

CHAPTER TWENTY-EIGHT

WITH NEVIN AND MARSHALL involved, things heated up quickly.[1] When the two investigators returned to Soda Springs in December, Joe Rice told Wojnicz that Elias was telling people in town that his lawyers were beating up on the government. This trip, however, was all about one thing: Robert Griffin.

Hilldorfer was surprised Griffin agreed to speak to them and even more surprised when he showed up the morning of December 1 at the Ameritel Hotel without a lawyer. Griffin had recently retired from Kerr-McGee but knew much about its operations, especially in Soda Springs.

Kerr-McGee began as an oil-drilling company in 1929 in Ada, Oklahoma. In the 1950s the company expanded from refining and marketing of oil into industrial chemicals. The Kerr-McGee plant in Idaho was located one mile north of Soda Springs, Idaho, and covered 158 acres near the western base of the Aspen Range. Since 1963 the nearby Monsanto Chemical Company and FMC in Pocatello supplied Kerr-McGee with the by-product ferrous-phosphate ore from which Kerr-McGee extracted vanadium. It was a symbiotic relationship between companies that mined the ore and chemical companies such as Kerr-McGee that try to get as much value out of the ore as possible. From the moment Griffin walked into their hotel room, Hilldorfer got the distinct impression he wanted to convey that he had nothing to hide. He had the confidence and glib manner of a salesman. Hilldorfer and Wojnicz decided to just let him talk.

Griffin said he had a degree in chemical engineering and had worked at Kerr-McGee since 1966. In 1985 he was transferred to Soda Springs. The plant was losing money, had shut down one of its furnaces, could not meet air-quality standards for running the plant, and had laid off a number of its employees. And those were not the plant's biggest problem. Its biggest problem was waste. The plant generated a number of liquid wastes and stored them in on-site ponds, the two largest holding 5.5 million gallons of industrial wastewater and 2,500 tons of tailings. The waste ponds were found to be leaking and on October 4, 1989, EPA Region 10 placed it on the National Priorities List as a Superfund clean-up site.[2]

Griffin said that if the EPA required a traditional clean-up—removing the waste and disposing of it at a hazardous waste disposal facility—the cost to Kerr-McGee could be $230 million. He told them his estimate was based upon an ongoing clean-up at a Kerr-McGee facility in Chicago that he said had cost $400 million to date.

One of Griffin's tasks was to find alternatives to such an expensive clean-up. To that end, sometime in 1988 he approached JR Simplot and Nu-West, and asked if Kerr-McGee could pay them to take the calcine tailings. Both companies declined, but Gary Dahms and Gary Greer, employees at Nu-West, agreed to form a company to help Kerr-McGee find a less expensive alternative to the traditional clean-up methods, fertilizer.

Griffin said he became acquainted with Elias when Elias was running AEI, Inc., in Pocatello and described Elias as very smart but a "stubborn son of a bitch." He said that at times he "would have liked to hit him in the head with a two-by-four. You can tell him something and he'll agree, but then he does whatever he wants."

When FMC stopped providing treater dust to AEI, Elias needed a different option. Kerr-McGee provided it. Griffin said he had Kerr-McGee's roaster/scrubber waste analyzed for silver content, determined it to be above the break-even point financially for the recovery process, and shipped four truckloads of the waste to AEI. Elias later told Griffin that his own tests showed the silver content to be too low to make the recovery economical.

Griffin said purchasing Evergreen was a huge windfall for Elias. He called the plant a "money pit" because Kerr-McGee would invest millions of dollars into Evergreen in its effort to avoid having to pay a potentially huge clean-up cost. "Kerr-McGee had a vested interest in Evergreen from day one," Griffin told the two agents. "Remember, this all comes down to one thing. It's all about money."

In 1992, Griffin said he learned that Kerr-McGee had potentially $30 million worth of phosphorus in its calcine tailings, and came up with the idea to have Evergreen develop a process to make phosphoric acid fertilizer. Kerr-McGee needed to get a plant up and running to show the EPA that the process could work. Elias, however, did not have the knowledge to do it, so Kerr-McGee went to a research and development company in Toronto that had expertise in fertilizer. The company developed a process, but it proved too expensive to implement. Another company came to the same conclusion.

Kerr-McGee and Evergreen went back to square one. Griffin said the next idea was to turn the waste into a solid fertilizer and, in essence, Evergreen became Kerr-McGee's research and development facility. Ironically, Griffin told the agents that Kerr-McGee hired Dahms and Greer as consultants to look over Elias's proposal for making food-grade phosphoric acid fertilizer out of the calcine tailings. He said the two men were shocked with the proposal, said it would never work, and wanted nothing to do with it, saying the fertilizer would be disastrous for the community. Griffin said Kerr-McGee officials toured Dahms and Greer's fertilizer plant in Arkansas and ran tests to determine if their process was feasible on Kerr-McGee's waste. According to Griffin the tests proved promising, but Evergreen, in its dilapidated condition, could not meet the capacity requirements desired by the EPA, and Kerr-McGee decided they would build their own fertilizer plant on-site. This change in plans, however, required Kerr-McGee to renegotiate its original agreement with Elias, which Griffin said included a noncompete clause regarding the production of fertilizer. Kerr-McGee, which had already paid Elias $1.5 million, less a $200,000 loan, and was paying him in the neighborhood of $41,600 a month, had to advance $500,000 on a fertilizer distributorship contract between Kerr-McGee and yet another Elias company, Western Fertilizer.[3] The deal was contingent upon Kerr-McGee and Evergreen finding a way to successfully make fertilizer from the waste. Elias was under no obligation to perform until March 1998.

After Dominguez's injury, Elias told Griffin that OSHA and the EPA were investigating him and that he might go to jail. Griffin said Kerr-McGee had told the EPA that they would soon be processing 150 tons of the waste at their new fertilizer plant, and it needed Evergreen working to determine if the process was feasible before they spent millions constructing their own plant. So, if Elias needed a pump, Kerr-McGee would get one. If he needed heavy equipment, Kerr-McGee would divert a construction job at Kerr-McGee and send over a crane, bulldozer, or whatever else was needed. The billing would then be processed through Kerr-McGee.

"Evergreen was our linchpin," he said, adding that Kerr-McGee "would do anything to keep Evergreen running and Elias out of jail."[4]

AFTER THE INTERVIEW Hilldorfer and Wojnicz sat in the hotel room shaking their heads, in one respect amazed at Griffin's forthrightness and in other respects not surprised at all. Griffin had summed up the history of environmental crimes in one short sentence: "It's all about the money." He was honest about it because he was right. Since December 2, 1970, when the EPA opened its doors, it had sparked an inevitable battle between American business seeking to generate as much profit as possible and environmentalists seeking to keep them from polluting America's skies, waterways, and lands.

At its birth the EPA was far from the eight-hundred-pound gorilla that was supposed to take down America's corporate polluters. It faced daunting challenges not unlike those confronting the recently established Office of Homeland Security. It had to establish itself amid a plethora of bureaucracies fighting for federal funding, blend multiple agencies into one coherent authority without alienating all, and fight a stealth opponent that if not found and neutralized could kill indiscriminately. Environmental crimes were often performed under the cloak of darkness. By the time they were discovered it was too late, the damage was unleashed.

They were also well behind in the fight. After World War II, as America's industry turned from military to domestic production, the amount of hazardous waste skyrocketed. It increased further with the organic chemistry industry's development of new products like plastics, electronic components, and modern construction materials and their chemical waste by-products, which were not biodegradable and could remain toxic for thousands of years. In addition there were too few hazardous waste disposal sites in the country to handle the waste and the contents; locations and disposal practices of those that did exist were largely unknown. America was sitting on hundreds of hazardous time bombs without any reasonable way to determine where they all were, when the next would go off, and how bad the damage would be.

But if the unknown was disconcerting, what was universally accepted as fact was downright scary. The EPA was realizing that massive quantities of toxic contaminants had already been released into the environment and the polluting wasn't likely to end soon. The primary reason?

Greed.

Disposing of a fifty-five-gallon drum of hazardous waste at a hazardous waste facility cost ten to a hundred times more than disposing of it at a nonhazardous waste facility.[5] Companies chose to dump it onto the ground and into pits, ponds, and lagoons, to dispose of it like household trash in landfills or pay a subculture of illegal hazardous waste haulers. These "sludge runners" dumped it in city sewers, left barrels and boxes in shopping center parking lots and rented warehouses, delivered it to fictitious addresses, buried it in pits, mixed it with dirt and passed it off to unsuspecting developers as landfill, sold it in contaminated oil to be burned in apartment houses and hospital furnaces, or simply drove down the highway on rainy days with the spigots on their tanks open.

The transformation of mining waste into fertilizer was, in Hilldorfer's mind, just another approach to getting rid of a hazardous waste.

February 1998
AEI, Inc.
Pocatello, Idaho

CHAPTER TWENTY-NINE

FOLLOWING A HUNCH, Hilldorfer and Wojnicz made a February trip to AEI. Just west of the city of Pocatello near the airport and visible from Highway 86, AEI was a single-story, block-shaped building surrounded by a chain-link fence and a yard of dead grass. It looked like a rural penitentiary and sat in the immense shadow of the smokestacks of the FMC and JR Simplot phosphate mining operations.

Bill Brugger, the president of Tesco, had not exaggerated when he told the two agents that Elias gutted AEI. Pigeons and pigeon droppings were everywhere. Equipment had been removed. There were holes in the walls. Pipes had been yanked free from the ceiling. An old mattress, articles of clothing, and the smell of human urine also indicated that the building, close to the rail lines, had become a refuge for the homeless.

They found what they were looking for shoved into a closet beneath a dark stairwell—a strange place to store a valuable product when the buildings had been stripped of everything else of even the slightest value: a fifty-five-gallon drum of cyanide. HAZMAT popped it open, revealing white briquettes. Wojnicz wrote down the name of the supplier off the label, Van Waters & Rogers, and over the course of the next couple of weeks he set to work tracking down the salesman who did business with AEI, a man named Bill Stout. Stout recalled selling tons of sodium cyanide to Elias and said he had been very concerned about Elias's handling of the material. In particular, he said he was concerned about a potential release of hydrogen cyanide gas because Elias had refused to purchase any caustic soda, which Stout explained was used to adjust the pH of cyanide solutions to prevent such a release. Because of this concern he repeatedly offered Elias free safety training for his employees.

Elias declined.

"He told me he knew everything he needed to know about cyanide."[1]

WHILE THE EVIDENCE against Elias was building, the biggest scientific hurdle remained: The waste did not meet the levels necessary to be termed *reactive* for cyanide under SW846. Early that March, Hilldorfer and Jim Oesterle flew to the National Enforcement Investigation Center (NEIC) in Lakewood, Colorado, for the long-awaited opportunity to meet "The Wizard," Dr. Joe Lowry.

At one time an armory, the NEIC facility still looked like a military installation. A security gate, chain-link fences, and guards ringed cookie-cutter-square, unremarkable buildings. Hilldorfer and Oesterle presented credentials to a guard behind a bulletproof window but, though expected, could not be admitted without their escort, EPA attorney Chuck Ashwanden, who took Hilldorfer to meet the man behind the curtain.

Hilldorfer expected a typical scientist—a thin, bespectacled man wearing a tweed coat with patches on the elbows smoking his famous pipe—but the man who stood from behind his desk and ambled over with an outstretched hand had a shock of copper brown hair and a full beard sprinkled with flecks of gray. Though soft, his deep voice resonated.

"Hello, Joe. Good to meet you. I've been anxious to talk to you. We've been doing a lot of work on this case."

The NEIC had not only been testing the tank samples, it had also been comparing the samples of waste found at AEI with the samples suspected to have been trucked to Evergreen.

"Have you ever been here before?"

Hilldorfer hadn't.

"Let's go on a tour." Lowry took Hilldorfer through pristine hallways of sparkling linoleum floors and pointed out half-million-dollar microscopes and other equipment. He also introduced Hilldorfer to what he referred to as "the boys"—the scientists working the Elias case.

When they returned to his office they made small talk about the NEIC for a few moments while Lowry chewed on a pile of sunflower seeds. "They're taking the place of my pipe," he said.

There was a picture on the wall of Bozo the Clown with a line through it and the words *No Bozos*.

"I understand you've worked with David Uhlmann before?" Uhlmann told Hilldorfer he and Lowry had worked together on the John Morrell case in South Dakota. Uhlmann considered Lowry nothing short of brilliant.

"Yes, I have. He has a golden Lab, too." He nodded to a photograph on his bookshelf of a golden Lab next to an attractive woman Hilldorfer assumed to be Lowry's wife. "He got him fixed too early though. The dog's bone structure didn't mature as it should have. Do you want some sunflower seeds? I don't usually take time for lunch."

Hilldorfer declined the seeds and got to the point. "I looked up the regulation. It says, 'Any cyanide waste with pH conditions between 2 and 12.5 that can generate toxic gases, vapors or fumes that present a danger to human health or the environment is a characteristic waste.' We know that this didn't just present a danger to the environment. It injured four workers and damn near killed Scotty. What am I missing?"

Lowry listened politely to Hilldorfer's rudimentary understanding of the regulation then laughed. "Because the test is flawed."

"The test is flawed?"

"When SW846 was written and placed in the regulations, someone, in essence, put the decimal point in the wrong place. There's more to it than that, of course, but essentially the test is flawed. I've spent ten years trying to get the Bozos to rewrite the testing procedure and correct the error. Maybe a tragedy like this will finally get someone's attention."

Lowry explained that the test only measured 1 to 3 percent of the actual cyanide potential of a sample because it failed to take into consideration certain scientific principles, something called Henry's Law. "Had the Manchester Lab adjusted the findings for Henry's Law, it would have found that the sample proved to be extremely reactive and well over the threshold. This is a very hazardous substance and SW846 isn't the only test that can be done to determine whether cyanide waste presents a danger to the environment or to human life. There are a number of tests that could have been done and I've read all of your reports and it doesn't look like Allan Elias bothered to do any of them. The tank he sent them in was a death chamber and I can prove it."

"How?"

"Using Scott Dominguez's medical records, what the employees said, and what Allan Elias told you, I can build a scale model of the tank and put a sample of the material you got from Evergreen into it. To be conservative I'll use an amount equivalent to the tonnage Elias estimated to be in the tank, though the employees indicated there was actually quite a bit more. Then I'll monitor the air inside the tank for the length of time Scott was in there, and we'll see what it tells us."

"What will it tell us?"

"Well, you've read all the reports and you've seen Scott's blood work. It was three times the lethal dose for cyanide. Science doesn't lie, Joe."

"But at this point we don't know for certain."

"At this point we don't know for certain," Dr. Joe agreed. "We'll all have to wait and see."

The words brought Hilldorfer little comfort. He also knew that a model demonstration would be dicey. There was never a guarantee that an experiment would meet the rigid federal evidentiary standards to be admitted at trial. They could assume that Marshall and Nevin would vigorously oppose it.

"Come out in a month or two with David when we're done running the tests." Lowry stood. "I'll walk you out."

As they walked out Lowry pulled Hilldorfer into a room with walls lined with photographs. He pointed to photographs of the brilliant yellow hexavalent chromium at Boomsnub. "You remember that?"

Hilldorfer didn't meet Dr. Joe back then. Lowry and all his work never made it to the courtroom. He wondered if it would this time.

"I've tried to forget it."

◆   ◆   ◆

HILLDORFER RETURNED to Seattle and began preparing for the prosecutorial review in Washington, D.C., on May 26–28. Colleagues of Uhlmann at the ECS would review the evidence gathered against Allan Elias and the charges being recommended and play devil's advocates, trying to poke holes in the legal theories to see if the charges could be sustained. After hearing Sandy Smith's horror story about PureGro, Hilldorfer wanted to be present and McClary had approved the expense, but when he got home that night Joanne met him at the door.

"Dad's had a heart attack," she said. "He collapsed in his doctor's office."

They flew the following morning to Honolulu and drove straight to the hospital. The news got worse. The doctors told them that her father aspirated as they attempted to intubate him. He had lapsed into a coma and was expected to die. For the next forty days they held a bedside vigil at the hospital with her mother. Hilldorfer used a pay phone to get updates from Wojnicz, who said the pros review went off without a hitch. Otherwise he and Joanne spent the time talking and reading to her father to try and get him to open his eyes. The doctors were not optimistic. They suggested her father be taken off life support. When they declined, the doctors advised that people on ventilators could stay in comas for years and told them it might be wise for them to return to Seattle, and their lives. They felt terrible leaving, but realized they had no choice.

Hilldorfer returned to work the next day still preoccupied. When he walked in the door Wojnicz was stoked. The prosecution had approved the knowing endangerment charge.

When Hilldorfer got home that night Joanne again greeted him at the door, this time with a smile.

"Mom just called. Dad opened his eyes and asked 'Where are the kids?'"

CHAPTER THIRTY

THE INSIDE OF Judge B. Lynn Winmill's courtroom in Boise was wood-paneled walls and an elevated bench, the grandeur of the room tempered only by a robin's-egg-blue carpet. Hilldorfer and Wojnicz sat in the gallery. Counsels' tables were positioned in an *L* shape, with the defense table facing the jury box, the government table perpendicular to it, facing the elevated bench.

Uhlmann and Breitsameter would present a five-count indictment against Elias. Days before, the grand jury had returned a true bill, which meant they had indicted Elias on each of the five charges. In addition to the knowing endangerment charge it included two RCRA disposal charges for illegally dumping the tank contents, a charge for submitting the false confined-space permit to OSHA, as Breitsameter had promised, and a charge for illegally burying the AEI treater dust at Evergreen.

If there was ever a defendant who deserved to be dragged out of bed in handcuffs, it was Allan Elias, and Wojnicz was itching to do it, but he and Hilldorfer knew that wasn't going to happen. This was an environmental crime. Elias was allowed to appear voluntarily, and he walked into the courtroom alone, seemingly untroubled by the whole affair but unhappy to be bothered. Nevin met him at the wooden railing and put an arm around his shoulder, sharing private words.

Judge Winmill stepped in from a door to the right of the bench and climbed to his high-back leather chair. Perhaps an inch over six feet with a slender, athletic build and youthful, boyish features, Winmill was an Idaho native. He grew up in Pingree, a small town in southeast Idaho near the Snake River, and attended college at Idaho State University in Pocatello, where he was student body president. He left the state to attend Harvard Law School but returned to Pocatello to live and practice law. A Mormon, Winmill was the father of four and active in the Democratic Party. He practiced for ten years in Pocatello, until 1987, when Governor Cecil Andrus appointed him to the bench in the Sixth Judicial District of the State of Idaho. Eight years later, in August 1995, he was a Clinton appointee to the federal bench. Breitsameter and Miller told Uhlmann that Idaho prosecutors and the defense bar universally considered Winmill extremely bright and even-handed. He was a judge who labored over his decisions, frequently taking matters under advisement rather than ruling from the bench, and he often conducted his own legal research to ensure the accuracy of his decisions.[1]

Winmill shuffled papers on his desk and attended to preliminary matters, then the indictment was read. After the knowing endangerment charge it was Nevin, not Elias, who stepped forward to plead.

"Counsel may well make assertions that this case involves violence. I will say now that this is a charge which will not be sustained. I deny that charge."[2]

Uhlmann remained silent, but made a note on his legal pad and underlined it twice. After the indictment was read he requested that Elias be jailed without bail, arguing Elias's considerable history of worker injuries made him a threat to the community. It was a long shot, but it gave the government a chance to preview for Winmill Elias's significant disregard for his worker's safety. Not to be outdone, Nevin described Elias as a distinguished businessman in the community, married for forty-two years, and the father of three successful children.

Winmill denied the request for bail and did not impose a bond. He ordered that Elias surrender his passport and weapons permit, report regularly to a probation officer, and refrain from contacting witnesses. Then he set trial for August 31, 1998.

Outside the courtroom, the trial team huddled for a moment.

"I've never heard an attorney answer an indictment," Hilldorfer said.

Breitsameter explained that the Boise U.S. Attorney's Office referred to Nevin as "The King of Vouching" because he had a habit of offering his opinion on his clients' innocence. "He tries to take control of the courtroom and he tries to get the jury to think of him as the defendant so that if they like him they'll like his client."

"Get the jury to like Allan? He doesn't need to be a lawyer to do that," Hilldorfer said. "He needs to be a magician."

Uhlmann smiled but he had not been amused by Nevin's statement. He wrote it on his notepad, along with a note to bring a motion to prevent him from vouching for Elias in front of the jury. But what had really struck a chord was Nevin's bold proclamation that the evidence would not sustain the charge. It was like an athlete predicting a win. Uhlmann took it as a challenge. He decided right then that Nevin would not take control of the courtroom, and he would do everything within the law to see that the charge would be sustained.

June 1998
Seattle, Washington

CHAPTER THIRTY-ONE

FOUR DAYS AFTER the indictment, June 30, Nevin and Marshall filed a motion to continue the trial to April 1999. The August trial date was unrealistic for the government or the defense, but the delay was more than the government was willing to concede and Uhlmann was not happy that the motion accused the government of withholding discovery. It galled Uhlmann because Elias had refused to produce Evergreen Resources' corporate records to the grand jury and had taken the matter all the way to the Ninth Circuit. The records were not turned over until a federal district court judge ordered that a bench warrant would be issued if they were not produced to the grand jury.[1]

Both sides eventually agreed to continue the trial to January 19, 1999, but there was no lingering doubt that the prosecution from here on out would be a battle.

The trial continuance gave Hilldorfer and Wojnicz some needed respite. They made a weeklong trip to Boise in July, but otherwise spent the summer working the phones and reviewing documents. Their to-do list included finding Sean Stevens, the former Evergreen employee Elias ordered to bury the tank sludge. They learned he was working for a company removing underground storage tanks in Las Vegas, but no one could, or would, provide them with the name of the company or Stevens's address. Hilldorfer wasn't about to ask McClary to spend his dwindling travel budget so he and Bob could drive around Las Vegas on a wild-goose chase, so it came as a shock when McClary showed up in Hilldorfer's cubicle in late September and said there was money in the travel budget that needed to be spent before the end of the fiscal year.

"You got any trips you need to make?"

◆   ◆   ◆

THEIR PLANE LANDED at Las Vegas International Airport at 5:14 P.M. on September 23. Hilldorfer had never seen the infamous Las Vegas strip with its juxtaposition of architecture and artificial night sky. He thought he had landed in a foreign country. For Bob there was a "screaming deal" to be found on every billboard, and he seemed determined to find every one. He somehow managed a free upgrade on their rental car, and he and Hilldorfer cruised into town in a silver Lincoln Town Car.

"We look like a couple of pimps," Hilldorfer said, though he was glad for the air-conditioning and the extra room.

They went to dinner that night and did a bit of sightseeing, but if there was any thought the trip would be a vacation it died the following morning when they set out looking for Stevens in the blinding Las Vegas summer heat. As with his pursuit of the cyanide salesman, Bill Stout, Wojnicz had been creative. He ran a search and determined there was a gas station franchise in Las Vegas under an EPA edict to replace their underground storage tanks. The gas company gave him the name of the company they contracted to do the work, and Wojnicz hit pay dirt. Stevens was on the payroll. Unfortunately, the company couldn't be specific about Stevens's whereabouts on a given day because the crew moved from station to station. The best it could tell them was the suburb where he might be working.

The suburb was a true slice of Americana, cookie-cutter homes with red-tiled roofs plopped in the middle of the desert and surrounded by strip malls. "I feel like I'm in a Steven Spielberg movie," Hilldorfer said.

They drove for hours, but that afternoon they hit the jackpot—a station with a big hole in the ground. They stepped out of the car into a blast of heat and found the foreman. Hilldorfer quickly assured the man that they were not a part of the EPA's UST (Underground Storage Tank) program. "We just need a few minutes with one of your men, Sean Stevens. He's not in any trouble and didn't do anything wrong. He worked at a plant in Idaho where another employee was hurt."

Noticeably relieved, the foreman pointed to the hole. "He's over there."

The young man who looked up at the two agents from under a crop of blond hair could have stepped out of a high school class photo. Stevens climbed out of the hole and they talked in the air-conditioned convenience store attached to the gas station. Stevens couldn't believe they'd found him, though it was clear he wasn't hiding. Married with children, he needed the work and told them that in September 1996 he called Vaughn Smith, a contractor in Soda Springs, looking for construction work. Smith sent him to Elias. He'd heard about Dominguez's injury and of Evergreen's reputation and it concerned him, but like many of the employees the agents had interviewed, Evergreen was all he could find.

Stevens rubbed the dirt from his arms and hands and gave clipped, matter-of-fact answers. He was a confident kid. He wasn't intimidated and he didn't take a lot of time to think before answering, but Hilldorfer noticed almost a twinkle in his eye, like he was sitting on something good and waiting for them to ask the right questions. He confirmed that Elias had him bury waste from the tank and that he had to dig it up when they found out Idaho DEQ was coming.

"Did you know EPA was investigating Allan?" Hilldorfer asked.

"Yeah. He thought you guys were a bunch of dumb shits."

Wojnicz shrugged. "Been called worse."

"And he knew you were coming to do that search warrant."

"Did he?" Hilldorfer asked. "How do you know that?"

"Cause he was frantic running around screaming at all of us that EPA was coming. He had us set up lockers in one of the rooms and sent us scrounging around trying to find anything we could call safety equipment, which was pretty slim."

Bingo.

"What did you find?"

"Some old oxygen bottles. Some rain gear that had so many holes in them they looked like a mesh T-shirt."

"And Allan told you to put them in the lockers?"

Stevens nodded. "Yeah, with everything else we could find. He took off for a while and then he had some safety harnesses, some shields or something, I can't remember exactly, safety equipment that he got."

"Had any of that equipment been available at Evergreen when you worked there?"

"No," Stevens said matter-of-factly. "It was just a setup to make it look like he had a safety program because he knew you all were coming."

The trip to Vegas had been a gamble, but Sean Stevens had paid off handsomely.[2]

CHAPTER THIRTY-TWO

ON THE AFTERNOON of October 2, during a monthly debriefing, Uhlmann and Breitsameter advised Hilldorfer and Wojnicz that the defense had filed eleven pretrial motions. The most significant was a motion to suppress any evidence Hilldorfer obtained during his first visit to Evergreen, including the samples from the tank. Elias was arguing that Evergreen had been improperly seized without a search warrant. He submitted an affidavit claiming he had repeatedly told Kelly O'Neil he did not consent to EPA sampling the tank and only agreed after he was told the samples would be "split" so he could test them.

"When I went to Special Agent Hilldorfer and asked him for my split samples, he just shrugged."[1]

Hilldorfer's alleged shrug became a running joke among the team, but Elias's affidavit was anything but funny. Because Elias disposed of the tank contents and had Ivan Williams cut up the tank, the government could not obtain any other samples. If the court suppressed the samples taken the day after the accident as improperly seized evidence, it would be near impossible to prove the material in the tank was hazardous, and without that underlying pin the other charges, including knowing endangerment, wouldn't stand.

Marshall had also not missed the SW846 problem. He filed a motion that the regulation was too vague to be enforced and that all of the samples taken that day had passed that guideline, but that the EPA changed the guideline to "get Elias." Uhlmann thought the argument disingenuous given that Elias had never performed any test to determine if the material in the tank had cyanide. How could he argue that a test he never used was too vague? The mistake in the regulation was sheer serendipity. Nevertheless, Marshall had written an excellent brief and Uhlmann knew it would be the biggest legal hurdle in the case.

Shortly after the conference call, Wojnicz received a telephone call from Joe Rice. He and another Soda Springs police officer, Rick Anderson, had been subpoenaed by Elias's attorneys to appear at the suppression hearing. Suppression hearings were fairly common in criminal matters, but it was clear the defense intended to put a lot of energy into the hearing.

THE TWO AGENTS returned to Soda Springs the following week to interview additional Caribou County volunteer firemen who had rescued Dominguez. As was their custom they stopped to talk with Jackie and Scott. They wanted to show Scott a form from Evergreen that indicated he had received safety and hazardous material training. Smith and Thornock both denied signing the form or receiving the training. They assumed Scott would say the same thing.

When Jackie answered the door she looked run-down and troubled. "Scott's not home," she said and it was clear she was not happy about it.

"How's he doing?" Hilldorfer asked.

Hamp shook her head. "Not good. He's having problems, Joe." She told them she'd let Scott know they stopped by.

Late the following day Hilldorfer and Wojnicz returned and stood waiting for Dominguez in Hamp's living room while Jackie told them someone was in town following Scott around. "I think he's videotaping him. He's rented an office right across the street from my dry cleaners."

Hilldorfer told her it was not unexpected, but that he and Bob would check it out.

"Scott's been running with the wrong crew," she said. "He's been down since Theresa left, but he's getting some help now."

As she spoke, Dominguez appeared at the end of the hallway with the fall sun glistening through a window, a bright beam of light over his left shoulder that silhouetted his form like a shadow emerging from a tunnel of darkness. The image was surreal. A halo of light encircled his head. Dominguez's hair had grown considerably since their last visit, now shoulder-length. Bedraggled and thin, he had also grown a scraggly goatee. The young kid with the million-dollar Tom Cruise smile suddenly looked more like a suffering Jesus Christ.

Hilldorfer tried to shake the image as Dominguez stepped into the living room. "Hey, Scotty."

Dominguez seemed to take longer to respond. It was evident his speech had deteriorated. "Um um um um um . . . Hi."

Hilldorfer didn't know what to say. He thought of his conversation with Joanne the weekend after he had met Dominguez, when he wondered what it did to a young man to have so much potential taken away from him so suddenly. Perhaps this was his answer. Perhaps Dominguez was coming to the realization that there was nothing anyone could do to give him back the life he once had. Hilldorfer knew he certainly couldn't do that, but perhaps he could give the young man something to focus on, something to motivate him to continue to try to get better, whatever that might be.

"I just wanted to stop by and shake your hand and tell you I was in town," Hilldorfer said. Then he went out on a limb. "There's going to be a trial soon, Scott. I know this is taking a long time, but I need you to be strong. I told you you're my hero for how hard you've been fighting this, and I want you to keep working because I want to be in that courtroom when you get up on that stand and tell everyone what Allan did to you. Will you do that for me, Scott?"

Dominguez seemed to brighten at the thought. "Um um um um um um um . . . Yhheeeesss."

They spoke for a few more minutes, then Jackie walked Hilldorfer and Wojnicz back to the door and thanked them for coming.

"You might want to have him get a haircut and shave before the trial," Wojnicz suggested.

Hamp said she would, thanked them again, and closed the door.

Hilldorfer remained shaken, perhaps by the image, perhaps because he had made the young man a promise he couldn't guarantee. As they walked back to the car he turned to Wojnicz. "God, he looked just like Jesus Christ for a moment."

If the image had been as apparent to Wojnicz he didn't let on. "Yeah, he needs a haircut," he said.

IN DECEMBER, as the January 19 trial date approached, Hilldorfer and Wojnicz took a break from preparing trial exhibits and finishing witness statements to have coffee with Mike Burnett and Glenn Bruck in the breezeway between the Union Square buildings. Bruck was a hydrogeologist by education and longtime EPA employee in the civil program. Sometime in 1997 the EPA decided it needed experts to assist the criminal investigators with obtaining samples during search warrants. Bruck was that person during the second search warrant at Evergreen and he had devoted extensive time comparing the samples he took at Evergreen with samples he took at AEI to prove Elias illegally shipped and buried the treater dust. He wasn't going to be happy with the news.

"We're dropping Count Five," Hilldorfer said.

Bruck's jaw nearly hit the table. "What? Why?"

Which charges to include in the indictment against Allan Elias had been the subject of much debate, and that debate continued as the government prepared for trial. The trial team had recently met in the cherry-wood conference room of the Boise U.S. Attorney's Office to discuss the evidence supporting each charge, Uhlmann standing at a large white easel making notes, though distracted. Despite the prior agreement reached to continue the trial to January 19, the defense had filed a second motion requesting that the trial be continued to April 1, 1999. Nevin and Marshall argued that the case was extraordinarily complex scientifically, legally, and factually, and that it involved novel issues of law and fact. They called the prosecution's allegations "far-reaching," adding, "Perhaps the government really believes that Mr. Elias is the devil incarnate."[2]

"They'll get no argument from me," Wojnicz replied.

When the trial team reached Count 5, Uhlmann stopped writing. "I'm considering dropping it." After the initial consternation, he explained that much of the defense's motion for a continuance was predicated on the complexity of Count 5. Dismissing it could preserve the trial date, but that wasn't the only reason he was contemplating it. Judge Shoob had always admonished that "The less time an attorney spends in front of a jury, the less time for things to go wrong." Proving Count 5 would require extensive scientific testimony and could extend the trial by weeks, bogging it down in a complex scientific analysis. Uhlmann was concerned Nevin would use it to distract the jury from the tragedy that befell Scott Dominguez and his family.

"This case needs to be about what happened to Scott," Uhlmann said. Hilldorfer, becoming more and more comfortable with Uhlmann, agreed.

Bruck wasn't as comfortable. He sat at the table in the breezeway shaking his head. "The cadmium waste is a hazardous waste; there's no doubt about it, Joe. It's ten times higher than you need to prove. You don't even know yet how the judge will rule on the SW846 test. You're giving up your easiest, clear-cut charge."

Bruck was right. By dismissing Count 5, the government was narrowing its aim, with Elias squarely in the crosshairs. Everything would revolve around the knowing endangerment charge. If that charge failed, it was unlikely the others would be sustained. It raised the stakes significantly. The government was going for broke.

March 4, 1999
Federal Courthouse
Boise, Idaho

CHAPTER THIRTY-THREE

HILLDORFER STOOD outside the oversized wooden doors to Judge Lynn Winmill's courtroom staring at a picture of George Washington dressed in resplendent military gear. The nation's first president knelt in prayer in the snow at Valley Forge, an enormous gray stallion towering behind him snorting white breaths of air. Hilldorfer would not be going into battle that morning at the suppression hearing. The government did not want to give the defense a chance to cross-examine him before trial. Judge Winmill had granted the defense's second request that the trial date be continued and it would now not begin until April 12. Kelly O'Neil would refute Allan Elias's affidavit alleging that he had not consented to the agent's request to take samples.

Hilldorfer pulled open the door and took a seat in the gallery next to Wojnicz. Uhlmann, Breitsameter, and Miller sat at the government table perpendicular to the jury, and Nevin, Marshall, and Elias sat at the table parallel to and facing the jury box. Promptly at 9:00 A.M., with the gallery filled with twenty students from a high school mock-trial class taught by Breitsameter and Miller, the court clerk called the matter to order and Judge Winmill took his seat behind the bench.

Nevin wasted no time dropping the gloves. He stated that he wanted either Hilldorfer or Wojnicz excluded from the hearing, citing federal rules that only allowed one investigator to be present. Sensing he was about to lose his front-row seat Wojnicz turned a beet red. Winmill quickly defused the situation, stating the rules also allowed him some discretion and he would exercise it at the hearing.

The issue temporarily rectified, Breitsameter called Sergeant Bill Reese to the stand. The government had to prove Evergreen wasn't seized, which would be in violation of Elias's Fourth Amendment rights and potentially render the samples taken that day inadmissible at trial, but instead had been closed for public safety.

Reese took the stand looking tough as nails in his indigo blue, Idaho State Police uniform and testified that Daren Schwartz, the incident commander from the Caribou County Fire Department, made the decision to close Evergreen to protect the public from a dangerous condition. He said Schwartz had little choice given that Elias had disappeared, something Soda Springs Police Officer Rick Anderson said was a pattern of behavior when the police had been called out to Evergreen to investigate reported acid spills. The obvious question was what, in the midst of this tragedy, Elias considered so important that it couldn't wait. Reese answered it. The foreman of a Union Pacific Railroad switch crew had stopped Reese as he was leaving Evergreen that night and reported that Elias had cornered one of his workers near Monsanto.

"Mr. Elias demanded that they go down and take those two sulfuric acid cars away from his facility. He wanted them gone from his facility. And he apparently made threats to, you know, this railroad worker that he was going to sue him—and other things, if he didn't."

Hilldorfer had heard this before, but hearing Reese testify to it in court, in full uniform, somehow gave it great weight.

Breitsameter was just as advertised—nothing fancy, but efficient and persistent with his questioning. Marshall's cross, by contrast, seemed disjointed, unfocused, and designed more to educate the court about future trial issues, like the defense's position that the responders knew early on that the material in the tank could be cyanide and that there had been a breathing apparatus at the site. Brietsameter objected that both issues were irrelevant to a suppression hearing. Winmill agreed. When Marshall persisted Winmill didn't waver.

"Why is that relevant to the suppression motion? Let's move on."

O'Neil took the stand that afternoon and Uhlmann walked him through how he arrived in Elias's office trailer with Officer Clements.

"I told Mr. Elias that he was not under arrest, no arrests were contemplated, and our presence was not in any way to interfere with the conduct of his business."

"What, if anything, did Mr. Elias say to you when you told him he was free to conduct his business activities that day?"

"Mr. Elias said that we would not be interrupting his business activities as he had sent his workers home following this incident until the end of the Labor Day weekend."

O'Neil disputed Elias's affidavit that he was in any way coerced into giving samples. "Mr. Elias was clearly in control. I was there in a consent mode." He testified how Elias came and went from the trailer to talk with the DEQ and OSHA inspectors, to talk to Darren Weaver in private, and to help the fire department get to a nearby brush fire.

The day came to an end, but not without some fireworks. Outside the courtroom, Marshall cornered Breitsameter in the hallway, upset at what he perceived as disrespectful demeanor during his cross-examination. Brietsameter pleaded innocence, but his ribs ached from Miller and Uhlmann elbowing him during Marshall's cross-examinations. He appeared out of practice and not just to the government attorneys. The students from Breitsameter's trial class asked him after the hearing what Marshall did before becoming a lawyer, apparently convinced he was a recent admittee to the bar.[1]

O'Neil retook the stand the following morning. Knowing Elias would not testify at the hearing, Uhlmann did the next best thing. He took out the affidavit and used O'Neil to attack each statement.

"Is the statement that you wanted to take samples from the tank on Mr. Elias's property, but he declined to allow you to do so, true or false?"

"False."

"It continues, 'Mr. O'Neil said repeatedly that it would be better for me if I cooperated.' Is that statement true or false?"

"It is false."

"And it concludes, 'He also promised that if we were allowed to take samples, the samples would be split; that is portions of each sample would be separated out and provided to me for independent testing.' Is that statement true or false?"

"False."

Nevin stood and dispensed with any introduction. "Your whole purpose for coming there was to investigate whether or not there had been a crime committed and whether or not a prosecution could be instituted, is that right?"

"I don't think I was thinking down the road to prosecution, I was thinking it was something that Idaho State Police had asked that we assist on. I thought it was worthy of at least a preliminary investigation."

Nevin persisted. "But that preliminary investigation was directed toward determining whether or not a crime had been committed, in your opinion?"

"That's what I do for work." O'Neil's cheeks flushed red.

"Could you tell the court what efforts you made to secure a search warrant prior to arriving at Evergreen Resources that morning?"

"None," O'Neil said with noticeable defiance.

"You didn't try to contact some of the assistant United States attorneys here in the District of Idaho?"

"No."

"Didn't make any effort to contact a judge in Pocatello?"

"No."

"And not the county prosecutor in Soda Springs?"

"No."

"No effort to acquire a telephonic—"

Uhlmann rose. "Objection, asked and answered, Your Honor."

"Overruled."

"Did you make any effort to acquire a telephonic one?"

"No."

"Did you ask anyone else to do that for you?"

"No."

"Why not?"

"We didn't have probable cause at that time. I didn't think to apply for a warrant. I didn't know what we had. The reason for going there was to determine what facts surrounded this incident. That was my reason for interviewing Mr. Elias."

Like Marshall, Nevin also asked a series of questions that Uhlmann considered an improper attempt to obtain discovery. Upon Uhlmann's second objection, Winmill agreed, but Nevin's reputation in the Pacific Northwest was readily apparent in their dialogue.

"Counsel, the problem is— I very strongly feel that motions to suppress should not properly be used or cannot properly be used for general discovery purposes. And I'm not even suggesting that that is what you were doing, but you may be shirking your duty if you are not trying. So I feel some obligation to rein you in. I don't want to second-guess your thought processes, but you're going to have to show some relevance to the matter at hand or I am going to sustain the objection."

"I understand, Your Honor."

"All right. With that rather candid— I find you guilty of doing your job."

"I think I'm going to puke," Wojnicz whispered to Hilldorfer.

"Get your own pot."

It was what the Boise U.S. attorneys referred to as "The Nevin Effect." With his brow furrowed meaningfully and his voice impassioned with sincerity, Nevin had an uncanny ability to get judges to buy into his arguments, or at least seriously consider them, the implied understanding being that he would take the matter up with the Ninth Circuit Court of Appeals if they were wrong.

When O'Neil stepped down, that left the two Soda Springs police officers, Rice and Anderson. Miller and Hilldorfer had met with both the night before the hearing to discuss their recollections. Both said unequivocally that the site was closed for public safety and that Elias left. Rice also said he spoke with Elias earlier the day of the accident and Elias told him there was nothing in the tank that could harm anyone. For that reason, when Marshall began to question Rice on the topic, Miller did not object that it was irrelevant to the suppression hearing. It would be powerful evidence for Winmill to hear.

"Did you have any conversation with him, Captain Rice?" Marshall asked.

"Briefly."

"And at that time did you tell him you needed to know what was in the tank?"

"Yes."

"Did he refuse to tell you?"

Rice hesitated. "Did he refuse to tell me what was in the tank, is that the question?"

"Yes."

"No, he didn't refuse to tell me what was in the tank."

Hilldorfer almost fell out of his seat. Miller turned her head and looked at him over the top of her reading glasses with an expression that clearly said, "What the hell just happened?"

"He told you he would get the information you were asking for and would let you know, did he not?"

"Yes, sir."

"And in fact, isn't that what he did?"

"The following day, yes, sir."

Rice also faltered when asked why the site was closed and Marshall did not waste the opportunity. "And it's true, is it not, that as part of your agency—your understanding as to why you were providing security—was no one could go and monkey with it before they could fully process it?"

"Yes, sir."

"The term *process* is commonly used in your profession, isn't it?"

"Yes, sir."

"And it generally refers to processing a crime scene, isn't that correct?"

"That is correct."

When Miller stood she had to quickly change strategies. She went back to Rice's conversation with Elias. "Did he tell you there was cyanide sludge in the tank?"

"No, he did not."

"Did he tell you he had used the tank in a business, a prior business, in a cyanide-leaching process?"

"The following day, when I interviewed him he did tell me that."

Miller became impatient. "Would it have been helpful for you to have learned on that date the contents of the tank, prior uses of the tank, rather than wait until the next day to obtain that information from Mr. Elias?"

"It may have been helpful to the victim, I'm not exactly sure if—"

"And you as a responder are there to help the victim?" She phrased it a question, but it was clearly a statement.

"Yes. Yes. Of course, I could have relayed the information if I knew the exact contents of the tank to medical personnel, but I did not. I didn't know that."

"Thank God," Hilldorfer said.

Anderson followed Rice and, much to Hilldorfer's and Miller's frustration, he also wavered in his answers. Miller did her best to rehabilitate him, but like Rice, it had not gone well.

Marshall followed Anderson by calling OSHA compliance officer Barb Franek. The government had considered using Franek at the hearing but decided against it. Marshall sought a curious admission from Franek, asking her if it was true that Elias had a long history of refusing to allow OSHA inspectors onto his site. The obvious inference was that Elias also would not have consented to allow the OSHA inspectors or the EPA special agents on his site, let alone consent to their taking samples. The admission, however, came with a risk and Breitsameter pounced on it.

"So Mr. Elias is familiar, is he not, with his legal rights with regard to people accessing his premises, correct?" Breitsameter asked.

Franek gave an emphatic "Yes."

Breitsameter then asked Franek about a videotape she made of the facility that morning. Franek confirmed she and Joe Eizaguirre had videotaped the site and contrary to any implication that Elias would have objected to their presence, she noted that it had been Elias who walked them around the facility and at no time did he voice such an objection on the tape. It had been an unexpected bonus that somewhat tempered the government's concern with the two officers' testimony.

After the hearing, Rice approached Hilldorfer in the hallway outside the courtroom, aware his testimony had not gone well. "Damn, those guys are good," he said. "I don't envy you guys at trial. I've never been turned around like that on the stand."

Friday, March 12, 1999
EPA Region 10 Headquarters
Seattle, Washington

CHAPTER THIRTY-FOUR

THE FOLLOWING FRIDAY, after the suppression hearing, Hilldorfer crossed University Avenue on his way back to the office from a workout. At 5:00 in the afternoon winter darkness entrenched Seattle like a moonless night and a light rain glistened in the headlights of commuters fighting traffic to get home. As he approached the building he noticed the familiar red glow of a cigarette tip. Dixon McClary was having a smoke.

McClary made eye contact and raised his chin as Hilldorfer approached, a signal that he wanted to talk. Hilldorfer was tired, hungry, and just wanted to get home.

"What's up, Dixon?"

McClary turned his head and blew smoke out of the corner of his mouth so that it would not be in Hilldorfer's face. "Heard you got good news today."

They had. Judge Winmill had issued a twelve-page Memorandum of Decision denying the defense's motion to suppress the samples. He also denied the defense's motion to dismiss the charges against Elias on the grounds that the RCRA statute was too vague. That would continue to be an issue at trial.

"We're all set to go," Hilldorfer said. "It's going to be a long trial."

McClary took another drag on the cigarette. "You think so?" He tilted his head. "I smell a plea, Joe."

Hilldorfer shook his head. "Not this time, Dixon. There's too much at stake and there's nothing for Allan to plea because we dismissed Count Five. Besides, Allan would never plea; his ego is too big."

McClary raised his eyebrows as if to say "I don't know." "I smell a plea," he said and turned and walked back inside the building.

Still wearing shorts and sweating from his workout, Hilldorfer crossed his arms against the damp cold and watched traffic inch down Sixth Avenue onto the on-ramp to Interstate 5 North. If there was going to be a plea, McClary was right, now would be the time. With the suppression hearing completed and trial looming, reality hit most defendants in the face, and with it the possibility of being convicted. Things changed for the attorneys as well. Defense counsel had squeezed a substantial sum of money out of the turnip, and the prosecutors had to quit talking tough and start acting tough. Hilldorfer didn't think Breitsameter or Uhlmann, whom he and Wojnicz had nicknamed "The Pit Bull," would back down, but he couldn't deny the fact that McClary had begun his "I smell a plea" mantra just before the U.S. attorney faxed the Boomsnub Corporation's plea deal to the Region 10 offices.

Uhlmann had been up-front with the agents about the possibility of a plea bargain. Trials were notoriously uncertain, as Uhlmann's first trial in Wyoming clearly demonstrated, and a prosecutor would be remiss to ignore that uncertainty to gratify his own desire for a conviction, particularly since environmental crimes and RCRA sentences remained an evolving area of the law. Uhlmann knew this as well. He was one of the attorneys setting the standard. He had recently secured a sentence against the owner of a drum-recycling facility in Memphis, Tennessee, for dumping scores of drums containing toxic, flammable, and corrosive chemicals and solvents in the middle of a poor residential neighborhood. The sentence was the longest criminal sentence for an environmental crime, forty-one months. He told the two agents that doing justice meant considering reasonable pleas. If a defendant was willing to plea to a reasonable sentence for his crime, the prosecutor was obliged to consider it.

Breitsameter agreed with Uhlmann for those reasons and one other. While a body of federal case law said courts should not consider payments to victims in exchange for reduced jail time, Breitsameter had tried enough white-collar criminals to know that too often only the defense lawyers got rich. The victim never saw a nickel. What Scott Dominguez and his family needed now was money to pay his significant and unrelenting medical bills and to hire someone to help care for him. Could the government, in good conscience, refuse to consider a lesser jail sentence if Elias offered Dominguez, say, a million dollars? Who would they be punishing, Allan or Scott and his family?

It never became an issue.

During the grand jury phase Uhlmann sent a "target letter" to Elias through David Marshall, then called Marshall to ask whether Elias wanted to make an appearance before the grand jury. Elias declined. Uhlmann used the opportunity to ask Marshall if Elias wanted to talk about a plea. Normally the defense initiated that conversation.

Marshall's response had not been encouraging. "Well, I'll always take back to my client whatever the government is willing to consider."

Uhlmann told Marshall he wasn't going to waste time putting together a plea agreement unless Elias indicated some willingness to plea to a felony and significant jail time. Uhlmann was considering a deal of between three and seven years for a felony RCRA charge. Again, it wasn't an issue; he never heard back from Marshall.[1]

Hilldorfer looked at the revolving doors leading to the illuminated lobby of his building. He'd intended to go back to his office, but now decided against it. If there was a fax on his chair from the U.S. Attorney's Offices, it could wait and ruin tomorrow.

CHAPTER THIRTY-FIVE

THE DAY AFTER he watched the Baltimore Orioles defeat the Tampa Bay Devil Rays 10–7 on opening day at Camden Yards, Uhlmann packed his bags at his Silver Spring, Maryland, home, kissed his wife and three children, and slid into a taxi for Dulles Airport and a multi-stop flight to Pocatello. He busied himself on the plane with trial briefs and the impending pretrial motions, trying to keep his mind off the thought that he would not likely see his family for at least a month, if not more.

For Uhlmann, the investigation and prosecution of Allan Elias had been a shining example of how the Environmental Crimes Section had evolved from the dark days of the congressional hearings and the internal controversy. After those hearings, Attorney General Janet Reno had ordered an independent investigation of the Environmental Crimes Section.[1] The subsequent report defended the section's decisions to decline certain prosecutions and the allegations that the declinations were politically motivated. It did, however, acknowledge there had been a breakdown in management and the inherent difficulties of prosecuting federal environmental crimes.

Environmental prosecutions involve multiple federal agencies, the EPA, the ECS at Main Justice in Washington and local U.S. Attorney's Offices, as well as state and local environmental quality agencies. In addition, the federal environmental program had initially been almost exclusively focused on the imposition of civil and administrative enforcement sanctions. The change to criminal enforcement met significant impediments. While politicians gave great comment to the need to protect the environment, they didn't back it up with funding. The EPA/CID and the ECS faced daunting challenges in terms of the sheer number of polluters, and the cost of scientific and technical expertise needed to convict them.

It led to a self-perpetuating cycle. EPA agents were advertised to be the best of the best, trained law enforcement agents who were also highly educated. Many, like Hilldorfer and Wojnicz, had advanced degrees. They had the guts to kick down doors, the brains and stamina to take on complicated fact-checking and research-intensive investigations that could take years, and the attitude required to interview educated and savvy corporate executives one day and slap handcuffs on them the next. As the "brick cops" who walked the environmental beat, they, more than anyone, saw the abuses in a system that allowed corporations to cause significant damage to the environment and walk away without any officers sentenced to significant jail time. It was a kick in the teeth. For some it got to be too much; it became easier to "pick the low-hanging fruit"—the easy environmental cases they could refer to the Department of Justice to get their bean without having to give blood, sweat, and tears to a doomed investigation. The low-hanging fruit, in turn, were exactly the kinds of cases the Department of Justice had no interest in prosecuting. As a result, they continued to decline more cases than they prosecuted.

Congress had also fallen into a chronicled legislative cycle of reacting only after catastrophes and near catastrophes, when public outrage for the environment and concomitant publicity was at its peak. It sent mixed messages. The message intended for the public was aggressive prosecution of environmental crimes. But at roughly the same time that the Dingell committee was skewering the ECS, Congress was entertaining a series of bills to restrict the enforcement of environmental regulations and to grant legal privileges and immunity to corporations and corporate officers who voluntarily disclosed environmental violations. The unspoken but widely understood impetus for the bills was that environmental regulations hindered the nation's businesses and private property rights.

The Environmental Crimes Section took several steps to break the cycle. In 1994, Uhlmann became part of a six-person review committee that generated a "blue sheet," a document that set out Department of Justice policy. The committee called it "the Peace Treaty" because it ended Main Justice's control over environmental criminal prosecutions and allowed local U.S. Attorney's Offices to indict cases without the need to seek approval. In addition, Cartusciello stepped aside and Ron Sarokin, an aggressive environmental prosecutor, became chief of the section. Sarokin brought a different approach to management. ECS's focus shifted to providing needed resources and expertise to help local U.S. attorneys prosecute and convict environmental offenders.

The Elias prosecution illustrated that working relationship. The trial would hopefully demonstrate the results such cooperation could achieve.

Uhlmann drove straight to the Federal Courthouse to file the government's motions. Leaving the clerk's office he ran into David Nevin in the lobby. It was cordial, but there existed an underlying tension neither could dismiss between two men about to step into the ring and do battle. Each admitted to having nervous energy, but only about getting started, not about the outcome. Then they shook hands and went their separate ways.

Uhlmann worked in the U.S. Attorney's Office on the first floor of the courthouse. The three offices and conference room in the recently constructed building were furnished but not yet occupied and would be the government's workspace for the trial. By the time Uhlmann got back into his car, checked in at the Ameritel Hotel, unpacked his things and organized his suite, it was 11:30 at night, 1:30 A.M. on the East Coast, too late to call his family. He set a photograph of his wife and youngest daughter, Emily, now approaching three, on the table next to his bed and considered them for a moment. Whether it was the thought he would not see them for an extended period, the stress before trial, or the added pressure of trying a case that embodied all of the reasons he chose a career prosecuting white-collar crime, David Uhlmann sat down on the bed, considered his surroundings, and cried.

Wednesday, April 7, 1999
First Pretrial Conference
Federal Courthouse
Pocatello, Idaho

CHAPTER THIRTY-SIX

THE TRIAL OF Allan Elias would be held in Pocatello. A city of 105 churches, half of them Mormon, Pocatello spread across 35 square miles with 54,000 residents living in nice homes that could still be purchased for $80,000. At 4,448 feet in the western foothills of the Rocky Mountains, the city was synonymous with the history of the Wild West— founded on land inhabited by Indians but coveted by white men venturing west in search of opportunity and fortune.

The city derived its name from Chief Paughetello, the leader of the Shoshoni tribe that once owned the 1.3-million-acre Fort Hall Indian Reservation. A railroad telegrapher has been credited with giving

"Pocatello" its present spelling, a fitting attribution since Pocatello's very existence, like many western towns, has been attributed to the great railroads.

Called the "Gate City," Pocatello is strategically located on the long, narrow Portneuf Valley—the eastern portal to the Snake River plain and much of the Pacific Northwest. Despite its key location, for much of the 1800s, Pocatello did not exist, and but for certain circumstances, might not today. The meandering Portneuf River and lava formations left behind by a prehistoric ocean made road building and travel difficult. Settlers heading west across southern Idaho for Oregon and California swung around the valley to Fort Hall—a fur trading post at the confluence of the Portneuf River and the Snake River—fifteen miles northwest of Pocatello.

In the mid-1860s, with the start of the Montana Gold Rush, wagons, stagecoaches, and freight companies began to haul merchandise and supplies from the Utah Territory through southeastern Idaho to the mining districts of western Montana. As the volume of freight increased, Mormon Church leaders looked to the railroad as a more economical and more efficient way to transport large quantities of commodities. Eventually, Pocatello became the junction for the Union Pacific and the Oregon Short Line. Retail and commercial stores sprang up along with a bank, a newspaper, a school, several churches, and multiple saloons compacted near the freight depot along Front Street. Painted a dark red brindle and set on a dusty, sagebrush-covered plain, the buildings must have resembled the bleak and barren appearance of a town in a Clint Eastwood western.

In 1999 the Union Pacific Junction no longer operated in Pocatello except for a hub branch and crew change-point. The tracks, however, still divided the more modern commercial area of town—a long strip of concrete with retail businesses and fast-food restaurants—from the old western town of the 1800s. The new Federal Courthouse, a brick facade structure with a four-column colonnade and the grandeur of a Southern plantation mansion, is located not far from those tracks. From its steps beneath a beige portico one can still hear the boxcars slam together like the roar of distant thunder and see the smokestack bearing Union Pacific's name, though certain of the red letters, vertically positioned from top to bottom, have faded to a pale pink or disappeared entirely, like an unfinished answer to a crossword puzzle.[1]

◆   ◆   ◆

ON WEDNESDAY MORNING, April 7, Hilldorfer and Wojnicz walked into Judge Winmill's courtroom on the second floor to the smell of fresh paint and polished wood. The only blemish was the same robin's-egg-blue carpet as the Boise Federal Courthouse.

"They must have got a deal on the carpet," Wojnicz observed.

United States v. Allan Elias would be the new Federal Courthouse's first criminal trial, and Judge Winmill would referee the proceedings from atop an elevated dark wood bench positioned directly beneath a bronze cast seal, an eagle ringed by the words *United States District Court, District of Idaho.* The elevated witness stand was to his immediate right. Beyond it, in the far corner, would sit his law clerk, Michael Fica. Directly below Winmill, in the "well," would sit his court reporter, Joe Roden, and to Roden's left, the court clerk, LaDonna Garcia. Counsel tables faced the bench, two on each side of the courtroom, one behind the other. Counsel's lectern was between them. Facing the bench, the elevated jury box was to the left with blue, high-back chairs beneath an oversized round clock that seemed better suited to a three-masted schooner. A solid wood railing and swinging gate separated the combatants from the gallery, five benches deep on each side. Overhead, modern globe chandeliers hung from chains.

The pretrial hearing was not unlike a technical rehearsal for the opening of a play. The new court was wired with the latest in technology, computer terminals at the bench, at the clerk's desk, and at counsel's tables. Exhibits could be downloaded onto the system and displayed on the computer screens. If Judge Winmill admitted the exhibit into evidence it was published to the jury on an enormous movie screen that dropped from the ceiling behind the witness stand. Winmill seemed particularly proud of the technology and eager to show it off.

"Does anyone have a photograph we can put up on the screen?"

None of the attorneys had thought to bring a trial exhibit. Uhlmann pulled out a photograph from his briefcase. "This is all I have, George. Do you have anything?"

Breitsameter looked ecstatic. "Use that."

"Are you sure?"

"Use it. Use it."

Uhlmann addressed Winmill. "I have a photograph, Your Honor. It doesn't relate to this trial though . . ."

"That's okay."

Winmill walked them through the steps and within less than a minute the smiling faces of Uhlmann, his wife, and daughter, Emily, at her second birthday party filled the giant screen.

Winmill smiled. "What a beautiful family."

Breitsameter stood trying not to look smug. Having the chance to let Uhlmann, the government prosecutor from Washington, D.C., introduce himself as a family man to the judge had been just too good an opportunity to pass up.

Their euphoria didn't last long. By the time they got downstairs to the U.S. Attorney's Office they had received the defense's pretrial motions. One in particular landed like a bomb at Joe Hilldorfer's feet.

THE FOLLOWING MONDAY, April 12, with all engines revved and ready to go, the government heard the words lawyers usually dread on the scheduled first day of trial.

"You're trailing."

A wrongful death civil action was being tried in Winmill's courtroom and it had not yet finished. Uhlmann was actually relieved. Pocatello had been hit over the weekend with a late snowstorm, and he'd been hit with a horrific stomach flu. It forced him to stay in bed for two days and left him dehydrated and nauseated.

Tuesday morning he dragged himself from bed early to argue the pretrial motions in Winmill's court. As anticipated, the defense sought to exclude Lowry's testimony and his simulated tank and requested a Daubert hearing—a hearing outside the jury's presence to challenge the scientific principles upon which Lowry's opinions were based, which they were calling "voodoo science." The government brought a motion to prevent the defense from attacking the credibility of several of the government's witnesses by bringing up minor criminal offenses. Winmill had already ruled that the only employees who could testify were those who, like Dominguez, had been similarly injured working in confined spaces at Evergreen. He had also precluded the government from introducing the cyanide drum found at AEI.

The motion that caused the government, particularly Hilldorfer, the most angst was to prevent Scott Dominguez from testifying. Nevin argued that the government couldn't have it both ways; if it was going to argue that Scott Dominguez had a severe and permanent injury—brain damage—it couldn't also argue he was competent to testify. They wanted Winmill to submit Dominguez to a competency examination. Uhlmann argued just as vehemently that while Dominguez had incurred a severe brain injury, medical experts would opine that his cognitive abilities to reason and to understand remained intact. He argued the contradiction was the defense's conceding Dominguez had been injured but not conceding it was from cyanide. They claimed the mask put on Scott's face had caused oxygen deprivation.[2] Winmill told the attorneys he wanted the issue briefed.

As he sat in the courtroom listening to the argument, Hilldorfer grew upset. Worse, he felt clammy and dizzy and his stomach was cramping. It wasn't nerves. He was getting sick.

Following the hearing the trial team reconvened in the conference room of the U.S. Attorney's Office. Breitsameter remained steadfast in his faith in Winmill, before whom he had appeared numerous times. "There is no way he will not allow Scott to testify," he said.

Without similar experience to draw from, Uhlmann didn't have the same confidence and he knew Scott desperately wanted to testify and that it was important to the young man and to his family, as it was to most victims of crime.

"Five- and six-year-old kids are allowed to testify," he said. "He should be, too."

To convince Winmill, the government would need declarations from Dominguez's doctors and others who had spent time with him, including Hilldorfer, attesting to Dominguez's ability to understand and respond to questions. Getting those affidavits normally fell to Hilldorfer and Wojnicz, but Hilldorfer was now racked with chills and thought he might pass out.

"I can't do it," he said. "I'm sick. I have to go back to the hotel."

By the time Wojnicz dropped him at the Ameritel he had to race to his room. Whatever was in his stomach came up, and nothing else stayed down. As much as he wanted to sleep, his body would not let him. He spent most of the afternoon on the bathroom floor shaking so violently

Scott Dominguez, age 14. Born in Soda Springs, he had an engaging smile and a passion for sports and the Idaho outdoors.

In his junior year at Soda Springs High, Dominguez fell in love with Theresa Cole, a senior.

Upon his graduating, Dominguez and Cole moved into an apartment together and planned to marry.

Allan Elias, a native of Great Neck, New York, made a fortune in Arizona real estate in the 1970s before moving to Soda Springs and founding Evergreen Resources. *(Photo courtesy Andrew Scutro, Boise Weekly)*

Featured on the cover of a Tucson magazine, Elias was described as that city's "financial Bruce Jenner," referring to the former Olympic champion.

From Superstar to Super Coach!

Allan Elias, Tucson's mystery player, has racked up an incredible record as a one-man Superstar. Testing his strength and maneuverability, in the last ten years Elias has become Tucson's financial Bruce Jenner. His entrepreneurial Decathlon includes many of Tucson's prime commercial properties.

Elias was an eager 30-year-old unknown when he arrived in Tucson in 1968, equipped with a Wharton School of Finance diploma earned at the age of 19, and the confidence of having trained in that camp of killers and climbers, the Big Apple.

Within his first year in Tucson, he enrolled at the University of Arizona Law School and took his first financial stride with the purchase of the Catalina Foothills Estates Apartments. A humble beginning that would lead to the acquisition of some of Tucson's prime commercial real estate bought and sold by the Superstar.

In 1969 the fans took notice when he dazzled the marketplace with his "four-on-one leap" a single purchase contract that made Elias owner of Campbell Plaza Shopping Center, Casas Adobes Shopping Plaza, Pueblo Plaza Shopping Center, and Wilmot Medical Building. It wasn't until the early '70's that his record began to get attention, when, without working up a

TUCSON MAGAZINE

On August 27, 1996, Elias ordered Dominguez to clean out a massive storage tank once used in a failed cyanide leaching process, claiming the tank contained only sludge and water.

The only way in or out of the tank was a twenty-two-inch-diameter hole.

Volunteer fireman Daren Schwartz led a massive rescue effort after Dominguez collapsed in the tank.

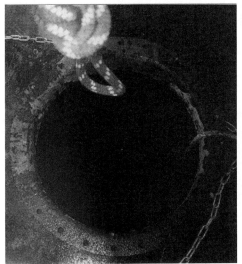

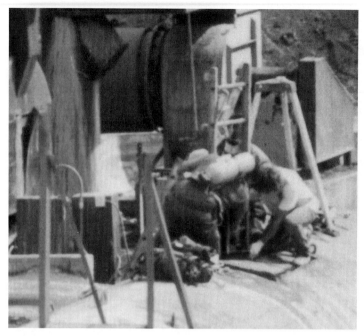

Atop the tank Schwartz and the rescuers encountered a potentially dangerous problem. The hole was too small for anyone wearing necessary safety equipment to fit through.

Fellow Evergreen employees who tried to save Dominguez also succumbed to the hydrogen cyanide fumes inside the tank.

EPA Special Agent Bob Wojnicz
took the call about a possible tragedy
in Soda Springs, Idaho.

EPA Special Agent Joseph
Hilldorfer, a former FBI agent, led
a two-year investigation of Allan
Elias from Seattle across southeast
Idaho, to Salt Lake City, Utah;
Denver, Colorado; and Las Vegas
and Moapa, Nevada in pursuit of
evidence. *(Photo by Gabe Palmer)*

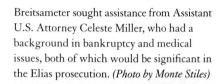

Breitsameter sought assistance from Assistant U.S. Attorney Celeste Miller, who had a background in bankruptcy and medical issues, both of which would be significant in the Elias prosecution. *(Photo by Monte Stiles)*

Assistant U.S. Attorney George Breitsameter, a senior litigator at the U.S. Attorney's Office in Boise, had the difficult task of prosecuting Elias. *(Photo by Monte Stiles)*

Assistant U.S. Attorney David Uhlmann, from the Environmental Crimes Section of the United States Department of Justice, had developed a passion for prosecuting white-collar criminals and wanted the Elias case. *(DoJ Official Photo/Craig Crawford)*

The newly constructed Federal Courthouse in Pocatello, Idaho.

U.S. Federal District Court Judge B. Lynn Winmill, a native of southeast Idaho. Prosecutors and defense attorneys considered him fair and hardworking. *(Photo courtesy Burns Studio, Boise Idaho)*

Outside the courthouse. Left to right: George Breitsameter, Ron Hamp (Scott's father), Bob Wojnicz, David Uhlmann, Jim Oesterly, Scott Dominguez, Joe Hilldorfer, Celeste Miller and Jackie Hamp.

Joe Hilldorfer (right) continues to live in Seattle, but his thoughts are never far from Scott Dominguez and his family in Soda Springs, Idaho, and the life they should have had.

his teeth chattered. When Wojnicz returned with medication to prevent vomiting Hilldorfer threw it up.

"How's David?" he asked.

"Better than you. He's on the floor at the U.S. Attorney's Office writing a brief and organizing trial exhibits. I don't know what's making him more sick, the flu or talking to Marshall and Nevin." The relationship had become so disagreeable only Jim Oesterle had a working dialogue with the defense. "If that doesn't make him sick," Wojnicz said, "nothing will."

Later that afternoon Breitsameter came to Hilldorfer's hotel room with a notary public to get Hilldorfer's signature on an affidavit recounting his numerous discussions with Dominguez. Breitsameter was unable to suppress a smile at how pathetic Hilldorfer looked standing at the door in his underwear holding a bowl.

"Anything I can get you, Joe?"

"A gun."

THE NEXT MORNING, still weak, Hilldorfer crawled from bed. He and Wojnicz drove to the courthouse early to move Dr. Joe's scale-size model of the storage tank into the courtroom. The tank would be concealed in the corner of the room beneath a hospital-blue blanket looking like a small child's coffin until, and if, it was admitted. Though the new courthouse had an elevator from the first to the second floor, moving the bulky tank remained a chore. Wojnicz disappeared, likely succumbing to a well-timed gastrointestinal attack, leaving Hilldorfer to struggle with the model while trying not to scratch the unblemished, cherrywood courtroom doors. By the time he got the tank in place and sat down in the gallery he had broken into a fevered sweat. Behind him he heard the courtroom door open and turned expecting to see Wojnicz.

Nevin stepped in surveying the room like a facile actor might a stage. He strode down the aisle, pushed through the bench railing, and sat down at the table positioned closest to the jury—the table traditionally reserved for the government. If Nevin knew that to be the case, he didn't care, pulling out a stack of papers and a notepad from his briefcase and settling in. Hilldorfer contemplated warning Breitsameter and Uhlmann, but he realized the courtroom was not his battleground. It was theirs.

At 8:50 A.M., Breitsameter entered the courtroom in a brown suit. Uhlmann stepped in behind him looking like one of the local Mormon choirboys in a dark blue suit and white shirt. Both spotted Nevin at about the same time.

BREITSAMETER DID NOT deliberately avoid what he considered "silly battles" with opposing counsel, but he also didn't seek them out. Looking at Nevin, he said to Uhlmann, "He's in our spot."

Uhlmann's mind was already churning. He'd tried environmental crimes in five different federal judicial districts and all throughout the District of Columbia. In every courthouse the government sat next to the jury. In Boise and the old Pocatello Federal Courthouse the counsel tables were arranged differently than most. The defense table was perpendicular to the government table and parallel to the jury box so the defendant faced the jury. But even as his mind tried to rationalize Nevin's act, Uhlmann knew Nevin's choice of seats had nothing to do with the particularities of trial practice in the District of Idaho. It had to do with Nevin trying to psychologically wrestle control of the courtroom, as Uhlmann had been forewarned.

"What are we going to do?" Breitsameter asked.

"We're going to sit at our table. He's not going to take our spot."

Uhlmann took off down the aisle in the determined gait of a man about to miss his train, pushed through the wooden railing, pulled out the chair directly next to Nevin, and threw himself into it. "You're sitting at our table."

Nevin gave him a brief look. "What makes you think it's your table?"

"Because in every courthouse I've ever been in the government sits at this table."

Nevin shrugged. "Not in every courthouse I've ever been in."

Breitsameter sat in the third chair while Uhlmann opened his briefcase and arranged his papers. "I guess we'll let the judge work this out."

"I guess we will," Nevin replied.[3]

WOJNICZ STEPPED INTO the pew next to Hilldorfer and nodded to Uhlmann and Nevin fighting for elbow room. "This ought to be good."

Hilldorfer shook his head. "Let's hope not. Hopefully the judge kicks his ass out of there."

Marshall entered the courtroom after Breitsameter and Uhlmann had taken their seats. If Nevin had told him his intention on seating arrangements, Marshall hid it. He walked down the aisle looking confused, and with no room at the inn, as Wojnicz said to Hilldorfer, he stood at the table in the rear.

Winmill entered the courtroom from the far right, took the bench, and spent a moment adjusting his papers before calmly folding his hands and addressing counsel as if there were nothing out of the ordinary, despite the lopsided appearance of his courtroom.

Nevin stood.

"Mr. Nevin, you're standing. I assume you have something you want to say."

"Yes, Your Honor. It's very important that the defendant be allowed to sit by the jury. It is highly prejudicial to my client not to sit here."

Winmill looked to Uhlmann. "Mr. Uhlmann?"

Uhlmann adjusted his glasses. "Your Honor, I've tried cases in federal courts all over the country, and this is how it is done in every single one of those courts. The government always sits on the left. There is nothing out of the ordinary with the way this courtroom is configured. If it isn't prejudicial to every other defendant in every other courthouse, it isn't prejudicial here." He pointed to the empty tables. "The defendant sits over there. As much as we like Mr. Nevin we don't want to share a table with him."[4]

Because the tables were wired for computers they could not be rearranged, but Winmill brokered a compromise. He said the government would sit at the table the first week of trial and the sides would alternate each week thereafter. Hilldorfer was not happy, thinking the compromise was a further illustration of the "Nevin effect," but Uhlmann wasn't that upset. While Nevin had obtained something to which Uhlmann believed he was not entitled, Uhlmann thought it a classic example of the adage "Be careful what you wish for." Not the usual spit-and-polish white-collar criminal, Elias could be demonstrative and histrionic with his facial expressions and hand movements. Uhlmann suspected it wouldn't play well to a jury. Still, he was glad it was Nevin and Marshall picking up their things and moving that morning.

The battle in the courtroom, however, did not end there. Uhlmann had successfully excluded Elias's longtime counsel, Craig Jorgensen, from the courtroom on the basis that Jorgensen could be a potential witness. Jorgensen had prepared Weaver's and Ivan Williams's affidavits. Hilldorfer and Wojnicz interviewed him in his office on Second Avenue in Pocatello to determine if there had been any witness tampering to warrant an obstruction of justice charge. Jorgensen professed not to know how Elias obtained Weaver's recorded conversation, though he said he sent the typed affidavit back to Elias, who made "corrections" before Weaver saw it. He also denied any knowledge of Andrus delivering Weaver's affidavit to the U.S. Attorney's Office.[5]

The interview was largely uneventful, except for Wojnicz, who always had his unique perspective on things. As Jorgensen walked the two agents out of the building, which was in the historic section of Pocatello, he told them it had at one time been a bank and, at another, a whorehouse.

"No kidding," Wojnicz said surveying the interior. "Some may say it still is."[6]

Perhaps in response to Uhlmann's exclusion of Jorgensen, Nevin renewed his request that one of the agents be excluded. As Uhlmann argued against the request Breitsameter walked back and leaned over the rail. "If one of you has to be excluded, it's going to have to be you, Bob."

Wojnicz clenched his jaw. "Fuck that, George, I ain't leaving. I spent two years waiting to see this goddamn thing. Fuck 'em."

Winmill again exercised his discretion for the hearing and allowed both agents to stay, but he told the two sides to work it out for the trial.

THE FOLLOWING DAY, jury selection, the courtroom again leaned decidedly to the left with all counsel seated at the tables closest to the jury, something Winmill acknowledged on the record as "unusual" but which he would allow for the purpose of selecting the jury.[7]

The government had spent a considerable amount of time discussing juries in Idaho. It had come up during the prosecutorial review in Washington, D.C. Uhlmann's peers wanted to know how jurors would perceive the U.S. government going after a local businessman, especially on the heels of the Ruby Ridge fiasco. Breitsameter remained the optimist, as unwavering in his defense of southeast Idaho jurors as he was of Winmill. He said they were not like northern Idaho, which was more commonly associated with the antifederal-government sentiment. Southeastern Idaho shared a border with Utah and was predominantly Mormon. The religion placed a great emphasis on families and the obligations of employers to care for their employees. He believed strongly that a Mormon jury would be offended by Elias's actions.

"Don't believe everything you hear," he had told Hilldorfer. "They're blue-collar, hardworking people who take their jobs as finders of the truth seriously. They're good people. They'll do the right thing."

As Uhlmann stood that morning questioning prospective jurors from the jury pool, he made an analogy to a baseball game and the score being zero to zero at the start. Nevin stood and objected. In Uhlmann's experience it was verboten to object to an attorney's voir dire unless the attorney said something egregious, and concluded it was an intimidation tactic by Nevin in his quest to control the courtroom. After Uhlmann sat down, Nevin stood and attempted to explain to the jury that he had objected because Uhlmann's analogy was wrong. Uhlmann stood and interrupted him.

"Your Honor, I should just make clear, I said the same thing. I said the defendant starts not guilty, there is no score."

Uhlmann might not get control of the courtroom, but he wasn't about to concede it to Nevin. At worst it was going to be a standoff.

The jury picked, they were about to find out.

Friday, April 16, 1999
Opening Statements
Federal Courthouse
Pocatello, Idaho

CHAPTER THIRTY-SEVEN

AT JUST AFTER 8:15 in the morning on the first day of trial, Hilldorfer sat alone in the first pew on the left side of the courtroom. It reminded him of the spartan pews in the Church of the Annunciation on Pittsburgh's North Side where he spent Sunday mornings with his grandfather, who liked to say more people "found religion" in courtrooms than in churches. Hilldorfer considered the empty seats in the jury box and wondered if the jurors would give Allan Elias a strong dose of religion. Voir dire produced no real surprises. Breitsameter described the jury as "fairly typical" for southeast Idaho.

Feeling physically better, Hilldorfer tugged at the sleeves of his French cuff shirt, clasped at the wrist with his father-in-law's black pearl cuff links, and straightened a gold-and-blue-speckled tie. He wore his best suit, a pinstriped Barney's label from his days working undercover in New York City. The government decided to "dress up" during the trial to show respect for the proceedings—even if it didn't accurately reflect their government salaries. If this were to be a heavyweight fight—and it was taking on that type of tension—they would be well dressed for it; Hilldorfer hadn't looked this good since his wedding.

The government would enter the ring confident but cautious. To convict Elias they had to convince all twelve jurors beyond a reasonable doubt that Elias knew there was cyanide in the tank when he ordered Weaver and Dominguez to clean it out. Uhlmann told them he believed that as the lead count in the indictment, the knowing endangerment charge would set the tone for the entire trial. It was the count on which the attorneys, and therefore the jurors, would focus their energy. If the government failed to prove it, the chances of a conviction on the other charges would greatly diminish.

Unlike the government, the defense didn't need to convince any of the jurors that Elias was not guilty. To get a hung jury they only needed to cause one juror to doubt for a moment the government's case.

As if on cue, Nevin stepped in wearing a green-brown wrinkled sport coat, mismatched slacks, and a cheap sports watch—the underpaid defense lawyer representing the indigent defendant. Scott Dominguez entered shortly thereafter, holding Jackie's hand as he made his way down the aisle in the halting walk and trembling gait of an elderly man. He had cut his hair and trimmed his goatee. Dressed in white Dockers, a polo shirt, and new tennis shoes he looked like the angelic kid Hilldorfer first met.

The family slid into the pew behind Hilldorfer—Jackie and Scott followed by Scott's stepfather, Ron, his aunts, grandparents, and his sister and two brothers. Jackie smiled, but she looked apprehensive and tired. With the hour drive from Soda Springs and the three hours it took Scott to get ready in the morning, they had likely been up very early. Even with the extra effort by Uhlmann and Breitsameter to bring the family to court during trial preparation they looked intimidated, talking in whispers, like mourners at a funeral. Power was wielded in courtrooms, and justice dispensed in a manner most laypeople only knew from television courtroom dramas.

Seeking to ease their tension, Hilldorfer leaned over the pew and shook Scott's hand. "Glad you could make it, Scott. You get to see big-shot Allan before he starts wearing an orange jumpsuit."

Scott let out a yelping laugh that caused the family to break into smiles and sit back noticeably more relaxed.

Wojnicz joined Hilldorfer in the front pew. Dressed in a navy blue, two-button suit, starched white shirt, and a tie knotted in a Windsor knot, he looked like an English gentleman having tea.

"Nice suit," Hilldorfer said.

Wojnicz tugged at the knot of his tie. "Got a screaming deal at the Bon, but the shirt is pinching the shit out of me." He swiveled like a kid in church. "Here comes the frog man."

Elias slumped up the aisle in a gray jacket, open-collared shirt, cowboy boots, and a look of disdain. Marshall and two paralegals followed. Marshall's attempt at dressing down was to wear billowy pants that folded over the top of his Gucci loafers.

"Must have borrowed those pants from a circus clown," Wojnicz said.

Hilldorfer kept an eye on the door for Matt Christiansen and Daren Schwartz. After considerable debate about the order of their witnesses, the government decided to start with the two volunteer Caribou County emergency firefighters. Everyone loved firemen, and both Schwartz and Christiansen were prototypical—big, strong, and good-looking. They were also articulate. Uhlmann wanted them to paint a picture for the jury of the scene they came upon, their desperate attempts to rescue Scott, and Elias's unwavering statements that he knew of nothing in the tank but mud and water. It was Hilldorfer's job to make sure the government's witnesses appeared when scheduled, and he was relieved when Schwartz entered. Hilldorfer's relief evaporated, however, when Christiansen followed Schwartz through the doors. Normally a hulking figure, he entered pale and bent over. He looked to be in considerable pain.

"What's wrong with him?" Wojnicz asked.

Hilldorfer's first thought was the stomach flu. "I don't know." He walked to the back of the courtroom. "Everything all right?"

Schwartz nodded to Christiansen. "We had to rush Matt to the emergency room. He's got a kidney stone."

Hilldorfer resisted the urge to overreact. "Are you going to be okay to testify?"

Christiansen straightened with a grunt. "Yeah. Don't worry. I plan to stay right here." He looked past Hilldorfer to the pew with Scott and his family. "It's not right what happened to Scott."

Hilldorfer led them both to a pew outside. Witnesses were not allowed in the courtroom before testifying.

At 9:35 A.M. the paneled wooden door behind the bench opened and Judge Winmill strode through with the hint of a white collar and blue tie showing beneath his flowing black robe. Mike Fica, his law clerk, stood and bellowed like a carnival barker.

"ALL RISE. THE COURT WILL NOW HEAR CRIMINAL CASE No. 98-070-E, THE UNITED STATES VERSUS ALLAN ELIAS."

Winmill's first order of business was to put an agreement on the record regarding the defense's motion to exclude one of the agents. Uhlmann had made a calculated response, arguing that Elias's wife, Midge, who sat in the middle of the courtroom looking southern California trim and tan, had to leave since she was a potential defense witness. The defense exchanged Midge for one of the agents.[1]

After Winmill denied Nevin's request that the trial be delayed to the following Tuesday because an alternate juror had called in sick, Uhlmann stood and inquired about Dominguez's right to testify. At the mention of his name, Dominguez began a monotonic moaning, like the drone of an air conditioner. Jackie's job was to keep Scott under control. Despite Breitsameter's faith, the government suspected Winmill was leaning against allowing Scott to testify. Any sudden outburst in the courtroom could be fatal.

Winmill told Uhlmann he would withhold his decision until he could personally observe Dominguez on the witness stand. It left the government in a bind. Breitsameter had planned to mention in his opening statement that Dominguez would testify. If Winmill ultimately ruled Dominguez could not, the jurors would be left to wonder why he had not done so.

Nevin then sought permission to move about the courtroom during his opening argument as opposed to having to stand at the podium. Breitsameter stood and sought the same freedom—like Uhlmann, not willing to give Nevin an inch. After several minutes, Winmill looked up at the large wall clock.

"Counsel, we are going to proceed. What I am going to do is bring the jury in. My instructions will take perhaps ten minutes. I'll allow Mr. Breitsameter to make his opening statement. Then I'm going to tell the jury that I am giving Mr. Nevin the option . . ." Winmill looked to Nevin. "I don't want to put you in a bad light because I think the timing of this morning has put you where you have to make the jury choose between hunger and allowing Mr. Breitsameter's eloquence to ring in their ears through the lunch hour."

Nevin stood. "Judge, could I suggest we do it this way: Let's simply wait and see how long Mr. Breitsameter's opening statement takes, and if you would just inquire from me at that point, I will simply give you an indication either way, if that's all right."

"All right, that's fine. We will proceed that way. Let's bring the jury in, if you would, please, Mr. Fica."

Fica disappeared through the door near the jury box and reemerged followed by the thirteen jurors, twelve in the box and one alternate. After they had settled into their seats Winmill apologized for the delay and proceeded with his preliminary instructions. Halfway through, a juror's persistent cough forced another fifteen-minute recess. Hilldorfer felt like a fighter coming off his stool at the first-round bell only to have the referee tell him to return to his corner.

When the jury returned Winmill finished his preliminary instructions. Then, without fanfare, he turned to Breitsameter. "Mr. Breitsameter, you may make your opening statement to the jury."

Uhlmann had been torn about whether to give the opening or the closing, but he and Breitsameter agreed that Breitsameter should give the government's opening. It was not just that Breitsameter was the local assistant U.S. attorney. His entire presence gave him the down-home feel of a country lawyer—Jimmy Stewart in a courtroom. Breitsameter had never rehearsed an opening statement in his career but Uhlmann had insisted. The opening needed to set out a road map of the evidence and the government's themes. Uhlmann would hit those themes when he gave the government's closing argument, making the entire trial come full circle.

Breitsameter believed in the "rule of three"—that people only remembered three things. The three points he wanted the jury to remember from his opening were: (1) Elias had specialized knowledge regarding cyanide; (2) Scott's injury was not an isolated incident—an accident— as the defense would argue; and (3) Elias lied to the emergency personnel and the emergency room doctor as Scott lay dying. He rehearsed his opening to the trial team at the courthouse after the jury selection. It did not go well. Uhlmann thought it too disjointed and perhaps *too* understated. To Hilldorfer it appeared Breitsameter was trying to do the whole thing off the top of his head. Breitsameter listened politely, then went back to his hotel across the street from the Ameritel and reworked it. Later that night they all met again in David Uhlmann's suite and he tried again. It was better, but still needed work.

Breitsameter stood, pushed back his chair and approached the jury, notepad in hand. Hilldorfer closed his eyes and listened as Breitsameter thanked the jurors, and began.

"This case, the United States versus Allan Elias, is about the dignity of human life," Breitsameter started. "Specifically, it is about how the defendant, Allan Elias, sent employees into a storage tank on August 26 and August 27, 1996, in utter disregard of those individuals' human life, exposing them to cyanide, and exposing them to the risk associated with this storage tank without taking any basic, fundamental safety precautions to ensure that this was done safely."

Breitsameter looked at his notes. If his nerves made him lose his place it was fortuitous because the pause was dramatic. "As a result of what the defendant did that day, on August 27, one of those employees, a young twenty-year-old individual from Soda Springs, Idaho, sustained permanent and severe brain injuries. That's what this case is about."

It was a strong opening. Emotional without being melodramatic, it rang with sincerity. Everything about Breitsameter said to the jury "I'm telling you the truth. You can trust me." He gave the jury a detailed accounting of the charges being brought against Elias, the elements the government would be required to prove, and the evidence that would support each element. He slipped once, despite—or perhaps because— they had all emphasized the need to avoid calling what happened to Scotty an "accident." He was quick to correct his error.

"You may hear witnesses describe what happened that day as an accident. A tragic accident. And it is tragic, but it was not an accident. This was a course of conduct by this defendant over a period of time in which he had knowledge of the dangers, had knowledge of the risks, and he knowingly sent his employees into that tank without taking basic safety precautions. This was not an isolated occurrence."

Breitsameter turned his attention to Elias. It was a trial tactic to anticipate the defense's opening and undermine it, and he anticipated Nevin would try to humanize Elias as a dedicated family man and business entrepreneur.

"He is an intelligent individual," Breitsameter said, not just conceding but adopting that fact. He kept one hand on the podium. "He's knowledgeable about scientific processes, chemical processes. He holds a patent. He has a patent on a system, which you'll hear testimony about, a cyanide leaching system, which basically he uses to leach or to draw silver out of materials by using cyanide. And so he knows about how those processes work. He is also an attorney, and he knows about the liabilities of an admission, accepting responsibility for what happened.

"You will hear he's also an individual with the financial resources to provide safety equipment. On August 26 and 27, he had the ability to ensure, the financial resources to ensure, that he could send those employees into that tank safely. That equipment could have been obtained for free by going to Kerr-McGee. You will hear about Soda Springs and a community that is very committed to the safety of their employees. And if the defendant simply went to Kerr-McGee they would have gladly and voluntarily provided Allan Elias, the defendant, or anyone else, the safety equipment that could have prevented what happened that day to Scott Dominguez." Again he paused. "That's the defendant."

Hilldorfer watched the jurors. At least a few of them shifted their gaze from Breitsameter to Elias, who sat beside Marshall frowning and shaking his head.

Breitsameter saved Elias's lies to the emergency responders to near the end, hoping it would indeed ring in the jurors' ears while Nevin gave his opening. Breitsameter spoke of Daren Schwartz, who bore the burden of trying to save Scott Dominguez that day. "He needed to know what was in the tank. He asked the defendant on three occasions, 'What was in the tank?' " Breitsameter raised a finger with each response.

" 'It's only water.'

" 'I don't know.'

" 'I don't know what happened.'

"He asked the defendant, 'Could it be cyanide?'

"He answers 'No.'

"It was a lie to protect himself. At that moment, the defendant was more concerned about protecting himself than saving Scott Dominguez."

Breitsameter summarized the testimony doctors would give regarding Dominguez's condition and his prognosis. Knowing what followed, Hilldorfer sat forward. Behind him, Scotty's rhythmic moaning increased in volume and intensity. Hilldorfer hoped Jackie had a firm grip on her son's hand.

"Scott Dominguez will testify," Breitsameter said, "and he will have difficulty. You may have difficulty hearing him, but he will describe to you why he went in that tank that day, why he went in without protection." Breitsameter paused to let the jury consider the question and the potential answers, then he said, "He trusted the defendant. . . . He trusted . . . the defendant. He thought that he would not send him into this type of condition. I ask that you listen very patiently to Scott as he testifies. He will not testify that he consented to what happened to him that day as may be suggested to you here by the defendant."

With that, Breitsameter concluded, thanked the jury, and sat down.

Hilldorfer felt a sense of relief. It was a good showing, not a knockout but solid.

Winmill looked to Nevin, and, as they had prearranged, he gave Nevin the option of not having to force the jury to sit through the lunch hour. "Mr. Nevin, we've put you in a difficult situation. Do you want to go now or would you rather delay and go after lunch? It's at your option." He said it without it sounding rehearsed.

Nevin shot out of his chair like it was spring-loaded. "Your Honor, I believe I would like to go now."

"Would you?" Winmill sounded almost surprised. "All right."

Nevin moved across the courtroom like he might climb right over the railing and get in the jury box with the jurors. "Members of the jury, I am glad to fight with my opponent, the prosecutors in this case, but I am ordinarily loath to fight with hunger, yours or mine. And a big, big part of me, as Judge Winmill just looked at me, said, 'Let's go to lunch. Let's have everybody go to lunch and get something to eat and come back and talk about this afterward.' But I just cannot let the things that Mr. Breitsameter just said to you go unanswered, even for lunch. I'm going to try to do it quickly and I'm going to try to do it succinctly, but I ask your indulgence in allowing me to do it now because I think it's that important."

Hilldorfer shook his head. Nevin had taken a routine issue like whether or not to break for the lunch hour and used it to imply a sense of urgency to correct the government's lies. He was clearly as good as his reputation. He was very, very good.

Nevin attacked Breitsameter's suggestion that Elias failed to properly test the sludge in the tank and said any argument that Elias only tested it for silver was nothing short of ludicrous. Throughout his opening he commanded the courtroom, his arm cocked over his hip, hand at the edge of his pocket like a gunslinger about to draw. He was both theatrical and eloquent in his attack. "And if you heard Mr. Breitsameter slip at one point and refer to this as an 'accident,' and tell you that he expected that I would refer to it as an 'accident,' I do. It was an accident. It was a freak accident. It should not have happened. Nothing about this situation reasonably indicated to Allan Elias that it would happen. He had tested it and he had tasted it. And he also knew some things about that material that was in that tank."

He turned his attention to the morning of the accident and said Elias held a two-hour safety meeting. "The evidence is going to be that Allan Elias told the employees 'Do it by the book.' That's what he told them." He added that Elias had relied on Thornock and Smith, experienced workers, to do the job safely.

For Hilldorfer, the hardest part of having an intimate knowledge of the facts and evidence was hearing things he knew to be untrue, and wondering if the jurors would buy it. The uncertainty—the crapshoot that made trying cases a risk—was both the adrenaline rush good trial attorneys fed on, and the thing that kept them awake at 3:00 A.M. feeling nauseated.

"Let me take a minute and introduce you to Allan Elias." Nevin turned to Elias. "Allan Elias is a man sixty-one years old. He has been married since 1958 to Midge Elias, who is the lady seated right back there." Nevin pointed to Midge Elias, dressed in a dark blue pantsuit. She gave an almost imperceptible nod of her head. "Allan and Midge have been married for forty-one years. They have three children: a boy, Eric, who's forty, who is a physicist in California; a son who's thirty-nine, Ryan, who is a television news reporter; and a daughter, Batina, thirty-four, who is a lawyer in New York City. Batina's husband is an assistant United States attorney."

Hilldorfer wondered if bringing up Elias's family was a mistake. Like all good defense lawyers Nevin wanted to personalize his client to the jury, to remove the stigma of the villain, but Hilldorfer couldn't help but notice that none of Elias's children were present in the courtroom. He wondered if the jurors did, too.[2]

Nevin then began a long discourse about leaching silver from mining waste using cyanide and Elias's attempts to make money doing it before the bottom fell out of the silver market. His elaboration wasn't overly technical, but it was academic and his audience was a group that had been denied lunch, and whose blood sugar level was probably rapidly waning. Hilldorfer thought it a mistake. Perhaps Nevin did also. He interrupted himself and said, "I have got about ten more minutes, I think."

Judge Winmill looked at the jurors. "Mr. Nevin, I will leave it up to you. We could take a short break and then come back and let you use that ten minutes after lunch, at your option. But if it's much more than ten minutes, I think we'll need to take a break because there may be hypoglycemic jurors here that need some food."

"There's clearly a hypoglycemic lawyer in the room, maybe even more," Nevin responded, not losing the chance to interact with Winmill in front of the jury. "Yes, I think I can do this in ten minutes and then we can go get something to eat," he said, making it sound almost as if he and Winmill would be dining together.

Nevin was true to his word, finishing his discourse on the cyanide leaching process in ten minutes.

"I believe you will find that Allan Elias would never have endangered his workers in that way. And that he did not, in fact, do that. And for all these reasons, I anticipate at the end of this trial, I will be here again and I will be asking you to return verdicts of not guilty on all these counts."

Winmill told the jurors not to discuss the facts of the case with each other or anyone else, then dismissed them.

Wojnicz flipped closed his legal pad. "Where're we going for lunch? I cut out some coupons for the Smith deli."

Hilldorfer stood. "That sounds fine." He turned for the door and saw Christiansen and Schwartz in the doorway. Christiansen looked pale white. Whether it was remnants of the flu or a foreboding, Hilldorfer had suddenly lost his appetite.

◆   ◆   ◆

DAREN SCHWARTZ took the stand at 2:27 P.M., his goatee neatly trimmed. He was dressed in a white starched shirt and slate gray pants. He knew he was the government's first witness and thought it a heavy burden, but his testimony was clear and powerful. As Uhlmann took him through his testimony he paused and thoughtfully rolled his eyes to the ceiling as if re-creating the events that day for the jury. Uhlmann used Schwartz's considerable knowledge about proper safety procedures at industrial plants to spell out what safety equipment Elias should have, but did not have at Evergreen the day of the accident. They had an expert on this topic, but having a fireman and employee of Monsanto specifically detail the equipment made a much more powerful point—people who worked at these facilities knew how things were supposed to be done, and the tragic consequences that could result when they were not.

As the five o'clock hour approached, Uhlmann chose to end with another powerful contrast he wanted the jurors to consider over the extended weekend—trial would not resume until Tuesday. Schwartz testified that normally when responding to an accident or fire the owner of a facility overwhelmed the firefighters with information trying to help.

"How did the defendant, Allan Elias, react to you?" Uhlmann asked.

"He offered no information. When we asked for information, we got no details. I got the same answers each time, that it was only water and sludge material in the tank. I did not find my conversations with him to be helpful in identifying the material in the tank."

With a warning to the jurors not to discuss or read about the case, Winmill recessed until Tuesday.

Saturday, April 17 to Wednesday, April 21, 1999
Federal Courthouse
Pocatello, Idaho
United States v. Elias, Trial Days 2 and 3

CHAPTER THIRTY-EIGHT

HILLDORFER AND WOJNICZ spent the long weekend trying to track down and interview witnesses on an extended list provided by the defense. They were interested in two in particular—a former Elias employee and current Kerr-McGee employee named Kenny McAllister, and Dick Anderson, an employee in Kerr-McGee's lab. In between their attempts to talk to the witnesses, Wojnicz's mission in life was to buy a huge diesel generator to prepare for the impending Y2K. Hilldorfer went to clear his head at the gym in town, but it wasn't easy. He'd climb on a StairMaster only to find Nevin running on a treadmill or Marshall walking beside him reading legal briefs. Craig Jorgensen would also wander in and the three men would huddle in a corner and whisper.

WHEN SCHWARTZ RETOOK the stand Tuesday morning, Uhlmann had to continually fend off Marshall's objections and frequent sidebars— discussions with the judge at the bench outside the juror's hearing. Attorneys were cognizant of preventing their opponents from getting into a rhythm, and objections were a good way to do it. Most judges, however, did not take time for sidebars. It slowed the proceedings.

"They get together so much they should start dating," Hilldorfer said to Wojnicz.

"Maybe Winmill thinks they'll eventually get sick of being that close to each other," Wojnicz replied.

Uhlmann ended Schwartz's testimony on a high note.

"Finally, Mr. Schwartz, Mr. Nevin referred to this as a freak accident. From what you saw that day, would you say this was a freak accident?"

"No, I would not. There are plenty of safety procedures that are out there that should have been followed that would have easily prevented this incident from occurring."

Marshall stood and took the lectern. "Mr. Schwartz, do you drink milk?"

Schwartz looked like he hadn't heard the question correctly. "Yes, I do."

"Do you ever go on vacation?"

Again he paused. "Yes, I do."

Wojnicz elbowed Hilldorfer in the ribs, each remembering Marshall's ineloquent cross-examinations during the suppression hearing. "Where the hell is he going with this?"

The prosecutors were equally perplexed.

"And sometimes when you go away for a couple of days, you come back and you open your refrigerator and you find some milk in there, right?" Marshall asked.

"That is correct."

"Can you tell me that you have never tasted or smelled what's in a milk carton in your refrigerator to determine whether or not that material is suitable for serving to your children?"

"I have probably smelled it and accidentally tasted some stuff I wish I wouldn't have, yes."

"Please," Hilldorfer said, realizing Marshall was trying to analogize smelling and tasting the milk to Elias's claim that he tested the sludge by smelling and tasting it. Hilldorfer had asked Dr. Joe about the argument and Lowry dismissed it as a cheap ploy. The danger, Lowry said, wasn't putting the material in your mouth; it was the reaction created when the acid mixed with the cyanide to cause hydrogen cyanide gas. Another government expert, Daniel Titlebaum, said Elias's putting the material in his mouth and calling it as safe as "ordinary shampoo" was "like taking the rattle off a rattlesnake." It made the employees think it was harmless when it remained very dangerous.

Marshall continued. "And you—in those circumstances—you don't think of that as being dangerous, correct?"

"Not necessarily dangerous, no. Unhealthy, yes."

"Because you know what the material is in your refrigerator, right?"

"Correct."

"And so, if you taste the milk in your refrigerator and it tastes sour, you know it's sour milk, but it's not going to hurt you any, correct?"

Uhlmann stood. "Your Honor, I will have to object at this point, we've gone far enough. The relevancy is beyond me."

"Well, it's cross-examination, I'll give counsel some leeway, objection is overruled."

It also became readily apparent that the defense would place the blame for Dominguez's injuries on everyone except Allan Elias. Marshall insinuated Schwartz knew early during the rescue that the tank possibly contained cyanide and communicated that knowledge to hospital personnel. The clear implication was that Obray and the hospital staff were somehow slow to treat Dominguez. He insinuated that the Evergreen employees had also screwed up, then suggested Schwartz had also failed to follow safety procedures, endangering the men in his command.

Schwartz's face reddened and he wanted to ask Winmill, "What is wrong with our legal system?"[1] But he bit his tongue and responded that he made his decisions and took some risks because otherwise they stood no chance of saving Dominguez.

"But you have acknowledged here today that you personally feel that you made a mistake?" Marshall said.

Uhlmann was on his feet. "Your Honor, I will object, asked and answered."

"Sustained. Counsel, it has been."

Marshall persisted. "You have not been charged with knowingly endangering—"

"Your Honor."

"Sustained." Winmill looked down at Marshall. "Counsel."

"You made a mistake, but you didn't do it on purpose, right, Mr. Schwartz?"

"Your Honor . . ." Uhlmann started.

"Overruled, I will allow it. The witness may answer this question."

"In the speed and the atmosphere of the conditions we were in, I did not have the time to clearly sit down and develop a plan and do things the way I would have liked to have, no," Schwartz said.

When Marshall concluded Uhlmann charged back to the lectern and gave Schwartz the chance to explain the difference between making mistakes in an emergency situation, with a life at issue, and not taking safety precautions during a routine cleaning operation. Then he asked Schwartz if Elias had assured him there was nothing dangerous in the tank.

"As you are testifying here today, is there any question in your mind as to whether you asked Allan Elias whether there was cyanide in the tank?"

"No, there is not."

"Is there any question in your mind about how he answered?"

"No, there is not."

"How did he answer?"

"He answered that there was nothing in the tank that could have harmed anybody, basically that there was water and sludge material."

Christiansen followed Schwartz, noticeably more comfortable than the agents had seen him on Friday with the kidney stone. Christiansen painted a similarly vivid picture of the rescue operation and Elias's lack of cooperation. Following Christiansen, Breitsameter called Roger Sears, a muscular, balding Sean Connery look-alike with a thin mustache. A captain with the Pocatello Fire Department, Sears had provided the government with one of the funniest moments in their trial preparation. Hilldorfer cold-called him and asked if Sears would meet the prosecutors at the Old Federal Courthouse. Sears said he was in the middle of a training exercise. "What's this about?"

"Scott Dominguez."

"Hang on."

Minutes later the trial team looked out the window to see a fire engine hauling down the street into the parking lot. Four to five firemen got out in full gear, running up the flight of stairs to the courtroom like it was on fire. Sears walked in, a commanding presence in full gear. He turned to his men. "You guys sit there."

They sat.

Then he turned to Hilldorfer and extended a hand. "What do you need?"[2]

Breitsameter had Sears contrast the type of safety equipment he and his men wore while taking samples of potentially hazardous materials with the equipment Elias had provided his employees. Sears also testified there was no indication the sludge was going to be reused, an important point to refute the defense's argument that the material was to be used in the fertilizer process, making it a product and not a waste. Sears was also supposed to testify that the samples from the tank showed high concentrations of cyanide, but Nevin objected that Sears could not testify until Winmill decided whether the sampling procedure was valid. It was the SW846 problem again. Winmill agreed. Breitsameter would have to get another witness to testify what the samples revealed.

Breitsameter tried to do that the following morning when he called Victor Baron to the stand, but Nevin again objected. After a sidebar Winmill cleared the jury and he did not hide his displeasure at the pace of the proceedings.

"Well, Mr. Nevin, my concern is— I don't want to send the jury home and conduct a two-day Daubert test right now, a Daubert hearing. I guess if we have to, we have to, but you better pack your bags because we are going to be here until about probably the end of July before this trial is completed."

After a spirited argument, Winmill brokered a compromise. He'd allow Baron to testify that the tests showed cyanide, but not the levels they contained until after Dr. Lowry testified and Winmill decided the testing was scientifically accepted.

When the jury returned, Baron testified the tests showed hydrogen cyanide. Unable to ask him about the levels, there was nothing more Breitsameter could do.

Brian Smith followed.

The government would paint Smith and Thornock's efforts to save Dominguez as truly heroic. Sensing this, and seeking to undermine it, the defense sought to discredit Smith in his small Mormon community with evidence he'd been fired from a previous job for refusing to take a drug test. Winmill took the matter up that morning outside the jury's presence and told the defense that unless they could link Smith's past use of marijuana to the accident he would not allow it.

Smith took the witness stand in dark blue jeans and a plaid shirt, a white T-shirt visible below the neckline, and his ponytail pulled back. As Uhlmann walked him through his background Smith appeared tentative and nervous and had to be reminded to keep his voice up. Smith had told Hilldorfer he didn't want to say anything wrong. He felt like he'd let Scott down when he'd been unable to get him out of the tank and had to live with that the rest of his life. He didn't want to let him down again.

Smith explained that a standard day at Evergreen started with a meeting in the trailer where Elias parceled out assignments. He set up the morning of the accident by discussing the previous afternoon when Elias sent Weaver and Dominguez into the tank without safety equipment. He said he had expressed his concerns about the lack of safety equipment to Elias, but Elias ignored him. Then Smith talked of his efforts to rescue Dominguez. His posture became rigid, his voice cracked, and his eyes watered.

Uhlmann let the jury know how frustratingly close Smith came to getting Dominguez out. "How close did you get to Mr. Thornock?"

"About two ladder rungs away is as close as I could get," he said, visibly upset. "At that point I didn't have enough strength to keep ahold of the ladder and keep ahold of Scott, too."

"How come you didn't have enough strength?"

Smith shook his head and pinched his lips. "I didn't have any oxygen.

There was— When I first entered the tank, one of the first things I noticed was a burnt-almond odor inside the tank."

"Do you know what a burnt-almond odor is?"

Smith nodded. "That's what cyanide smells like."

Nevin wasted no time on cross using Smith's experience and knowledge against him. As anticipated, he tried to paint Smith as a "foreman" and blame him for what happened. It was particularly upsetting to Smith because he had felt powerless to stop Elias.

"Did you know they were going into the tank?"

Smith paused. "Yes, I knew they were going into the tank."

"Allan wasn't there when they went into the tank, was he?"

Smith dropped his eyes. The words rolled off his tongue with bitterness. "No, he wasn't."

After Smith stepped from the stand, Miller called Dr. John Wayne Obray. The government wanted to follow Smith's emotional testimony with their evidence that Elias had denied there was cyanide in the tank to Obray while he tried to save Dominguez's life—possibly the most damaging witness against Elias.

Obray took the witness stand in a sport coat, solid-colored tie, and dark-colored slacks. For a big man he was soft-spoken. Miller took him through his medical background to the fateful day he was on call in the Caribou County Memorial Hospital emergency room. She had Obray explain the dramatic moments as he struggled to save Dominguez's life, and his tense, personal attempt to figure out what could have possibly caused the injury. Having set up that life-and-death struggle, Miller asked, "At some point during the early afternoon of August 27, 1996, did the defendant, Mr. Elias, come personally to your hospital?"

"Yes, he came to the emergency room while Mr. Dominguez was receiving treatment."

"And did you again speak to him there?" Miller asked.

"Yes, I did."

"And what did you ask him?"

"Well, he asked what Scott's condition was and I told him it was very bad, in fact, I thought he was going to die. And I asked him, you know, 'Do you have any more information about what could be in the tank, because, you know, I think it's cyanide.'" Obray paused, the courtroom as quiet as a sleeping child. Hilldorfer looked over at the jurors. Some were sitting forward, focused on Obray. "And he didn't have any more information of what was in the tank."

Miller looked at her notes, letting the implication seep in. "Has he recovered from the injuries?"

Obray shook his head as if to say "you silly girl." "Oh, no, no. From the first time I saw him after the return from the rehabilitation unit, he has deteriorated, in my opinion, and that would be the opinion that I have gotten by correspondence from the University of Utah as well. He has more difficulty with spasticity of his muscles, has more difficulty with his speech, and that was kind of what they had expected when they first saw him."

"And are these circumstances permanent?"

"Yes," Obray said solemnly. "And progressive."

Thursday and Friday, April 22–23, 1999
Federal Courthouse
Pocatello, Idaho
***United States v. Elias,* Trial Days 4 and 5**

CHAPTER THIRTY-NINE

THERESA COLE flew in from Dry Prong, Louisiana, making numerous connections to reach Pocatello. Cole was attending Louisiana State University, studying biology and pursuing her dream of becoming a dentist. She had been back to Soda Springs just once—to attend her father's funeral. Gene Thornock had attended with Scott Dominguez and Thornock told Hilldorfer that when Cole walked into the funeral service Dominguez moaned as if struck with pain.

"If ever there was true love," he said, "that was it."

The government had debated putting Cole on the stand. They were concerned it might appear to the jury that they were tugging on heartstrings. On the other hand, Cole had relevant testimony about Scott's condition the night before and the morning of the accident. She could also speak to prior incidences when he had been burned by acid. And no one was denying that Cole would serve to illustrate the full extent of Scott's loss. She walked into the courtroom, no bigger than a minute, as Hilldorfer's grandfather liked to say, in a tight-fitting, dark blue dress, black stockings, and heels. Dominguez moaned at the sight of her and it was as Thornock had described it, a haunting, wounded wail. Cole winced, looked over, acknowledged the family with a tentative smile, and continued to the stand.

Sensing Cole was nervous, Brietsameter attempted to ease her into her testimony, but Nevin would have none of it. He objected repeatedly from the start and asked for multiple sidebars to argue Cole's testimony was not relevant. If it was Nevin's intent to disrupt Breitsameter's flow and Cole's emotional impact, it worked. Her direct examination was rough and disjointed. She testified about the two occasions in which Dominguez had been sprayed with acid and how he had refused to go to the doctor for fear Elias would fire him. Breitsameter asked her to describe how the accident changed Dominguez's life. She wept openly, her voice catching.

"Before Scott's accident, Scott was so charming and very physically active, so funny and sweet and kind and bright. After Scott's accident, the significant amount of brain damage that he received because of his accident, he's still so sweet, but Scott is very, very, slow, still very kind. He's in a lot of pain a lot of the time. He doesn't really function like an adult anymore. He's not healthy. He has a lot of physical problems. He used to be so very independent and now he's not independent at all. He has to have somebody take care of him all the time. But Scott has always remained very stubborn, very sweet."

Nevin declined to cross-examine her.

As Cole left the stand, Breitsameter gave Hilldorfer and Wojnicz a frustrated shake of the head. Sensing that Cole felt the same way, Hilldorfer left the courtroom and met her in the U.S. Attorney's Office. She was crying, blotting her eyes.

"How did I do?" she asked.

"You did great, Theresa. Thanks for coming. I know it was difficult for you to get here."

She shook her head. "No. Thank you, Joe. I've wanted to do this for so long. I'm so relieved I had the chance to tell the family how bad I felt about having to leave."

AFTER COLE the government changed focus. They wanted to prove Elias knew about the search warrant, staged the locker room of equipment, and forged the safety manual and confined-space permit. That brought Sean Stevens to the stand, the confident kid from the hole in the ground in Las Vegas. Stevens testified about the staging of the locker room and burying the waste. He also said Elias had him sign a document indicating he had safety training and received safety equipment, neither of which was true.

Marshall tried to use the evidence to imply Stevens was dishonest, but Hilldorfer's instincts about Stevens proved accurate. He didn't appear intimidated by the process or Marshall's attack. When Marshall asked, "So, when you put your initials down there you were putting something down that was false, isn't that right?" Stevens shot back. "When I put my initials down there the only thing I had ever done is set foot in the trailer, I'd never even been on the plant before. He told me he would show me where they were at, which I was never shown."

Marshall's final line of questioning was the most curious. He spent an extended amount of time asking Stevens exactly where he buried the cyanide sludge and implied it contradicted what he had told Hilldorfer and Wojnicz.

"Who cares?" Hilldorfer said. "What does it matter exactly where he buried it?"

BEFORE COURT FRIDAY morning, counsel met Winmill in his chambers. Marshall was sick, likely the unfortunate recipient of the flu that felled Uhlmann and Hilldorfer. Nevin requested he be allowed to explain Marshall's absence from the courtroom to the jury. Winmill agreed. Uhlmann believed it improper for an attorney to address the jury for any reason except in opening and closing statements. He viewed Nevin's request as another small psychological ploy to interact with the jurors, but instead of objecting he held it as a chit to be cashed in later.

After Nevin explained Marshall's absence to the jury, Uhlmann called Lorinda Wallace to the stand. Uhlmann remained uncertain how an Idaho jury would react to federal agents descending on a local business and wanted to soften that impact through Wallace, who was female, young, and attractive. She was also competent. Wallace no longer worked for the EPA/CID. She had moved on to the Department of Defense, working on top-secret projects. She confirmed that during the search warrant Hilldorfer asked Elias for all of his testing materials and equip-

ment and that the only thing Elias produced was the box of pH strips, saying, "This is all the sampling information that I have."

Wallace also confirmed that the agents had seized a safety notebook,
an MSDS notebook, and a Kerr-McGee safety manual found in the back
of Elias's home office. It seemed a curious introduction by Uhlmann, but
the reason became readily apparent, as did his choice to have Wallace
follow Stevens's testimony that Elias had been tipped about the search
and had staged the locker room. Uhlmann asked Wallace to show the
Evergreen safety book to the jury and she explained how the references
to cyanide had been whited out, implying that a rushed and harried Elias
had copied Kerr-McGee's book but didn't think or have the time to re-
copy the pages he'd doctored. Uhlmann also had Wallace review the employee handbook that supposedly recorded that each employee had
received safety training. Wallace testified that every signature from 1992
to 1996 was in the same handwriting, and next to each signature were the
initials "AE."

Nevin's cross-examination of Wallace focused not so much on the content of the safety book but on the fact that Elias had one at his Evergreen
office. Uhlmann repeatedly objected that Nevin's questions bordered on
argument. Winmill agreed, but Nevin again made his points without so-
liciting answers from Wallace.

"If a person said to 'Do it by the book' would you think that they might
well have been referring to something like this?" he asked holding up the
safety manual.

Uhlmann shot out of his chair. "Objection, calls for speculation."

"Sustained."

Bill Reese, who inspected the lab with Wallace, followed her to the
stand. He detailed the testing and safety equipment they collected. Breitsameter had Reese take the Air-Pac, which the defense was calling a "self-
contained breathing apparatus," from the trunk and confirm it had been
manufactured in 1958.

"Does the label itself reference the conditions that that Scott Air-Pac is
not appropriate for use in?" Breitsameter asked.

Reese took a moment to consider it, though he knew the answer. "Yes.
It says it's not appropriate for use in a cyanide atmosphere."

Winmill had requested that they end the day at 4:00 P.M. to allow jurors and his court staff an early start on their commute home for the
weekend. Reese's examination was anticipated to be lengthy and techni-

cal. Wanting to comply with the judge's request and to send the jurors home for the weekend with something powerful to consider, Breitsameter interrupted Reese's testimony. He called Boyd Schvaneveldt, Kerr-McGee's production maintenance superintendent, the number two man at the facility in Soda Springs.

In 1996, Schvaneveldt had been the staff safety and health specialist and had implemented new OSHA regulations and safety rules. Under Schvaneveldt, Kerr-McGee had become a Star Facility, meaning it had an exemplary safety program. It also cooperated with the other Soda Springs companies to ensure worker safety. All of this seemingly explained Schvaneveldt's presence at Evergreen immediately after the call from dispatch that a man had gone down in a tank, but that wasn't why the government called him.

"Did you know the defendant, Allan Elias?" Brietsameter asked.

"I knew Allan," Schvaneveldt said, using the past tense.

Hilldorfer and Wojnicz had interviewed Schvaneveldt at his ranch. He looked like a science-type, short hair and glasses, but was also a horse-breeder. He had a Kerr-McGee attorney present and had been careful to distance Kerr-McGee from Evergreen, characterizing the relationship between the companies by saying that Elias was buying "product," though in reality Kerr-McGee was paying Elias.

"And how did you know the defendant, Allan Elias?" Brietsameter asked.

"Allan and Evergreen Resources was buying by-products from us and he would come to Kerr-McGee frequently to discuss sampling and the things that were going on between the companies."

Breitsameter knew Schvaneveldt was walking a difficult line. He had allegiance to his employer but also seemed to have genuine sympathy for what had happened to Scott Dominguez. Though there were things Breitsameter could do to highlight the relationship between Kerr-McGee and Elias, he made a calculated decision to focus only on Elias.

"Okay. And did he know that you were the safety person at Kerr-McGee at that time?"

"Yes."

"Did he ever come to you to talk about safety matters prior to August 27, 1996?"

"No."

Despite this, on the morning after the accident Elias showed up at

Schvaneveldt's Kerr-McGee office at 6:00 A.M. talking about confined-space permits. Schvaneveldt said he gave Elias the Kerr-McGee safety manual and told him the requirements and equipment needed for a confined-space permit and Elias left. At 2:00 P.M. that same day, Schvaneveldt drove back to the Evergreen facility. He said it was to discuss a "research and development project" with Elias, a curious act given what had happened the day before, and his testimony that he had never gone to the Evergreen facility prior to August 27, 1996.

Brietsameter handed Schvaneveldt the confined-space permit that Elias said he had filled out the morning of the accident. "Could you tell the jury just briefly how it is that you saw that, what's been represented as a confined-space entry permit. How did you see it on the occasion at Evergreen Resources on the twenty-eighth?"

"When I was down there Allan was just sitting at his desk and he showed me the permit. Let me look at it."

"Did you ask to see it?"

"No."

"Had you had some discussion with him about the permit before he provided it to you?"

"Just early that morning about a confined space, the requirements for a confined-space permit."

"Did he ask you to review it to determine whether it was in any way appropriate?"

"No, he did not."

"And so, do you know why he showed it to you at that time?"

"No."

The implications were clear. Elias went to Kerr-McGee to learn what he needed to know to prepare a confined-space safety permit, then went back to Evergreen and used the Kerr-McGee safety manual as a template. Nevin had his work cut out for him. On cross he had Schvaneveldt discuss the inadequacies of Elias's confined-space permit, including the fact that none of the employees had signed it, as required. It seemed a curious line of inquiry until Nevin asked the ultimate question.

"And there was every opportunity for him to have made this exactly the same way as the way you do it if he had wanted to, isn't that correct?"

Breitsameter objected that Nevin was arguing, but Winmill overruled him. The objection, however, was well-timed. Schvaneveldt asked Nevin to repeat the question. Instead, Nevin rephrased it.

"There would have been every opportunity if Mr. Elias were about the business of making a phony confined-space entry permit, for it to have been identical to—"

Brietsameter was up in a hurry. "Your Honor, objection."

Winmill was not pleased. "Mr. Nevin, you went over the edge. I will sustain the objection."

Again, however, Nevin had made his point.

THE FOLLOWING MORNING, Saturday, April 24, Hilldorfer was working in the U.S. Attorney's Office conference room when paralegals working for Marshall and Nevin brought over a box of beaker bottles, allegedly given to Elias by Dick Anderson, the employee in Kerr-McGee's lab. The defense intended to argue the bottles contained chemicals commonly used in a titration test to check a sample for cyanide. The implication was that Elias tested the sludge before he sent Weaver and Dominguez into the tank. Uhlmann had anticipated the argument but dismissed it because the only "testing equipment" Elias had produced was the box of pH strips and because Wallace had testified that the glass equipment in the back of the trailer was covered in dust and dirt, indicating no recent use. Hilldorfer pulled out the beaker bottles from the box. They had a problem.

He and Wojnicz jumped in the car and took a ride out to Thatcher, Idaho, about twenty-five miles south of Soda Springs. Dick Anderson's home, a meticulous white rambler with a porch, was in the midst of large fields. The woman who answered the door didn't blanch when told they were federal agents. Dick Anderson was not home. They told her they'd wait outside.

When Hilldorfer pulled the beaker bottles from the box the first thing he noticed was someone had written a date on them. *June 1996.* It implied Elias received the beakers, and ran a titration test before he sent Dominguez and Weaver into the tank in August.

"There's no good reason for anyone to write the date on the bottles," Hilldorfer said to Wojnicz while they waited for Anderson in the sweltering summer sun. "It's just too damned convenient."

Late in the afternoon a car drove up and a man and young boy got out. Anderson looked like a Midwestern farmer born to ride a John Deere tractor—rawboned and balding with callus-rough hands. He told the agents that he recalled giving the beakers to Elias but could not recall when he did so. He said nothing about writing the date on the bottles. Both agents thought Anderson appeared evasive, but there was not much more they could do.

They returned to the Ameritel Hotel late at night, tired and frustrated. As they drove into the parking lot of the L-shaped building they saw a familiar light on in a familiar room on the third floor at the back of the lot. Uhlmann paced in front of the window, reading.

"Should we tell him tonight?" Wojnicz asked.

"You want to sleep or you want to win?" Hilldorfer said, repeating one of Uhlmann's favorite expressions, and they got out to tell him about the beakers.

Monday and Tuesday, April 25–26, 1999
Federal Courthouse
Pocatello, Idaho
United States v. Elias, Days 6 and 7

CHAPTER FORTY

THAT MONDAY, the government began its attempt to discredit the defense's argument that the incident was an unfortunate accident. To do this, they needed to get into evidence Elias's long history of OSHA violations and injuries to other employees working in confined spaces. Uhlmann started with Danny Rice, who continued to live in the community but no longer worked in Soda Springs. He was flying to the Bay Area auditioning for stunt work in the movies. Hilldorfer had tracked him down through Rice's girlfriend.

Rice testified about his own injury as well as an injury to a co-worker named Fred Mancini. He told the jury about Elias's telephone call to the hospital when Elias swore at Rice and told him if he wasn't back at work he was fired. Uhlmann attempted to solicit from Rice that he had told OSHA someone at Evergreen was going to die, but Nevin objected and after a sidebar Winmill did not allow the testimony.

Nevin attacked Rice as an untruthful and bitter former employee, suggesting he didn't like Elias because Elias honored an order from the State of Idaho that Rice's wages be garnished to pay past child support. Nevin also suggested Rice was dishonest because he refused Elias's offer to have his job back because he wanted to continue to receive workmen's compensation benefits. It was a mistake. It gave Rice the chance to say what Winmill prevented on direct examination.

"Workmen's Comp said that he had a job for me in the tool room and I told them I'd rather be unemployed than go there and be killed."

One of the problems Nevin faced in cross-examining the former Evergreen employees was that his attack highlighted the government's argument that Elias preyed on low-income workers who were financially desperate and couldn't get jobs elsewhere. Uhlmann stood for redirect examination and immediately asked, "You testified on direct examination and on cross about the lack of safety equipment at Evergreen Resources and the concerns that you had while working there. And I guess I'm wondering why you worked there if you thought it was such an unsafe environment?"

"Well, I needed a job. I had child support to pay and I needed a place to work and that was all there was at the time." Rice said he was trying to get a job at other companies without luck. He stuck with Evergreen because "I had no choice."

Breitsameter followed Rice with David Mahlum, an OSHA inspector who testified that there had been numerous OSHA violations at Evergreen and that during an inspection in 1993, Elias told them no one worked in confined spaces. Mahlum said he provided Elias with written safety materials for employees working in confined spaces. Celeste Miller followed Mahlum with Bill Stout, the Van Waters & Rogers salesman who had sold sodium cyanide to Elias at AEI, Inc. Stout looked like a salesman in a light-colored suit, his dark hair combed straight back off his forehead. He testified that he sold Elias 40,000 to 45,000 pounds of cyanide each year, routinely provided him with MSDS sheets, and made repeated overtures to give the employees free training seminars. Elias refused.

"He told me that he knew more about cyanide than I did and that he didn't need my help and I was invited to leave."

Marshall stood to cross-examine Stout, but even before he began it appeared to Hilldorfer that the trial, and perhaps his recent illness, was wearing on Marshall. When Stout testified that Elias wouldn't let him on the premises to do the training, Marshall objected, then added a chance comment, "We have an unhappy salesman here." That led to a particularly heated sidebar at which Uhlmann objected to the comment and Marshall shot back that Uhlmann should not have been present at the sidebar since Stout was Miller's witness.

Marshall continued his examination by painting Stout as a disgruntled salesman and implied that Elias was protecting his confidential manufacturing processes. The attack lost its luster, however, when Stout said that Elias was the only client to ever turn down the free training, and that Van Waters & Rogers signed confidentiality agreements to ease employer concerns about manufacturing secrets.

"Good find," Hilldorfer told Wojnicz as Stout left the stand. "He was a good witness for us."

Breitsameter ended the day with Joe Eizaguirre, the OSHA inspector who inspected the AEI plant in Pocatello and Evergreen after the accident. Eizaguirre told the jury that AEI had drums of cyanide on-site, and there had been complaints that employees were being exposed to gasses without protective equipment. He said Elias did not have a cyanide antidote kit on site and that OSHA had cited him for storing acid containers in the same room as the cyanide.

TUESDAY WAS BILLED as Fred Mancini day, and Hilldorfer was anxious for the self-proclaimed rehabilitated former bad boy to testify. Mancini had sustained a head injury while working in a confined space at Evergreen in January or February 1995, which made his testimony relevant, but at the time of his employment he had also been on probation for assault on a peace officer. Uncertain as to what kind of witness Mancini would make, in December 1998, Hilldorfer and Wojnicz had made a drive out to Preston, a small town on the Utah-Idaho border. They found Mancini kneeling in a closet hard at work fixing a water heater for "his girls"—his wife and three-year-old daughter. When Mancini stood he gave the agents a wide grin and said the bad boy who had ended up in jail was long gone. He now worked for the railroad and was a member in good standing of the Mormon Church.

Mancini confirmed that a heavy piece of machinery had fallen on his head while he worked in a confined space at Evergreen and that he went into convulsions right at the plant. He didn't go to the hospital though because he was afraid Elias would fire him, and being on probation, he needed to keep his job.

"What did you do?" Hilldorfer asked.

Mancini beamed, animated. "I just crawled home and laid in bed all weekend like a sick cat! Thought I was going to die, but come Monday morning I went back to work."

Mancini said that when he returned to Evergreen Elias was waiting for him in the trailer and tried to "convince" him he had not been hurt and did not need to go to a doctor. Mancini never did, but he could not physically finish the day. He told the agents, "I tried to cowboy up, you know, but I was too sick to work and my head was all swelled up. I went home."

Elias told the employees that he fired Mancini for using marijuana on the job.[1]

The two agents' concern, despite Rice and Thornock's confirmation that Mancini had been hurt, was that he had no hard evidence to prove his injury.

Mancini just smiled like a kid with a secret. "You want proof?" he asked, and broke into a contagious laugh.

MANCINI WALKED TO the witness stand flashing the same broad smile beneath a mop of jet-black hair and dark eyes that sparkled like a child's. On the witness stand he lost none of his humor. At one point he professed to being nervous, then looked to his wife in the gallery. "I think it was the Dr Pepper before I came in." He laughed. He was nonplussed when Winmill called him Mr. Martini and apologized for "butchering his name" and he referred to Miller as "ma'am" and to Nevin as "sir."

When he explained how he had been injured but tried to "cowboy up" the jurors smiled at the expression, and Hilldorfer sensed Mancini was a welcome respite from the tension of the trial.

Not wanting to let Nevin bring up the assault on the police officer Miller asked about the incident herself. Mancini didn't shy away from it.

"Who was that peace officer?"

"Officer Robert Lawman."

"With what police entity?"

"Corporal at the ISP."

"Idaho State Police?"

"Yes, ma'am."

"And have you made amends with Officer Lawman?"

Mancini's voice boomed. "Bob Lawman's one of my very best friends."

Nevin asked Mancini a series of questions that implied Mancini had not really been hurt, that he and Rice concocted the entire incident to get even with Elias for firing them. Hilldorfer and Wojnicz looked at each other and smiled.

"Now, you also said one of the reasons that you didn't go to the doctor is because Allan didn't want you to go?" Nevin asked.

"Yes, sir, that's the understanding he made me have, sir."

"Well, that couldn't have made any difference to you after you quit the job; could it?"

"No, sir."

"What did you care after you have left the job if he doesn't want you to go to the doctor?"

Mancini shrugged, ever smiling. "I was hurt and I was trying to mend up, sir, and I probably made the wrong choice there, sir."

"You probably made the wrong choice not to go to the doctor?"

"Yeah, I probably should have went."

"Mr. Mancini, if you had really been seriously hurt, you would have gone to the doctor, wouldn't you?"

Wojnicz muttered to Hilldorfer under his breath. "He's going to do it."

"No," Mancini said. "Now I would have. At that time I wouldn't have."

"Back then you didn't go to the doctor when you were hurt?" Nevin's tone was incredulous.

"Come on," Wojnicz uttered.

"Nope," Mancini said.

"Okay, Mr. Mancini, isn't it true that you weren't really hurt that bad?"

"Bingo," Hilldorfer said.

Mancini gave Nevin the same coy smile he gave Wojnicz and Hilldorfer, then he lowered his head so the jury could see it as he rubbed his hand over an indentation. "I still got a dent in the top of my head, sir, if you would like to feel it."

It brought smiles to the courtroom. Several jurors had to raise their notebooks to cover their faces. "Feel My Head Fred," Hilldorfer said to Wojnicz, the nickname they had bestowed on Mancini the moment he made them the same offer.

For once, Nevin seemed at a loss. "No, I will pass on that," he said, asking a few more questions before sitting down.

Wednesday, April 28, 1999
Federal Courthouse
Pocatello, Idaho
United States v. Elias, **Day 8**

CHAPTER FORTY-ONE

HILLDORFER GRABBED a hard-boiled egg and a yogurt from the Ameritel Hotel breakfast bar, far less than he usually ate, and pulled up a chair at Uhlmann's table.

"You doing okay?" Uhlmann asked.

Hilldorfer was scheduled to testify, but that wasn't the reason for Uhlmann's question. Though Mancini had left the courtroom laughing, the pressure of long days and nights was catching up to everyone, as was the flu. Celeste Miller had been sick and not in good temper. Hilldorfer and Wojnicz shared one of the three U.S. Attorney's Offices with Miller, and after Mancini ended the day Hilldorfer went there to call witnesses. When Miller walked in she looked at the voluminous witness reports scattered over the desk and snapped.

"Get that shit off my desk."

It hit a raw nerve but Hilldorfer bit his tongue, hung up the telephone, and walked out.

"Are you comfortable with Celeste? Do you want me to do your direct examination?" Uhlmann asked.

"I'm fine, David. Nothing is going to throw me off-mission here. Don't worry about it."

"Okay." Uhlmann changed topics. "How do you think Gene's going to do?"

Thornock was also scheduled to testify that morning, and while all acknowledged "the caveman" could be a powerful witness, a man who risked his life to rescue Dominguez, they were also apprehensive. What made Thornock a good witness also made him a loose cannon. He was brutally honest. He told the OSHA investigators on tape that he "wanted to kick Allan's ass" and during trial preparation he had become unnerved when Uhlmann put him through a mock cross-examination. Uhlmann challenged him about minor inconsistencies between what he had told OSHA and what he recalled three years after the event. Thornock grew noticeably more irritated with each question and finally asked Uhlmann if he wanted to step outside. Uhlmann called Hilldorfer to intervene. If Thornock lost his temper on the witness stand it would make him easy pickings for Nevin.

The government needed to hold it together because it appeared that Marshall was becoming increasingly frustrated. Tuesday had ended with a bang. Breitsameter called Greg Boothe to testify that Elias had placed his employees in imminent danger of death or serious bodily injury. Marshall objected before the first question and requested a sidebar. He argued Boothe, though an expert, could not testify about what Elias knew or didn't know. Winmill agreed. But because the ruling was made at sidebar, Breitsameter had no opportunity to advise Boothe. After sidebar he tried to phrase his questions appropriately but Boothe again began to answer that Elias had "knowledge." Marshall shot out of his chair and asked for another sidebar.

"Defendant Allan Elias hereby moves for a mistrial in this case based on the government's express disregard of the court's instructions earlier."

Winmill denied the request. Breitsameter and the rest of the government trial team thought it an indication the defense was concerned things weren't going well and getting desperate.[1]

THORNOCK STEPPED onto the stand in a T-shirt and jeans, looking as if he'd come straight from work, which was perfect. Given the animosity with Uhlmann, Breitsameter would do the direct examination. Before Breitsameter began Uhlmann stood. He was about to cash in the chit he believed Winmill owed him for letting Nevin address the jury, and he got his money's worth. With Winmill's permission, he turned to the jury to explain why Miller was ill and would not be in court.

"As she put it this morning, she tried to 'cowgirl up' and make it through the day today, but she has gone to see the doctor."

The reference to Feel My Head Fred Mancini's testimony brought smiles to the jurors' faces.

Breitsameter walked Thornock through the events leading to the morning of August 27. As Thornock talked about his inability to rescue Scott Dominguez he faltered, like Brian Smith, which made his testimony even more compelling. Breitsameter asked him about returning to work at Evergreen the Friday after the accident and a meeting Elias held that day.

"And do you recall what Mr. Elias indicated at that time?"

Anger shaded Thornock's voice. "He indicated that it was Scott and Darren's own fault."

When Breitsameter returned to his seat at counsel table Uhlmann leaned over and whispered in his ear. "Fasten your seat belt."[2] Breitsameter ordinarily limited his objections during cross-examinations, believing too many objections made it look like the government was trying to hide information. As Nevin's cross-examination of Thornock progressed, however, Uhlmann kept jabbing him with elbows and telling him to "get ready to object." Then Nevin began an inquiry they all knew was coming.

"Now Mr. Thornock, do you recall telling the folks from OSHA that you were really angry at Mr. Elias?" Nevin's voice dripped with indignation.

Thornock sat back from the microphone and crossed his arms in a defensive posture. "Yeah, I do."

"And do you remember the words that you used to describe that?"

Thornock rocked once in his chair. "Yeah, I would have liked to have kicked his ass."

"You told them that didn't you?"

"Yes, I did," he said with conviction.

Nevin had him. He could now argue to the jury that Gene Thornock was simply an angry man who did not like Allan Elias and his testimony reflected his desire to get even with him. But Nevin didn't stop.

"And you still feel that way today, too, don't you?"

Thornock seemed to pause for just a moment, as if surprised by the question. "Do I?"

"Yes, sir."

Hilldorfer felt the left side of the courtroom shift forward, waiting for the shoe to drop. Breitsameter was on the verge of objecting when

Thornock suddenly uncrossed his arms and his entire body seemed to relax, as if releasing a held breath. He adjusted in his chair to look at the jury, his voice calm. "No," he said. "I feel that justice will be settled right here."

For a moment no one moved. The response had come completely out of the blue.

Sitting in the gallery, Hilldorfer looked at Wojnicz, disbelieving. "The caveman came through," he said. "He came through for Scott."

Thursday and Friday, April 29–30, 1999
Federal Courthouse
Pocatello, Idaho
United States v. Elias, **Days 9 and 10**

CHAPTER FORTY-TWO

HILLDORFER AWOKE early the next day and called Joanne looking for some comfort and reassurance. "It's been a long time since I testified. I don't want to say anything that could hurt Scotty's case."

Because of the length of Thornock's testimony, Hilldorfer's appearance on the stand at the end of Wednesday had been brief, just enough time to get out his credentials.

"You're great on the witness stand," Joanne assured him. "Everyone has always told you that. Just be yourself and don't worry about anything else."

He and Miller made a tactical decision to keep his testimony short and hard-hitting. They wanted to contrast Elias's explanation to Hilldorfer and Wojnicz about a stratum of cyanide in the tank with his telling the emergency responders and Dr. Obray that there was only mud and water in the tank. They also wanted to emphasize Elias's complete lack of remorse, telling Hilldorfer, "You can't manage stupidity."

The only potentially sticky issue involved a statement Elias made to Hilldorfer during their initial meeting. Elias said he had performed a titration test. Hilldorfer had not written the statement in his witness report because at that time he didn't know what a titration test was, or its significance, if any. He knew both now, and he knew after reviewing the beakers and talking to Dick Anderson that it would be one of Elias's primary defenses.

He had testified approximately twenty-five times in his career, each time adhering to his grandmother's admonition when he was a boy: "Tell the truth, shame the devil."

"I want you to bring it up on direct," he told Miller, meaning Elias's statement that he performed a titration test.

As a representative of the government anything he said that even looked like a lie would be equated to the entire trial team and he didn't want that. It could also effectively end his career. An officer found to have lied under oath was required by law to disclose that perjury in any subsequent trial, which made it highly unlikely he would ever testify again, which made it unlikely he'd ever be given any significant cases. The agent was put out to pasture, like an old horse. Miller agreed. She brought out the omission during Hilldorfer's direct examination.

When Marshall stood to cross-examine him, Hilldorfer realized his brief time on the stand the day before had been a blessing. What anxiety he felt had vanished. He felt in control.

When Marshall tried to impeach Hilldorfer with Kelly O'Neil's written report of their meeting with Elias, Hilldorfer calmly stated it wasn't his report and Miller objected it was improper impeachment. Winmill agreed. Dr. Joe Lowry had told Hilldorfer that the most effective witnesses always remained calm. Rather than get angry at a question, they downplayed it, making the attorney look stupid for asking it. Hilldorfer took the advice and throughout Marshall's cross-examination he was as polite and formal as a Southern gentleman, addressing him repeatedly as "Mr. Marshall." He also knew from experience that good attorneys jabbed at a witness with a series of meaningless questions to get them in the rhythm of saying "Yes," then slipped in the damaging question. Like a boxer, Hilldorfer took Marshall's jabs, tried to avoid the damaging blows, and looked for opportunities to counterpunch.

Despite the defense's argument at the suppression hearing that Elias did not consent to the search but had been bullied by O'Neil and Hilldorfer, Marshall now painted Elias as a cooperative owner who willingly provided the investigators with critical information. Hilldorfer had no way to point out the inconsistency of the two positions to the jurors.

"And when you spoke to Mr. Elias on that day, if I understand correctly, you didn't have a search warrant or anything to be on his premises, right?"

"No, we did not."

"And he consented to your being on his premises, correct?"

"Yes, he did."

"And didn't throw you off his premises?"

"No, he did not."

Marshall stood looking satisfied; his palms open toward the ceiling like they were old friends having a conversation. "So you learned from Mr. Elias some important facts relating to the case, including the possibility of cyanide having been in the tank in Pocatello, without any hesitation on Mr. Elias's part, he told you about that cyanide, didn't he?"

"Yes, he did."

Marshall then asked Hilldorfer about Elias's comment that Weaver and Dominguez hit a pocket of cyanide. "Isn't it possible, sir, that the day after a tragic incident, Mr. Elias in discussing with you the facts relevant to your inquiry, might have been trying to figure out what happened and why?"

There was the right hook, but it was sweeping and Hilldorfer didn't miss his chance to punch back. "Mr. Elias was trying to figure out how to protect himself from liability."

Marshall's face reddened. He crossed his arms like an unhappy parent. "You are obviously speculating with respect to that, based on your personal impression as a law enforcement officer, correct?"

"Well, the question was speculative in nature and that was my answer . . . Mr. Marshall."

Marshall persisted. He insinuated that Elias's use of the term *pocket* was an explanation for what happened that day.

"That's Mr. Elias's explanation for what happened. I don't think that's what happened."

Frustrated, Marshall went back to the lectern, the courtroom quiet as he considered his notes. He asked Hilldorfer about the tin can of bluish-green material at the site. "And you could have seized it if you wanted to, right?"

Hilldorfer saw another opening. "No, I could not have seized it if I wanted to. I would have had to have asked permission of Mr. Elias. I think, as you mentioned, I was there in regard to his consenting to us being there that day and any samples we took were pursuant to his consent; so I couldn't have seized it."

Marshall continued to highlight Elias's cooperation.

"When Mr. Elias was discussing this with you, he was discussing it with you openly, correct?"

Hilldorfer was now enjoying the banter. "Mr. Marshall," he said almost apologetically, "there were some things he discussed openly; when he was asked some questions, at times he would refuse to give us answers or he would give us various answers."

Marshall gave Hilldorfer a patronizing smile. "Mr. Hilldorfer, I don't mean to be rude, but you are not answering the question I asked you. If you wouldn't mind."

Before Hilldorfer could respond Winmill stepped in. "Counsel, I'll caution the witness if that needs to be done. Restate the question."

Marshall gathered himself. "Isn't it possible, Agent Hilldorfer, that again, this is a man, after a tragic accident, trying to figure out what happened and why and what he might have done wrong?"

It was another roundhouse punch. Hilldorfer ducked and came up swinging. "There's a lot of things possible, Mr. Marshall."

Marshall went back to the lectern. "During your conversation with Mr. Elias that day, it's true, is it not, that Mr. Elias told you that, based on the sampling that he had done in the tank, he felt that the conditions in the tank were safe enough for him to sit in a rocking chair and read a book?"

It had been a cavalier comment by Elias, and Hilldorfer wanted to respond, *Yeah, that's what he said, but guess what, he never stuck his fat ass in the tank once to find out for himself, did he? He just kept sending his employees in.*

He bit his tongue. "That's what Mr. Elias said, yes."

KYLE SCHICK, the owner of the Salt Lake City lab where Elias had sent the samples from the tank, followed Hilldorfer later in the day. Uhlmann made a tactical decision to keep Schick's testimony short. He was the ideal witness to prove Elias chose not to test the sample for cyanide. He was not a "government witness" like Joe Lowry, and if Schick was going to be beholden to anyone, it would have been Elias, his client. Uhlmann used Schick to end the nonsense that the test of the sample for silver was somehow a test to determine cyanide. He asked Schick if Elias sent him a sample in 1996 and asked that it be tested for silver. Schick agreed.

"Did the defendant in any way indicate to you, when he sent you that sample, that he was trying to figure out whether the sample had cyanide in it?"

"No, not at that time."

"Does a fire assay test tell you whether there is cyanide in the material?"

"No, not at all."

Uhlmann continued a few questions later. "And what did you find out in terms of whether the sample that Mr. Elias had sent you had any silver value, if you will?"

"It had no detectable levels of silver in it at the levels we were testing for."

Uhlmann concluded on a powerful note. "How much did it cost or how much did you charge the defendant for this analysis?"

"Twenty-five dollars."

"And if he had asked, could you have also had cyanide analysis performed for him?"

"Yes."

"And how much would that have cost?"

"Fifty."

Uhlmann cocked his head as if he hadn't heard the answer. "Fifty dollars?" he asked, incredulous.

There was nothing wrong with his hearing. He not only heard Schick, he knew the answer before he asked the question. It was in Hilldorfer's report.

Schick's eyes widened behind his wire-rimmed glasses as if to say I don't understand it either. "Yeah."

"Thank you. No further questions, Your Honor."

The implication was that Elias didn't think Scott Dominguez's life was worth $50.

Nevin attempted to ask Schick about other samples Elias had sent his lab, but Uhlmann quickly objected that, since he did not ask about the other samples in his direct examination, Nevin could not bring them up on cross. This caused yet another sidebar and it appeared Winmill was finally losing his patience.

"I wonder what the wear guaranty is on this carpet? It seems like we're up here a fair amount."

Winmill sustained Uhlmann's objection and told Nevin he'd have to put Schick on the stand in the defense case, if he so chose.

After Schick stepped down, Winmill excused the jury for the day. It was showtime for Dr. Joe Lowry and his death chamber.

HELD OUTSIDE the presence of the jury, a Daubert hearing was the defense's opportunity to challenge Lowry's efforts to simulate the conditions within the tank on the morning of the injury and his explanation as to why the sludge was hazardous despite being below the SW846 threshold. Daubert hearings prevent an expert from espousing a theory as fact when the scientific community does not accept it as such. For Marshall it was another opportunity to argue to Winmill that the samples met the SW846 threshold and that Lowry's tests were "manufactured" by the government to "get Elias." Marshall knew the regulations, and he knew the tests. This was where he was expected to shine.

Uhlmann had no such pretensions. He'd nearly flunked freshman calculus and his instructor made it quite clear after his final exam that math and science were not his forte. His abilities had not gotten any better during his career at the ECS, but he had learned to use his shortcomings. If he could get Lowry to explain the scientific principles in simple enough terms that even he could understand, he was certain the jury would also. But that was putting the cart before the horse. He first had to get Winmill to understand it. He'd know immediately if the judge didn't. When confused or frustrated Winmill had a habit of pressing his palms flat against the side of his face, mouth open, in what Uhlmann called the "silent scream" because it resembled the Edvard Munch painting.

To avoid that response Uhlmann had traveled to Dr. Joe's lab in Colorado multiple times during trial prep, and for the past week he had spent late hours in his suite with Lowry giving him a tutorial. Hilldorfer and Wojnicz sat in each night eating Popsicles from Uhlmann's fridge. They called the sessions Science 101. Wojnicz found them fascinating, Hilldorfer felt like he was listening to a foreign language, and Uhlmann developed headaches. He'd lower his head and begin banging it on the round table.

"Stop! Joe, stop! I'm an idiot! I don't understand anything you're saying. It doesn't make sense. You have to be able to explain it to me, Joe, so I can understand it or I'm never going to be able to explain it to the judge."

Lowry had the patience of Job. He would laugh like a great uncle teaching his nephew. "It's simple, David," he'd say, and start the tutorial over again.

After a week of very late nights Uhlmann got it.

The afternoon of the Daubert hearing the rest of the trial team, as well as Nevin, had departed, the prosecution team going back to the U.S. Attorney's Office to begin preparations for the next day. When Uhlmann put Lowry on the stand they broke down a complex process into five steps that ended with converting the amount of cyanide in a sample to a volume of hydrogen cyanide. By determining the amount of hydrogen cyanide in a sample it was then straight math for Lowry to determine how much hydrogen cyanide was in the tank the morning of the incident.

During his direct Uhlmann knew Winmill was following him because the judge was asking his own questions and nodding. Uhlmann sat feeling gratified that all the hard work had paid off.

Marshall stood. He didn't challenge the science Lowry used to conclude the hydrogen cyanide content of the sludge was well beyond the necessary threshold for being considered a hazardous waste. Instead, he argued the sample taken from the tank the day after the accident was not representative of the sludge in the tank as a whole, calling it a "grab" sample from one location. Confused, but suspicious of where Marshall was going, Uhlmann objected that whether the sample was representative had nothing to do with whether the scientific methodology Lowry used to run the test was reliable and accepted in the community. That was the question during a Daubert hearing.

Winmill agreed.

But Marshall continued, and Uhlmann quickly concluded Marshall was using the hearing to cross-examine Lowry without the jury present to learn how he would answer specific questions. At one point Marshall went so far as to state that he was not challenging the methodology, but arguing that the experiment was completely irrelevant to the case because of flaws in the assumptions. Uhlmann jumped on this, hoping to put an end to the proceeding.

"I think he's conceding the science issue, this witness will say it's representative."

Winmill allowed Marshall to continue, but if his purpose was to cross-examine Lowry it was an uphill battle, and Lowry was king of the hill. While answering Uhlmann's questions Lowry's voice had been a deep baritone. He spoke slow and crisp, like he wanted his words to seep into the court's conscious. On cross-examination he mumbled and his answers were so soft that at times he was inaudible. They also had a very subtle bite, as if he was politely insinuating at the end of every answer, "You just don't get it, you dumb ass."

Lowry refused to admit that the sample was not "representative." He said that so long as it contained cyanide it was representative because the issue was whether the material in the tank presented an acute hazard.

Clearly frustrated, Marshall interrupted. "But that's not the question I asked you."

"Well, that is the question," Lowry responded.

"That's your question, not mine."

"That's the reactivity characteristic."

Marshall turned to Winmill, saying he "didn't want to fence" with Lowry. Winmill was unsympathetic. He said Marshall and Lowry were not going to agree because they were not on the same page.

At 5:00 Winmill continued the hearing to the morning and left the bench. Uhlmann was livid. The government had lost time it could have otherwise used to put on evidence to the jury, and he had been up late each night for a week killing himself to learn the science because the defense requested the Daubert hearing. But that wasn't what the hearing had been about at all. They just wanted to take a free crack at cross-examining Lowry. It was another incident of what he considered improper tactics by the defense, what he called "sharp elbows."

As Marshall packed his things for the day Uhlmann walked across the room and confronted him. "I thought you wanted a Daubert hearing to challenge his science. That's what I prepared for and that's what I did on direct, but that isn't what you intended at all. I never would have bothered wasting the court's time."

Marshall smirked. "Well, far be it from me to get some free discovery of your expert."

The response set Uhlmann off. "I'm getting tired of you pulling this nonsense. You're a better lawyer than that. You don't need to engage in those kinds of tactics."

Whether it was the frustration of the day, the proceedings in their entirety, his recent illness, or the fact that Elias had apparently stopped paying Marshall's legal bills, Marshall lost his temper.[1] Blistering red in the face, he stepped around the table and advanced on Uhlmann. "I don't need any lectures from you. I'm sick and tired of your lectures. You're a piece of shit and you've been a piece of shit for years. You once filed a motion when I was on vacation and told you I would be out of the country."[2]

Uhlmann was dumbfounded. The motion Marshall referred to had been made when he was prosecuting the Wilber Ellis case. It had prompted a vitriolic attack by Marshall in a responding pleading, but they had talked about it and Uhlmann considered it a misunderstanding they had resolved. Apparently not.

Thinking Marshall was angry enough to take a swing at him, Uhlmann stepped back. "I'm not going to stand here and listen to this. From this point forward I'm not dealing with you. I'll deal with your co-counsel. I get along fine with him. I'm through with you."

BY THE TIME Uhlmann stormed into the conference room in the U.S. Attorney's Office where the rest of the trial team had already gathered, he was shaking with anger. He considered it a great indignity to be called a "piece of shit" in a federal courtroom in front of the judge's staff.

"Where were you guys?"

"What happened?" Hilldorfer asked. Uhlmann looked and sounded like a kid who picked a fight with the schoolyard bully and turned to find his backup had deserted him.

Uhlmann told them the story. "Marshall just lost it. He called me a piece of shit in front of the judge's staff."

"Damn it." Wojnicz said, then looking at Hilldorfer, "I can't believe we missed it." He sounded like he'd been cheated out of the best part of a movie.

They tried to convince Uhlmann that what had happened was a good thing.

"They're frustrated, David," Breitsameter said. "Things aren't going well."

Uhlmann dismissed it. "I'm through dealing with him. I'll deal with Nevin."

They sat down to prepare for the following day, everyone but Uhlmann hiding a sheepish grin. After a moment of uncomfortable silence Hilldorfer looked at Wojnicz. "Maybe he meant it as a compliment."

They all looked at him like he was crazy.

"You know, like a Native American name."

Wojnicz smiled back. "Yeah, like 'Walks with the Gods' or 'Dances with the Sun.' "

"Piece o' shit," Hilldorfer said. The nickname stuck for the better part of the rest of the trial.

THE FOLLOWING MORNING, as Uhlmann approached the courtroom, Marshall called to him in the hall. "I'd like to talk to you."

Uhlmann shook his head. "I don't want to talk to you. I have nothing to say to you."

"Please," Marshall said. He gave a heartfelt apology.

Uhlmann had talked with his wife and heeded her advice to let it go, though he wouldn't act like nothing had happened. "David, you can put me on the long list of people in my office who want nothing to do with you."[3]

Before court Winmill called counsel into chambers and asked if there was anything that needed to be discussed, a reference to the blowup his staff had apparently reported. Uhlmann said there was not and they proceeded back to court.[4]

They concluded the Daubert hearing, at which time Winmill told the attorneys he would allow Lowry to testify. "I feel that there's really not a serious question about whether this expert's testimony reflects scientific knowledge," he said. "I don't think that's been seriously challenged."

With the jury back and perhaps the biggest legal hurdle finally behind them, Uhlmann called Kim Barnett, the former AEI employee. Barnett testified that the solids in the tank had never been cleaned out during his four years at AEI, a refutation of Elias's claim that the tank was empty when he had it moved to Evergreen. He said that whenever OSHA came to the plant Elias instructed them to "turn out the lights and lock the doors and lock the gate" so he could tell them he was in research-and-development mode only. With regard to the safety rules and other regulations OSHA provided Elias, Barnett said he watched Elias throw them against the wall. "He said we didn't have to comply with them."

Miller concluded the day with Dr. John Roberts, Scott's neurosurgeon, who looked like a rusty-haired kid from a Norman Rockwell painting. From an evidentiary standpoint Roberts was to testify that Dominguez's symptoms indicated a serious injury caused by cyanide, but there was another reason for his testimony and the order in which the government called him to testify.

"Dr. Roberts, does brain tissue regenerate?" Miller asked.

"No, it does not regenerate."

"Is Scott Dominguez's condition permanent?"

"Yes, it is permanent."

"What is his long-term prognosis?"

Nevin objected. Winmill overruled him.

"Scott's long-term prognosis is not good for recovery. Brain damage is permanent. A person cannot regenerate these types of brain cells, so these injuries will always stay there. Unfortunately, Scott will stay about the same the rest of his life."

"And there's nothing that medicine can do to change that?"

"Not in 1999, no."

It was a sobering thought, especially with Scott and his family sitting in the courtroom listening, but as Dr. Roberts delivered his heartfelt prognosis, it remained what it was, a doctor giving a clinical analysis. On Monday a very vivid and personal illustration of what had happened August 27, 1996, would bring everything into certain perspective.

Scott was going to take the stand—if Winmill allowed him.

Monday, May 3, 1999
Federal Courthouse
Pocatello, Idaho
United States v. Elias, Day 11

CHAPTER FORTY-THREE

AT THE END of the proceedings on Friday, Winmill had instructed the jury not to discuss the case. "Over the weekend, simply put the matter out of your mind. You are not to give any further thought on it."

For the government, Hilldorfer and Uhlmann in particular, that was not about to happen. Hilldorfer had used the promise that Scott would be able to testify to keep him focused on his rehabilitation and to not lose faith because of the extended length of the investigation. He'd feel horrible if that didn't happen. Uhlmann was equally committed to doing everything in his power to see that Dominguez testified.

MONDAY MORNING, Miller opened the day by walking Jackie Hamp through an emotional direct examination. Hamp had shown remarkable strength, but on the stand she struggled to hold back the tears she had held for three years, and had to stop several times to regain her composure. Miller moved at a deliberate pace, letting a mother's pain for her son permeate the courtroom.

When she had finished Nevin stood to cross-examine Hamp and established that she had filed a civil lawsuit against Elias, Evergreen Resources, and Kerr-McGee on behalf of her son. The only reasonable implications were that Hamp's testimony was somehow tainted by the prospect of getting money, or to let the jury know Elias was going to be punished financially. To Hilldorfer it seemed a large risk for a very small reward. Hamp's demeanor on the stand, reserved and deferential, made her appear anything but opportunistic, and though he had no children he couldn't imagine a single juror would have changed places with Hamp for any amount of money.

Lowry followed Hamp and testified until the court broke for lunch. When they returned Winmill did not immediately bring in the jury. He told counsel he wanted to discuss Nevin's request that Dominguez be subjected to a competency exam before being allowed to testify. It caught Uhlmann and Breitsameter off-guard. At the conclusion of Friday's court proceedings all the attorneys had met in Winmill's chambers to discuss the matter and they had presented affidavits that Dominguez's injury did not render him incompetent to testify. The defense had offered nothing in opposition.[1] Uhlmann and Breitsameter thought the issue of Dominguez's competence to testify had been put to rest. Uhlmann stood and pointed this out in court, and he beseeched Winmill not to subject Dominguez to a competency exam.

"I don't want to make this too overly dramatic, but no other witness who has been called to testify in this matter has been required to first demonstrate his or her competency," he said, his voice impassioned. "Mr. Dominguez has been clearly horribly victimized already and it just seems to us—again, I don't mean to be overly dramatic—but it just seems to us to be unfair to Mr. Dominguez to subject him to that . . ."

Winmill listened to the argument, then disagreed.

Hilldorfer became angry. While he understood defense lawyers had a job to do, and he respected Nevin and Marshall's right to do it, they were now trying to use the injury that Elias had inflicted on Scott to keep him from testifying. There was something horribly unjust about Elias robbing Scott of his future and then robbing him of his moment to talk about it. It left a taste in his mouth ten times as bitter as the taste left from Boomsnub.

At 4:00 in the afternoon when Lowry stepped off the witness stand Uhlmann turned and faced the bench. He could have said there was a matter to take up outside the jury's presence, but he decided he wanted the jury to know the government intended to put Dominguez on the stand.

"Your Honor, the United States calls Scott Dominguez."

Winmill told the jurors he had a matter to take up with counsel and dismissed them. After they were gone he turned to the gallery. His voice reverberated like the great and powerful Oz ordering the Tin Man to "come forward."

"Mr. Dominguez, you may come forward, please."

Dominguez hesitated at the mention of his name then stood. He faltered as he stepped from the pew, shuffling forward like a prisoner shackled about the ankles and waist. As he approached the gate, Hilldorfer stood and held it open. Dominguez stepped through and again hesitated, eyes wide. It caused Hilldorfer's chest to tighten as if from a sudden shot of adrenaline.

"Mr. Dominguez, if you will step right up into here, please," Winmill said, directing him to the witness stand.

Uhlmann stood waiting patiently at the lectern, all sound sucked from the courtroom, like the silence that follows a percussive blast. By the time Dominguez reached the witness stand ninety seconds had passed. To Uhlmann it felt like ninety hours.

The court clerk asked Dominguez to state and spell his name for the record.

Dominguez did not immediately respond. When he did speak, it was inaudible.

Uhlmann stepped from the lectern. "Your Honor, can I just help him move forward?"

"Yes," Winmill said quickly.

Uhlmann slid Dominguez's chair closer to the microphone.

The clerk repeated her question. "Sir, could you please state your name."

Dominguez's face remained a blank mask.

Inside Uhlmann was urging him to speak. They had worked hard to get to this point. Twice his family had brought Scott to the old courthouse to get him acclimated with the courtroom, but ethically Uhlmann could not tell Dominguez what to say, couldn't script his questions and answers. This was Scott's moment to succeed. There was nothing more any one of them could do for him. All he could do was wait, like everyone else.

A stillness permeated the courtroom like a held breath. Hilldorfer sat rigid, his hands on his thighs. The tip of the pen in Wojnicz's hand, ever scribbling across the notepad in his lap, rested silently. Behind them Dominguez's family sat resolute, painful as it must have been, giving Scott their full attention. Only Elias, scrunched down in his chair and partially obscured by trial binders and paper, seemed unwilling to look at the young man on the witness stand.

Dominguez grimaced and swallowed. The words trickled out in the now familiar haunting gasp of air. "My name is Scott Dominguez."

Winmill turned to Uhlmann. "You may inquire. Mr. Dominguez, if you could speak as loudly as you possibly can."

Uhlmann sighed in relief. He had made a decision to keep Dominguez's testimony short, not wanting Winmill to think the government was using Dominguez like some sort of exhibit. He wanted Winmill to see Scott as they all saw him, a gentle, decent person. He had written out his questions, something he never did, but he felt the clearer and more precise his question, the better chance Scott had to answer it. Nerves intervened, however, and his first question out of the box was wrong. He had to correct it.

"Mr. Dominguez, in the fall of 1990—I'm sorry, in the fall of 1994, did you go to work for Evergreen Resources?"

Dominguez swallowed. "Um, yeah," he whispered.

"And who hired you at Evergreen Resources?"

"Allan Elias."

After a problem with the microphone Uhlmann continued, speaking in as even a cadence as he could, doing everything within his power to will the answers from Dominguez. "And who was your boss at Evergreen Resources, Mr. Dominguez?"

"Allan Elias."

"How would you describe Evergreen Resources in terms of safety?"

Scott swallowed and grimaced. "Very, very poor."

His voice was so soft it was like trying to listen to a flowing stream.

"Did you ever talk to the defendant about your safety concerns?"

"Um, um, um, um, yes."

"And how did he respond?"

"He, he, he, he never did anything."

"Did you ever receive safety training at Evergreen Resources?"

"Um, um, um, um, no."

"If the defendant wrote your name down in a book and said you had received safety training would that be true or false?"

"That would be false."

Uhlmann looked to Winmill, certain Dominguez had established his competence and feeling somewhat vindicated. "How much of my exam do you want me to go through?"

"That's fine." Winmill turned to David Nevin. "Mr. Nevin."

Nevin stepped forward. Uhlmann had come to feel protective of Dominguez, but he knew this was what the judicial system required. Scott would have to stand on his own.

"Scott, do you remember the events of August 27, the day that you were injured in the tank," Nevin asked.

"Yes."

"Do you remember the days after you were removed from the tank?"

"Um-hmm."

"Do you remember who your doctors were who treated you?"

"Um-hmm."

"Who are they?"

Dominguez paused. His stutter became more pronounced, like a chant echoing from the court's PA system. "Um, um, um, um, um, um, um, um, um, it was John Obray and, and, and, John Roberts."

"Do you remember what time you went to work on the morning of the twenty-seventh, the day when the accident occurred?"

"Um-hmm, yes."

"What time?"

"It had to be at seven o'clock."

Nevin pursed his lips. "I don't have further questions. I have argument."

Perhaps convinced he could no longer argue Dominguez was not competent, Nevin argued Dominguez could offer nothing of evidentiary value. He said the purpose of having Dominguez testify was not to impart information to the jury but to elicit juror sympathy and prejudice. "I understand that he is the last or perhaps the next to last witness to be called in this case and I believe that that is being done for the purpose, to leave the jury with that very strong impression."

"Son of a bitch," Hilldorfer said to Wojnicz. "This is such bullshit."

Winmill turned to Uhlmann and asked that he explain the topics Dominguez would testify about. Trying to hide his annoyance, Uhlmann noted again that the defense had made several arguments that Dominguez would refute. With each argument he jabbed his thumb at the air, like sticking a sword in a bull, his voice impassioned. Dominguez would refute the defense's positions that Elias told him and Weaver to only go in the tank one at a time, that there was more than one ladder, or that Elias told them to wear safety equipment.

Winmill put his head in his hands and admitted to being torn, calling the decision "more difficult than I anticipated. I had not seen Mr. Dominguez until he appeared here. I want to mull it over just a bit. I'm going to join the jury in a short recess."

Dominguez began to moan. Soft at first, it grew progressively louder, from a haunting moan to a plaintive wail. In the small confines of the courtroom, with the PA system echoing, it was like an air-raid siren had gone off unexpectedly and everyone was scrambling to find the switch to turn it off.

Winmill asked Dominguez if he could calm down.

Dominguez didn't.

Winmill turned to Uhlmann and told him to calm him.

Uhlmann couldn't.

It was the best thing the defense could have hoped for, exactly the type of thing that could prejudice the jury beyond any probative testimony. Nevin renewed his objections to Dominguez's testifying.

Winmill stood from the bench. "Mr. Uhlmann, I'm going to take a break to consider this. Get your witness under control."

Hilldorfer sat in the front row as though he had come upon the scene of a horrible accident, uncertain what to do. He looked to the family; Jackie had lowered her head in her hands. Breitsameter had joined Uhlmann, who stood with his arm around Dominguez, trying to gently calm him. It didn't work.

Breitsameter turned to Hilldorfer. "Joe, come up here and talk to Scotty."

Hilldorfer stood and pushed through the gate. His training had taught him the worst thing to say to a person in an emotionally agitated state was "Calm down"; it only confirmed they were out of control and could make the situation worse. As he approached Dominguez, he didn't know what to do.

IN CHAMBERS there was a different discussion occurring. Winmill's two clerks had separate, adamant opinions about whether Dominguez should be allowed to testify. One thought him competent, with probative information. The other thought the potential prejudice to Elias from having the jury witness Scott's pain, outweighed the probative value of what he could offer. Winmill, ever dutiful, listened to them both in earnest. Then the judge went into his chambers and did something he rarely did. He closed his door.[2]

STANDING IN COURT, Hilldorfer recalled a moment during Dominguez's trial preparation.

"Hey, Scott, show me how to use your monitor."

Dominguez looked at Hilldorfer, unblinking. Whatever sense of imminent despair or loss had overcome him, it disappeared as suddenly as it came on.

"Remember the monitor? Show me how to use the monitor," Hilldorfer said.

Dominguez looked at the monitor. Uhlmann had shown him how to use it to draw, likening it to the football commentator John Madden, diagramming plays on a teleprompter. Dominguez had smiled broadly at the reference.

Hilldorfer walked to the stand. "Can you draw something for me?"

Dominguez drew a circle with his finger.

"That's cool, Scott. What else can you draw?"

Dominguez struck the monitor three times with his finger, dotting in what looked like two eyes and a nose. Hilldorfer, Uhlmann, and Breitsameter released nervous laughter.

"Hey, that looks like a face," Hilldorfer said.

Dominguez drew two pig ears.

"Shit, that looks like David Marshall," Hilldorfer joked.

Breitsameter stepped forward and drew horns and a forked tail and they laughed harder until Celeste Miller approached suddenly and stuck her head into the group, visibly anxious. "The ... mike ... is ... on. Everyone in the courtroom can hear every word you are saying."

Winmill pulled open the door and retook the bench as Hilldorfer and Breitsameter returned to their seats. Uhlmann went back to the lectern. Winmill gave Dominguez a quick glance. He was no longer crying. Winmill gathered himself and told them it was not an easy issue to resolve, that he had spent a considerable amount of time over the weekend researching case law on the competency of witnesses.

Nobody doubted that he had.

"In view of the affidavits that have been filed without any opposition or at least no opposing affidavit suggesting to the contrary, based upon the witness's ability to respond to questions here, the court cannot conclude that the witness lacks competence to testify in this proceeding."

It was the first step. Hilldorfer heard a "but" coming and didn't have to wait long.

"However ..."

Winmill said that he had not given as much thought to Nevin's new argument, that Dominguez could offer no probative testimony. As he spoke it sounded as though he was justifying the decision he was about to make. He noted that with eleven and a half years on the bench he had as much if not more trial experience than any local judge. He said victims of crime always engender sympathy from the jury. "The other side of the equation in terms of the probative value of the evidence is that I think there is, or rather there are, certain areas upon which this witness is unique in his ability to testify concerning, for example, safety training that he himself received, matters of that sort. Some of the questions would be cumulative, some would be simply corroborative and some would be unique. Given those circumstances, I'm going to permit Mr. Dominguez to testify. . . ."

Hilldorfer clenched his fist. Uhlmann showed no outward emotion, but inside he was churning—happy, relieved, and anxious.

Now it was up to Scott.

With some limiting instructions on what Uhlmann could and could not ask, Winmill instructed Fica to bring the jury back, waited until they were seated, then instructed Uhlmann to proceed.

Uhlmann focused on Dominguez. "Now, Scott, during 1996, did Allan Elias, the defendant, direct you and Darren Weaver to go into the tank to clean it out?"

"Um, yes."

"And did he tell you and Darren Weaver to go into the tank together?"

"Um, yeah."

"Did you and the other Evergreen employees ask the defendant, Allan Elias, for safety equipment before he sent you into the tank?"

"Um, yeah."

"Did he tell you that he was going to get that safety equipment?"

"Um, yes."

"Did he tell you to start working inside the tank while he went to get the safety equipment?"

"Um, yeah."

Uhlmann didn't know how the jurors were reacting because he did not take his eyes off Dominguez. Listening to Scott was like hearing a foreign accent for the first time; it required effort to understand but became easier with time. He was trying not to rush, but inside he felt a sense of urgency to get through the examination, like a clock was ticking down in his head to an impending explosion.

"Did he ever come back with the safety equipment like he said he would?"

"No."

Dominguez's hands gripped the arms of the chair. His mouth moved up and down like someone with no teeth gumming food. He was holding on.

"Are you okay to go on?" Uhlmann asked.

Dominguez began to moan.

Perhaps anticipating the worst, Winmill quickly called for a break and cleared the jury. He pressed Uhlmann on how much he had left. Uhlmann said he would limit it. After a moment, Dominguez calmed. Winmill brought the jury back.

"Did you follow all of Allan Elias's instruction when you went into the tank?" Uhlmann asked.

"Um, um, um, um, um, um, yeah."

"Did he ever tell you he had used that tank to store cyanide solution?"

"Um, um, um, um, um, um, no."

"Did you know that the tank had cyanide in it?"

Dominguez's stuttering became almost hypnotic, like the chant of an African tribe to the beating of drums. "Um, um, um, um, um, um, no."

"Would you have gone into the tank if you had known it had cyanide in it?"

"Um, um, um, um, um, um, um, um, no way."

"Were you scared when you went into the tank?"

"Um, no."

He pressed for another question. "Can you tell us why you weren't scared?"

"Um, um, um, I, I, really, really, really did, really did trust Allan."

Uhlmann stopped and looked at his notes. That was it. That would do. Emotionally spent, he sat down. Winmill looked to Nevin.

"No questions," Nevin said.

Winmill directed Dominguez to step down and as he did Hilldorfer heard stifled sobs of relief and grief. Jackie was in tears, as was the rest of Scott's family. Several jurors also wept; others sat with pinched expressions. The judge's clerk, LaDonna Garcia, wiped tears from her cheeks.

When Dominguez reached the gate he looked to Hilldorfer, who had stood again and held the gate open, an act so symbolic it was hard to miss. After nearly three years, Scott was putting the anxiety of testifying behind him. He had stood tall, not just for Hilldorfer or for his family, but for himself. As he passed through the gate, the young man and the agent looked to one another and Hilldorfer gave him a slight nod of the head, a silent, nearly imperceptible gesture that reverberated louder than any spoken words ever could.

"You did good, Scott. You did real good."

CHAPTER FORTY-FOUR

THE DEFENSE OF Allan Elias began Tuesday, May 4. Nevin and Marshall called former employees of Evergreen Resources and AEI, Inc., in rapid-fire succession. Their problem, however, was the witnesses they called had worked at Evergreen in the early 1990s, which had little bearing on 1996. The safety equipment they described as being at Evergreen was either the equipment at the plant when Elias bought it, or limited to rain gear, boots and gloves, and the 1950s Air-Pac. On cross-examination they also had to admit that the extent of their safety training was Elias saying "Be safe" or "Be careful."

Marshall then called Ivan Williams, the man who transported the tank to Evergreen in the early nineties, then cut it up for Elias after Dominguez's injury. Williams said that before he moved the tank from AEI to Evergreen he looked in it and it was empty. Hilldorfer could only marvel at Williams's testimony. Could anyone really dispute that on the morning of the accident there was sludge in the tank that contained cyanide? If it had not come from AEI where had it come from?

Breitsameter cross-examined Williams the next day, Wednesday, May 5, and Williams admitted his testimony was different from his grand jury testimony. He also admitted certain statements in the affidavit he filed to contradict Hilldorfer had been suggested to him by Allan Elias and that certain of those statements had proved not to be accurate. As to whether he had looked in the tank before moving it, however, Williams would not budge.

The defense then called Richard Gallucci, the environmental consultant and geologist they hired to be at Evergreen during the search for the buried treater dust. His appearance was brief. Uhlmann objected that Gallucci's testimony was not relevant since the government dropped Count 5 of the indictment. At a sidebar Winmill admitted Gallucci seemed a curious witness.

"If I'm Mr. Uhlmann, I'm sitting there thinking, 'Now what is that crafty Mr. Nevin up to now?' "

But Uhlmann suspected he knew what Nevin was up to. He was going to paint a picture of an extensive search at Evergreen that did not find cyanide sludge, then argue that Sean Stevens had lied about burying the waste. "[T]hey weren't looking for cyanide, they were looking for treater dust," Uhlmann told Winmill. "And I'm entitled, I think, to make that clear so that they can't go argue that there was no cyanide found when they went and did all this sampling, because it's totally taken out of context."

Winmill agreed and let Uhlmann establish the search was not for the material in the tank.

After Gallucci, the defense called a series of former AEI employees who also said the tank was empty at that facility. Again, however, their testimony didn't hold up on cross. It became a near circus. One witness, John VonSchriltz, testified the tank at AEI had no solids, only liquids. This was a total turnaround from what VonSchriltz had told Hilldorfer and Wojnicz just the day before, when he had called Elias a "shady character" who "almost killed" him and another employee at AEI when a sulfuric acid tank exploded.[1]

"Do you recall being interviewed by agents from the Environmental Protection Agency?" Uhlmann asked.

"Yes, sir."

"They talked to you as recently as last night, right?"

"Yes, sir."

Uhlmann pressed him. "Okay. I just want to make sure we understand, though. Because I thought you said there wasn't any sludge in the tank. So you're just saying you don't know whether there was sludge in the tank, is that right?"

VonSchriltz blurted, "I also told them I had never looked in there, so I wouldn't know."

The defense then recalled Hilldorfer. Marshall began a series of questions about Hilldorfer's interview of Sean Stevens. Hilldorfer now knew Marshall wanted to argue Sean Stevens lied and had never buried any cyanide waste at Evergreen. Marshall tried to get Hilldorfer to admit that Stevens's testimony about where he buried the waste was different from what he told the two agents. Hilldorfer had to admit it was. Marshall then asked about the second search, though he didn't call it that. He used words like "sampling activities" and "sampling personnel."

"Did you inform the sampling personnel as to where you believe or you understood from employees at Evergreen that the materials from the tank had gone?"

Feeling Marshall had opened the door to the second search, Hilldorfer punched back. "The focus of our search warrant was to find other contaminated material that was brought to the site and that is what I was asking people to find that day."

Despite the answer, Marshall didn't let it go.

"Are you aware of whether anyone found any material from the tank during the search that was executed that day in 1997?"

"They did not," Hilldorfer said, knowing that Marshall had just given Uhlmann the chance to kick down the door.

Uhlmann did. He stood and asked Hilldorfer about the intent of the 1997 search warrant. Hilldorfer took on the role of Dr. Joe Lowry, his voice even and calm, almost tutorial. "In the course of my investigation, I, of course, interviewed a number of Evergreen Resource employees and after getting information pertaining to Mr. Dominguez's injury, a number of employees told me information about in excess of thirty truckloads of other waste coming to the facility that came from Mr. Elias's Pocatello Plant—"

Marshall shot from his chair waving his hands like a traffic cop trying to stop the rush of cars. "Your Honor—"

"And as a result of that—"

Winmill jumped in. "Just a moment."

Red in the face, Marshall asked for a sidebar and objected that the testimony was only relevant to Count 5, which the government dropped. He got no argument from Uhlmann, who was all too happy to point out that relevance had been his objection.

Winmill agreed with Uhlmann and declined to strike Hilldorfer's testimony.

That brought John Stoor to the stand, one of the rescuers who had carried Dominguez from the tank. Stoor testified that when he carried Dominguez out of the tank, Dominguez was wearing a face mask cinched tight and that when Stoor removed the mask he noticed Dominguez took a breath. The testimony supported Elias's defense that Dominguez's brain injury was not caused by cyanide but from a lack of oxygen, that his well-meaning co-workers had suffocated him. Stoor said he told this information to Hilldorfer and Wojnicz, and to the government attorneys, but he believed they dismissed the information as unimportant.

Hilldorfer leaned into Wojnicz. "What a bunch of bullshit." In fact, when Stoor told Uhlmann the information Uhlmann stopped the interview with Stoor and called Hilldorfer to listen. Hilldorfer had to write up a report that was turned over to the defense.

Dick Anderson, the Kerr-McGee chemist who allegedly gave Elias the chemicals in the beaker bottles, followed Stoor. Though he had told the two agents he did not remember when he gave Elias the chemicals, he testified he gave the chemical reagents to Elias in the summer of 1996. Nevin introduced the bottles and Anderson confirmed the writing on the bottles, June 1996, was his. Displeased by the turn of events, Uhlmann stood. He normally used cross-examination to first get whatever constructive information he could from a witness before proceeding to destructive cross-examination, but there was little Anderson could give him. Uhlmann suggested that the block writing on the bottles was very similar to Elias's block writing, implying it was Elias who wrote the dates on the bottles. It was a stretch, and coming at the end of the day, Uhlmann was not pleased. He felt the government was ahead on points, but that didn't diminish the danger that they could get sucker-punched. All it took was one well-placed fact to get a juror off-track. They could not let their guard down. When the trial team gathered in the U.S. attorney's conference room he decided to make that point clear, shouting at Hilldorfer. "I thought you told me he said he didn't remember when Elias gave him those bottles?"

Hilldorfer had no answer for him. "That's what he told me, David. He said he couldn't recall it."

Thursday, May 6, 1999
Federal Courthouse
Pocatello, Idaho
United States v. Elias, Day 14

CHAPTER FORTY-FIVE

THE FOLLOWING DAY, after Nevin examined Wojnicz, Marshall called Kenny McAllister, another former Evergreen employee who worked for Kerr-McGee. Hilldorfer and Wojnicz had interviewed

McAllister and found him evasive. They did not have a good feeling about him.

In response to Marshall's questions, McAllister testified that he worked at Evergreen in the early nineties, quit for a period, then went back and worked there until the summer of 1996, immediately before Dominguez's injury, when he quit again and returned in September. Then he started carpet bombing the government's case. He said that while he worked at Evergreen he looked inside the tank.

Uhlmann looked to Breitsameter as if perhaps he had not heard McAllister correctly.

"And can you tell us when you looked inside the tank what you saw inside the tank?" Marshall asked.

"Just kind of rusty, flaky."

"Was it full of a ton or more of sludge?"

"Not that I seen."

"Was the tank empty?"

"I believe it was."

Uhlmann seethed. So did Hilldorfer and Wojnicz, who sat burning holes through McAllister. He told them none of this. Worse, he was now the only witness to testify that he had actually looked in the tank while it was at Evergreen. His testimony would allow Nevin to argue in closing that the material in the tank when Dominguez was injured could not have come from AEI's cyanide leaching system, but instead was just wash water from Evergreen's fertilizer process. This was the sucker punch about which Uhlmann had warned. McAllister, however, wasn't finished. He said that during the summer of 1996 Evergreen had rubber boots, raincoats, face shields, glasses, and gloves available to all the employees—as well as respirators.

"Did you have those things available to you in the summer of 1996 before Mr. Dominguez—the incident with Mr. Dominguez?"

"Yeah, we used them clear back in ninety-three, ninety-four, when we were preacidifying for the granulation plant."

Marshall later asked, "And do you remember seeing Scott Air-Pacs there during the period of your first employment?"

"Yes, I do."

McAllister also testified there was a safety harness at Evergreen in the summer of 1996 hanging in the tool room and that Elias held safety training at the plant. His final assertion, however, may have been the most damning. He testified that he, not Sean Stevens, scooped up the sludge material drained from the tank.

"What did you do with it?" Marshall asked.

"I scooped it up with a Bobcat and mixed it in the feed in the plant."

"You used it as feedstock for product, is that right?"

"Yup."

McAllister had provided Elias with a complete defense.

Uhlmann stood like a man charging into battle. It was show. He was actually trying to find a way to retreat to regroup. He confirmed McAllister had met with Marshall prior to trial and that Marshall took notes during the interview. Marshall had not produced those notes to the government. He was not obligated to do so unless the notes differed from McAllister's testimony, but Uhlmann knew Winmill could not make that determination without a recess to review the notes. When Uhlmann asked that the notes be produced, Winmill ordered a review in chambers and Uhlmann got his recess.

He raced out of the courtroom, catching up to Hilldorfer in adjacent urinals of the men's bathroom on the first floor. "You told me this guy wasn't going to be a problem," he seethed. "What the hell is going on?"

"He didn't tell us any of that," Hilldorfer said, teeth clenched. "He didn't say anything even close."

Uhlmann washed his hands at the sink like a surgeon scrubbing for surgery. "I have to rip this guy a new asshole. I have to destroy him," he said, flinging the paper towels at a waste can. Their discussion spilled into the first-floor foyer and continued into the conference room while Uhlmann rooted through boxes of materials until he found the file he was looking for. He quickly opened it, scanning the pages and checking his watch. He had precious minutes.

"I knew it," he said snapping the file shut. "I knew it."

BACK IN THE COURTROOM, Uhlmann displayed none of the anger he flashed downstairs. He appeared almost in good humor as he asked McAllister for specific detail about the dates he was employed at Evergreen. Hilldorfer and Wojnicz sat in the front row watching. McAllister looked like a man sitting on his front porch having a casual conversation on a warm summer day. He had no idea there was a runaway truck careening down the highway, and it was aiming right for him.

Uhlmann showed McAllister a picture of the storage tank. "You were there when it was delivered?"

"Yeah."

"You were working at Evergreen Resources at that time?"

"Yeah."

Uhlmann's voice had a hint of incredulity to it, without being sarcastic. He took his time with his questions, like a man savoring a sixteen-ounce steak. Through it all McAllister remained in appearance to be completely unconcerned. "And you actually recall Mr. Williams coming and delivering it, right?"

"Yup."

"You all assisted Mr. Williams in removing the tank from his vehicle, correct?"

"Yes."

Uhlmann had McAllister testify in detail about the delivery of the tank. McAllister willingly obliged. The runaway truck kept closing in.

"And after doing that, later that day, you were curious about what was in the tank, right?"

"Yup."

"So you looked inside?"

"Yup."

Uhlmann casually put a photograph on the projector. It was digitally dated, but the date had been redacted at Marshall's insistence. Marshall now told the court he did not object to the date being unredacted. But Uhlmann did not immediately publish the picture. He asked McAllister to be even more specific about how he had looked in the tank. McAllister calmly testified it was late in the afternoon, just before leaving for the day, when he and all of the other workers looked in the manhole.

"And all of this happened sometime after September of 1992?"

"Yeah. Probably spring of ninety-three, I'm thinking."

"Spring of ninety-three?"

"Yeah."

Hilldorfer turned to Wojnicz. "Here comes the truck."

"Ms. Miller, could you show us Exhibit 48-1?" Uhlmann asked.

Exhibit 48-1 was the same picture Marshall had showed McAllister but with the date no longer redacted. It showed the storage tank to be clearly at Evergreen.

"Same picture, right?"

"Right."

"Could you zoom on the lower right-hand corner, Ms. Miller."

Miller did.

"What's the date?" Uhlmann asked McAllister.

The truck bore down. McAllister looked like a deer caught in its head-lights, frozen, no time to get out of the way. He hesitated. "It is 3/24/92."

Uhlmann paused. "You didn't work at Evergreen Resources in March 1992, did you, sir?"

"Wham," Hilldorfer said under his breath.

The file Uhlmann found was McAllister's employment file at Evergreen. McAllister wasn't working at Evergreen when the tank was delivered. He looked stunned, disoriented. "No, I didn't," he said quietly.

"And yet that tank is right there in that photo, isn't it?"

McAllister's face twitched in confusion. "Yup."

Uhlmann could have sat down. Judge Shoob would have screamed at him to sit down, but he had other bones to pick with McAllister and he sensed the kill. He started with McAllister's statement that he had received safety training, his questions no longer friendly. They had a distinct bite. "And would it be fair to say you never had any confined-space training at Evergreen Resources that first time you were there?"

"No, not really."

"You didn't have any confined-space training?"

"No, not really."

"Not really?" Uhlmann sounded like a parent upset with his teenage child.

"No."

"It is 'no,' right?"

"Yeah."

Uhlmann then set to work on McAllister's testimony that Elias had a locker room full of safety equipment. "Didn't have those lockers during the summer of 1996 when Scott Dominguez was injured working at Evergreen, did you?"

"Nope."

On a roll now, Uhlmann hammered McAllister about the discrepancies between his testimony and what he told Hilldorfer and Wojnicz. McAllister admitted he told the agents Elias told his workers not to operate when OSHA inspectors were around, then blurted, "But I didn't think I wrote it in stone." It brought audible laughter. "[B]ut I could have. I guess I did, I don't know. I don't remember if we was operational or not." McAllister looked uncertain of just about everything.

Finally, Uhlmann attacked the testimony that the waste was mixed with feed, McAllister admitting that Evergreen was not even making a product when he worked there. Not quite done, Uhlmann left the jury with a further reason to doubt the veracity of McAllister's testimony. "And you only came back to Soda Springs when the defendant paid to bring you back there, right?"

"Well, he hired me. He didn't pay, he borrowed me the money to move back to Soda Springs."

When Uhlmann sat down, Marshall stood. Hilldorfer likened it to a man coming upon the scene of a disaster. Marshall couldn't save the victim, but he also couldn't leave him bleeding on the side of the road. Marshall suggested McAllister's memory was correct and the date on the photograph was somehow erroneous or that someone had changed it. It was like putting a Band-Aid on a compound fracture. McAllister quietly left the witness stand as the court broke for lunch.

When they returned, Nevin stood. "Your Honor, members of the jury, Mr. Elias rests."

They would give closing arguments in the morning.

Friday, May 7, 1999
Federal Courthouse
Pocatello, Idaho
United States v. Elias, Day 15

CHAPTER FORTY-SIX

HILLDORFER AND WOJNICZ arrived at the courthouse early the following morning. Wojnicz went to the U.S. Attorney's Office. Hilldorfer went into the courtroom and sat alone, as he had on the first day of trial. Though he remained nervous for Uhlmann, who would give the government's closing, and concerned about what wizardry Nevin would offer for the defense, he had a sense of peace he had not felt in some time. The night had been restful. After nearly three years there were no witnesses to track down, no statements to take, no exhibits to prepare, and no direct examinations to sit in on. Keeping to routine, he and Bob went across the street from the hotel to Prospect Pies for dinner, chili for Hilldorfer and split pea soup for Wojnicz, all you could eat, of course. Then he spent a quiet evening in his room watching television.

He'd done his job. It was all he ever really wanted the opportunity to do. He had investigated what happened and turned the evidence over to the Department of Justice. They had carried the ball to the goal line. Uhlmann would carry it across that morning.

WINMILL TOOK THE BENCH at 8:14 A.M. He denied a defense motion to dismiss the case for lack of evidence and took up last-minute discussion on jury instructions. There were no stock jury instructions for knowing endangerment. Mike Fica, the judge's clerk, had called the administrative offices of federal district courts all around the country looking for one, but struck out. Eventually they fashioned one the parties agreed upon.[1] The preliminary matters completed, the logistics decided, Winmill called for a brief recess.

Uhlmann set his pen down on his legal pad. He'd been so focused on the jury instructions he'd forgotten about his closing, which was probably a blessing, because normally the anticipation made him nauseated. When Winmill left the bench Uhlmann turned and nearly gasped. The courtroom had quietly filled behind him, looking like attendees at a lopsided wedding. The gallery on the left was full—perhaps fifty people sat behind the government, including Scott, his entire extended family, and familiar faces from Soda Springs. On the other side of the courtroom Midge Elias sat alone.

Uhlmann spoke to Celeste Miller. "Oh my God, talk about pressure."

Miller put a hand on his shoulder. "It's not pressure. It's support."

"Easy for you to say."

He pulled out his closing and started to feel sick. It was his practice to type his closing a week in advance, then tweak it as the final testimony was admitted into evidence. He sent it home to Virginia for her comment and practiced it twice for the trial team in his hotel room, solicited their input, then went into seclusion to create an outline and memorize the first few minutes and the order of the issues he would discuss. As he paced his hotel room, practicing, he drew his inspiration from Scott Dominguez and his family, and their unwavering belief that justice would be done. He had to have the same confidence. He did not want to let them down.

Winmill retook the bench.

"Mr. Uhlmann."

Uhlmann stood and put a hand to his chest, not to calm the beating of his heart, but to touch a piece of his family, his great-uncle Michael's tie. An immigrant from Poland, his uncle had escaped Nazi occupation and become a plastic surgeon in the land of opportunity. They had been very close. When his uncle died his aunt Berta gave him the tie and now when he touched it he heard his uncle's voice.

"Good luck, David. I'm looking forward to hearing your closing argument."

He'd also worn his navy plaid suit, his lucky suit that he'd worn for every closing he'd ever given. He pushed back his chair. As always, his final thought was of his wife and three children and the comfort that even if he failed miserably they would still love him. He gathered his notes and made his way to the lectern, already beginning to feel the adrenaline rush.

TO JOE HILLDORFER, Uhlmann looked like a coiled spring, a man who could not wait to get started. He stood before the jury fumbling with the clip-on microphone, joking that it was "the court's leash." Intended or not, and Hilldorfer believed it intended, the stumble gave the performance that was to follow the appearance of being spontaneous.

UHLMANN TOOK a breath, arranged his notes on the lectern, addressed the court and his opposing counsel and faced the jurors. "Three weeks ago today, Mr. Breitsameter stood before you and told you this was a case about the defendant's disregard for the decency of human life. On August 26 and August 27, 1996, the defendant, Allan Elias, sent his workers into one of the worst environments imaginable: a twenty-five-thousand-gallon steel storage tank that had been used to store sodium cyanide solution and phosphoric acid, materials which react to form deadly hydrogen cyanide gas.

"The defendant did so even though he had been warned for years about the dangers associated with confined-space entries, even though he had been warned for years about the dangers associated with cyanide. He ignored the pleas of his workers for safety equipment to protect them against the hazards of that confined space. He ignored the pleas of his workers to test the air to make sure that there weren't any hazards inside that tank. Instead he ordered them into the tank without any testing, without even the most basic safety precautions, all to save him a few dollars of railcar storage fees."

Uhlmann could feel the energy in the room building like electrical impulses.

"On August 27, 1996, wearing just jeans and a T-shirt, twenty-year-old Scott Dominguez descended into that tank on a ladder with his whole life ahead of him. Two hours later, covered in sludge and barely breathing, Scott Dominguez came out of that tank on a stretcher, his life shattered because of the defendant's knowing disregard, blatant disregard for the health and safety of his workers. Scott Dominguez has severe and permanent brain damage from cyanide poisoning. His life will never be the same."

THOUGH UHLMANN HAD the slight build of a runner and appeared to have lost even more weight over the course of the trial, there was a power that resonated from him, like an actor given a powerful script determined to do the writing justice. Hilldorfer felt confidence radiating from Uhlmann to every corner of the courtroom. Rather than getting emotional, he stated the facts. Rather than being over the top, he understated his fury. He spoke with ease, never rushing. His movements were fluid and languid, never looking rehearsed. When he talked of Scott Dominguez he spoke to each juror as if he were talking about a relative they had come to care for. Some began to cry. When he pointed his finger at Allan Elias it was like the hooded Ghost of Christmas-Yet-to-Come passing judgment on Scrooge for the injustices he had wrought in his life. Elias recoiled.

Hilldorfer had never experienced anything like it in a courtroom. At that moment, he sensed he was in the presence of greatness.

◆   ◆   ◆

HIS OPENING COMPLETE, Uhlmann discussed the charges against Allan Elias. He never looked at his notes.

"You have heard all of the evidence and I submit to you that Allan Elias is not innocent. An innocent man does not lie to rescuers trying to save one of his employees from a storage tank. An innocent man does not lie to doctors who are trying to save a twenty-year-old man's life. An innocent man does not falsify safety documents to conceal his criminal acts. And an innocent man certainly does not stage safety equipment for a search warrant to make it appear that he had provided adequate protection to his workers."

He scoffed at the notion that the defense would argue the tank was empty. "If the tank was empty, why is Scott Dominguez permanently brain damaged? How can he come into this courtroom and say that stuff?"

He went through a chronology of the tank to make his point, then turned to some of the witnesses, to the men who had minor criminal charges, or child support obligations, the men who had no luck working at the other plants in Soda Springs. "But they deserve this much: They deserve to be able to go to work in the morning and they deserve to be able to come home at night safe and sound like all the rest of us."

He challenged Nevin to prove that Elias tested the tank for cyanide. He challenged him to stand before the jury and "insult all of our intelligence" by arguing that the sludge was a product to be used at Evergreen as opposed to a waste. He talked about the men and women of Caribou County who risked their lives to save Scott Dominguez while Elias offered a series of lies to the rescuers, to Hilldorfer, to the OSHA investigators, and to Dr. Obray. "In a way, ladies and gentlemen, that says everything you need to know about Allan Elias."

Despite this, he told them not to decide the case based upon sympathy for Scott Dominguez, but on the evidence.

"The final thing I want to say to you is that this case is a case that never should have happened. What Allan Elias did to Scott Dominguez never, ever should have happened in the United States of America, not in 1996, not in 1986 or 1976 or 1966, not anytime in the last fifty years. What the defendant, Allan Elias, did to Scott Dominguez is an eerie and harrowing reminder that no matter how far we have come as a nation, no matter how industrialized our society, no matter how much most of us care about worker safety, there's still some people who think workers are expendable and that their lives do not matter. One of those people is the defendant, Allan Elias. And that, ladies and gentlemen, is why we have been here the last three weeks."

Uhlmann thanked them, gathered the notes he had never used, and sat down. It was, bar none, the best closing Hilldorfer and Wojnicz had ever heard. Like all of the witnesses at trial, David Uhlmann had risen to the occasion.

AFTER A BRIEF RECESS, David Nevin stood and walked toward the jury box. "I would like to begin talking with you essentially right where I left off at the time of the opening statement. Counsel has accused me of having said some things in the opening statement that were false and he's quoted me in certain ways in the opening statement. What I said to you in the opening statement was that Allan Elias was not substantially certain that the tank cleaning operation would injure his employees; he was substantially certain that it would not."

Nevin told the jury he had used those words because it was the burden the government was required to meet but did not. He had the John F. Kennedy hand in the pocket. "Substantially certain is the barrier through which the government must go, must convince you in order to convince you to convict Mr. Elias. And I submit to you, ladies and gentlemen, the evidence absolutely does not establish that. It absolutely does not establish that Allan was substantially certain that this risk would flow from this tank-cleaning operation."

He looked as comfortable as Uhlmann, more demonstrative in his movements, and seemingly determined to lock eyes with every juror, to pull just one of them onto the boat of reasonable doubt with him. He told them that contrary to the government's statements the evidence was that Elias had performed a titration test. He cited Elias's statements to the Idaho State Police officers, Joe Hilldorfer, and OSHA and said that Elias tasted the material. "He would never put it in his mouth if he thought there was cyanide in it."

He took Uhlmann's challenge and continued to beat the drum that Elias had the material tested for silver because silver was a marker for cyanide. He maintained that the tank was empty when it left AEI, citing Ivan Williams's testimony and the testimony of Kenny McAllister, conceding McAllister might have been confused about some things, but not about looking in the tank. He called Dominguez's injury a "freak accident," and took aim at Brian Smith and Gene Thornock for not doing the job "by the book." He refrained from blaming the hospital personnel but suggested Dr. Obray knew early on in treating Dominguez that there was cyanide in the tank, and therefore what Elias said and didn't say was a "red herring."

Despite the government's motion to prevent Nevin from vouching for Elias's innocence, he did just that, offering his personal opinion that Elias didn't commit the crimes. "Now, was he wrong? Yes, he was wrong. It was cyanide in the tank and I wish it were otherwise and he wishes it were otherwise, no one doesn't wish that it were otherwise. But that is different from being substantially certain. That is different from knowing that it's probable that the waste is going to be harmful to the human health and environment. That's different. And because of that, because of those facts alone, he is not guilty of Counts One through Three."

He implored them to follow the jury instructions and told them it was not their job to determine what Allan Elias knew or didn't know. "If you have a reasonable doubt about these matters, then you must acquit him. And I will say, if there's not a reasonable doubt present on this set of facts, then I suspect there never will be. Ladies and gentlemen, it would be wrong to convict Allan of these offenses, it would be wrong and I ask you, please, do not do that. Find him not guilty because he is not guilty. Thank you."

Though it was noon, Winmill decided to have Uhlmann give his rebuttal rather than break for lunch. Uhlmann was scribbling furiously. Part of him wanted the lunch break to organize his rebuttal, but that wasn't going to happen. He stood and went back to the jury, talking as he crossed the carpet and clipped on the microphone.

"I scribbled an awful lot of notes while Mr. Nevin was talking and I promise you I won't review all of them with you," he told the jury. "But I had to restrain myself not to shake my head because I wondered, as I listened to him, where he had been the last three weeks?"

He attacked the "freak accident" argument, which he had anticipated, comparing Elias's operation of Evergreen to a driver knowingly driving a truck without brakes. "I say to you that an accident waiting for a place to happen is not an accident." Hilldorfer smiled at Wojnicz. Hilldorfer had made the analogy so often during the past two years he was certain Uhlmann was sick of hearing it.

"It is tragic, it is horrible, and I believe that Mr. Nevin is sincere when he stands before you and says that he is sorry about what happened. But Mr. Nevin standing before you today and saying that Mr. Nevin is sorry about what happened is no substitute and no excuse for what Mr. Elias did. Mr. Elias was playing a game of Russian roulette with the lives of his employees. It was simply a matter of time before somebody was seriously hurt."

Uhlmann concluded as he had concluded every closing he had ever given, with a statement he believed in despite being the kid who grew up in Washington, D.C., watching the race riots and hearing the news that Bobby Kennedy and Martin Luther King had been shot. It was a statement he believed in despite having his perception of Atticus Finch shattered while working as a young law clerk. It was a statement he believed in despite having his enthusiasm for prosecuting environmental offenders squashed by a federal judge in Wyoming during his first environmental trial. He still believed in the judicial system. He believed in justice.

"After you eat lunch you will begin your deliberations," he told the jury. "On behalf of the United States I ask you only one thing: When you retire to deliberate on your verdict, bring back a verdict that speaks the truth. Bring back a verdict that speaks for justice." He considered every juror. "The only verdict that speaks for truth in this case, the only verdict that speaks for justice, is that Allan Elias is guilty as charged in the indictment."

With those final, familiar words, he was done. It had been one hell of a ride.

After he sat, Winmill instructed the jury and dismissed them. He turned to the attorneys and expressed his gratitude for the professional manner in which they had conducted themselves, calling it "unrivaled," then asked, "If there is nothing else, Counsel?"

Amazingly, no one spoke.

"We'll be in recess," he said.

CHAPTER FORTY-SEVEN

T HEY MET IN the U.S. Attorney's Office. To Hilldorfer it felt like being let out of school after a long and trying year. Uhlmann began the difficult process of trying to decompress while still feeling like he had sugar running through his veins and was walking on a trampoline. Judge Shoob and Neil Cartusciello, the former chief of the Environmental Crimes Section, both told him it was important for a trial attorney to begin letting go of a case after closing argument, to accept that their job was done, that it was the jury's job to convict. It was a necessary survival technique. Waiting for a jury could be maddening.

Hilldorfer approached Uhlmann and stuck out his hand. Uhlmann gripped it. Then the two men embraced. Hilldorfer told him it was the best closing he'd ever heard. Uhlmann thanked him, then he stepped back and took a moment to exhale. He looked at the trial team and was about to tell them all that, win or lose, they had all done one hell of a job. The room stilled. Uhlmann turned. Scott Dominguez and his family stood at the door.

Ron Hamp stepped in. "Scotty wants to give you all something."

Scott stepped forward and handed Uhlmann a card. Breitsameter stood with Uhlmann as he opened the envelope and slid the card out. On the front was a cartoon of an elephant climbing a limbless tree, a rope around its waist and a potted plant wrapped in its trunk. A dinosaur sat atop the tree sleeping.

"Scott chose this card himself," Jackie said smiling, "and he spent the longest time looking for it. He went through just about every card in the store."

Uhlmann opened the card. The Elephant had reached the top of the tree and had given the plant to the grinning dinosaur. He read the printed note aloud.

"You really went out of your way for me! Thanks."

Below the print, Dominguez had scrawled a personal note.

*Well, this card is self-explanatory, except I haven't really had
the chance to tell everyone how much I appreciate how
everyone really went out of their way for me.*
                              Thanks again, Scott.[1]

Dominguez chose to say thank you without knowing the verdict.
The thought was sobering. Uhlmann embraced him. Hilldorfer and the
rest of the trial team followed.

"Let's go outside," Breitsameter said. "I want to get a picture of all of
us so we can remember this day."

They took the photograph in front of the courthouse, lingered for a
few moments, then split up and went to lunch. After lunch they met again
in the U.S. Attorney's Office, making telephone calls and watching
the clock. When it neared four in the afternoon it became unlikely they
would get a verdict. The judge's staff had a three-hour drive back to
Boise. They'd have to wait until Monday, at the earliest. Breitsameter
wanted to buy a pair of cowboy boots from a nearby Indian reservation.
Uhlmann, in search of presents for his family, and Wojnicz, always looking for a screaming deal, joined him, along with David Overy, the young
attorney from the Environmental Crimes Section who had done much of
the research and motion work.

Feeling the need to burn off nervous energy, Hilldorfer begged out
to go to the gym.

AT AMERICAN FITNESS Hilldorfer told the woman at the counter
who he was and asked her to page him in the unlikely event someone
called looking for him. He changed into his workout clothes and rode a
stationary bike for twenty-five minutes, then moved to the free weights,
pressing sixty-pound dumbbells when he heard his name over the gym
intercom and nearly dropped the weights. As he rushed back to the front
counter he ran into Roger Sears, the Pocatello Fire Department captain
who was walking out of the locker room buttoning his shirt.

"Hey, they're calling you."

"I heard," Hilldorfer said.

The woman spoke before he reached the counter. "They want you
back in court. Right now."

◆   ◆   ◆

THE TRADING POST was on the Shoshone-Bannock Reservation fifteen miles north of Pocatello at the Fort Hall turnoff. Breitsameter picked out a pair of cowboy boots while Uhlmann sized moccasins for his two daughters and called Virginia to get the appropriate size. Then they all piled back into Uhlmann's green Subaru Outback, stopping at a gas station to fill up, since Uhlmann would need the car for at least one more weekend. As Uhlmann stood outside the car pumping gas his cell phone rang. It was the judge's staff.

"The jury is back. It has a verdict."

He repeated the words out loud and everyone and everything froze for an instant then started again as if on fast-forward. Uhlmann pulled the hose from the tank, quickly screwed back on the cap, and jumped behind the wheel looking at his watch.

They were at least twenty minutes away.

HILLDORFER didn't bother to shower, throwing his clothes on, splashing water on his face and rushing out the door with his tie unknotted around his neck and his mind spinning. There was so much science in the case and so many witnesses. How could the jury have come back so quickly? He feared they had found it incomprehensible that anyone could have done what Allan Elias did, acquitted him of the knowing endangerment charge and found him guilty on the lesser charges. That, however, would be contrary to Uhlmann's experience that the lead charge dictated the findings on the lesser charges, and Hilldorfer didn't even want to consider that possibility.

He bounced the car over the curb into the Federal Courthouse parking lot and parked at an angle near the front, jumping out and knotting his tie as he bounded up the steps. He presented his credentials to the court security officers as he stepped through the metal detector then hurried across the marbled foyer to the U.S. Attorney's Office.

No one was there.

He sprinted up the steps to the second floor and pulled open the courtroom door as Mike Fica stepped in at the front of the room.

"ALL RISE."

The gallery was full. Uhlmann, Breitsameter, and Miller sat at the table closest to the jury, Breitsameter in the middle. Uhlmann sat across the aisle from Nevin, Elias between him and Marshall.

Hilldorfer slid into a pew next to Wojnicz. "What do you know?"

"They have a verdict."

Hilldorfer looked to the jurors reentering the room. They were pokerfaced, eyes locked on Winmill.

"I will note for the record that the jury has advised the bailiff that they have arrived at a verdict. I'm having a hard time finding Mr.— Who is the foreperson?"

Juror Boyd Greenlee stood. "I am, your honor."

"Mr. Greenlee, has the jury, in fact, unanimously agreed upon a verdict?"

"Yes, we have."

Hilldorfer's pulse rushed in his temples like the wind through a seashell and everything came to a slow roll, each movement noticed and registered.

"All right. Mr. Greenlee, would you please hand the verdict form to Mr. Fica."

Fica walked to the railing, took the form from Greenlee's outstretched hand, and handed it to Winmill. Every head in the courtroom followed the slip of paper. The judge opened it like a gambler considering his cards. His face revealed nothing.

"Ladies and gentlemen, at this time I'm going to give the verdict to Ms. Garcia and ask that she publish it by reading it," he said, referring to his court clerk. "As it is read I will ask you to listen carefully to the verdict, since you may be polled individually to ensure that this is, in fact, your verdict. Mr. Elias, if you will please stand."

Elias pushed back his chair and stood, hands clasped behind his back, Nevin and Marshall at his side. Garcia opened the piece of paper and leaned toward the microphone.

"In the matter of the United States of America versus Allan Elias, Criminal Case No. 98-0070-E . . ."

Hilldorfer shut his eye, listening. He sat rigid, hands resting on his thighs. The first charge was for knowing endangerment. Everything else would revolve around it.

Garcia continued. "We the jury find the defendant as to Count One of the indictment: guilty."

Hilldorfer opened his eyes, turned, and glanced at Jackie and Ron Hamp. There were no smiles, just exhausted expressions of relief at the end of a tortured ordeal. Scott Dominguez sat between them, his face blank but his eyes radiating that he understood what had just happened.

At the verdict Uhlmann felt a rush surge across his chest but remained outwardly stoic, his face a mask of ambivalence. Under the table he clenched his fist. He glanced at the defense table. Nevin looked ashen, stricken, as did Marshall. Elias stood between them sweating profusely, as if reality was flowing from his pores. Normally a big man, he suddenly looked very, very small.

Nevin put a hand at Elias's back as Garcia continued.

"As to Count Two of the indictment: guilty.

"As to Count Three of the indictment: guilty."

It was like a drum beating. "As to Count Four of the indictment: guilty."

Every count, Hilldorfer said to himself. They'd got him on every count.

Winmill thanked Garcia and turned to Elias. "You may be seated, Mr. Elias. Ladies and gentlemen of the jury, is this your verdict, so say you one, so say you all?"

They responded in unison. "Yes."

"Counsel, do you wish to have the jury polled?"

Nevin stood. "Yes, your honor."

"All right. Ladies and gentlemen, I will ask each of you individually if this is your verdict, if you will please indicate whether this is your individual verdict in all respects, that is, the verdict finding the defendant guilty on all four counts, Counts One, Two, Three, and Four."

The jurors did not waver. Each responded, "Yes, Your Honor" or "Yes, it is" twelve straight times. The drum continued to beat.

Several of the jurors looked to the two agents and nodded.

Breitsameter and Uhlmann advised the court that they had a matter to take up with the court and Winmill, rightfully anticipating they would request that Allan Elias be detained in jail until sentencing, thanked the jurors and excused them. As they left, Breitsameter walked to the railing and spoke to Hilldorfer and Wojnicz.

"Go out in the lobby and stand there. Sometimes the jurors here want to talk to you. Don't approach them but if they want to talk to you let them. It's important they know we appreciated their service."

As much as they wanted to see Elias handcuffed and led away, the two agents went outside and stood in the hall like two kids at a high school dance trying not to look conspicuous. Wojnicz stuck out a hand. "Good job, Joe."

Hilldorfer took the hand and patted him on the shoulder. "You, too, Bob."

Ten minutes later the jurors filed out of the jury room. Some walked by quickly. A few nodded or said hello and Hilldorfer and Wojnicz thanked them for their hard work. The jurors dismissed it and thanked the two agents. One of the last jurors to leave was a woman who had been a copious note taker. She approached Hilldorfer with a smile and outstretched hand.

"I want to shake your hand," she said. "I usually only get to read about guys like you in books."[2]

INSIDE THE COURTROOM Winmill set sentencing for August 2 and took up the matter of detaining Elias. Breitsameter argued that Elias, sixty-one years old, was facing a considerable incarceration and was sophisticated and financially well-off.

"There was a financial investigation done, as the court's aware from pretrial matters, which established that [Elias] had received over $2 million from Kerr-McGee. There was difficulty tracing funds. I can represent to the court that it appeared that money may have been going offshore, which gives us reason to believe he would be a flight risk."

In addition to being unable to trace Elias's money, Breitsameter said Elias had no ties to the Soda Springs community and had residences in California and Wyoming and had not lived with his wife, who resided in Beverly Hills, for many years. He also had displayed erratic, or defiant, behavior, sometimes calling his probation officer at 3:00 in the morning.

Nevin dismissed the notion of Elias being a flight risk. "Mr. Elias had every opportunity of fleeing if that were something that he had made a choice to do, while the case was in its pendency, but he's not done that. He's made every court appearance and he's been faithful in doing that."

At 7:10 P.M. on a Friday evening, Winmill didn't appear inclined to hear a lot of argument. He set a further detention hearing for May 17, ordered Elias to surrender his passport, contact his probation officer daily, wear an electric monitor, and restrict his travel. After the high of the verdict, it was tough for Uhlmann and Breitsameter to watch Allan Elias walk out of the courtroom free.

They met the rest of the trial team and Scott Dominguez and his family in the U.S. Attorney's Office, offering high-spirited congratulations and hugs. Jackie Hamp asked the question on all their minds.

"How long will it be until he's sentenced?"

Breitsameter told her three months was not unusual. "By the end of the summer, early fall at the latest, Allan should be in jail."

Wednesday, June 16, 1999
Environmental Crimes Section
Department of Justice
Washington, D.C.

CHAPTER FORTY-EIGHT

DAVID UHLMANN sat in his office on Pennsylvania Avenue staring out the window at the magnificent rotunda and eight Roman columns of the National Gallery of Art. The weather in Washington was becoming seasonally warm, hazy and humid, and he was settling into his old routine, but Pocatello, Scott Dominguez, and Allan Elias were never far from his mind. He turned from the view and considered the small table between the two chairs across from his desk. Prominently displayed with framed family photographs and trinkets from other cases stood the card given to him by Scott Dominguez.

Uhlmann had not returned to Pocatello for the detention hearing on May 17. Breitsameter had handled it alone. Breitsameter believed sufficient grounds existed to detain Elias, including the legitimate concern he would flee. Ron Hamp had called Hilldorfer in Seattle and Hilldorfer had advised Breitsameter that Elias had been seen around town using pay phones. The U.S. Attorney's Office was having trouble tracking his money. It was not out of the realm of possibility that Elias was hiding money and making plans to disappear. If he did, they would likely never get him back. Many jurisdictions did not recognize environmental crimes for extradition.

But Breitsameter was also a realist. He knew judges in the District of Idaho detained the fewest individuals pending sentencing in the Ninth Circuit and were proud of that fact. It was peculiar given that it was the failure of Randy Weaver to appear for trial that resulted in the bloody Ruby Ridge standoff, the incident in northern Idaho when federal agents descended on a farmhouse to arrest white separatists and a gun battle erupted that left Weaver's wife and a federal agent dead.

At the detention hearing Breitsameter had called Special Agent Mike Ryan of the IRS. Ryan testified that he had not been successful in tracking all of Elias's money, which Breitsameter argued to the court was "some evidence of the shell game here that's occurred."[1] At various times Elias kept bank accounts in Alabama; Evanston, Wyoming; Idaho; California; New York; and the Bank of Malad, Ireland—which ironically had a branch in Soda Springs. He would retain cash from transfers, or write checks to his personal bank account, to one of his businesses, to his children and to his wife. He had even sent money to Mike Griffin, Bob Griffin's son in Alabama. Ryan identified more than $80,000 in cash withheld, and said he could not account for another $320,000. He also noted that Elias, despite his conviction, continued to be paid roughly $41,600 a month from Kerr-McGee.

Elias filed an affidavit stating that Evergreen no longer operated. He was now operating Western Fertilizer as a distribution center for Kerr-McGee's fertilizer. Western Fertilizer was a large warehouse. Despite the monthly payments, Elias said he had less than $5,000 available cash, had an outstanding obligation to his father of $400,000, and had paid lawyer fees exceeding $750,000.[2]

Winmill had ruled from the bench, finding insufficient evidence Elias was a flight risk and setting him free. "I trust Mr. Elias will not abuse the trust that I am showing him."

LATE IN THE afternoon, June 16, Uhlmann took a call from Breitsameter to discuss Elias's impending sentencing and to discuss preparing the government's sentencing memorandum. It would advise Winmill on the base number of months Elias should serve for each count convicted, as well as appropriate enhancements under the federal sentencing guidelines.

"It might be helpful to talk to one of the jurors and find out what resonated with them," Breitsameter said, suggesting what resonated with the jurors might also resonate with Winmill.

Some districts did not allow attorneys to speak to jurors, even after the trial. Idaho was not one of those. Breitsameter had spoken with perhaps half a dozen jurors after trials he had lost, but had never spoken to a juror after a case he had won. Uhlmann, always mindful of Judge Shoob's advice, thought it a good idea. They decided to call the obvious choice, foreman Boyd Greenlee.

Greenlee was not home but they left him a message and he called back an hour or so later saying he was happy to hear from them. "I was hoping to have an opportunity to talk with someone about the case. I was hoping somebody would call."

They talked for about forty-five minutes, discussing the trial and Greenlee's experience as a juror. He complimented the prosecutors and said he hated to "hang" Elias, but based on the evidence he felt Elias deserved it. They asked Greenlee what evidence had resonated with him. They had been influenced by the evidence that Elias knew what was in the tank but hadn't bothered to get proper safety equipment. The two prosecutors talked with him for perhaps half an hour, then Uhlmann and Breitsameter thanked Greenlee for his time. He again said he was happy to have had the chance to talk to them.

"I had to be very careful to avoid contact with all of you when I'd see you in the hallway and such." Greenlee had stayed at the Ameritel Hotel during the course of the trial. "Elias said 'hello' to me a few times, though, and to some of the other jurors. And one time he winked at me, maybe like he was trying to win us over, or something, I don't know."

Uhlmann was not surprised.

"And then when he knew he was going to get hung, he asked one juror what it would take to buy her off."[3]

Uhlmann couldn't believe it. He asked Greenlee if he knew which juror. Greenlee didn't know her by name but described her as "the alternate with blond hair. She was sitting just to my right."

The alternate was Janet Scott. As an alternate, she had been dismissed prior to the jury deliberations. Uhlmann asked what was said.

"I didn't hear it. He said it to her and I knew about it, but we didn't discuss it much, you know, since the court told us not to discuss anything concerning the case. She just came into the jury room and mentioned it, and we thought it was just really, that he was joking about it. But it wouldn't have mattered. He could have paid us each a million dollars and it wouldn't have changed the verdict."

Uhlmann was disturbed but not shocked. Elias had evaded regulations for a whole host of noxious actions for years and he didn't expect Elias to suddenly start playing by the rules. It was the reason the government had kept him on a short leash during the trial. Twice they asked Winmill to admonish Elias, once for making faces and gestures during witness testimony, and once when Midge Elias walked into the well during an attorney sidebar to give him a hug and rub his back in front of the jury. The comment to the juror increased Uhlmann's concern Elias would never voluntarily report for sentencing. He saw it as a further basis to ask the court to detain him.

They thanked Greenlee and ended the call. As Uhlmann stewed waiting for Breitsameter to call him back, another realization suddenly hit him. The jurors probably should have reported the incident to the court when it happened. An uneasiness enveloped him and he snatched the phone on the first ring. Breitsameter, still thinking in terms of using the information to detain Elias, said, "I don't think this is really something we should pursue further."

"George, I don't know that we have the choice. I think it's something we have to tell the court about."

Upon further discussion, Breitsameter agreed. Anything with the potential to impact a jury was possible grounds for a new trial. Breitsameter knew of a recent case in the district in which the Ninth Circuit Court of Appeals had set aside the verdict because a juror read about the trial in the newspaper. He also told Uhlmann that Winmill had two other cases pending before him that involved jury issues. It was ridiculous to think Elias could orchestrate an appellate issue, or even get a new trial through his own misconduct, but in a case in which every issue seemed to be on the cutting edge of the law, nothing was far-fetched. They agreed to talk to their respective supervisors and call each other back.

Breitsameter spoke with Deerden. Uhlmann talked to his section chief, Steve Solow, then called his mentor in Montana, Assistant U.S. Attorney David Kubichek. All advised the responsible thing to do was to tell the court. It was not their prerogative to decide what was and wasn't important. By not disclosing the comment they could potentially draw more significance to it than it deserved if it came out down the road.

Uhlmann and Breitsameter called Winmill's chambers in Boise at 5:00 P.M. that afternoon and spoke to Mike Fica.

"Mike," Uhlmann said, "do you know how some prosecutors never talk to jurors . . . Well, we did."[4]

Uhlmann said they were seeking the court's guidance. Fica hung up and spoke to Dave Metcalf, Winmill's permanent law clerk, then sent an e-mail to the judge. Fica called Uhlmann back a short time later. The judge wanted Uhlmann to call defense counsel and arrange a conference call to discuss the matter.[5]

The next day, as he drove his family minivan north on Interstate 95 to take his son and oldest daughter to summer camp, Uhlmann reached Nevin by cell phone. They spoke for a moment about the case; Nevin said he felt by the end of the trial the jurors were looking at him with fangs. Then Uhlmann advised Nevin of his conversation with Greenlee and said it concerned him enough that he was thinking of requesting that the court reconsider its decision not to detain Elias. Nevin defended his client, saying it was "something I'll look into" but that he was certain it was nothing untoward. They'd take the matter up further during the conference call with the court on June 23, 1999.[6]

Each side submitted briefs. Uhlmann and Breitsameter took an offensive position and suggested the court conduct a further inquiry of all the jurors to determine if Elias was guilty of improper conduct warranting his detention pending sentencing. As to any suggestion of a new trial, and there had been none by Nevin, they dismissed it as a nonissue. The allotted time for such a motion had passed, and Elias's improper conduct was not "new evidence" to justify such a motion.

During the telephone conference Winmill agreed that a further inquiry was appropriate and set the hearing for July 2, 1999.

THE FOURTH OF July weekend was Uhlmann's fourth wedding anniversary. Rather than tell Virginia that she'd be celebrating it alone while he was back in Pocatello again, he surprised her by taking her and Emily with him. They would spend the weekend in the Sawtooth Mountains white-water rafting. As their plane landed in Pocatello on July 1, Uhlmann looked out at the expansive horizon and broad countryside and felt a certain peace, like he was returning home. Neither he nor Breit-sameter were particularly concerned about the hearing. Both considered it just another saga in the prosecution of Allan Elias.

Winmill held the hearing in his chambers, which were modest. His desk faced inward, his back to the windows. He had rearranged the furniture so that the attorneys, and Elias, sat in a corner, but as on the first day in court Nevin and Uhlmann jockeyed for position until Winmill finally arranged them. The judge expressed concern that the jurors, called out of the blue, would worry that they had done something wrong. At the same time he believed it critical they be placed under oath. Until he determined what had actually happened only he would question the jurors. The strict rules of federal evidence did not allow inquiry into jury deliberations, but did allow a limited inquiry into what the jurors had heard and what impact, if any, it had on them. The distinction, Winmill said, "was an uncomfortable and unclear line."

Nevin wanted the opportunity to cross-examine the jurors and disagreed with the arbitrary line drawn by the court. "If we're not here on an issue of inquiring into whether or not there was something untoward that occurred with respect to this jury, then I question why we are here. That's exactly what we're doing here."

Winmill was not persuaded. After admonishing Elias not to make any nonverbal gestures, which he called his "habit," he told Fica to bring in Greenlee.

HILLDORFER AND WOJNICZ sat in their customary location in the first row of the courtroom, the jurors seated to their left.

"Déjà vu all over again," Wojnicz whispered.

Hilldorfer felt like he had just reached into his pocket for his wallet and found a hole. The fact that they were not allowed in chambers only added to that helpless feeling. Worse, the jurors that the two agents had last greeted in the foyer outside the courtroom with smiles, nods of the head, and handshakes, now sat in the jury box looking like they had been dropped out of an airplane blindfolded. The two agents could not approach them, and they could not explain why they suddenly had to ignore them. All they could do was sit, like statues, and watch as one by one the jurors stood and walked hesitantly through the side door that led to the judge's chambers.

◆   ◆   ◆

GREENLEE APPEARED relatively calm entering Judge Winmill's chambers. Perhaps in his forties, he was five foot nine with a short-cropped haircut and a neatly trimmed dark mustache. Throughout trial he had been extremely attentive and the government team was not surprised he became the foreman.

"Take a deep breath," Winmill soothed. He explained to Greenlee why they were there and asked him about his comment.

"She mentioned it to us jurors in the room, she just says Mr. Elias approached us—or approached me and just mentioned what would it take to turn her decision, and that was all that was said."

"Did you understand— What was your understanding as to the tone or nature of Mr. Elias's remark?"

"I kind of think maybe he was just joking. I wasn't there, so I didn't hear. This is just hearsay." He recalled Janet Scott telling them about it during a lunch recess, and though he couldn't recall what jurors were present, he said, "I'm sure a big majority of them."

Greenlee reiterated Elias would wink at him to acknowledge him, but said his decision was made solely on the evidence. With that, Winmill dismissed him.[7]

Janet Scott followed—a pleasant-looking woman perhaps in her late thirties with straight blond hair that came to her shoulders. She looked much more uncomfortable than Greenlee. Winmill asked, after she was sworn, whether she recalled having any conversations with Mr. Elias or anyone else associated with the case.

"No."

Winmill asked specifically if she recalled talking to Elias on a recess, bumping into him in the hallway or parking lot.

"Other than hello?" Scott asked. She sounded almost defensive.

"Yes."

"No."

Uhlmann gave Breitsameter a peripheral glance.

Winmill said, "I think I'm going to cut right to the quick. A statement was attributed and, frankly, the juror may have been confused possibly as to who the person was that made the statement even, but at least the suggestion was made that you may have indicated that Mr. Elias may have made some comment to you in the parking lot on the way in or perhaps in the hallway in which a specific statement was made, and you're telling me that no specific statements other than hello?"

"Other than greetings of some kind?"

"And greetings would be hello, how are you, something of that sort?" Winmill suggested.

Scott shook her head.

Winmill excused her and turned to counsel. Now they were all confused. Wanting to be certain that perhaps Greenlee had not attributed the statement to the wrong juror, Winmill said he would be even more specific. When Janet Scott re-entered he told her what Greenlee had represented she told the jurors.

"So my question is, first, do you recall or was, in fact, that statement made by Mr. Elias to you?"

"No."

He asked if she'd heard another juror make a similar type comment.

"I don't recall that."

Winmill thanked her. She left them all scratching their heads.

The next two jurors denied hearing anything like what Greenlee related, but juror Michael Burkhart confirmed that other jurors had mentioned bumping into Elias and Janet Scott was one of them, though he did not recall any specific comment. Juror Joyce Barrus followed and said Scott had mentioned Elias talked to her in the parking lot "midway" through trial. Barrus recalled that Scott said she tried to avoid Elias and when she walked back into the courthouse one of the marshals, who sat in the lobby with a view of the parking lot, asked her if Elias talked to her. According to Barrus, Scott responded that she was "trying not to have a conversation with him."

None of the other five jurors had any information.

At the conclusion of the hearing Uhlmann was convinced it was an interesting legal issue but of no consequence, and he believed Winmill had reached the same conclusion. Winmill told them it was his "inclination not to inquire further. I think that we have at this point exhausted as much as we need to pursue."

HILLDORFER AND WOJNICZ waited in the lobby outside Winmill's courtroom. When Breitsameter and Uhlmann emerged they gave them the *Reader's Digest* version. Breitsameter expressed regret for having called Greenlee and worried the issue could further delay getting Elias sentenced. It had already been continued to accommodate a European vacation by Marshall. The better news, however, was that based on what they'd just heard, neither Breitsameter nor Uhlmann had any concern about a new trial. As they talked, Hilldorfer found himself looking out the second-story window into the court parking lot where he spotted Nevin talking with Elias. Nevin reached out and gave Elias a hug. Despite Breitsameter and Uhlmann's assurances things were fine, Hilldorfer suspected the matter was not over.

Wednesday, October 20, 1999
EPA Region 10
Sixth and University
Seattle, Washington

CHAPTER FORTY-NINE

ELIAS'S SENTENCING was delayed, but not because of the juror issue. On July 26, Marshall filed a second request to continue the sentencing, this time because Marshall was not available until after September 15, 1999. Winmill rescheduled sentencing to October 1, 1999. Two weeks later, both Nevin and Marshall filed motions to withdraw as Elias's attorneys. Nevin's accompanying affidavit stated only that Elias no longer wanted him to represent him. Craig Jorgensen, Elias's longtime counsel, wasted no time trying to use the withdrawal to delay Elias's sentence still further, this time indefinitely. Jorgensen said Elias was contemplating filing a motion for a new trial based upon juror misconduct.

Uhlmann filed a brief calling the request another stall tactic to keep Elias out of jail. He said Jorgensen had represented Elias for years and had been involved with his trial; there was no reason he couldn't handle a sentencing still two months away.

On September 14, Winmill granted Nevin and Marshall's motions to withdraw—that was a given. But he didn't stop there. Winmill found that during the hearing of July 2, 1999, Greenlee's statement was "at odds with that of another juror, thereby raising credibility issues." He also granted the defense's request to conduct further discovery into Greenlee's credibility. The defense now alleged that Greenlee had failed to report a sixteen-year-old DUI conviction in Utah during voir dire, and said that had he done so, they would have challenged him. When Hilldorfer and Wojnicz read the motion they were spitting mad. They believed the only way Jorgensen could have obtained such obscure information was by someone improperly using the National Crime Information Center. The fact that the allegation was unsupported by an affidavit only confirmed their suspicion of wrongdoing. They wanted to conduct a criminal investigation into the matter.

Winmill's order acknowledged the allegation was unsupported, but in deference to Jorgensen, whom he called an "officer of the court," he granted the request. Sentencing was again put off, this time to December 10, 1999.

In late September, Hilldorfer was sitting in his cubicle when he got a call from Jim Oesterle.

"Joe, you truly have the gift of stirring up trouble."

He laughed. Oesterle's comment could have been directed at any number of things. "What did I do this time?"

Oesterle told Hilldorfer that Elias had armed himself with a new dream team of appellate lawyers from Seattle and Los Angeles and that they had filed two motions.

"If he's as indigent as he claims, who's paying his legal bills?" Hilldorfer asked.

"I don't know."

Oesterle told him that, to no one's surprise since Winmill's order had invited it, Elias filed a motion for a new trial on the grounds of juror misconduct. Elias argued that Greenlee either fabricated Juror Scott's comment, which made him biased and unfit as a juror, or the other jurors lied under oath when asked if the event occurred. Elias denied making the statement, and his counsel submitted that he had passed a polygraph test.[1]

"What a bunch of crap," Hilldorfer said.

Oesterle told him the appellate attorneys had also come up with a new strategy. Relying on an Appellate Court decision out of the Eighth Circuit, they filed a motion to have the hazardous waste disposal charges against Elias dismissed entirely.

"On what grounds?" Hilldorfer asked, bewildered.

"They're arguing the government never had jurisdiction to prosecute him."

"Well, it's a little late for that, isn't it?"

"Let's hope so," Oesterle said.

WHILE THE MOTIONS meant more work, Uhlmann was not concerned about either. He considered the attack on the government's
jurisdiction to try Elias as born of desperation, a request that essentially required Winmill to call into question nearly every RCRA conviction in the United States in the previous five years. He wrote a blistering
response to the motion for a new trial, pointing out that Elias's misconduct did not justify the tremendous societal cost of invalidat-
ing a three-and-a-half-week jury trial. He also scoffed at the suggestion
that the incident had not occurred. As to the allegation that Greenlee
lied in voir dire, he agreed with the court's observation that it was
"hard to imagine a more remote, irrelevant offense" and said the defense's belated argument that it would have challenged Greenlee was
hypocrisy. Several others in the jury pool, including two eventual jurors, reported prior DUI offenses. The defense did not challenge any of
them.

Ten days later, on November 11, Elias moved to again continue his
sentencing to allow for a court hearing on his two motions. Seemingly in
keeping with Uhlmann's belief that neither motion warranted much consideration, Winmill issued an order denying the continuance, saying a
hearing was not necessary. Uhlmann called Hilldorfer with the news, and
they both looked forward to seeing each other December 10 in Pocatello
for Elias's long-awaited sentencing.

Thursday, December 9, 1999
Honolulu International Airport
Honolulu, Hawaii

CHAPTER FIFTY

FOR HILLDORFER, Hawaii had always been a respite from the
wet Seattle winters and the hassles of everyday life. His mother- and
father-in-law adopted him like the "son" they never had, and he had

taken to calling them "mom" and "dad." Their home in Honolulu had very much become his home and the bond with his father-in law was particularly strong. They shared the same birthday; both were proud, driven men; and their most prized possession was Joanne. But since his father-in-law's illness and coma, Hawaii had become bittersweet. The trip that December was particularly melancholy. His father-in-law remained in a nursing home, still struggling with his medical problems and the psychological impact they had on a proud and self-made man. It made it that much more difficult to leave to return to Pocatello for Elias's sentencing. He felt guilty and worried he'd never see his father-in-law again, but he also knew he had to go. He needed to bring closure to the Elias case, to fulfill his promise to Scott and his family that they would see Allan Elias go to jail. He also needed the psychological boost of seeing a defendant he had investigated go to jail for his crimes.

Joanne dropped him off at the Honolulu airport and their embrace lingered a moment longer than normal. Then he stepped from the car to catch his plane to Salt Lake City.

Six hours, one movie, and a restless nap after he boarded, the pilot advised the cabin to prepare for their descent into Salt Lake City. When the plane rolled to the gate Hilldorfer stood with everyone else to gather his carry-on; a mass of humanity rushing to take three irrational steps only to stand and wait in an aisle. It was like watching weekday commuters without their cars. His back ached from the prolonged sitting, and he wanted only to get off the plane to stretch it and his legs.

"Would everyone please re-take their seats." The stewardess's voice came through the cabin. "I need everyone to please retake their seats."

Audible moans of displeasure greeted her request, but the passengers dutifully sat back down. When they had, the stewardess continued. "Joe Hilldorfer?"

For a second Hilldorfer was too puzzled to move.

"Joe Hilldorfer?"

He raised his hand.

The stewardess walked to him. "I need you to grab your luggage and depart."

"What's the matter?"

"You need to contact the airport police. They have a message for you."

Hilldorfer felt certain it was Joanne calling with bad news about his father-in-law and the guilt of leaving exploded inside him. He grabbed his carry-on and hurried down the aisle, every eye on the plane watching him depart. When he exited the gate there was an airport security officer waiting for him.

"Joe Hilldorfer?"

"Yeah."

"You have a message to call Dixon McClary at your office."

His office? Hilldorfer's thoughts shifted from his father-in-law to Allan Elias.

He'd fled.

He hurried through the terminal scanning the face of every man, irrationally searching for Elias. At the pay phone he called McClary on his government card, standing to continue to watch the travelers heading toward their planes.

"Joe?"

"Dixon, what's up?"

"I'm sorry to have to tell you this, Joe. I have bad news. They've delayed Elias's sentencing again."

As frustrating as that news was, Hilldorfer knew from McClary's tone that it was not the worst of it.

Not even close.

ON SUNDAY, DECEMBER 5, Uhlmann flew to Portland for a meeting of the Environmental Crimes Policy Committee. The Thanksgiving holidays had passed without an order from Judge Winmill denying Elias's motions, but ever confident, Uhlmann had been working with the U.S. Attorney's Office and the Office of Public Affairs coordinating a press release on the impending sentencing. The story of Elias's conviction had caught national attention. The *Washington Post* was sending a reporter to cover what was being called one of the most significant sentences in the history of the EPA and the Environmental Crimes Section.

In Portland, Uhlmann attended meetings all day Monday, then worked late into the night on the government's sentencing memorandum. On Tuesday he made a presentation on the Elias case, and discussed the Eighth Circuit decision on *United States v. Harmon* that Elias's new lawyers were relying upon for their unprecedented argument that it precluded any federal enforcement of the RCRA laws. The pending conviction of Allan Elias became the buzz of the conference and the excitement grew that the sentence would demonstrate the significance of environmental regulations. By the time Uhlmann left for the Portland airport Wednesday morning for his flight to Boise he received a groundswell of support, like he was going off to war.

He picked up some Chinese food at the airport in Portland and ate it on his flight to Boise, using his laptop to put the final touches on the government's sentencing memorandum. With an hour layover in Boise before his flight to Pocatello he found a bank of telephones and was retrieving his voice mail messages when he heard his name echoing overhead throughout the airport terminal. His mind immediately began to list the people who would know he was in Boise, and his first thought was that something terrible had happened to his family. Fighting to remain calm, he searched for an airport phone, found one, and identified himself to the operator.

"You have a message to call George Breitsameter in Pocatello."

Uhlmann's concern for his family dissipated but his relief did not last. He had a new feeling of dread. Elias had fled. He picked up a phone and called the U.S. Attorney's Office in Boise and was connected to Breitsameter.

"George, it's David. What's going on? Is everything okay?"

Breitsameter sounded like he had the weight of the world on his shoulders. "David, I'm sorry."

STANDING IN THE Salt Lake City airport terminal with a stream of travelers flowing past, Hilldorfer braced himself.

"What happened, Dixon?"

"Winmill issued an order finding that Elias has made out a prima facie case of jury tampering. He's ordered another hearing on his motion for a new trial. He put the sentencing off indefinitely."

CHAPTER FIFTY-ONE

RETURNING TO POCATELLO for more hearings rather than a sentencing was particularly bitter for Uhlmann, so instead he returned to Washington. On Monday morning, December 13, 1999, he walked down his driveway to find a front-page article in the *Washington Post* on Scott Dominguez and the trial of Allan Elias. While the article told of the terrible tragedy and conviction, it was supposed to have culminated with Elias's sentencing. Even Virginia couldn't help but ask, "When are you going to get that guy sentenced?"

He didn't know.

Winmill's thirteen-page memorandum acknowledged that the delays in getting Elias sentenced were significant and not attributable to the government. He also expressed reservations about using the term *jury tampering,* since there was a dispute whether any tampering or attempted tampering actually occurred. He called it a "perceived" tampering case. Nevertheless, he held that Elias had established a prima facie case that Greenlee *believed* Elias attempted to bribe a juror. The government had the burden to prove Greenlee was not prejudiced by that belief. He scheduled the hearing for January 7, 2000.

The day after Winmill's order Elias's new attorneys filed a motion to have the conditions of his release modified so he could travel to California to enjoy the holidays with his family. The arrogance caused Uhlmann to file a short, blistering response.

"The feelings of the victim and his family are entitled to at least as much consideration as the desires of a convicted defendant and his family," Uhlmann wrote. "Public confidence in the criminal justice system would be ill-served by providing less restrictions to a defendant convicted of such serious crimes."

Winmill wasted no time denying Elias's request.

For the next three weeks Uhlmann returned to working sixteen-hour days. He and Breitsameter called Miriam Krinsky, the appellate chief of the U.S. Attorney's Office in Los Angeles, considered the guru on Ninth Circuit Appellate authority. Her office handled the Keating Five Savings and Loan scandal in 1988 and that verdict had subsequently been set aside for juror misconduct. Uhlmann also talked to the chief of the appellate section of the Criminal Division of the Department of Justice, and with his two longtime mentors, Judge Shoob and David Kubichek. He also called Richard Lazarus, a law professor at Georgetown University. Lazarus had argued the leading U.S. Supreme Court case on jury tampering that defined the appropriate inquiry of jurors in such an instance. Between them, Uhlmann and Breitsameter read every case they could find on the issue and discussed what questions they could and could not ask. It was a tightrope. As with anything in the law, nothing was black or white. They couldn't inquire what happened in the jury room unless it was related to improper evidence brought into the deliberations and whether it had affected the jurors. For Uhlmann it was maddening that he couldn't just directly ask the jurors whether the comment by Scott, if she made it, affected them or not? In fact, Lazarus agreed with his interpretation that the Supreme Court decision allowed such an inquiry but that the appellate courts had subsequently misinterpreted the Supreme Court's decision. The case law was a mess. Was it juror misconduct? Jury tampering? Juror bias? No one seemed to know, and each was a separate legal category with different evidentiary burdens. If it was tampering, it was the government's burden to prove it didn't influence the verdict. If it was juror bias it was Elias's burden to prove the bias existed and that it affected the verdict. To make matters still worse, the Ninth Circuit had two weeks earlier reversed Winmill on a similar issue in a different case. The jurors in a bank robbery case had brought a newspaper article into the deliberations and though they were instructed to disregard it, the appellate court determined that the potential for bias existed and remanded the case to Winmill. Winmill was facing the prospect of retrying that case. Uhlmann was concerned Winmill would, as a result, be overly cautious and gun-shy.

On January 6, Winmill held a telephone conference with all counsel to discuss the hearing the following day. Darrell Hallett, one of Elias's new team of appellate lawyers from Seattle, handled the conference call. Hilldorfer and Wojnicz both knew him. They told Uhlmann they found him contentious and said he had a mean streak. It was clear during the

January 6 conference call with Winmill that the defense smelled blood. Unlike Nevin, who had wanted to question the jurors, they now argued there should be no further inquiry, a tactic designed to prevent the government from establishing their burden that the jury had not been prejudiced against Elias because of his misconduct. Later that day the water got a whole lot bloodier when Winmill issued a second order. While his prior order focused on jury tampering and the government's burden to rebut a presumption of prejudice, he now said the case actually involved potential jury tampering, juror misconduct, and juror bias. If the government proved there was no tampering or there was tampering but no prejudice, it still had to prove there was no juror misconduct. But it was the last sentence of Winmill's order that was truly troublesome.

"It is also difficult to understand how a trial could pass muster under the Sixth Amendment when one juror perceived that the defendant tampered with the jury. These are difficult issues the court is still struggling with."

AS HE WALKED into court the following morning, January 7, Uhlmann tried to maintain an air of confidence. It wasn't easy. Hilldorfer and Wojnicz sat in the front row looking morose and drawn. The *Washington Post* story had been picked up nationwide and reporters from the major news services also sat in the gallery. Meanwhile Hallett and the appellate lawyers were strutting around the courtroom like it was their game to lose, and Elias, who had appeared afraid the last time Uhlmann saw him at the jury verdict, looked like the alpha rooster of the chicken farm.

Uhlmann also felt like he was going into battle blindfolded. Three jurors had not been questioned during the July 2, 1999, hearing and no one had any idea what they might say. He and Breitsameter came up with a list of questions they believed passed muster under the federal case law, but they were uncertain which, if any, they'd be allowed to ask. They'd also come up with a strategy. They wanted to prove Elias made the comment, which would give Greenlee credibility, then wall it off as a nonissue. Beyond that, it was a blind crapshoot. The defense, which had wanted to delve into the issue with questions when Nevin was in Winmill's chambers, continued their one-eighty. They took the position that no further inquiry was required or appropriate, the intent being to prevent the government from proving its burden.[1]

After Winmill took the bench Uhlmann made it immediately known that while he would respect the Ninth Circuit, which governed Idaho, and therefore Winmill, he believed the U.S. Supreme Court saw the issue of what could and could not be asked differently.

"Frankly, Mr. Uhlmann, I sympathize with your concerns about where the Ninth Circuit is, but I am in the Ninth Circuit, so you're preaching to the choir somewhat, just having had my tail feathers singed in the Rasmussen case on a somewhat similar issue. I did not feel anything I had done was inappropriate, and I felt my decision was correct, but the Circuit saw it differently so we will retry that case."

With that ominous thought ringing in his ear, Uhlmann called Betty Connely, one of the three jurors who had not been questioned July 2. As can happen in the law, fortune changed with one question.

Connely said that near the middle to end of the trial Janet Scott walked into the jury room and told them Elias approached her in the parking lot, that she tried to avoid him, and that the court security officers questioned her about it.

Uhlmann's adrenaline shot up like someone rang a carnival bell. It gave Greenlee instant credibility.

"It was a female and she came in," Connely said. "We were just talking amongst us, and she said that when she came into the building, they had asked her—the security guards had asked her if she'd been approached or talked to him, and she said no. That is what I heard. She said, 'I did not speak with him at all.' He said, 'Well, you were moving your lips,' and she said, 'Well I did not speak with him.' That's all I know."

Uhlmann pressed Connely about the allegation, asking if Elias said, "What does it take to get a guy off?" or words to that effect, but she didn't recall them. Feeling he'd pushed her far enough and not wanting to get greedy, Uhlmann sat. Hallett asked no questions.

Juror Burkhart was the fourth witness and Breitsameter ran him through the same standard set of preliminary questions they'd asked each juror. "First, I would like to confirm your prior testimony that you were not aware of any out-of-court contacts between the defendant and jurors in the trial."

"I thought I mentioned I did hear something."

Breitsameter looked up from his notes. "Specifically what did you hear?"

"I think it was something to the effect that when they were coming back upstairs from lunch that the defendant had turned to one of them and said, 'What does a guy have to do to get out of this?' I don't recall but I thought I said that in July."

Burkhart hadn't, and it set off a firestorm. On cross-examination Hallett attempted to impeach Burkhart with his testimony at the July 2 hearing that he could not recall the specifics of what Scott had said, though he had recalled the incident.

Burkhart seemed at a loss. "I was pretty nervous when I came down here last time. I mean it does not sound like much of an excuse, but . . ."

Breitsameter followed with Juror Barrus, a calculated move because on July 2 Barrus confirmed hearing that Scott came into the lunchroom and told them Elias tried to talk to her and the court security officer questioned her about it. It buoyed Connely and Burkhart's testimony and all of them supported Greenlee.

When Barrus left the stand and Breitsameter sat down Uhlmann was feeling so good about the reversal of fortune he leaned over and whispered in Breitsameter's ear. "We need to seriously think again about requesting that he be detained for doing this."[2]

Boyd Greenlee was Uhlmann's witness. He remained steadfast that Scott said Elias approached her and asked, "What would it take to win your vote?"

Before the hearing Winmill ruled that the defense could ask Greenlee about his DUI conviction. Now, at a sidebar Uhlmann decided to let the court know that he disagreed, and that he was piqued. Prompted by Hilldorfer and Wojnicz, an FBI investigation led to a sheriff in Preston, Idaho, and revealed that the NCIC had in fact been used to obtain the information on Greenlee.

"We don't even know that it is a DUI conviction, all we know is on a NCIC run—which the defense obtained improperly, illegally—we know that it showed up. We are rewarding the defense for having the sheriff in Preston run a DUI check without the witness's authorization, sharing that information with the defense, and running the NCIC check two more times to help the defense try and locate records." He said that to ask Greenlee about the incident in open court in front of the media would only humiliate him.

Winmill was not swayed, but he did caution Hallett not to badger Greenlee.

Greenlee didn't hesitate when Hallett asked him about the conviction and on redirect Uhlmann took the opportunity to apologize to Greenlee for "even asking you about this." He asked if Greenlee could explain why he had responded "No" on the jury questionnaire and during voir dire. Greenlee said he believed the record had been expunged and he did not therefore have a conviction.

The last juror was Janet Scott. As Uhlmann approached the lectern he was still trying to figure out the best way to get Scott to admit, at the very least, that *something* had happened. Though he now felt a lot better about the issue, he still considered her testimony critical to prove the incident was not a figment of Greenlee's or anyone else's imagination or part of a scheme to "get Elias." He had barely finished his question when Scott responded that Elias had in fact approached her in the parking lot and that she had "avoided him at all costs . . . I really didn't want to say hello."

Scott didn't say Elias asked her what it would take to get a guy off, but Uhlmann was now confident they had exactly what they needed. There could be no doubt the incident occurred and that Elias had improperly initiated it. In addition, they had walled it off. Every juror that heard about it said they hadn't given it much thought or took it as a joke. Sensing the kill, Uhlmann pressed for oral argument right there, but the defense, now looking like they had been sucker-punched, did not want oral argument. They wanted to catch a flight out of town.[3]

Outside the courtroom the media cornered Uhlmann and Breitsameter. While they had to admit that some of the jurors had slightly altered their recollection of what happened, they reiterated that contact between Elias and a juror had no effect on jury deliberations and did not take away from the overwhelming evidence of his guilt.[4]

At Uhlmann's request Winmill set a tight briefing schedule and it was fast and furious. The defense again changed tactics, arguing that Burkhart's altered testimony further indicated the jurors were biased against Elias. Uhlmann filed his final brief January 19.

Then they all waited.

CHAPTER FIFTY-TWO

LATE JANUARY, UHLMANN awoke to a strange sound outside his Silver Spring, Maryland, home—utter and deafening silence. When he looked out the window he saw his neighborhood quieted beneath a blanket of deep, fresh snow. It flowed over the sidewalks and paved roads in gentle rolling waves and clung undisturbed to the branches of the leafless trees, over the tips of which a gray curtain hung with the promise of more snow. The local schools would certainly shut down, and his call to work revealed that the federal government had also closed. Uhlmann had an unexpected day off. He knew just what to do with it. But for their family trip to Jackson Hole, and despite living on the East Coast, his three-year-old daughter, Emily, was a snow novice.

As soon as she awoke he bundled her in snow clothes, grabbed a sled from the garage, and they set out together to the big hill just down the street, alternating between sledding, returning home for hot chocolate, and building a snowman in the front yard. They had just ventured back outside to continue work on their snowman when Virginia stuck her head out the front door.

"David, George is on the phone."

Uhlmann dusted off the snow, walked through the kitchen and went upstairs to the bedroom. Breitsameter sounded glib. "Sorry to disturb you. Virginia says you got quite a snowfall."

"No problem. Emily and I were just finishing up a snowman. What's up?"

"The judge issued his order."

Uhlmann had been pacing. He came to an abrupt stop. The snow had not only quieted the traffic, it had momentarily quieted his thoughts of Allan Elias. They came back in a rush. "What's the verdict?"

"He denied their motion for a new trial."

Uhlmann yelled and punched a fist in the air, which brought Virginia running upstairs to find out what happened, Emily trailing behind. Uhlmann had Breitsameter fax the order to his home and he read it carefully, confident it would hold up on appeal. Relying upon Juror Scott's testimony, Winmill found no tampering. On the more critical issue concerning Greenlee and Burkhart's bias, Winmill concluded they had misinterpreted Scott's interaction with Elias, but that they did not consider the comments seriously and it did not bias them.

Uhlmann called Hilldorfer in Seattle, who was both relieved and elated. Nine months after the verdict, the defense's far-reaching motion to dismiss Counts 1, 2, and 3 of the indictment, Elias's violation of the RCRA laws, was the only thing left standing between Allan Elias and jail.

Monday, March 27, 2000
Environmental Crimes Section
Department of Justice
Washington, D.C.

CHAPTER FIFTY-THREE

I N PREPARING ITS motion to dismiss, the defense was, ironically, aided by the EPA. Former EPA attorney Gene Lucero, working for the Los Angeles–based law firm Latham & Watkins, and Marcia Williams, the former EPA director of the Office of Solid Waste, working as a consultant with PHB Hagler Bailly, Inc., joined in the brief. They provided historical perspectives on the RCRA laws and their intended enforcement. The argument put forward was novel, but the theme it repeated, that the federal government should butt out of state environmental affairs, was not.

Relying upon *United States v. Harmon,* Elias argued that because the State of Idaho had established a hazardous waste management program, and because that program had received EPA approval, only Idaho, not the federal government, could indict or charge Elias. Since the indictment alleged no violations of Idaho State laws, it was invalid, mandating dismissal of the case. Elias further argued that had he been charged and tried under Idaho State law the violations would have been misdemeanors with a maximum sentence of one year for each alleged violation. The Idaho Department of Environmental Quality, he said, did not treat the handling of mining waste as a hazardous waste. Therefore his disposal of the tank contents was legal under Idaho law. In golfing terms, the defense was calling a Mulligan—a do-over.

Uhlmann found the position breathtaking not because he considered it even remotely accurate, but because it was so sweeping. If the argument was accurate, not only would Elias walk but the EPA's and ECS's criminal enforcement powers in the forty-seven states that had enacted their own hazardous waste programs would be in serious jeopardy. Because the majority of those state programs focused on civil and administrative remedies and did not have strong criminal programs, such a ruling would effectively end the prosecution of hazardous waste crimes throughout the country. Uhlmann's research did not reveal a single instance in which Idaho had prosecuted a criminal hazardous waste action.

Beyond that far-reaching and sweeping consequence, Uhlmann considered the motion absurd. It was contrary to legislative history, which clearly indicated Congress's intent to prevent midnight dumping, and decisions published by the First Circuit and Ninth Circuit Courts of Appeals. Moreover, if the argument had any validity at all, it was inconceivable to Uhlmann that David Marshall, one of the premier environmental defense attorneys in the Northwest, would have missed it. The motion was also ludicrously late. They had just completed a two-and-a-half-year investigation, battled through pretrial proceedings and a three-week trial, fought for nearly eight months over posttrial issues, and now Elias was telling the court it had all been a charade, an exercise.

There was no way Winmill would grant the motion.

Uhlmann told his trial team as much during a conference call. He told them the motion was hardly worth the time of day and that he wanted to treat it as a no-brainer, a complete nonissue. He sought their input, but because the motion involved environmental regulations and history, the opposition was his to handle. Compared to Elias's thirty-page brief, his response was a crisp eleven pages. He called the argument "bordering on the frivolous" and cited the Ninth Circuit Court of Appeals opinion that had rejected the argument.[1] Since Idaho was in the Ninth Circuit, the decision was binding precedent upon Winmill. To further emphasize his point, Uhlmann noted that no court had ever held that state criminal provisions supplanted RCRA's criminal provisions. As for *Harmon,* he wrote that it stood for the more limited proposition that the federal government could not initiate a *civil* enforcement action while a state civil enforcement action was pending.

With that, he considered the issue closed. Then he waited, and waited.

The defense originally filed its motion in October and the government responded in November. December and January had been consumed with Elias's motion for a new trial and the jury issue, but that was now over. A decision should have been imminent. January, however, became February, and February suddenly March. Elias remained free, and Winmill remained silent.

In Seattle, Joe Hilldorfer had become embroiled in the Olympic Pipeline disaster and was looking down the long road at an indictment of a consortium of petrochemical companies and individuals. In between his investigations he called Uhlmann.

"David, what's going on?

Uhlmann didn't have the answer. "I don't know, Joe. I have no idea."

Late in the afternoon of March 26, as Uhlmann sat in his office, the answer came. Breitsameter was on the phone.

"David," Breitsameter said in a voice that was eerily familiar. "I'm sorry."

UHLMANN HUNG UP the telephone and rushed down the hall to the office of Steve Solow, chief of the ECS. "You're not going to believe this."

Two minutes later he paced near the fax machine as it hummed and spit out Winmill's decision. Uhlmann was practically pulling the pages from the machine as they printed, scanning the words while Breitsameter's voice rang in his head.

"We got the decision and you're not going to like it. I don't really understand it. He dismissed some counts but not others. Let me fax it to you."

Winmill's decision hit like a tornado, sweeping and destructive. He granted Elias's motion to dismiss Counts 2 and 3 for dumping a hazardous waste, finding that the two sections of the RCRA statute had been supplanted by corresponding sections of the Idaho code. He further held that under Idaho law the disposal of mining waste was not a crime. He did not dismiss Count 1, the knowing endangerment charge, but that was little consolation. Without the underlying charges that Elias disposed of a hazardous waste, the knowing endangerment charge was fatally vulnerable on appeal.

Winmill reset sentencing for April 28, 2000, but it was now a hollow act.

IN SEATTLE, HILLDORFER sat in his cubicle talking on the telephone and staring up at a framed photograph Joanne had given him when he returned to Seattle to begin his career with the EPA. He loved the photograph for its ability to capture the sheer immensity of a moment in time and the stark reality that forces exist beyond man's control. The photograph depicted a lighthouse off the coast of Africa. Bleak white in the midst of a dark and ominous storm, it stood doing its job while, towering in the background, an enormous wave bore down upon it with impending and certain doom. Lost in the photograph amid the enormity of nature, unnoticed without closer inspection, a lone man stood clinging to a metal railing.

Dixon McClary walked into the room and handed him a document over the top of his cubicle with an arched eyebrow, then turned and walked away. Hilldorfer saw that the document was a printout of a news story on the Elias case. He finished his conversation, and hung up the telephone. It was an article being run over the business wire and as he read it Hilldorfer felt like the man in the photo.

Elias's attorney John Colvin did not mince words. He crowed that Judge Winmill's decision to dismiss the RCRA charges was the "first case in which federal criminal environmental charges were dismissed because they had been supplanted by state equivalents." Colvin called the decision another instance of the "EPA's civil and criminal enforcement programs coming under fire by the courts," and offered "This ruling could effectively end most federal criminal enforcement activity in states with authorized state programs, and return control of environmental affairs to state regulators."[2]

Hilldorfer felt as if he'd been kicked in the stomach, paralyzed with frustration. As bad as he felt for himself, it didn't even register on the scale of hurt he felt for Scott Dominguez and his family, who had put their complete and utter faith in the justice system.

BACK IN WASHINGTON, Uhlmann's phone was ringing off the hook. He read the article and Colvin's quotes and seethed. His case, a case that had meant so much to him and everyone involved, a case that would stand for the proposition that environmental crimes were real crimes and those convicted would face real jail time, a case that showed the potential power of an environmental criminal program that pooled its resources and worked in tandem, had suddenly become the case that could topple the Environmental Crimes Section of the Department of Justice. He had two choices. He could file an appeal to the Ninth Circuit or file a motion asking Winmill to reconsider his decision. Each had its problems; neither was particularly attractive. An appeal would take considerable time to put together and to get a date to argue before the Ninth Circuit. Elias would remain free for many more months. The appeal could also have national ramifications. If the Ninth Circuit Court of Appeals agreed with Winmill, an appellate decision would be binding federal authority in the Ninth Circuit and persuasive authority throughout the rest of the country. As for a motion for reconsideration, in the absence of some seismic event, they were almost certain losers, the functional equivalent of asking the judge, "Are you sure?"

Uhlmann had filed them. He'd never won one.

Uhlmann chose the motion for reconsideration. This time he would not do it alone. The EPA Office of General Counsel, the ECS Appellate Division, and the Civil Environmental Enforcement Section of the Justice Department, which had worked on the *Harmon* briefs, all assigned attorneys to help draft the motion.

Once again smelling blood in the water, Elias's lawyers circled and attacked. They filed their own motion and asked Winmill to reconsider his decision not to dismiss the knowing endangerment charge. As Uhlmann anticipated, they argued the disposal of a hazardous waste was a predicate to a charge that Elias knowingly endangered Dominguez. But their motion actually helped Uhlmann because he now would have three pleadings to convince Winmill his decision was wrong. He'd file the government's motion to reconsider. He'd file an opposition to Elias's motion to reconsider. And he'd file a reply to Elias's opposition to the government's motion. At the Environmental Crimes Section it was referred to as "the trilogy."

Over several weeks of very long days, Uhlmann wrote his brief while fending off questions from the other departments and generally getting fly-specked by the EPA, which had put programs on hold while they determined if they had any authority.

He filed the government's motion March 24 asking Winmill to reconsider what he called "a dramatic and unprecedented departure from nearly 20 years of criminal jurisprudence under RCRA." He used Colvin's quotes in the newspaper article against him to illustrate the far-reaching ramifications of Winmill's decision, including calling into question hundreds of convictions for hazardous waste violations, many having already been upheld by Courts of Appeal across the country. He elicited support from the Idaho DEQ and hinted coolly that the other forty-six states with hazardous waste programs would also be offering opinions if the United States was forced to appeal Winmill's decision to the Ninth Circuit.

With each brief his arguments became more and more refined, and after filing the government's reply to Elias's opposition, he was finished. The matter was out of his hands and back in Winmill's court, literally.

Wednesday, April 26, 2000
Federal Courthouse
Pocatello, Idaho

CHAPTER FIFTY-FOUR

EARLY ON THE morning of April 26, 2000, Uhlmann boarded a plane for Salt Lake City. When it landed he would take a puddle jumper to Pocatello. Beyond that, nothing was certain. Elias was to be sentenced Friday, April 28, but to what and for what he wasn't sure.

On the plane Uhlmann had dusted off his old sentencing memorandum and started working on potential scenarios. Under federal sentencing guidelines there were multiple levels a convicted defendant could reach for his conduct. Each charge had a base-level number of months in jail assigned to it. However, the court had discretion to add months to that base level for additional crimes, like obstruction of justice and filing false statements. It could also subtract months. Elias could get nothing or he could get twenty years.

When Uhlmann's plane circled for landing at the Pocatello airport the feeling of nostalgia again swept over him, but this time it wasn't the warm feeling of returning home, but more like the uncertainty he had felt when he arrived a full year earlier to try the most important case of his career.

He rented a car and drove past AEI, Inc. Visible from the highway, it remained a blight on the landscape beneath the monolithic configuration of steel and pipes and catwalks of the FMC and JR Simplot plants, a taunting reminder that nothing had yet been accomplished. Rather than stop at the hotel to brood alone in his room—Hilldorfer and Wojnicz were not expected until late that night and Breitsameter and Miller not until the next day—he drove straight to the courthouse to work on the sentencing memorandum at the U.S. Attorney's Office.

He parked in the parking lot and considered the colonial facade of the Pocatello Federal Courthouse and imagined the trial team as it had stood there after his closing argument, smiling into a bright sun. He had told them then that whatever the verdict they should be proud of their accomplishment. Sitting in the parking lot he tried to tell himself that again, that whatever the sentence imposed, it didn't take away from what they had all accomplished.

It wasn't working.

He grabbed his briefcase and started across the parking lot. As he did, the front doors to the courthouse opened and he recognized Pam Gross, a paralegal in the U.S. Attorney's Office, step out.

She stood on the steps waiting as he approached.

"Hi, Pam."

"Hi David," she said. "We just got the judge's order."

Thursday, April 27, 2000
Federal Courthouse
Pocatello, Idaho

CHAPTER FIFTY-FIVE

UHLMANN THOUGHT he had prepared himself for Winmill's inevitable denial of his motion by telling himself that they had a good shot at winning an appeal, but as he stood on the steps looking up at Pam

Gross he realized he had only been fooling himself. Losing would be a bitter taste that lingered in his mouth for a very long time, and the potential for an appeal was of little consolation.

"Pam?"

Pam Gross smiled. "He granted your motion for reconsideration. David, you've won!"

AS GOOD AS UHLMANN felt, he had no time to prop himself up on his laurels. He felt he'd received a reprieve from the governor and that only added to the pressure that he get the matter finished before some other unexpected turn of events. Everything shifted to fast forward. The next day, when Hilldorfer, Wojnicz, Breitsameter, and Miller huddled with Uhlmann in the U.S. Attorney's Office conference room, they mused briefly about Winmill's order, then got to work. Because it had been a year since the trial, Uhlmann and Breitsameter felt it imperative they recount the highlights of Elias's behavior for Winmill. Uhlmann believed Elias deserved the longest criminal sentence for an environmental crime, and it appeared that, ever so slowly, judges around the country were coming around to the idea that environmental crimes warranted serious jail sentences. When the government tried Elias in April 1999 the longest sentence had been seven years for a pesticide case in the Southeast. By August of that year a sentence of nine years was imposed in Georgia. A month later in Florida, a defendant found guilty of dumping toxic waste down a sewer received thirteen years as a repeat offender. In November a defendant had received fifteen years though that case had also involved the illegal manufacture of methamphetamines.

The prosecutors decided to put Hilldorfer on the stand to discuss Elias's environmental violations and worker injuries. Wojnicz would testify about Elias's attempts to obstruct justice. Dr. Joe Lowry would discuss the dangerous nature of cyanide waste. Glenn Bruck would testify about the clean-up costs at AEI and Evergreen, and an economist would detail the type and cost of Scott's lifelong care. They also wanted some of the employees to recount their injuries, and they wanted Brian Smith to recount his efforts to save Dominguez. Scott and his family also wanted to make statements to the court as victims, and Uhlmann would need to discuss the sentencing guidelines and argue that Elias should not be granted bail pending appeal or allowed to get his affairs in order and voluntarily report to serve his sentence. It was a lot to get prepared for in one day, but that was reality.

As they set to work they received a fax that changed the game plan. Jorgensen had filed an emergency motion to continue the sentencing, arguing there was inadequate time, given the recent series of events, for him to prepare.

"What's next?" Hilldorfer said, exasperated.

Uhlmann sighed, then set to work. As he, Breitsameter, and Miller sat down to plot out how best to respond to the latest motion, the fax machine spit out more papers.

Winmill wasted no time denying Jorgensen's motion. Elias, he said, had received more than a year to prepare for the sentencing.

Three and a half years after Scott Dominguez had stepped down a ladder into a black abyss of poison, and one year after a jury's verdict, Allan Elias would be sentenced. Whether he would ever spend a day in jail, however, remained to be seen.

Friday, April 28, 2000
Federal Courthouse
Pocatello, Idaho
United States v. Elias, Sentencing

CHAPTER FIFTY-SIX

HILLDORFER AWOKE and dressed for court. It remained surreal. He was in the same hotel, in the same city, at the same time of year. He wore the same suit and tie he'd worn on the last day of trial. He and Wojnicz met in the same breakfast room, which had not changed its decor or menu, then jumped into the car and drove the same route to the same Federal Courthouse. The court security officers greeted them as they passed through the metal detectors, and they crossed the marbled foyer and climbed the staircase to Judge Winmill's courtroom on the second floor. Everything was the same, but different.

♦   ♦   ♦

UHLMANN SLEPT LESS than four hours and awoke with a thousand thoughts running through his head. He wanted to recapture the emotion and momentum that had propelled them all like a slingshot through the two-and-a-half-year investigation and the extended trial. The familiarity of the surroundings played tricks with his mind, imploring him to believe everything was as it was then, but the nearly yearlong delay had created a disconnect. It was in some respects like going back to high school for a class reunion and trying to relive past glory. Everything appeared the same, but no one was.

WINMILL ENTERED his courtroom to a packed and charged gallery that now included half a dozen reporters. Mike Fica was gone, and Hilldorfer missed the way he had barked out "All Rise!" Hilldorfer and Wojnicz sat in their usual spot in the front row. Scott Dominguez sat in the back, perched on the wooden bench, elbows on knees, eyes forward, listening. Jackie Hamp sat next to him with her eyes closed, pinching the bridge of her nose. Extended family surrounded them, as did the witnesses expected to testify—Danny Rice, Brian Smith, Dr. Joe Lowry, Glenn Bruck, and Theresa Cole. Others who had taken a personal interest in seeing the outcome had also made the trip—Daren Schwartz, Matt Christiansen, Gene Thornock and his wife Stacey and their new baby, Joe Rice from the Soda Springs Police Department, even John Hatfield.[1]

The first question on everyone's minds was answered that morning when a sullen-looking Elias entered the courtroom. He sat at counsel table, shoulders hunched. Nevin and Marshall were gone, and the room seemed strangely empty without them. Elias's appellate dream team was also not present. It was left to Craig Jorgensen, Elias's longtime counsel, to handle the sentencing. Uhlmann thought it fitting that Jorgensen, who perhaps knew Allan Elias and his history better than anyone, would make Elias's final stand, an indication Elias could no longer command the big law firms and high-priced defense attorneys. Uhlmann did not consider Jorgensen to be in the same league with Nevin or Marshall. Whatever the ultimate reason, Uhlmann's alert went up a notch or two.

After Winmill settled at his desk Uhlmann stood and advised how the government intended to proceed with the presentation of witnesses. As Uhlmann spoke Hilldorfer looked around the courtroom, but except for Jorgensen and two paralegals, Elias did not appear to have a supporter in the group. The only people sitting on his side of the courtroom were re-porters.

He leaned against Wojnicz. "Midge isn't here."

Wojnicz swiveled and surveyed the gallery for Elias's wife. "Hmm."

"I have a feeling they don't think this is going to happen today," Hill-dorfer said.

As if on cue, Jorgensen stood. At least six foot five with dark brown, thinning hair, he had the broad-shouldered build of a basketball player but also the pained expression of a kid with a stomachache. He renewed his emergency motion for a continuance and objected to the government putting on any additional evidence at the sentencing.

Winmill overruled the objection. "I certainly intend to ensure your client's rights are protected, but I'm also mindful of the public's need to have this case resolved, and it has been pending far too long."

With that, Celeste Miller called Hilldorfer to the stand.

No longer limited by certain rules of evidence, including hearsay, Hill-dorfer freely told the court about his interviews with former employees of Evergreen and AEI and of the horrific working conditions and frighten-ing injuries they described. He told how, in response, Elias fired them. He spoke freely about the extent to which he believed Elias lied and fabri-cated his defense. They kept his testimony short, hitting the highlights in about twenty minutes.

Jorgensen stood and protested that he was hearing much of Hill-dorfer's testimony for the first time. He asked for time to get files from his office.

"Can you gather those on the morning recess?" Winmill asked.

Jorgensen nodded reluctantly. "Probably."

Winmill excused Hilldorfer. He retook his seat next to Wojnicz. "He's going to try to get this thing continued," he said. "I really think if Elias walks out of here today he's going to flee."

Wojnicz nodded. "I think you're right."

Uhlmann walked Rice through his testimony. Jorgensen again pro-fessed to be unable to cross-examine Rice without additional information he had for some reason not brought with him to court. Winmill grew less sympathetic and less patient, noting that Rice had also been a trial witness. He told Jorgensen he'd give him the morning recess to gather his files. "Then we're going to proceed. So this is the last witness you'll have a chance to do that with."

Breitsameter called Brian Smith and in workmanlike fashion walked Smith through his testimony. The morning had been, up until that point, almost clinical. Then Breitsameter asked Smith, "Could this have been prevented?"

It was classic Breitsameter—direct and unblemished.

Smith lowered his head. "I'll never forget it," he said, voice barely above a whisper, and he began to weep. As he did, so did others in the courtroom.[2] At that moment Brian Smith transported them all back to April 1999. With one simple sentence he reminded them all that while they had moved on with their lives, others, like Scott Dominguez and his family, had not. He recaptured the momentum the delays had depleted, and the passion and emotion that had been buried beneath the passage of time suddenly flickered and burst into flames.

Smith chastised Elias for refusing to listen to him that morning, and told him that if he had, everyone might have gone home that day instead of to the hospital in the back of an ambulance. His anger built with each word, like a slow burn.

"As far as I'm concerned, Mr. Elias deserves everything he receives here today and maybe a little more. If it was up to me he'd be on trial for murder because as far as I'm concerned he just as well as put a gun to Scotty's head and pulled the trigger. Scotty's still alive, but he took away his life and it could have been prevented."

From the back of the courtroom, Dominguez let out a haunting wail.[3]

Smith paused to gather himself. Breitsameter stood silent. Smith's voice softened and his sudden anger dissipated. He paused between sentences, contemplative, his words like waves offshore gaining momentum and rolling over the courtroom.

"Nobody has the right to play God with anybody's life. I don't care who you are or how much money you think you have in your pockets. . . . It's wrong. It should never have happened." He shook his head, then, almost in silence. "Never . . . Never."

The courtroom had frozen.

Wojnicz followed Smith and told of Elias's lies to the investigators. His testimony was particularly important because the government sought a Level 36 sentence. To reach it they needed the enhancements allowed for Elias's attempts to obstruct justice. Without them Elias would be at a base level of 34. The difference between the two levels was as much as thirty-seven months in jail.

As the court broke for its morning recess Winmill told them he had scheduling conflicts that afternoon. It made Hilldorfer all the more certain they would not finish. That left Elias the entire weekend to flee. He began making mental plans to stay in town and, if necessary, he and Wojnicz would sleep in the car and watch Elias around the clock. But just before the court broke for lunch, Winmill advised that he also had commitments in Boise the following week that would prevent him from returning to Pocatello to complete the hearing until the following Wednesday. Hilldorfer closed his eyes. There was no way he and Bob could sleep in a car and watch Elias that long.

They returned from lunch at 2:00 P.M. sharp. Dr. Joe testified that he calculated between six and ten pounds of cyanide in the tank, enough lethal doses to kill as many as 600,000 people. He also said eight hundred tons of cadmium waste remained buried at Evergreen with three times that amount at AEI, Inc., and that "it wasn't about to just disappear." To the contrary, he said the waste would continue to contaminate the ground and the ground water—particularly at Evergreen, which was near a creek—as well as the aquifer for Soda Springs. Given what had already happened to Dominguez, he said it was "stupid" not to clean it up, even if that meant "digging up the whole place." The clean-up cost was estimated to be $881,250 at AEI, Inc., and $364,750 at Evergreen.

Jorgensen then called Hilldorfer for cross-examination. It was brief and uneventful, as was his belated cross-examination of Danny Rice. But the hands of the big clock on the wall continued to move and it was 4:00 P.M. when Jorgensen informed the court he intended to call just one witness, Allan Elias, but said he anticipated his testimony to be lengthy. The gallery groaned, the length of the day and frustration readily apparent. The air was heavy and the mood intense, like someone had left a lid on a pot of water on slow boil.

Winmill called for a fifteen-minute recess, but before leaving the bench he surprised them by saying he could stay past 5:00 to as late as 7:00 P.M. Beyond that, the matter would have to be continued until the following Wednesday.

At 4:15 P.M., Allan Elias took the stand with a stack of notes. Jorgensen reiterated he could not promise they would complete his testimony even by 7:00 P.M.

"Why doesn't he just shut up and get going," Hilldorfer said to Wojnicz. "We'd be done already." But he knew why, now convinced that if Winmill continued the hearing it would be the last time they saw Allan Elias.

Elias began giving a dissertation of his business at AEI, Inc., stating that it stood for Argent Exploration, not Allan Elias, and that the process was ecologically perfect. He then broke out a videotape to explain the process, and said he wanted the court to see that AEI was a serious business, that he believed recycling would be the wave of the future until the laws changed, making treater dust a hazardous waste. As the tape played, Elias narrated, calling the process "a technical marvel" and the fertilizer "terrific with crops; just fabulous." He spoke directly to Winmill, offering that the tank couldn't possibly have contained any sludge. "I've heard testimony in the trial that it did. It can't. Hey, it's enough for me to tell you that and move on. Okay."

"Unbelievable," Wojnicz said. "You'd think the guy was in here trying to sell us all fertilizer."

"He's selling something," Hilldorfer said. "He's selling Allan Elias."

Uhlmann, who had never heard Allan Elias speak, was struck that his voice was higher pitched than he expected and had an almost whimsical quality to it. The man was clearly bright, but Uhlmann also sensed that Elias's view of reality was distorted and that he actually believed he could talk his way out of the whole affair. He was trying to sell the court as he had sold FMC and Kerr-McGee. When the video stopped Elias's testimony quickly deteriorated into the theater of the absurd. He rambled without prompting, his thoughts frequently disjointed and defiant. He maintained that the tank left AEI empty, and any statements attributed to him to the contrary were "fantasy." He said the material trucked to Evergreen from AEI was actually Kerr-McGee material he had previously trucked to AEI to turn into fertilizer and not the cadmium-bearing FMC material. He blamed the workers for their own injuries. He called OSHA overzealous and said they found no violations. He blamed Bill Brugger for the Tesco American litigation. At every opportunity he elevated himself and his efforts to get AEI and Evergreen working, saying it took "fortitude."

Mostly what he did was talk. The clock ticked.

Uhlmann became so frustrated and appalled that Elias was continuing to work the legal system that he stopped standing to object, something he considered a breach of courtroom decorum.

Winmill, too, seemed to grow frustrated, sustaining one of Uhlmann's objections and adding, "I'm afraid time is starting to wear my patience." When they reached the point for a break Winmill asked Jorgensen how much he had left.

"A lot," Jorgensen responded.

That brought audible groans from the gallery and Uhlmann's frustration boiled over. Outraged by what he considered further stall tactics designed to ensure that Elias was not sentenced, he shot out of his chair like coming out of a cannon.

"Your Honor, this is a filibuster. I mean this is an attempt that's been going on all week and much of this year to delay this sentencing. This man is maneuvering the legal system constantly over and over again. We have heard almost no relevant testimony from him. He's just going on and on . . . and he is just trying to delay this so you can't sentence him tonight. And the court has the authority to control him, and we would ask that you please do so."

There were shouts of agreement from the gallery. "That's right!" "Yeah!" "This is an outrage."

Winmill's response was direct and telling.

"Mr. Uhlmann, the court will impose sentencing tonight. One of the reasons I'm taking a recess is so that the court staff can obtain motel rooms if we need to stay until we are done."

Hilldorfer looked at Wojnicz for assurance, uncertain he'd heard Winmill correctly. Given his admonitions throughout the day that he could not stay beyond a certain hour the statement came out of the blue and it landed like a sledgehammer dropping on the courtroom.

Winmill, however, was not through. "I would also caution those in the audience that the alarms have been set for the building, and if you leave the building you won't be allowed to return." Winmill stood. "We will be in recess."

Hilldorfer hurried downstairs and spoke to one of the marshals to confirm a suspicion, then went to find Wojnicz in the courtroom. "I just talked to one of the marshals. He said Winmill ordered them to lock down the courthouse."

WHEN THEY RETURNED from the break Jorgensen again complained that he was feeling time pressured and that it was adversely affecting his client's rights. Winmill responded that the matter had been scheduled for some time, that his only witness was Elias, and that while he intended to let Elias be heard, "I don't see any reason why we can't complete this this evening, so I'm going to proceed."

Elias continued with what was frequently a monologue, but with Winmill's assurance that Elias would be sentenced, Hilldorfer and Uhlmann both found the spectacle amusing. It was also telling. Not once did Elias admit to any responsibility for what had happened to any employee. He had an answer for each OSHA citation. He scoffed at the notion that there remained tons of FMC treater dust to be cleaned up at AEI, but said if there was, it was FMC's responsibility to clean it up because they had given it to AEI. As for Evergreen, he denied any dumping. He said the treater dust came from Soda Springs Phosphate. He denied influencing Darren Weaver, and he said he had discussed the affidavits with "Governor Andrus," and it was Andrus who suggested the information be taken to the U.S. attorney.

Even as his ship took on more and more water, slowly sinking, Elias stood on the deck with a bucket, bailing, believing he could once again save himself by talking, by getting people to believe him, as he always had. When Elias finally finished, more than two hours had passed. Uhlmann did not even bother to cross-examine him. There was nothing he could extract to make Elias appear worse than he already did—a man without remorse who refused to accept any responsibility for what had happened.

Uhlmann said as much when he stood to discuss the sentencing guidelines, imploring Winmill to add the enhancements to the base sentence.

". . . [H]e has basically called everybody who testified in this case a liar. So either they're all lying or he's lying," Uhlmann said.

He asked the court to impose the maximum sentence—nearly twenty years in prison—and to order Elias to pay restitution to Scott Dominguez of more than $6 million and to clean up the Evergreen and AEI sites.

Jorgensen's response was brief. Like his client, he conceded nothing.

Allocutions—statements by the victims and the defendant to the court—followed. Uhlmann had never had allocutions in an environmental case.

Jackie and Scott could not bring themselves to speak. It was left to Scott's older brother, Anthony, to speak for the family. He stepped up to the rail, Uhlmann at his side, a painting of faces behind him. Anthony told the court how Scott's injury had permanently changed all of their lives and the awful toll it had exacted on them. His family sobbed as he read his statement. Despite it all, he said that as a family, "we can get through this."

Cole followed him to the railing, her voice emotionally taut and strained as she told the court that Scott was her "soul mate" and that she would never love another like him again. Behind her Dominguez wailed. To anyone in the court who had ever been young and in love, the raw emotion resonated. Cole expressed guilt for leaving Scott and his family and said that she thought of the morning of the accident, when Scott had said to her "I'm afraid to go to work today," and how she wished desperately that she had told him to stay home.

When Cole sat, Ron Hamp stood, but he did not approach the railing. His eyes were red and raw and his face streaming with tears. Bereft, he struggled to gather himself, unable to do so. He simply turned to Allan Elias and said without venom, "Allan, you are a very, very evil man."

Uhlmann took a moment to walk to the back of the courtroom to be certain everyone who wanted to speak had. Then he walked to the podium. He told the judge he was there to speak of the family's pain, to request the imposition of a long sentence, and to request that the court send a message to others who would consider doing what Elias had done.

"The Scott Dominguez that went to work the morning of August 27, 1996, would never come home again," he began. "At seven o'clock that morning, when he kissed his fiancée, Theresa Cole, good-bye, their life together was over."

He said that but for the heroic efforts of Dominguez's co-workers and emergency personnel, Dominguez would not be alive, and that, he said, is exactly what Elias intended when he lied to the rescuers and to Dr. John Wayne Obray.

"If it was up to the defendant, Scott Dominguez would not be here today. . . . In those critical moments after Scott collapsed on August 27, when Scott needed him most, Allan Elias was as calculating and cold-blooded as the most ruthless criminal. When Allan Elias should have been screaming to anyone who would listen that he had stored cyanide in the tank where Scott lay unconscious, Allan Elias was denying point-blank that there was any possibility there was cyanide in the tank."

Uhlmann then turned Elias's soliloquy against him, saying it was illustrative of why law enforcement had had such a difficult time shutting him down.

"The guile, the emotion, the intellect, the ability he had to keep people, everyone, at bay who would try and stop him. As a nation our laws require that employers provide a safe workplace for their employees. As a people we depend on employers to look out for their employees. Just as Scott was a beloved son, a brother, a nephew, a cousin, and a fiancé, every worker is someone's relative and friend. Every single one of them deserves to go to work knowing that they will return safely to their families when their work is done. But Allan did not believe that. To him the workers were an expendable commodity, just like the flue dust."

He pointed out the obvious, that Elias had never shown any remorse and instead called his employees lazy and stupid. He said that in the year that had passed since sentencing, and the four years since the injury, Elias continued to receive $41,600 a month from Kerr-McGee, yet he had again thumbed his nose at the law, at the court, and at Scott Dominguez by refusing to provide his probation officer or the court with any information about his finances—demonstrating again what was truly important to Allan Elias: money. He contrasted Elias's day of playing golf with Bob Griffin with Scott Dominguez's day at home, or the nights when he would scream out in pain, unable to even turn over.

Uhlmann reached inside himself for the passion that had driven him to the U.S. Justice Department and said Allan Elias had been given much and much, therefore, should not just be expected but demanded in return.

"The disregard that Allan Elias has shown for the law, for worker safety, and for the environment is all the more contemptible because Allan Elias has had every advantage in life and is more than capable of appreciating the wrongfulness of his actions."

In the end, Uhlmann was forced to say what everyone in the courtroom reluctantly knew to be true, despite all of their efforts. No one could truly save Scott Dominguez, but Scott Dominguez could save others.

"Unfortunately, justice for Scott and his family may not be possible in this case. What happened to them never should have happened, and what they may have lost cannot be replaced. But if the sentence you impose in this case, Your Honor, keeps Allan Elias and others like him from wreaking havoc on another American family, then Scott and his family will not have suffered in vain. Scott will be imprisoned by brain damage far longer than the defendant serves in any jail cell. Barring a medical miracle, Scott Dominguez has received a life sentence. The defendant, Allan Elias, deserves nothing less, Your Honor."

Uhlmann sat.

Elias stood.

He said that when Dominguez first came to Evergreen he turned him away as too young, but Scott persisted and "by the third day, we all had fallen in love with him."

The use of the word sent a shudder through the courtroom.

Elias said that Gene Thornock, who even now he persisted in calling a "foreman," took Dominguez under his wing, called him "the kid," and it "was absolutely exciting to see this young man flourish." He expressed dismay that his workers had turned on him, saying he had loaned them money to pay for their daughters' weddings, to pay their income taxes, and to buy property. He said "everybody has responsibility here," intimating again that the emergency workers and Dr. Obray had screwed up, as had the employees on the job that day.

"My share of this is if I had a two-hour meeting, then I must have known. I must have been concerned. And if I was concerned, I shouldn't have left the property. That was my mistake in judgment. If it was going to require a meeting that was seven times longer than the normal meeting, then it should have required me standing there and seeing that it was done the way we talked about. We've talked too much about how this got out of hand."

Then, in a bizarre, final twist, he turned to the back of the courtroom where the Dominguez family sat together.

"Scott, I love you, and I am so, so sad."

It rang so hollow, and neither Hilldorfer nor Uhlmann missed the fact that Elias used the word *sad*. He did not say "sorry."

As Elias's final words resonated, Hilldorfer still couldn't help but think that Elias believed he was going to walk out of that courtroom that night. That was also Uhlmann's concern. He stood for the final time and urged the court to detain Elias, to not allow him to post bond pending appeal or to give him seventy-two hours to get his affairs in order. He stated that any further argument that Elias had demonstrated trust by appearing at his court hearings no longer held true because "there will be no more court dates before you."

"I am sure as the day is long—and this is a long day—that we will never see him again."

Winmill began with restitution. He noted that Elias had refused to provide any financial information to the court or to law enforcement. "The court finds that the defendant has the ability to pay the sum and

will therefore order that the defendant pay the sum of $5,936,086 to
Mr. Dominguez pursuant to statute." He also ordered Elias to pay the
$364,750 cost to clean up Evergreen, bringing the total restitution to
$6,300,836.

The money matters out of the way, he looked down on Allan Elias.

"Now, Mr. Elias, if you'll stand I'll pronounce sentence at this time."

Elias drained a shot of water, the last left in the pitcher, from a white
Styrofoam cup, and stood, hands clasped behind his back.[4]

"Mr. Allan Elias, having been found guilty by a jury of Counts One
through Four contained in the indictment, and the court being satisfied
that you are guilty as charged, I hereby order and adjudge as follows.

"That pursuant to the Sentencing Reform Act of 1984, it is the judgment of the court that the defendant Allan Elias is hereby committed to
the custody of the Bureau of Prisons for a term of 180 months on Count
One, and terms of 24 months each on counts Two, Three, and Four,
those—the 24-month sentence to run consecutive to Count One, but
they'll run concurrent with each other—for a total term of 204 months."

Seventeen years.

"The court perhaps could find that the defendant does not pose a danger to the community. And I feel that perhaps the situation has been resolved where he is not operating a business like that involved with
Evergreen Resources," Winmill said.

"However, I cannot find by clear and convincing evidence that he does
not pose a risk of flight, and I think— Frankly, the circumstances now are
substantially different than they were following the defendant's conviction. And facing this substantial sentence, I think the risk of flight is real."

There would be no bond pending appeal.

"I find in addition that the defendant has had a very lengthy period
since his conviction and has had a great deal of time to get his affairs in
order. I will therefore not provide a delay in detention and permit him to
report, but will rather order his immediate detention and that he be taken
into custody this evening."

There would be no seventy-two-hour reprieve. Elias was going to jail.

Elias sat down seemingly stunned.[5]

Hilldorfer looked at the Dominguez family. Some had closed their
eyes, as if an enormous weight had been lifted from their shoulders. As
with the reading of the verdict, they expressed no joy. There were no
handshakes, no backslapping, no cheers. Winmill also remained digni-

fied. He did not, as Hilldorfer knew some judges to do, take Elias to task. He offered no personal opinions on what Elias had done and did not chastise him. Without ceremony, he simply adjourned the proceeding.

It was over.

Elias sat at counsel table with a look of total disbelief as two stone-faced U.S. marshals approached. He stood tentatively and looked behind him, catching Hilldorfer's eye for just a fraction of a second, but long enough that others in the courtroom that day would still recall it years later. Joe Hilldorfer's expression spoke for all of them.

"We got you."[6]

Elias turned and said something inaudible to Jorgensen. Then the two marshals handcuffed him and escorted him to the door at the right of the courtroom. He stepped through it and the door closed. Allan Elias was gone.[7]

As Uhlmann, Breitsameter, and Miller left the courtroom reporters quickly approached, rushing to meet deadlines. Uhlmann spoke of the significance of the sentence, but it was almost redundant given that out the courtroom windows he could see multiple television vans with satellite dishes and the courthouse parking lot was lit up like a Hollywood movie set. Word of the sentence had apparently trickled out to the reporters. The trial of Allan Elias had started as a fight for justice for one young man, but in the end it had become so much more than that, for all of them. For Uhlmann it would shine its own light on the Environmental Crimes Section of the U.S. Justice Department and the significance of the responsibilities with which it had been tasked.

As he walked out the glass doors of the courthouse, the cameras and future awaiting him, Uhlmann paused briefly and looked back over his shoulder, wanting to remember where he had been.

JOE HILLDORFER sat down in the pew and looked at his watch—9:30 P.M. He felt the tension of the day in his limbs. His head felt numb. Jackie Hamp would later tell him that she felt sorry for Allan Elias as she watched him being handcuffed and led away. Ron Hamp made a similar comment. Elias was the only man he'd ever seen sent to jail. He said it "made his stomach roll." Hilldorfer found the comments amazing in one respect, and completely consistent with the salt-of-the-earth people he had come to know and respect. There was a party scheduled for that night. The hotel had been expecting them at 5:00 P.M. The food would certainly be cold but the room warm.

In the morning the family would leave Pocatello, driving south on Highway 15, then east on Highway 30 back home to Soda Springs. It was a route Joe Hilldorfer and Bob Wojnicz had driven so often it felt, in some respect, like their own road home. But they would not take the Highway 30 turnoff east to Soda Springs; they would continue south to Salt Lake City where they would board a flight to Seattle. And when his plane landed at SeaTac International Airport, Joe Hilldorfer would drive home, arriving in time to sit on his deck with the picturesque view of the Puget Sound and have dinner and a glass of wine with Joanne. The sun would set behind them, making the glass facade buildings of Seattle glisten like the Emerald City it was said to be, and he would think of the end of the day in Soda Springs, the sun falling gently behind the jagged Blackfoot basalt ridge, the last light of day glistening gold and silver across the rolling mountains that cradled the precious elements that sustained the town and those who lived there.

Scott Dominguez would start life there, again, without Allan Elias.

EPILOGUE

A T THE END of the first decade of the environmental crimes program in 1992, the question remained whether the general public and the judiciary would ever accept environmental crimes as crimes in the traditional sense of the word. Scholars opined that until they did, the program would never achieve its greatest impact.[1]

That may never happen. It also may not be realistic. Environmental law will always be at the apex of the conflict between two politically charged issues: protecting the environment, and promoting industry and business. It is subject to the uncertainty caused by political conflict, changes in administrations and their environmental policies, and public opinion. The reality that EPA agents and ECS attorneys face is that what is considered essential and critical one day is forgotten the next. Like a movie star, the environment is too often the flavor of the week at one moment and a tired and worn-out issue the next.

As the third decade begins, the base criticism remains that the prosecution of environmental crimes continues to fall sharply, first during the Clinton administration and after President George W. Bush's first year in office. If the numbers are accurate, it is a startling revelation. But are the numbers accurate? It seems the statistics fluctuate wildly depending on who is reporting them, and therefore they may never be a true indication of the agency's impact. What cannot be denied are the statistics that in the thirty years since its creation, the EPA has decreased the number of polluted waterways, significantly reduced air pollution, improved the quality of drinking water for millions more Americans, and reduced the amount of generated hazardous waste by millions of pounds. Perhaps more importantly, with all of the controversies that have marked its thirty-year existence, at a minimum, the EPA did what it set out to do. It brought the environment into America's consciousness. It made Americans realize their planet cannot be treated like a huge garbage dump if man hopes to continue to exist.

As for the ECS, since 1995 there have been scant few articles like the proliferation of literature that criticized it in the early 1990s. Perhaps that is simply a function of it having found its place within the Department of Justice. As one former ECS chief acknowledged, bureaucracies, by their structure, are notably resistant to new endeavors, and that resistance is only exacerbated when the new endeavor requires interagency cooperation.

It may also reflect the change in policy that encouraged ECS attorneys to work with U.S. attorneys instead of supervising them. It may be a function of a change in leadership at the ECS to environmental prosecutors, people who have been in the trenches and experienced the idiosyncrasies associated with prosecuting environmental crimes. And it may simply be a reflection that the judiciary and the public are becoming more accepting of environmental crimes as real crimes and therefore more willing to hold those responsible as accountable as any common criminal.

In May 2000, David Uhlmann became chief of the ECS. As of the writing of this book he had served for four years, longer than any previous chief. He speaks frequently about the Elias case and how it illustrates the impediments of prosecuting environmental offenders, but also how those impediments can be overcome through a cooperative effort between EPA investigators, U.S. attorneys, and the ECS. When that occurs, the United States has at its disposal a much larger and better-armed arsenal to take down America's corporate polluters than it perhaps realizes, and that power can be wielded like a sledgehammer to convict even the most resourceful of environmental polluters so that, perhaps, what happened to Scott Dominguez need not be repeated.

At the EPA, change is also under way. On December 15, 2003, a management review was conducted on the Office of Criminal Enforcement, Forensics and Training, of which the Criminal Investigation Division is a part. The honesty of that report created quite a buzz. Among other things it recognized that the evaluation of regional offices and the special agents therein was too heavily weighted on quantitative measures such as the number of cases referred to the Environmental Crimes Section or the local U.S. Attorney's Office. The report said that such "bean counting," as opposed to a clearer mission that encouraged and rewarded agents on the quality of their investigation by recognizing the degree of environmental harm inflicted by the perpetrator, or the likely deterrent effect of an investigation and prosecution, led to a waste of limited resources. It acknowledged that a system dependent on quantitative statistics could have grave consequences, encouraging special agents to focus on insignificant crimes or not thoroughly work up cases for prosecutions, which in turn led to a high number of declinations by the Department of Justice and the resultant friction between agents and prosecutors. As a result, the report encouraged a continued evaluation of implementing changes to the referral system so that it served as an incentive, and not a disincentive, to special agents.

ON JULY 20, 2000, Allan Elias filed an appeal of his convictions to the Ninth Circuit Court of Appeals. Scott Dominguez and his mother flew to Seattle for oral argument and were present in the courtroom when Elias's appellate attorneys argued that the government failed to prove that the material in the tank was hazardous.

Justice Thomas Nelson sat in the middle of the three-panel bench. Upon hearing the comment he sat forward and asked with bewilderment, "Not hazardous? How many people have to die before it's considered hazardous?"

Four months later, on October 23, 2001, the Ninth Circuit denied Elias's appeal. He filed a petition for writ of certiorari, paper work requesting that the U.S. Supreme Court review his conviction. That petition was denied October 7, 2002.

Allan Elias remains incarcerated, inmate #09452-023. As of the writing of this book he is at the federal correctional facility in Big Spring, Texas.

On September 18, 2003, Jorgensen and Uhlmann appeared again before Judge Lynn Winmill. While the Ninth Circuit Court of Appeals upheld Elias's conviction, it reversed Judge Winmill's order that Elias must immediately pay Scott Dominguez the $5.9 million in restitution. It remanded the case to Winmill to change this portion of the sentence. The RCRA Statute, 42 U.S.C. §6901 does not allow for restitution to a victim of an environmental crime. Speaking to this, Justice Nelson reluctantly opined: "This latter offense is one of the few for which Congress has not sanctioned the imposition of restitution. Perhaps this case will change that."[2]

Scott Dominguez has not received a dime from Allan Elias.

There has been no effort to clean up the hazardous waste buried at Evergreen Resources or AEI, Inc.

AFTERWORD

IN THE STRUGGLE for environmental justice, there may never be any easy answers.[1] The EPA and ECS are often damned if they do and damned if they don't. There will always be those who argue environmental enforcement is overzealous and insensitive to economics, which is a way of saying it impedes American business and its ability to compete in a world market. They argue that the hazardous waste problem in America is simply too large and complex for any one agency to police, that reality mandates that companies be encouraged to self-police themselves without the threat that the disclosure and prompt remedy of misconduct will result in criminal prosecution.

Proponents of environmental protection argue with equal passion that the EPA does not do enough, and that expecting companies to "self-police" themselves is hopelessly optimistic without the threat of jail. Only through the vigorous investigation, prosecution, conviction, and punishment of particular violators will those subject to the environmental laws get the message that it is more painful to get caught than it is to comply.

Defense attorneys will continue to bemoan the complexity of the environmental regulations, particularly RCRA, and say it makes the fair imposition of prosecutorial discretion impossible. They'll say that discreet judgments about blameworthiness and moral innocence can't be left to a particular prosecutor's "whim" because the defense of an environmental charge can easily cost a company $250,000 in legal fees and put them out of business.

Prosecutors reject the suggestion, citing statistics that the majority of environmental prosecutions hardly require much discretion—cases against facilities and owners for deliberate acts of dumping obviously hazardous chemicals, or for failing to install antipollution technology then falsifying records or making false statements to avoid the expense of legal waste disposal.

While it makes for an interesting debate, it may also be like running on a treadmill, exhausting but getting nowhere. Perhaps more poignant is the fact that there remains disagreement on the very definition of a "white-collar crime" and on whether there should even be a separate criminal classification. Some are content defining white-collar crime as "a crime committed by a person of respectability and high social status in the course of his or her occupation." Others flatly reject this definition, calling it "a lion's den from which no tracks return," and a distinction that leads to disparate treatment of these individuals that undermines the public's trust in the justice system as a whole. They cite statistics that white-collar crime costs the communities in which it occurs more money than common crimes, but because white-collar criminals steal with a pencil they get away with it, while the eighteen-year-old kid who steals with a gun goes to prison for a long time. It reminds one of the old saying, "The rich get richer and the poor go to prison."

The disparity in treatment is particularly ironic given that a trip to jail for a hardened criminal is not likely to change behavior, but just the threat "puts the fear of God" in a white-collar criminal. It is also not a consequence most employees will accept as the cost of working for a particular company. As one writer has said, "Nothing screws up the old résumé like a criminal conviction."

The fact is, despite Congress's professed intent to impose stringent regulations, and despite the EPA's and the ECS's best attempts to enforce those regulations, most of the defendants are successful individuals who have ostensibly led exemplary lives or large companies that communities depend on to employ their citizens. They have the money and resources to hire the very best attorneys and lobby the highest politicians. Witnesses are understandably reluctant to bite the hand that not only feeds them but feeds their neighbors, and juries are lenient for the same reason. So, too, are some judges, who too often consider prosecution and the resulting public ridicule white-collar criminals face to be sufficient punishment and an adequate deterrent to curb repeat behavior. The advent of mandatory federal sentencing guidelines has removed some of this discretion, but judges can still make upward or downward departures from the set level of months a defendant receives for an environmental crime. As a result, some continue to impose sentences of straight probation or incarceration of less than a year for significant offenses. Overworked prosecutors, all too aware of this judicial ambivalence, are faced with a difficult decision. Do they accept a plea bargain that usually involves little, if any, actual jail time, or face the difficult burden and task of litigating a case, only to have a judge, in essence, plea the case for them? EPA investigators are faced with a similar dilemma, putting blood, sweat, and tears into an investigation that may ultimately not even be charged.

In the end, therefore, the successful prosecution of environmental crimes may not be so much about the complexity of the laws and the competence of those agencies struggling to enforce them, but rather about changing a fundamental reluctance in American society to accept white-collar criminals as true criminals. When that happens, they may start being treated as such.

WHERE THEY ARE TODAY

George Breitsameter—"The Trial Dog," is still trying criminal cases as a senior litigator with the U.S. Attorney's Office in Boise, Idaho.

Mike Burnett—is now the assistant special agent in charge of the EPA's Los Angeles office.

Lieutenant Bryce "Bob" Clements—is now a lieutenant with the Idaho State Police, Bureau Manager, Alcohol Beverage Control Bureau.

Scott Dominguez—lives with his mother and stepfather in a cabin-style home on top of a mountain in Lava Hot Springs, Idaho.

Allan Elias—remains incarcerated, inmate #09452-023 at the Big Spring Federal Correctional Facility in Big Spring, Texas.

Michael Fica—is now an assistant U.S. attorney in Pocatello, Idaho.

Jackie and Ron Hamp—live in a cabin-style home in Lava Hot Springs, Idaho, and care for their son Scott. Ron continues to work for the Monsanto Corporation. Jackie sold the B&H Cleaners to care for Scott full-time.

Joe Hilldorfer—remains a special agent with the EPA/CID in Seattle, Washington. Shortly after the Elias sentence, he became the lead investigator in the Olympic Pipeline rupture, which occurred on June 10, 1999, and received the Agency's Gold Medal. Hilldorfer continues to live in Seattle with his wife, Joanne.

Craig Jorgensen—continues to work in Pocatello, Idaho, and to represent Allan Elias.

Joe Lowry—"Dr. Joe" remains the chief deputy scientist for the EPA's National Enforcement Intelligence Center in Lakewood, Colorado. He still hunts with his golden Labs, cooks dinner for his wife, Barb, and coaches his sons' baseball teams.

David Marshall—remains a defense attorney in the Pacific Northwest. Among his clients is the Equilon Corporation, one of the petrochemical corporations that owned and managed the Olympic Pipeline.

Dixon McClary—is now retired and living in his waterfront house in Seattle, Washington.

Celeste Miller—remains an assistant U.S. attorney and acts as liaison counsel with the U.S. Bankruptcy Court.

David Nevin—is still considered one of the premier federal criminal defense attorneys in Idaho and the Pacific Northwest.

James Oesterle—remains a regional counsel attorney with EPA.

Kelly O'Neil—is the resident agent in charge of the EPA/CID office in Boise, Idaho.

Officer William Reese—has been promoted to sergeant with the Idaho State Police, the Commercial Enforcement and Hazardous Materials Division, and has relocated to Boise, Idaho.

Sergeant Joe Rice—is now the captain of the Soda Springs Police Department.

Daren Schwartz—retired from the Caribou County Volunteer Fire Department following the September 11, 2001, disaster. He is now the chief safety officer for the Monsanto Corporation.

Brian Smith—works for a family-run business, a road-paving company in Soda Springs, Idaho. He still resides in Grace, Idaho, with his wife, Cathy, and his dog.

Gene Thornock—"The Caveman," now resides is Pocatello, Idaho, with his wife, Stacey, and is the father of a new child. He is a laborer in a local plant.

David Uhlmann—"The Pit Bull," has been promoted and is now chief of the Department of Justice's Environmental Crimes Section. He oversees a team of trial attorneys that prosecute corporate polluters across the United States.

Lorinda Wallace—has obtained an MBA from Stanford University and is now working as a consultant in Dallas, Texas.

Judge B. Lynn Winmill—remains a U.S. district court judge in Boise and Pocatello, Idaho.

Bob Wojnicz—remains a special agent in Seattle, Washington. He also received the Agency's Gold Medal for his work on the Olympic Pipeline investigation. He was assigned to the FBI's Joint Terrorism Task Force.

ENDNOTES

In retelling the investigation, prosecution, trial, and conviction of Allan Elias, the authors considered writing the story in the first person perspective of Special Agent Joe Hilldorfer. They realized, however, that just as the investigation and conviction of Allan Elias required the collective efforts of numerous law enforcement agencies and individuals, the full telling of this story would require the re-creation of scenes and events at which Hilldorfer was not present or not intimately involved. To ensure the accuracy of these events the authors relied upon thousands of pages of sworn trial testimony and testimony at the sentencing of Allan Elias; transcripts of hearings and proceedings, pleadings and sworn affidavits filed with the U.S. Federal District Court in Pocatello, Idaho; sworn statements from deposition transcripts; contemporary witness statements taken by the Occupational Safety and Health Administration, interviews by EPA special agents; official reports by the Idaho State Police Department, the Soda Springs Police Department, and the U.S. Department of Labor; the official medical records of Scott Dominguez at the Caribou County Memorial Hospital emergency room, the Bannock Regional Medical Center, and throughout his arduous rehabilitation, including helicopter flight records; the personal calendars of Bogdan Wojnicz and the itineraries he kept for each trip related to the investigation; articles from newspapers throughout the nation from the *Caribou County Sun, Boise Weekly,* and *Idaho State Journal* to *The Washington Post* and *USA Today;* official publications by the Soda Springs Chamber of Commerce and books written on the history of that community; as well as hundreds of hours of independent interviews by the authors of key witnesses involved in these events.

In telling the history of the Environmental Protection Agency, the Environmental Crimes Section of the Department of Justice, and of the prosecution of white-collar environmental crimes in this country, the authors similarly relied upon articles written in legal journals, law review publications and newspapers, congressional reports, and internal reports, documents, and speeches published by the EPA and Department of Justice.

The endnotes set forth below represent only a small portion of the materials relied upon.

CHAPTER 1

1. In addition to the specific endnotes set forth herein, the information contained in Chapters 1 and 3 comes from the following sources: Brian Smith trial testimony, *U.S. v. Elias,* April 22, 1999; Brian Smith interview, August 29, 1996, Grace, Idaho; Darren Weaver OSHA transcript, August 29, 1996; Weaver interview, August 22, 1997, Soda Springs, Idaho; Gene Thornock trial testimony, *U.S. v. Elias,* April 28, 1999; Gene

Thornock OSHA statement, September 4, 1996; Theresa Cole trial testimony, *U.S. v. Elias,* April 22, 1999; Theresa Cole testimony at sentencing, April 28, 1999; Theresa Cole interview, June 12, 1997; Corporal Bob Clements, Idaho State Police incident report, supplemental, August 27, 1996; Corporal Bob Clements, Idaho State Police incident report, August 27, 1996—Weaver interview; Andrew Scutro, "A Case of Toxic Greed," *Boise Weekly,* July 22–28, 1999, p. 14; Mark Mendiola, "Fertilizer Worker Survives Bout with Toxic Fumes," *Idaho State Journal,* August 28, 1996; Mark Warbis, "Soda Springs Man Struggles with Injuries From Cyanide Gas Exposure," *USA Today* (AP), July 2, 2000; Roger Parker interview, April 3, 1997, Pocatello, Idaho; Roger Parker OSHA statement, September 4, 1996, p. 18; Officer Bill Reese, suppression hearing testimony, March 4, 1999; Roger Sears trial testimony, April 20, 1999, p. 1104; Soda Springs Police Department supplementary report.

2. Gene Thornock trial testimony, *U.S. v. Elias,* April 28, 1999.
3. Brian Smith trial testimony, April 28, 1999; Gene Thornock trial testimony, April 28, 1999.
4. Corporal Bob Clements, Idaho State Police incident report, August 27, 1996—Weaver interview; Darren Weaver OSHA statement, August 29, 1996, p. 21; Gene Thornock OSHA transcript, August 29, 1996, p. 7, and September 4, 1996, p. 11; Danny Rice OSHA transcript, September 5, 1996, p. 3; Shane Walker OSHA statement, August 29, 1996, p. 27.
5. Betsy Sommers OSHA statement, October 3, 1996, p. 15 (Evergreen employees told her that they were told that the tank material was as safe as shampoo); Betsy Sommers interview, February 8, 1998; Gene Thornock trial testimony, April 28, 1999, p. 2667; Darren Weaver interview, August 22, 1997.
6. Gene Thornock trial testimony, *U.S. v. Elias,* April 28, 1999, pp. 2596, 2602; Darren Weaver OSHA statement, August 29, 1996, pp. 31, 47.
7. Gene Thornock trial testimony, *U.S. v. Elias,* April 28, 1999; Gene Thornock OSHA statement, September 4, 1996, p. 12.
8. Gene Thornock trial testimony, *U.S. v. Elias,* April 28, 1999, p. 2597; Darren Weaver OSHA statement, August 29, 1996, p. 42.
9. Darren Weaver OSHA statement, August 29, 1996, p. 50.
10. Corporal Bob Clements, Idaho State Police incident report, August 27, 1996—Weaver interview (Elias said he'd go get some); Gene Thornock trial testimony, April 28, 1999, p. 2602; Gene Thornock OSHA statement, September 4, 1996, pp. 5, 12; Darren Weaver OSHA statement, August 29, 1996, p. 41.
11. Gene Thornock trial testimony, April 28, 1999, p. 2667; Betsy Sommers OSHA statement, October 3, 1996, pp. 15–18; Betsy Sommers interview, February 8, 1998; Darren Weaver interview, August 22, 1997.

CHAPTER 2

1. Judgment in Criminal Case, *U.S. v. Trimbo,* CR95-5129RJB-001.
2. Mike Burnett interview, October 3, 2003, Los Angeles, California.
3. Details of the Boomsnub investigation, indictment, and plea agreement come from multiple court documents including: Judgment in Criminal Case, *U.S. v. Boomsnub Corporation,* Case # CR95-5129RJB-001, March 15, 1996; Judgment in Criminal Case, *U.S. v.*

William Trimbo, Case # CR95-5129RJB-001, March 15, 1996; Judgment in Criminal Case, *U.S. v. Edward Takitch,* Case # CR95-5129RJB-001, March 15, 1996; Judgment in Criminal Case, *U.S. v. Jay Jurek,* Case # CR95-5129RJB-001, March 15, 1996; Complaint for Violation, *U.S. v. Jay Jurek,* No. 94-5040m, June 7, 1994; and newspaper articles including: Loretta Callahan, "EPA to Close Local Company," *The Columbian,* May 19, 1994, A1; Loretta Callahan, "Feds Will Spend $3.3M to Clean Up Boomsnub," *The Columbian,* May 20, 1994, A1; Loretta Callahan, "Boomsnub Decision Due Friday," *The Columbian,* May 26, 1994, A1; Loretta Callahan, "Plume Is Focus of Public Forum," *The Columbian,* May 26, 1994, A6; Loretta Callahan, "Environmental Laws Enforced by Possible Penalties, prison time," *The Columbian,* May 26, 1994, A3; Loretta Callahan, "Boomsnub: Remedy on the Way," *The Columbian,* May 26, 1994, A3; Loretta Callahan, "Boomsnub Rejects EPA Closure," *The Columbian,* May 29, 1994, A1; Loretta Callahan, "Boomsnub Open, Defying EPA; Court Showdown Likely," *The Columbian,* May 31, 1994, A2; Loretta Callahan, "Park Is Now Superfund Site," *The Columbian,* June 2, 1994, A3; Loretta Callahan, "State: Suspect Drums Have Been Hauled Away," *The Columbian,* June 2, 1994, A6; Loretta Callahan, "Boomsnub Manager Arrested in Incident," *The Columbian,* June 8, 1994, A10; Loretta Callahan, "Boomsnub Resumes Operation," *The Columbian,* June 9, 1994, A1; Loretta Callahan, "The Amazing Bouncing Boomsnub," *The Columbian,* June 9, 1994, A10; Loretta Callahan, "Boomsnub Site Soil Removed; EPA Works to Clean Up Aquifer," *The Columbian,* June 10, 1994, A1; "EPA Wants Update on St. Johns Cleanup," *Oregon Live,* June 27, 2003; Loretta Callahan, "Boomsnub Guilty," *The Columbian,* August 14, 1994, A1; Loretta Callahan, "Boomsnub Manager Arrested in Incident," *The Columbian,* June 8, 1994, A10; Loretta Callahan, "Boomsnub 3 Officials Indicted," *The Columbian,* February 19, 1995, A1; Cathy Kessinger, "Private Wells Threatened," *The Columbian,* June 1, 1994, A1; John Lancaster, "Idaho Businessman Is Jailed for Endangering Employees," *Washington Post,* April 30, 2000, A02; Cathy Kessinger, "Boomsnub Shutdown Postponed," *The Columbian,* May 22, 1994, A1; Cathy Kessinger, "Former Employee Blew Whistle," *The Columbian,* May 22, 1994, A3; Press Release, U.S. Attorney, Western District of Washington, "Vancouver Company and Corporate Officials Plead Guilty to Environmental Crimes Charges," August 30, 1995.

CHAPTER 3

1. Weaver interview, August 22, 1997, Soda Springs, Idaho.
2. Brian Smith trial testimony, *U.S. v. Elias,* April 22, 1999; Gene Thornock OSHA transcript, August 29, 1996, p. 2; Gene Thornock trial testimony, April 28, 1999, p. 2599.
3. Brian Smith sentencing hearing, April 28, 2000.
4. Gene Thornock trial testimony, April 28, 1999, p. 2608; Darren Weaver OSHA statement, August 29, 1996, p. 23. (Weaver claims to have lowered the Air-Pac to Thornock on a rope. But Thornock and others have said Thornock went into the tank two, and possibly three, times to try to rescue Dominguez.)
5. Darren Weaver OSHA statement, August 29, 1996, p. 30.
6. Brian Smith trial testimony, April 22, 1999.
7. Brian Smith sentencing hearing, April 28, 2000; Brian Smith trial testimony, April 22, 1999.

CHAPTER 4

1. Bob Wojnicz interview, September 3, 2003, Seattle, Washington.
2. Bob Wojnicz interview, September 3, 2003, Seattle, Washington; Bob Wojnicz, August 27, 1996, notes of telephone conversation with Dixon McClary.

CHAPTER 5

1. U.S. Geological Survey Minerals Yearbook—2000, the Minerals Industry of Idaho.
2. Ellen Carney, *Historic Soda Springs, Oasis on the Oregon Trail* (Traildust Publishing Co., 1998); Lula Bannard, Faunda Bybee, and Lola Walker, *Toshiba "Sparkling Waters"* (Daughters of Utah Pioneers, Camp Meads, 1958, third printing 1984). Andrew M. Scutro, "A Case of Toxic Greed, the 'Egregious Environmental Crime' that Destroyed a Young Man's Life," *Boise Weekly* 8, no. 2 (July 22–28, 1999); Soda Springs Geyser Park Information Center.
3. Daren Schwartz trial testimony, April 20, 1999, p. 865.
4. Ron Myers interview, October 7, 1998.
5. Theresa Cole trial testimony, April 22, 1999; Theresa Cole interview, June 12, 1997.
6. Theresa Cole interview, June 12, 1997.
7. Ron Myers deposition, January 13, 1999.

CHAPTER 6

1. Daren Schwartz trial testimony, April 16, 1999, p. 858; Daren Schwartz interview, May 17, 2003.
2. Daren Schwartz interview, May 17, 2003.
3. Sergeant Bill Reese, Idaho State Police incident report; Daren Schwartz trial testimony; Daren Schwartz interview, May 17, 2003.
4. Daren Schwartz's conversations with Allan Elias come from the following sources: Daren Schwartz OSHA transcript, August 29, 1996, pp. 6, 14; Daren Schwartz trial testimony, April 20, 1999; Daren Schwartz interview, May 17, 2003; Sergeant Bill Reese, Idaho State Police incident report, August 27, 1996.
5. Matt Christiansen's conversation with Allan Elias comes from the following sources: Daren Schwartz trial testimony, April 20, 1999; Matt Christiansen trial testimony, April 20, 1999; Matt Christiansen OSHA statement, October 2, 1996; Matt Christiansen's and Daren Schwartz's testimony is further confirmed by the testimony of Captain Joe Rice, Soda Springs Police Department, at the suppression hearing on March 5, 1999. Rice testified that he asked Elias "What was in the tank?" and Elias replied "It shouldn't have—there shouldn't have been a problem," pp. 288–289.
6. Dr. John Wayne Obray's personal history comes from his trial testimony of April 21, 1999.
7. Dr. Obray's treatment of the injured workers, including Scott Dominguez, comes from the following sources: John Obray trial testimony, April 21, 1999; John Obray interview, June 12, 1997; Sergeant Bill Reese, Idaho State Police incident report, August 27, 1996; Captain Joe Rice suppression hearing testimony, March 5, 1999; Caribou County Memorial Hospital Nurse's Notes; and Betsy Sommers, EMT, interview, February 8, 1998.
8. John Obray interview, June 12, 1997.

the

9. Betsy Sommers OSHA statement, October 3, 1996. Sommers confirmed that Elias came to the hospital and spoke with Obray.
10. John Obray trial testimony, April 21, 1999; John Obray interview, June 12, 1997.

CHAPTER 7

1. Newsline, "Enforcement Actions, EPA's 800-pound Gorilla," *EPA Journal* 17, no. 2 (March/April 1991); *The Guardian: Origins of the EPA,* U.S. Environmental Protection Agency.

CHAPTER 8

1. Joe Hilldorfer trial testimony, April 28, 1999.
2. The statement was confirmed in an interview of Bob Wojnicz, September 3, 2003, Seattle, Washington.
3. The comment of the Soda Springs Police Chief was confirmed in an interview with Bob Wojnicz, September 3, 2003, Seattle, Washington.
4. The substance of the statements made by Allan Elias to the EPA special agents inside and outside the construction trailer the day after the accident on August 28, 1996, were further documented in the following written statements: Kelly O'Neil interview, December 16, 2002; Kelly O'Neil testimony at suppression hearing, March 4, 1999; Kelly O'Neil interview notes of Allan Elias, August 28, 1996; Joe Hilldorfer interview of Elias, August 28, 1996; Kelly O'Neil affidavit, October 20, 1998; Corporal Bob Clements, Idaho State Police incident report, Supplemental, August 27, 1996; Joe Hilldorfer, Application and Affidavit for Search Warrant in the Matter of Search of Evergreen Resources, September 17, 1996; Joe Hilldorfer trial testimony, April 28, 1999; Bob Wojnicz interview, September 10, 2003, Seattle, Washington.
5. Captain Joe Rice of the Soda Springs Police Department testified at the suppression hearing, March 5, 1999, that on the day after the accident he interviewed Allan Elias and was told that the tank had been used in a cyanide leaching process.
6. Helen J. Brunner, "Environmental Criminal Enforcement: A Retrospective View," *Environmental Law* 22, no. 135 (1992).
7. "Worker Is in Critical Condition When Fumes Overcame Him While Cleaning Tank," *Caribou County Sun,* September 5, 1996, p. 1. (Elias told Soda Springs chief of police Blyn Wilcox that he held a safety meeting that morning and signed off on the work certificate.)
8. "Worker Is in Critical Condition When Fumes Overcame Him While Cleaning Tank," *Caribou County Sun,* September 5, 1996, p. 1. (Wilcox stated that Elias told him he tested the pH and it was low and no problem.)
9. The comment is further confirmed by the trial testimony of Joe Eizaguirre, April 26, 1999. (Elias told the OSHA inspectors he suspected his employees "hit a pocket of cyanide gas.")
10. The substance of the Allan Elias interview on August 28, 1996, including Darren Weaver appearing at the site and disappearing with Elias, and Elias's statement "there is nothing I can do about managing stupidity" is further confirmed in the notes taken by OSHA compliance officer Barb Franek during a walk-around inspection of Evergreen with Elias and with OSHA inspector Joe Eizaguirre on August 28, 1996, attached as Exhibit A to the Affidavit of Barb Franek filed October 22, 1998.

11. Testimony of Officer Bill Reese at suppression hearing, March 4, 1999; Bob Wojnicz interview, September 10, 2003, Seattle, Washington.

CHAPTER 9

1. The background of Allan Elias comes from the following written sources: Andrew M. Scutro, "A Case of Toxic Greed, The 'Egregious Environmental Crime' that Destroyed a Young Man's Life," *Boise Weekly* 8, no. 2 (July 22–28, 1999); the September 25, 1997, affidavit of Bogdan Wojnicz, "In the Matter of the Search of the Evergreen Resources Facility," *U.S. v. Elias*, witness interviews attached; Bob Griffin interview, December 1, 1997; Kim Barnett interviews, January 26, 1999, and February 6, 1998; Gary Dahms and Gary Greer interviews, February 6, 1998; Mark Cates interview, February 5, 1998; Dave Buttleman interview, June 17, 1998; William Moore interview, April 2, 1997; Hans Rasmussen interview, August 11, 1997; Bill Breuger interview; Chuck Prince interview; testimony of Bogdan Wojnicz, detention hearing, May 17, 1999; testimony of David Ryan, IRS Agent, detention hearing, May 17, 1999; testimony of Allan Elias, sentencing, *U.S. v. Elias*, April 28, 1999; deposition of Allan Elias, October 17, 1990; deposition of Allan Elias, November 14, 1994; proof of claim, U.S. Bankruptcy Court—Idaho District, December 14, 1989, Southeast Idaho Council of Government, Inc.; security agreement, Allan Elias and Southeast Idaho Council of Government, Inc., February 6, 1989; testimony of Craig Jorgensen, Esq., detention hearing, May 17, 1999; sentencing hearing, April 28, 2000; the deposition of Midge Elias, August 14, 2000, *U.S. v. Elias*; Bob Wojnicz interview, August 7, 2003, Seattle, Washington; and the articles, "From Superstar to Super Coach!", *Tucson Magazine*; *Tucson Weekly* and the *Skinny*, May 11–17, 2000, *http://www.tucsonweekly.com/tw/2000-05-11/skinny.html*.

2. The conversation with Allan Elias in front of his Soda Springs home is further confirmed by the OSHA walk-around inspection of accident scene report, August 28, 1996, Exhibit A, to the October 22, 1998, affidavit of OSHA compliance officer Barb Franek; Bob Wojnicz interview, September 10, 2003, Seattle, Washington.

3. Gene Thornock interview, August 28 and 29, 1996, Bailey Creek, Idaho; Bob Wojnicz interview, September 10, 2003, Seattle, Washington.

4. Brian Smith interview, August 29, 1996, Grace, Idaho; Bob Wojnicz interview, September 10, 2003, Seattle, Washington.

CHAPTER 10

1. The treatment of Scott Dominguez comes from the following written sources: Flight Record 8/27/96 Flight 3221; John Wayne Obray trial testimony, April 21, 1999; John Ratcliffe interview, February 5, 1997; "Worker Is in Critical Condition When Fumes Overcame Him While Cleaning Tank," *Caribou County Sun*, September 5, 1996, p. 1; Bannock Regional Medical Center medical records, history and physical; Dr. John Roberts trial testimony, April 21, 1999.

CHAPTER 11

1. George Breitsameter background from interview, December 16, 2002, Boise, Idaho.
2. See also, Duff Wilson, *Fateful Harvest* (Harper Collins, 2001), pp. 209–210.
3. Lorinda Wallace trial testimony, April 23, 1999, pp. 1694–1695.

CHAPTER 12

1. George Breitsameter interview, December 16, 2002, Boise, Idaho.
2. Lorinda Wallace trial testimony, April 23, 1999; Government Trial Ex. 22–3.
3. Lorinda Wallace trial testimony, April 23, 1999; Government Trial Exs. 22–1 and 22–2.
4. Lorinda Wallace trial testimony, April 23, 1999.
5. Lorinda Wallace trial testimony, April 23, 1999.

CHAPTER 13

1. The meeting between George Breitsameter and David Uhlmann comes from Breitsameter interviews in December 2002 in Boise, Idaho, and multiple interviews with David Uhlmann in July 2003 in Washington, D.C.
2. The ECS history comes from: Judson W. Starr, "Turbulent Times at Justice and EPA," *George Washington Law Review,* April 1991; Theodora Galacatos, "The United States Department of Justice Environmental Crimes Section: A Case Study of Inter- and Intrabranch Conflict Over Congressional Oversight and the Exercise of Prosecutorial Discretion," Fn. 2, *Fordham Law Review,* November 1995; William Greider, "Fines Aren't Enough; Send Corporate Polluters to Jail," *Rolling Stone,* March 29, 1984; Kathleen F. Brickey, "Environmental Crime at the Crossroads: The Intersection of Environmental and Criminal Law Theory," *Tulane Law Review* 71, no. 487 (1996); Richard J. Leon, "Environmental Criminal Enforcement: A Mushrooming Cloud," *St. John's Law Review,* Summer 1989; Colleen C. Murnane, "Criminal Sanctions for Deterrence Are a Needed Weapon, but Self-Initiated Auditing Is Even Better: Keeping the Environment Clean and Responsible Corporate Officers Out of Jail," *Ohio State Law Review,* 1994.
3. *U.S. v. Timothy Sinskey & Wayne Kumm,* 119 F.3d 712 (published 1997).

CHAPTER 14

1. George Breitsameter interview, December 16, 2002, Boise, Idaho; Bob Wojnicz, notes of February 5, 1997, meeting at Boise U.S. Attorney's Office; Joe Eizaguirre trial testimony, April 26 and 27, 1999, pp. 2151, 2225, 2226.
2. See Steven Solow, "Environmental Crime Update: What Is the State of Federal Environmental Crime Enforcement," American Bar Association Section of Environment, Energy and Resources, 32nd Annual Conference on Environmental Law, Keystone, Colorado, March 13–16, 2003; Theodora Galacatos, "The United States Department of Justice Environmental Crimes Section: A Case Study of Inter- and Intrabranch Conflict over Congressional Oversight and the Exercise of Prosecutorial Discretion," Fn. 175, *Fordham Law Review,* November 1995, citing William J. Corcoran, U.S. Department of Justice, Internal Review of the Department of Justice Environmental Crimes Program.
3. Helen J. Brunner, "Environmental Criminal Enforcement: A Retrospective View," *Environmental Law* 22, no. 135 (1992).
4. Richard J. Leon, "Environmental Criminal Enforcement: A Mushrooming Cloud," *St. John's Law Review,* 1989; Judson Starr, John Cooney, and Joseph Block, "More Criminal Environmental Prosecution?", Electric Law Library, *http://www.lectlaw.com/files/*

env18htm; Theodora Galacatos, "The United States Department of Justice Environmental Crimes Section: A Case Study of Inter- and Intrabranch Conflict over Congressional Oversight and the Exercise of Prosecutorial Discretion," Fns. 52 and 175, *Fordham Law Review,* November 1995, citing William J. Corcoran, U.S. Department of Justice, Internal Review of the Department of Justice Environmental Crimes Program.

CHAPTER 15

1. *U.S. v. Iverson,* 162 F.3d 1015; Bob Wojnicz interview, September 3, 2003, Seattle, Washington.
2. Bannock Regional Medical Center History and Physical Report, Addendum, prepared by J. Schott, M.D., Resident, dictated August 27, 1996.
3. John Roberts interview, June 20, 1997; J. Schott interview, June 16, 1998; Life Flight record, August 27, 1996.

CHAPTER 16

1. Scott Dominguez's medical status comes from the Bannock Regional Medical Center, Nursing Progress Reports, Consults Reports, Discharge Summary, and Physician's Progress Reports; University of Utah Medical Center records; John Obray trial testimony, April 21, 1999, pp. 1378–1384; Bannock Regional Medical Center, Discharge Summary and Physician's Progress Reports.
2. John Roberts trial testimony, April 21, 1999, p. 3199.

CHAPTER 17

1. Jackie Hamp trial testimony, May 13, 1999, pp. 3264–3265.
2. Jackie Hamp interview, March 6, 1997, Soda Springs, Idaho; Scott Dominguez interview, March 6, 1997, Soda Springs, Idaho.
3. The EPA history comes from multiple sources: Kathleen F. Brickey, "Charging Practices in Hazardous Waste Crime Prosecutions," *Ohio State Law Journal* 62, no. 1077 (2001): fn. 8; citing to the EPA's Criminal Enforcement Program: Hearing before the Subcommittee on Oversight and Investigations of the Committee on Energy and Commerce, 102nd Congress 106 (1992) and 103rd Congress 2 (1993); "Environmental Crime at the Crossroads: The Intersection of Environmental and Criminal Law," *Tulane Law Review* 71, no. 487 (1996); Kathleen F. Brickey, "The Rhetoric of Environmental Crime: Culpability, Discretions and Structural Reform," *Iowa Law Review* 84, no. 115 (1998): 113; Kathleen F. Brickey, "Environmental Crime at the Crossroads: The Intersection of Environmental and Criminal Law Theory," *Tulane Law Review* 71, no. 487 (1996). Author's note, a five-year study by the GAO concluded that the success rate for ECS tried cases between 1988 and 1993 was 100 percent. Theodora Galacatos, "The United States Department of Justice Environmental Crimes Section: A Case Study of Inter- and Intrabranch Conflict over Congressional Oversight and the Exercise of Prosecutorial Discretion," *Fordham Law Review,* November 1995. Lee M. Thomas, "Environmental Regulation: Challenges We Face," *EPA Journal* 14, no. 2 (March 1988): 3; Richard J. Leon, "Environmental Criminal Enforcement: A Mushrooming Cloud," *St. John's Law*

Review, (Summer 1989); Jane F. Barrett, "Green Collar Criminals: Why Should They Receive Special Treatment," *Maryland Journal of Contemporary Legal Issues* (Fall/Winter 1996–97); Lauren A. Lundin, "Sentencing Trends in Environmental Law: An 'Informed' Public Response," *Fordham Environmental Law Journal* (Fall 1993); Colleen C. Murnane, "Criminal Sanctions For Deterrence Are a Needed Weapon, But Self-Initiated Auditing Is Even Better: Keeping the Environment Clean and Responsible Corporate Officers Out of Jail," *Ohio State Journal* (1994); "RCRA's Criminal Sanctions: A Deterrent Strong Enough to Compel Compliance?," *University of Hawaii Law Review* (Spring 1997), and Helen J. Brunner, "Environmental Criminal Enforcement: A Retrospective View," *Environmental Law* 22, no. 135 (1992). Judson Starr, director, Environmental Crimes Unit, November 1984, memo to F. Henry Habicht II, assistant attorney general, Land and Natural Resources Division, Talking Points on Management Study Involving EPA's Investigators. Judson Starr, January 6, 1985, Memo Summary of Criminal Case Activity; Richard J. Leon, "Environmental Criminal Enforcement: A Mushrooming Cloud," *St. John's Law Review* (Summer 1989); Colleen C. Murnane, "Criminal Sanctions for Deterrence Are a Needed Weapon, but Self-Initiated Auditing Is Even Better: Keeping the Environment Clean and Responsible Corporate Officers Out of Jail," *Ohio State Law Review* (1994). Ken Rademaker, "Eco-Cops," *Occupational Hazards,* September 1991; Lauren A. Lundin, "Sentencing Trends in Environmental Law: An 'Informed' Public Response," *Fordham Environmental Law Journal* (Fall 1993). "EPA Steps Up Enforcement," *Chemical Marketing Reporter, New York* 244, no. 25 (December 1993): 13; "Enforcement Stats Set Records," *Occupational Hazards* (Cleveland) 56, no. 2 (February 1994): 20.

4. Helen J. Brunner, "Environmental Criminal Enforcement: A Retrospective View," *Environmental Law* 22, no. 135 (1992). Author's note: Each of the sources located providing statistics on environmental prosecutions contained a caveat that 100 percent accuracy was not possible because not all prosecutions and convictions were reported. The number of referrals by the EPA, the number prosecuted, and the number convicted can also depend upon who is doing the reporting. TRAC, an organization at Syracuse University that tracks federal enforcement, staffing, and spending, provides different overall numbers, but confirms the percentages of criminal cases prosecuted—less than 40 percent—and the average sentence—less than six months. The DOJ, by comparison, prosecutes about half of the cases referred by the FBI, but the percentage of persons convicted and doing jail time is 75 percent and the average length of sentence is about five years. TRAC, Syracuse University, *www.trac.syr.edu,* April 3, 2003.

CHAPTER 18

1. Casey Johnson interview, March 18, 1997, Eagle Idaho.
2. Roger Parker OSHA statement, September 4, 1996, p. 18; Roger Parker trial testimony, April 29, 1999, p. 2815; Roger Parker interview, April 3, 1997, Pocatello, Idaho.
3. Danny Rice trial testimony, April 26, 1999; Danny Rice OSHA statement, September 5, 1996; Danny Rice interview, June 11, 1997.
4. The interview of Vance Turner was conducted later in the year on June 16, 1998, in Montpelier, Idaho; it is told here to facilitate the telling of this story.

5. Darren Weaver OSHA statement, August 29, 1996; David Uhlmann interview, July 24, 2003, Washington, D.C.
6. Jerry Farrel is not this witness's real name. To prevent any undue embarrassment, the name has been changed. Interview, June 11, 1997, Soda Springs, Idaho.

CHAPTER 19

1. Theresa Cole interview, June 12, 1997, Soda Springs, Idaho; Staff Notes, Rehabilitation Records, University of Utah, and records from Neurocare, Rehab without walls.
2. See Duff Wilson, *Fateful Harvest* (HarperCollins, 2001), p. 208. (In 1997, Geddes was the chairman of the agricultural committee of the Idaho State Senate.)
3. John Obray trial testimony, April 21, 1999, p. 1370.
4. John Obray interview, June 12, 1997; Betsy Sommers OSHA statement, October 3, 1996, pp. 18, 22–23 (EMT Betsy Sommers confirmed Elias came to the hospital and that Obray asked him directly about cyanide and Elias said there should not be any in the tank); John Obray trial testimony, April 21, 1999.

CHAPTER 20

1. Kyle Schick trial testimony, April 29, 1999; Kyle Schick interview, June 19, 1997.

CHAPTER 21

1. According to David Uhlmann the decision to accept a misdemeanor plea agreement had nothing to do with David Marshall, who had withdrawn as counsel for the company at the time the plea was agreed to. Uhlmann said the decision was based upon problems that developed with the evidence, including his evaluation of the strength of the potential testimony of employee witnesses. One had backtracked from earlier statements he had made to EPA agents.
2. David Uhlmann telephone interviews, June 19 and 27, 2003, Washington, D.C.
3. The meeting was confirmed by David Uhlmann in telephone interview, June 27, 2003, Washington, D.C.

CHAPTER 22

1. Frank Edward Allen, "Few Big Firms Get Jail Time for Polluting," *Wall Street Journal,* December 9, 1991, p. B1; Karen Heller, "Clamping Down on Environmental Crime," *Chemical Week* (New York) 150, no. 13 (April 1, 1992): 22; Lauren A. Lundin, "Sentencing Trends in Environmental Law: An 'Informed' Public Response," *Fordham Environmental Law Journal* (Fall 1993); Kathleen F. Brickey, "Charging Practices in Hazardous Waste Crime Prosecutions," *Ohio State Law Journal* 62, no. 1077 (2001): Fn. 8; citing to the EPA's Criminal Enforcement Program: Hearing before the Subcommittee on Oversight and Investigations of the Committee on Energy and Commerce, 102nd Congress 106 (1992) and 103rd Congress 2 (1993); "Environmental Crime at the Crossroads: The Intersection of Environmental and Criminal Law," *Tulane Law Review* 71, no. 487 (1996); Karen Heller, "Clamping Down on Environmental Crimes," *Chemical Week*

(New York), April 1, 1992; Kathleen F. Brickey, "The Rhetoric of Environmental Crime: Culpability, Discretions and Structural Reform," *Iowa Law Review* 84, no. 115 (1998), citing to Hearing Before the Subcommittee on Oversight and Investigations of the House Committee on Energy and Commerce, 102nd Congress 9 (1992); Lois J. Schiffer, "Criminal Enforcement in a Cooperative Environment," SB43 ALI-ABA 297 (1997); Theodora Galacatos, "The United States Department of Justice Environmental Crimes Section: A Case Study of Inter- and Intrabranch Conflict over Congressional Oversight and the Exercise of Prosecutorial Discretion," *Fordham Law Review,* November 1995.

2. David Uhlmann telephone interview, October 3, 2003, Washington, D.C.
3. Theodora Galacatos, "The United States Department of Justice Environmental Crimes Section: A Case Study of Inter- and Intrabranch Conflict over Congressional Oversight and the Exercise of Prosecutorial Discretion," *Fordham Law Review,* November 1995.
4. Smith testified before the subcommittee, as did, among others, representatives from the Washington State Attorney General's Office, and the surviving members of the Downs family. However, according to the Congressional Report, ECS trial attorney Rick Filkins, ECS unit chief Criselda Ortiz, and ECS chief Neil Cartusciello, who the subcommittee deemed to have "substantial involvement" in the matter, were less responsive to the subcommittee's request to be interviewed. The report states that because of, among other things, "the plea from the senior political leadership of the department for closure on this investigation," the subcommittee did not subpoena them. They sent written statements instead. The subcommittee provided a complete history based on its own interviews and investigation. It concluded that the handling of the PureGro matter within the ECS was replete with managerial failure and dysfunction, and noted that its own internal documents had deemed it, for more than a year, one of the section's most important cases, a case that ranked with the *Exxon Valdez* and Rock Flats in terms of significant investigations before the "abrupt and inexplicable about face." It also concluded there was "inefficiency and wasted resources, serious internal morale problems, bitter infighting, deep suspicion and distrust on the part of other agencies which were obliged to work with the ECS. . . ."

   "The PureGro experience," the subcommittee report stated, "while extreme, was not unique."

CHAPTER 23

1. The interview of William Moore actually took place on April 2, 1997, but is included here to facilitate the telling of this story.
2. Mark Warbis, "Soda Springs Man Suffers Long After the Accident," Associated Press, January 3, 2000; "Idaho Boss to Be Sentenced in Worker Cyanide Poisoning," *Seattle Times,* January 9, 2000; "Negligent Employer Shatters a Life Victimized by Idaho's Walking, Talking, Three Mile Island," *Hartford Courant,* January 10, 2000.
3. Elias history at AEI, Inc., and at Evergreen and the special agents' interviews of witnesses are summarized in the September 25, 1997, Affidavit of Bogdan Wojnicz, In the Matter of the Search of the Evergreen Resources Facility, *U.S. v. Elias,* filed in Idaho federal court; Bob Griffin interview, December 1, 1997; Kim Barnett interviews, January 26, 1999, and February 6, 1998; Gary Dahms and Gary Greer interviews, February 6, 1998; Mark Cates interview, February 5, 1998; Dave Buttleman interview, June 17, 1998;

William Moore interview, April 2, 1997; Hans Rasmussen interview, August 11, 1997; Bill Breuger interview; Chuck Prince interview; testimony of Bogdan Wojnicz, detention hearing, *U.S. v. Elias,* May 17, 1999, pp. 102–132; testimony of David Ryan, IRS agent, detention hearing, *U.S. v. Elias,* May 17, 1999, pp. 5–50; testimony of Allan Elias at sentencing, *U.S. v. Elias,* April 28, 1999, pp. 228–313; deposition of Allan Elias, October 17, 1990; deposition of Allan Elias, November 14, 1994; proof of Claim, U.S. Bankruptcy Court—Idaho District Court, December 14, 1989, Southeast Idaho Council of Government, Inc., Security Agreement—Allan Elias and Southeast Idaho Council of Government, Inc., February 6, 1989; testimony of Craig Jorgensen, Esq., detention hearing, *U.S. v. Elias,* May 17, 1999, pp. 72–99.

CHAPTER 24

1. Government Trial Exhibit 80-3 (note from Andrus to Deerden); Andrew M. Scutro, "The Andrus Connection," *Boise Weekly,* July 22–28, 1999; testimony of Allan Elias at sentencing, April 28, 1999; George Breitsameter interview, December 16, 2002, Boise, Idaho.
2. Affidavits of Darren Weaver, February 21, 1997, and March 6, 1997.
3. Darren Weaver interview, August 22, 1997; Darren Weaver testimony before grand jury as testified to by Bob Wojnicz at the sentencing of Allan Elias, *U.S. v. Elias,* April 28, 1999.

CHAPTER 25

1. Darren Weaver's testimony before the grand jury comes from the September 25, 1997, Affidavit of Bogdan Wojnicz, In the Matter of the Search of Evergreen Resources Facility, *U.S. v. Elias* §62 and the Testimony of Bogdan Wojnicz, Sentencing of Allan Elias. *U.S. v. Elias,* April 28, 1999, pp. 79, 80–82, 84.
2. The interview of Cecil Andrus and the information concerning his involvement comes from the following sources: Cecil Andrus interview, September 10, 1997; Bob Wojnicz interview, September 27, 2002; Andrew M. Scutro, "The Andrus Connection," *Boise Weekly,* July 22–28, 1999; Government Trial Exs. 80-3 (Andrus Note to Deerden) & 80-5 (Check No. 1024).

CHAPTER 26

1. Staff Notes, Rehabilitation Records, University of Utah and Neurocare, Rehab Without Walls records.
2. The fact that Ivan Williams was subpoenaed, appeared before the grand jury, and testified that he cut up the tank at Allan Elias's direction comes from George Breitsameter's cross-examination of Williams at trial.

CHAPTER 28

1. If there was any doubt the matter was going to be hotly contested it ended when the government subpoenaed Evergreen's corporate records. Elias objected, and when the district

court ruled against him he filed an appeal to the Ninth Circuit. When the Ninth Circuit rejected his argument he asked for a stay to petition the U.S. Supreme Court for certiorari. The Ninth Circuit denied the request for a stay, finding it was for the purpose of delay. The records were not turned over until February 1998, after District Court Judge Lodge ordered that a bench warrant would be issued if the subpoenaed corporate records were not produced to the grand jury.

2. *www.kerr-mcgee.com/history/html,* April 4, 2003; EPA Region 10, ID # IDD041310707, *Yosemite.epa.gov;* Fact Sheet, Kerr-McGee Chemical Corporation, U.S. Environmental Protection Agency, "Kerr-McGee Superfund Site Update; EPA Checkup Confirms Safe Cleanup," November 2002; EPA, "NPL Site Narrative for Kerr-McGee Chemical Corp.," National Priorities List, *www.epa.gov,* April 4, 2003; EPA Record of decision, Kerr-McGee Chemical Corp., *www.epa.gov;* U.S. Environmental Protection Agency, Region 10, Emergency Response Unit Pollution Report, Kerr-McGee Site, Soda Springs, September 10, 2001; EPA Superfund Fact Sheet, "Revised Proposed Plan, Kerr-McGee Superfund Site," May 2000. "Chamber Hears Plans to Shut Down Kerr-McGee Plant; Cap Tailings," *Caribou County Sun,* April 27, 2000, p. 1. See also, Duff Wilson, *Fateful Harvest* (HarperCollins, 2001), pp. 209–210.

3. See also, Allan Elias testimony at Debtor Exam, June 7, 2000.

4. Robert Griffin interview, December 1, 1998, Ameritel Hotel, Pocatello, Idaho; Bob Wojnicz interview, September 19, 2002. In 2000, Kerr-McGee shut down its vanadium and fertilizer plants in Soda Springs. Kerr-McGee said the fertilizer operation was not profitable, having lost $5 million to $6 million in 1999. It foresaw similar losses for at least ten years. At the time, Kerr-McGee had a million tons of calcine tailings and said it would cost between $40 million and $80 million a ton to truck the material off-site. Instead, it was submitting a plan to EPA to cap the tailings and leave them on site. "Chamber Hears Plans to Shut Down Kerr-McGee Plant, Cap Tailings," *Caribou County Sun,* April 27, 2000, p. 1.

5. Kathleen F. Brickey, "Charging Practices in Hazardous Waste Crime Prosecutions," *Ohio State Law Journal* 62, no. 1077 (2001); Kathleen F. Brickey, "The Rhetoric of Environmental Crime: Culpability, Discretions and Structural Reform," *Iowa Law Review* 84, no. 115 (1998); and "Environmental Crime at the Crossroads: The Intersection of Environmental and Criminal Law Theory," *Tulane Law Review* 71, no. 487 (1996): Fn. 110.

CHAPTER 29

1. Bill Stout interview, June 10, 1998; Bob Wojnicz interview, October 15, 2002; Bill Stout trial testimony.

CHAPTER 30

1. George Breitsameter interview, December 16, 2002, Boise, Idaho; Michael Fica interview, May 17, 2003, Pocatello, Idaho; Celeste Miller interview, May 20, 2003; *http://www.id. uscourts.gov/history/winmillbio.thm;* Press Release, September 9, 2002, New Appointment for Chief District Judge B. Lynn Winmill; Pocatello Courthouse Dedication Ceremony, June 4, 1999, Historical Perspective by Judge B. Lynn Winmill.

2. Government's Motion in Limine, *U.S. v. Allan Elias,* CR 98-070-E-BLW, Transcript of

Arraignment, June 26, 1998, p. 13; Magistrate Minute Entry; Order Setting Conditions of Release; George Breitsameter interview, December 18, 2002, Boise, Idaho.

CHAPTER 31

1. See, *Elias v. United States,* 134 F.3d 377 (1998).
2. Sean Stevens trial testimony, April 22, 1999, pp. 1579–1779; Sean Stevens telephone interview, June 3, 1998, and Sean Stevens interview, September 24, 1998, Las Vegas, Nevada.

CHAPTER 32

1. Affidavit of Allan Elias, October 1, 1998, in Support of Motion to Suppress.
2. Second Motion to Vacate Trial and for Finding of Excusable Delay.

CHAPTER 33

1. George Breitsameter interview, December 16, 2002, Boise, Idaho; Celeste Miller telephone interview, May 2, 2003, Boise, Idaho.

CHAPTER 34

1. David Uhlmann telephone interview, July 2, 2003, Washington, D.C.

CHAPTER 35

1. Theodora Galacatos, "The United States Department of Justice Environmental Crimes Section: A Case Study of Inter- and Intrabranch Conflict over Congressional Oversight and the Exercise of Prosecutorial Discretion," *Fordham Law Review* (November 1995); Kathleen F. Brickey, "Charging Practices in Hazardous Waste Crime Prosecutions," *Ohio State Law Journal* 62, no. 1077 (2001); "Environmental Crime at the Crossroads: The Intersection of Environmental and Criminal Law," *Tulane Law Review* 71, no. 487 (1996). Jane F. Barrett, "Green Collar Criminals: Why Should They Receive Special Treatment," *Maryland Journal of Contemporary Legal Issues* (Fall/Winter 1996–97); Rena I. Steinzor, "EPA and Its Sisters at 30: Devolution, Revolution, or Reform?" *Environmental Law Reporter* 31, News & Analysis, September 2001; Lois J. Schiffer, "Reform of Environmental Regulations: Three Points," WTR Natural Resources and Environment 12, no. 175 (1998). Ken Rademaker, "Eco-Cops," *Occupational Hazards,* Cleveland, September 1991. Richard J. Leon, "Environmental Criminal Enforcement: A Mushrooming Cloud," *St. John's Law Review* (Summer 1989). Lois J. Schiffer, "Reflections on the Role of the Courts in Environmental Law," *Environmental Law* 27, no. 327 (1997); Steven P. Solow, "Audit Privilege and Immunity Legislation and the Department of Justice Policy on Voluntary Disclosure," *SD19 ALI-ABA* 21 (1998).

CHAPTER 36

1. Gary Wolf, "Origin of Pocatello's Name Buried in History," *Pocatello Journal,* August 4, 2001; *The Early History of Pocatello, Idaho* (Bannock County Historical Society & Pocatello Public Library, February 1981); Robert L. Wrigley, "The Early History of Pocatello, Idaho," *Pacific Northwest Quarterly* (October 1943); A. L. Lillibridge, *The Origin of Pocatello* (Pocatello Public Library, undated).
2. David Uhlmann telephone interview, July 7, 2003, Washington, D.C.; George Breitsameter telephone interview, July 3, 2003, Boise, Idaho.
3. David Uhlmann telephone interview, July 2, 2003, Washington, D.C.
4. The interaction between counsel and Judge Winmill was not transcribed. However, the argument about where to sit and what was said was confirmed in the trial transcript, April 15, 1999, and by Judge Winmill in the transcript of the detention hearing, May 17, 1999, as well as interviews with George Breitsameter, December 18, 2003, Boise, Idaho; David Uhlmann telephone interview, July 2, 2003, Washington, D.C.
5. Craig Jorgensen testimony at Elias detention hearing, May 17, 1999, pp. 93–94; Craig Jorgensen interview, February 8, 1998.
6. Bob Wojnicz interview, September 27, 2002.
7. April 15, 1999, Transcript of Hearing. Speaking to the jury, Winmill stated, "At this point don't worry about the fact that we have all the attorneys on one side of the courtroom. They are doing so at my direction."

CHAPTER 37

1. David Uhlmann telephone interview, July 7, 2003, Washington, D.C.
2. Breitsameter Opening Statement, Transcript of Jury Trial Held Before Honorable Winmill, April 16, 1999; Joe Hilldorfer interview, September 12, 2002, Seattle, Washington. In a May 17, 1999, Declaration of David Marshall in Opposition to the Government's Motion for Detention, Marshall stated, "I am also aware that the only reason Mr. Elias's children did not attend the trial was a personal request by their mother that they not disrupt their own lives by doing so."

CHAPTER 38

1. Daren Schwartz interview, May 17, 2003, Bailey Creek, Idaho.
2. Roger Sears also confirmed these events in a conversation in a supermarket in Pocatello, September 18, 2003.

CHAPTER 40

1. Danny Rice trial testimony, April 26, 1999; Fred Mancini trial testimony, April 27, 1999.

CHAPTER 41

1. George Breitsameter telephone interview, July 3, 2003, Boise, Idaho; trial transcript, *U.S. v. Elias,* April 27, 1999.
2. David Uhlmann telephone interview, July 10, 2003, Washington, D.C.

CHAPTER 42

1. David Uhlmann interview, June 27, 1999, Washington, D.C. During the trial Marshall told Uhlmann that he had not been paid in some time; at his debtor's examination, Elias testified that he owed Marshall's firm more than $300,000.
2. David Uhlmann interview, June 27, 2003; Michael Fica interview, May 17, 2003—Fica confirmed that Marshall called Uhlmann "a piece of shit. You've always been a piece of shit."
3. David Uhlmann telephone interview, June 27, 2003, Washington, D.C.
4. David Uhlmann telephone interview, June 27, 2003, Washington, D.C.

CHAPTER 43

1. Trial transcript, May 3, 1999, p. 3362; David Uhlmann telephone interview, July 7, 2003, Washington, D.C.; George Breitsameter telephone interview, July 3, 2003, Boise, Idaho.
2. Mike Fica interview, May 17, 2003, Pocatello, Idaho.

CHAPTER 44

1. J. VonSchriltz interview, April 3, 1997, Pocatello, Idaho.

CHAPTER 46

1. Michael Fica interview, May 17, 2003, Pocatello, Idaho.

CHAPTER 47

1. Card from Scott Dominguez; David Uhlmann telephone interview, August 19, 2003, Washington, D.C.
2. George Breitsameter telephone interview, July 3, 2003, Boise, Idaho; Bob Wojnicz interview, September 19, 2002.

CHAPTER 48

1. Detention hearing transcript, May 17, 1999, 133–134.
2. Affidavit of Allan Elias, *U.S. v. Elias,* May 17, 1999.
3. David Uhlmann telephone interview, August 26, 2003, Washington, D.C.; George Breitsameter telephone interview, July 10, 2003, Boise, Idaho; Telephonic Status Conference Held Before the Honorable B. Lynn Winmill, *U.S. v. Elias,* June 23, 1999; Government's Post-Hearing Brief in Opposition to Defendant's Motion for a New Trial, *U.S. v. Elias,* January 19, 2000; Michael Fica interview, May 17, 2003, Pocatello, Idaho.
4. Michael Fica interview, May 17, 2003, Pocatello, Idaho.
5. Michael Fica interview, May 17, 2003, Pocatello, Idaho; David Uhlmann telephone interview, August 26, 2003, Washington, D.C.

6. David Uhlmann telephone interview, August 26, 2003, Washington, D.C.; order dated June 17, 1999, CR No. 98-00070-E-BLW.
7. Memorandum Decision, *U.S. v. Elias,* December 9, 1999; Jury Inquiry Held Before the Honorable B. Lynn Winmill, July 2, 1999; Government's Response to Defendant's Motion for New Trial, *U.S. v. Elias,* November 1, 1999.

CHAPTER 49

1. Motion for New Trial, *U.S. v. Elias,* October 20, 1999.

CHAPTER 51

1. David Uhlmann telephone interview, August 28, 2003, Washington, D.C.; January 3, 2000, Evidentiary Hearing.
2. Transcript of Evidentiary Hearing, January 7, 2002; David Uhlmann telephone interview, August 28, 2003, Washington, D.C.
3. Ibid.
4. "Assistant U.S. Attorney Conceded Jurors Have Modified Stories," Associated Press, January 11, 2000; George Breitsameter telephone interview, July 10, 2003, Boise, Idaho.

CHAPTER 53

1. Government's Opposition to Defendant's Motion to Dismiss Counts 1, 2, and 3 for Lack of Jurisdiction, *U.S. v. Elias,* November 1, 1999; *Wyckoff Company v. Environmental Protection Agency,* 796 F.2d 1197, 1199–1201 (1986).
2. "Precedent-Setting U.S. Court Ruling Announced: EPA Barred From Bringing Federal Criminal Charges to Enforce State Environmental Laws," *Business Wire,* March 21, 2000.

CHAPTER 56

1. Andrew M. Scutro, "Brain Damage, Polluter Gets Prison in Cyanide Poison Case," *Boise Weekly.*
2. Ibid.
3. Ibid.
4. Ibid.
5. Ibid.
6. Daren Schwartz interview, May 17, 2003, Bailey Creek, Idaho.
7. Andrew M. Scutro, "Brain Damage, Polluter Gets Prison in Cyanide Poison Case," *Boise Weekly.*

EPILOGUE

1. Helen J. Brunner, "Environmental Criminal Enforcement: A Retrospective View," *Environmental Law* 22, no. 135 (1992); Kathleen F. Brickey, "Environmental Crime at the Crossroads: The Intersection of Environmental and Criminal Law Theory," *Tulane Law Review* 71, no. 487 (1996); David Uhlmann telephone interview, September 5, 2003,

Washington, D.C.; Public Employees for Environmental Responsibility, "Uneven Justice, & Environmental Enforcement Plummets Under Bush," January 2002, *www.peer.org*; Judson W. Starr, "Turbulent Times at Justice and EPA," *George Washington Law Review* (April 1991); Management Review of the Office of Criminal Enforcement, Forensics and Training, U.S. Environmental Protection Agency, December 15, 2003.

2. *U.S. v. Elias,* 269 F.3d 1003 (2001).

AFTERWORD

1. William K. Reilly, "Interview a Vision for EPA's Future," *EPA Journal* 16, no. 6 (September/October 1990); see Colleen C. Murnane, "Criminal Sanctions for Deterrence Are a Needed Weapon, but Initiated Auditing Is Even Better: Keeping the Environment Clean and Responsible Corporate Officers Out of Jail," *Ohio State Law Review* (1994); Laura M. Litvan, "The Growing Ranks of Enviro-Cops," *Nation's Business* (Washington) (June 1994); William Greider, "Fines Aren't Enough; Send Corporate Polluters to Jail," *Rolling Stone,* March 29, 1984; Jane F. Barrett, "Green Collar Criminals: Why Should They Receive Special Treatment," *Maryland Journal of Contemporary Legal Issues* (Fall/Winter 1996–97); Jane Barrett, "Sentencing Environmental Crimes Under the United States Sentencing Guidelines—A Sentencing Lottery," *Environmental Law* 22, no. 1421 (1992); Kathleen F. Brickey, "The Rhetoric of Environmental Crime: Culpability, Discretions and Structural Reform," *Iowa Law Review* 84, no. 115 (1998); Judson Starr, et al., "More Criminal Prosecution," The 'Lectric Law Library, *www.lectlaw.com/files* (April 1994); Kathleen F. Brickey, "Charging Practices in Hazardous Waste Crime Prosecution," *Ohio State Law Journal* 62, no. 1077 (2001); Lois J. Schiffer, "Reflections on the Role of the Courts in Environmental Law," *Environmental Law* 27, no. 327 (1997); Travis Hirschi and Michael R. Gottfredson, "The Significance of White-Collar Crime for a General Theory of Crime," *Criminology* 27, no. 359 (1989): 362–363; Lauren A. Lundin, "Sentencing Trends in Environmental Law: An 'Informed' Public Response," *Fordham Environmental Law Journal* (Fall 1993). Helen J. Brunner, "Environmental Criminal Enforcement: A Retrospective View," *Environmental Law* 22, no. 135 (1992).

INDEX

ABOUT THE AUTHORS

Robert Dugoni graduated Phi Beta Kappa from Stanford University with a degree in journalism and was an intern with the *Los Angeles Times*. He then earned his doctorate of jurisprudence from the University of California at Los Angeles and practiced law in San Francisco and Seattle for fifteen years. He is intimately familiar with the intricacies of legal strategy and trial procedures. Since moving to Seattle he has won awards for his writing.

Joseph Hilldorfer is a special agent for the Environmental Protection Agency and a member of the National Counter-Terrorism Evidence Response Team. He has been involved in high-profile environmental investigations in the Pacific Northwest since 1992, including the Olympic Pipeline disaster. Prior to joining the EPA, Hilldorfer was a distinguished special agent with the FBI in Seattle and New York City working high-profile cases such as the Green River Killer and undercover for the Counter-Espionage Squad. He has an M.A. in criminal justice administration from Indiana University at Pennsylvania and a law degree from the University of Pittsburgh School of Law. He is a member of the Pennsylvania bar. He lives in Seattle, Washington.